THEY MARRIED ADVENTURE

THEY
MARRIED
ADVENTURE

The Wandering Lives of
Martin and Osa Johnson

Pascal James Imperato
AND
Eleanor M. Imperato

RUTGERS UNIVERSITY PRESS
NEW BRUNSWICK, NEW JERSEY

Library of Congress Cataloging-in-Publication Data

Imperato, Pascal James.
   They married adventure : the wandering lives of Martin and Osa
Johnson / Pascal James Imperato and Eleanor M. Imperato.
     p.   cm.
   Includes bibliographical references and index.
   ISBN 0-8135-1858-X (cloth)
   1. Johnson, Martin, 1884–1937. 2. Johnson, Osa, 1894–1953.
3. Photographers—United States—Biography. 4. Explorers—United
States—Biography. 5. Wildlife cinematography. 6. Nature
photography. I. Imperato, Eleanor M. II. Title.
TR140.J63I46   1992
910'.92'2—dc20
[B]   92-4696
                                                          CIP

British Cataloging-in-Publication information available

Design by John Romer

For our children
Alison, Gavin, and Austin
with love

CONTENTS

INTRODUCTION

Martin and Osa Johnson were acclaimed pioneer filmmakers and still photographers of both wildlife and vanishing cultures during the first half of the twentieth century, when relatively few Americans traveled overseas, much less to exotic corners of the world. They were a popular couple who brought adventure and faraway places into American homes through their books, magazine articles, and highly personalized travel documentaries. It was not merely the lure of strange peoples and the high drama of the African plains that drew audiences to them, but also the fact that they so well represented the American ideals and values of their time. Their popularity rose on the tide of early twentieth-century America's intense admiration for explorers and adventurers. Along with Richard E. Byrd, Frank Buck, Richard Halliburton, and Charles A. Lindbergh, they were heroes to millions, especially young people, for whom their names became household words.

Martin's public image was a combination of Peck's Bad Boy and a Horatio Alger hero whose bravery, sincerity, resourcefulness, and respect for American values enabled him to succeed. Yet in reality, he was a very complex man who embodied both virtues and faults. His virtues stemmed more from family values than from religious instruction. According to Osa's mother, both he and Osa believed in God, but were not "church-going people." He was kind and extremely generous, as when he paid the medical bills of an impoverished child who needed to have a harelip surgically corrected. But he was also shrewd in business matters, and was an experienced showman who sometimes reworked the facts in order to increase the popularity of his films. Yet his basic decency and sincerity were never compromised. His commitment to the life of a wanderer was constant and complete. Not surprisingly, he used his wealth to sustain a life of almost perpetual travel.

Martin's hero and model was Jack London, with whom he sailed across the Pacific in 1907–1908. Jack's influence on Martin's life and career was powerful and pervasive. Martin not only embraced many of Jack's values and attitudes, but also emulated his formula for success. Like Jack, Martin became a man of action who did not shrink from self-promotion. Both men were pugnacious and outspoken and could be terribly frank and even abrasive. At the same time, they were also sensitive and modest and given to self-pity and enormous generosity.

Osa's mother and grandmother instructed her in all of the domestic arts, at which she eventually excelled. They also taught her that a wife's role was defined by her husband's wishes. While she adhered to this belief for most of her married life, she did at times assert her independence, which brought her into sharp conflict with Martin's attitudes and those of relatives and friends. His public acknowledgment that she was "the best pal a man ever had" summed up his perception of her as a helper. Yet Osa was far more than that. Although Martin outclassed her as a cinematographer and photographer, she had no equal when it came to tracking wildlife and organizing the logistics of complex safaris. She was also a crack shot who had few equals in East Africa. As Martin moved in close to film potentially dangerous game, his life often depended on Osa's marksmanship.

Crack shot that she was, Osa was not a tomboy. She was beautiful, photogenic, charming, and poised. That she was also a risk-taker and enjoyed high adventure set her apart from most women of her time. She wore Parisian creations when in Europe and America, was always well coiffed when out in the bush, and rarely failed to put on her makeup, even when meeting headhunters in the South Seas. Because of her stage presence and elegant wardrobe, she was named one of the twelve best-dressed women in America in 1940. Martin's artistry and technical skills as a cinematographer were not the only reasons his work enjoyed wide acclaim in his lifetime. Osa was the star of most of his movies. Although audiences enjoyed the thrilling scenes of charging animals and were awed by the strange customs of exotic peoples, it was she who captured their hearts and who kept drawing them back to the box office. Yet, despite her prominent contributions, she always appeared with her husband under the name Mr. and Mrs. Martin Johnson, or alone as Mrs. Martin Johnson. The appellation was more than just a matter of semantics; it reflected not only Martin's dominance, but also the norms of a male-dominated society.

Martin and Osa had no pretensions about being either anthropologists or animal behaviorists. Anthropology had barely emerged as a science when they began to record the vanishing cultures of the South

Pacific in 1917, and animal behaviorists were not to walk the trails of East Africa for almost thirty years after the Johnsons had left them. However, the Johnsons viewed their filming of African wildlife as an essential part of the historical preservation mission of the American Museum of Natural History, whose scientists were predicting mass extinctions within a few years.

Martin and Osa responded to the peoples of Africa and the South Pacific as did most Americans and Europeans of their time. They traveled to Africa and Melanesia with a white ethnographic perspective infused with both innocence and arrogance. As a result, their films and books frequently reflect an unquestioned belief in white superiority. These attitudes were then the norm for American and European society, and pervade the literature and cinematography of that time.

There was little financial incentive for the Johnsons to present a complete and sympathetic picture of Africans as they were. Thrills, the exotic, and the unusual were what packed the movie houses and provided them with the capital they needed to continue their work. Their success very much depended on market forces and a commercial film industry that knew the entertainment value of racial stereotyping. Although their portrayals of Africans were sometimes unsympathetic, they dramatically changed America's image of Africa in other ways. The Africa they presented in their films and books was a land of beauty, tranquility, and sunshine, accessible to many and not just to the privileged few. This truthful depiction represented a radical departure from the tales that had been told by numerous travelers over the previous decades. These travelers had frequently presented a distorted image of Africa as a land of savage tribes and ferocious beasts, sometimes because they actually saw it that way, but often in the interests of inflating their own accomplishments. As Ernest Hemingway cogently observed in his short story "The Short Happy Life of Francis Macomber," the Johnsons "debunked the image of Darkest Africa by lighting it up on the silver screen."

Martin and Osa developed a great respect for many of the Africans who worked with them, often under very trying conditions in the bush. They expressed enormous admiration for Boculy, their elephant guide in Kenya, and were high in their praise of Bukhari, their headman, whom they frequently treated as an equal. Within the context of the colonial era, they were considered far too democratic and generous with their African staff, and were sometimes criticized on this account. Yet their close relationships with some Africans do not often forcefully emerge in their writings and films because they were to some extent the captives of the commercial forces that determined their success.

Despite their numerous films and writings, and their prominent position in American society in the 1920s and 1930s, the Johnsons have never been the subjects of a serious and comprehensive biography. Contemporary documentation of the various facets of their lives and careers is dispersed in numerous archival holdings that require much time and effort to retrieve. Their own published writings are consistently vague and imprecise about critical aspects of their careers and offer little help to anyone trying to establish a chronology of their travels. Compounding matters is the fact that all of Osa's and some of Martin's books for adults were entirely ghosted by writers who took significant liberties with facts in the interests of producing entertaining reading. Osa's 1940 memoir, *I Married Adventure*, which covers their lives up to Martin's death in 1937, was ghosted by a radio scriptwriter, Winifred Dunn. She fabricated entire sections, and distorted facts and chronologies to create a hero and heroine bound to appeal to readers of the early 1940s. Secondary sources are of little help in piecing together the story because they are often based on what the Johnsons had to say about themselves.

Martin and Osa's careers were extremely complex because they were not only travelers, but also documentary filmmakers, still photographers, the authors of numerous books and magazine articles, and popular celebrities whose lives inspired many. A critical biography had to take into account not only these aspects of their careers, but also their personal lives and marital relationship, and present them within a larger historical context.

Our objective was to rely as much as possible on primary source materials, and to gather as much contemporary documentation as possible about their lives, films, books, and still photographs. This process began in a sporadic fashion following a meeting with Osa's mother, Belle Leighty, in 1964. In 1974, our efforts became more methodical, and continued unabated for the next fifteen years in Africa, Europe, and the United States. We read or reread all their books and major periodical articles, and spent hundreds of hours gathering and photocopying materials in various archives and libraries. We viewed their major films several times over, studied the film scripts contained in the copyright descriptive material in the Library of Congress, and retrieved unindexed contemporary reviews from both the popular press and film industry publications. The latter were especially important to us since they documented the judgments of contemporary experts in the industry and provided us with insights into the commercial forces behind the Johnsons' productions. We twice viewed the 8,485 Johnson photographs stored on a laser video disc produced by the International Museum of Photography at George Eastman House, and examined the photographic collections of the American Museum of Natural History, the Martin and Osa Johnson

Safari Museum, and the Museum of Modern Art. A number of photographs reproduced in this volume have never before been published.

Our most important primary source was the Johnsons' correspondence, which is found in several archival holdings. Taken together, this material enabled us to document their personal relationships and business arrangements, and to establish a chronology of their month-to-month activities. Several collections of newspaper clippings and newsreels from various periods of their lives helped corroborate and enhance the information in the letters. The *New York Times* regularly covered their careers for the thirty-two-year period from 1921 until 1953. However, the index lists many news and feature stories under the general term "portrait." All of the *New York Times* articles had to be examined on microfilm and copied, a process that alone took several days.

We were fortunate that, when we started, Osa's mother, Belle Leighty, and Osa's second husband, Clark H. Getts, were still alive, as were a number of others who had been associated with them. Long interviews, conducted over many years, provided us with much crucial information not documented elsewhere. We also interviewed the descendants of several people who had worked with the Johnsons in Africa. These individuals knew a great deal about the Johnsons from what their parents had told them, and corroborative documentation confirmed that most of their information had not been distorted during generation transfer. Friends in East Africa kindly interviewed other individuals whom we were unable to reach during our visits there.

Several years of living and working in Africa, combined with a broad knowledge of East African history, exploration, and wildlife conservation, gained over many years from other research studies, enabled us to evaluate the Johnsons within several larger contexts. Other writers and scholars working in related research areas in East Africa provided us with additional useful insights.

The writing of this biography required three years during which all of the interviews, primary source materials, and published sources were synthesized with insights and analyses. Presenting Martin and Osa as they were instead of as they were perceived required our probing beneath the myths they and others had created. What emerged from our efforts was the essential Americanism of two courageous and determined people who left lasting impressions of sincerity, kindness, and generosity wherever they traveled.

ACKNOWLEDGMENTS

We can never adequately thank the numerous people who over a period of many years freely gave of their time and knowledge, patiently answered incessant questions, and provided us with steady encouragement. We owe a special debt of gratitude to Belle Leighty, Osa Johnson's mother, without whose support and friendship this book would not have been possible. Clark Hallan Getts, Osa's second husband, graciously shared his memories and insights with us, without which we could not have fully documented her later years. Margaret Cripps Sachs, Martin Johnson's niece, kindly provided us with valuable information about the Johnson family. Many associated with the Martin and Osa Johnson Safari Museum in Chanute, Kansas, have been of help in numerous ways. They include former museum directors Sondra Updike Alden, John C. Awald, Keith Bollwahn, and David L. Rabe. Anna Lou Mattix, the museum's first director, the late Dorothy Wilson, and the late Margaret Bloomhart were very close personal friends of Osa's mother and shared their vast knowledge of the Johnsons with us. The late Dr. James Butin assisted us on our early visits to the museum and our friends Don and Evelyn Abbuehl have been unstinting with their support for close to a quarter of a century. The late Vern L. Carstens and his wife Wilma gave us both friendship and excellent insights into the Johnsons' lives, for which we are very grateful. Over the years, a number of museum officers and volunteers have helped us in various ways. Among them are Dale Fairchild, Richard W. Good, Barbara Henshall, James W. Kensett, Mrs. Dale W. McCoy, Jr., and Christopher H. Morton. Kenhelm W. Stott, Jr., an honorary trustee of the museum, shared with us his personal memories of the Johnsons and his knowledge about their careers.

In East Africa, we are deeply grateful to our friends Errol and Sbish Trzebinski, who have tirelessly helped us for many years. They have not only dug into archives, newspapers, and people's memories on our behalf, but have also constantly given us their encouragement. Edward Rodwell, the dean of Kenya's journalists, has been a good friend and supporter who quarried government documents on our behalf, searched old cemeteries for headstones, and interviewed some who knew the Johnsons. William G. Dixson put us into contact with many who knew the Johnsons, and as only a true friend could, did everything from searching property records in Nairobi to arranging guides for us on Mount Marsabit. We are very grateful to our friends Cynthia and the late Sydney Downey, who gave us much help and encouragement. Father Paolo Tablino of the Maikona Catholic Mission in the Marsabit District of Kenya did much to assist us in our research and has been a steady supporter of our work.

Elspeth Huxley gave us steady encouragement and kindly helped us in many ways. Margaret D. Kummerfeldt, A. Blayney Percival's daughter, not only helped us in our efforts and cheered us on, but also read portions of the manuscript and made valuable suggestions. We want to thank Kevin Brownlow for reading the original manuscript proposal and for his suggestions about the final draft. We are grateful to I. Milo Shepard for his encouragement and for permission to use the Jack and Charmian London Collections at the Henry E. Huntington Library. We are very thankful to Sara S. Hodson, associate curator of Literary Manuscripts at the library, for her assistance, encouragement, and excellent suggestions. David Kuhner not only carefully studied Charmian London's 1907–1908 diaries for us, but also provided many good suggestions. The staff of the American Museum of Natural History, Department of Library Services, has been extremely helpful to us for many years. Barbara Mathe and Carmen Collazo photocopied large quantities of materials from the museum's archival holdings, and Andrea La Sala, Special Collections librarian, assisted us in accessing Johnson photographs. Penelope Bodry-Sanders, Carl E. Akeley's biographer, was of great help to us in retrieving materials from several collections in the museum's archives and has given us much encouragement, for which we are very thankful. Andrew Eskind, Katharine Bassney, Barbara Puorro Galasso, and Kathy Wolkowicz of the International Museum of Photography at George Eastman House provided us with access to the Johnson-Eastman correspondence and to Johnson photographs in the museum's collections. Gene M. Gressley, former director, and Emmett D. Chisum, research historian at the University of Wyoming, American Heritage Center, allowed us to study the Clark H. Getts Collection. We are deeply grateful to Mr. Chisum not only for providing us with numerous photocopies of newspaper articles concerning Osa's later life and career, but also for his support over a period of several years.

We are very grateful to Karen Reeds, our editor at Rutgers University Press, for both her enthusiastic support of this project and for her many excellent suggestions. We are thankful to Marilyn Campbell, Managing Editor at Rutgers, for her many useful suggestions and to Alice Calaprice for her careful copyediting of the manuscript. We want to especially thank Lois Hahn for her patience and careful preparation of several drafts of the typescript. We express our gratitude to our children, Alison, Gavin, and Austin, for their tolerance and acceptance of what at times was a less than normal family life because of this commitment.

We thank the following individuals for their help, and apologize for any names we have overlooked: Yusuf Abdulgani; Alec and Alison Abell; Ella Abney; Marthe "Barbie" Adcock; Willa Klug Baum; Rob Grahame Bell; Lady Sheila de Bellaigue; Evelyn and Frank Belletti; Jane Blades; Judith Block; Evelyn Bolte; J.D.T. Breckenridge; Monty Brown; Connie Budreau; Bartle Bull; Glenn E. Burch; Joe Chege; Joan M. Considine; Mary Corliss; Pat Cottar; Mervyn Cowie; William Cox; Dorothy Davison; Norman and Camille Dee; Anthony Dyer; Elizabeth Marshall Erickson; Elsa and the late Henry Evans; Lesley E. Forbes; Sir Vivian Fuchs; Dorothy Getts; the late Fitzhugh Green; the late J. R. Gregory, M.D.; Wako Halake; Thelma Constant Harmon; Pat Helm; Jane Hogan; the late Alfred A. Imperato, M.D.; Gerard A. Imperato, Esq.; Louis G. Imperato, Esq.; Anne Jaynes; Karl Kabalac; Edward and Judy Kennedy; Joan Kennedy; Dilawar Khan; Russ Kingman; the late James Laneri; the late C.F.D. McCaldin, M.D.; Mervyn Marciel; Susan Marshall, Esq.; David R. Martin; Rita W. Matthews, Ph.D.; Marion Miller; Iris Roberts Mistry; the late Agnes Newton Keith; the late Brother Andrew Noud, F.S.C.; Festo Ochogo; Douglas L. Oliver, Ph.D.; Dorothy Percival; D. Strother Pope, M.D.; Delwin J. Rathbun; Lady Alys Reece; Kathleen J. Reich; J. M. Richmond; Dorian Rocco; the late E. A. Ruben; the late DeWitt Sage; Lillian Schiff; Helena and the late Ladislas Segy; Don Silverek; Frank E. Smith, Jr., M.D.; Cecile Starr; Clarice Stasz; Joseph Tilton; the late Lowell Thomas; the late Minnie Thomas; the late William Thomas; Jack Topchick; Judith Thurman; Paula Vogel; Helen Wauchope; the late John C. Willey.

The following institutions and organizations kindly assisted us: Academy of Motion Picture Arts and Sciences; California Department of Parks and Recreation; Carnegie Library, Lincoln, Kansas; The Explorers Club Library; Great Neck Public Library; Humbolt Public Library, Humbolt, Kansas; Independence Public Library, Independence, Kansas; Kenya National Archives; Library of Congress,

Motion Picture Division; McMillan Memorial Library, Nairobi, Kenya; Manhasset Public Library; Medical Society of the State of New York, Albion O. Bernstein Library; The Museum of Modern Art, Film Stills Archive; The New York Public Library, General Library and Museum of the Performing Arts (Lincoln Center); New York Times Pictures; National Zoological Park; Port Washington Public Library; Rollins College, Department of Archives, Special Collections and Records Management; Royal Archives, Windsor Castle; Smithsonian Institution Archives; St. John's University Law Library; State University of New York, Health Science Center at Brooklyn Library; University of California, Berkeley, Bancroft Library; University of Durham Library; University of Rochester, Rush Rhees Library; University of Wyoming, American Heritage Center; Wide World Photos; Women's Independent Film Exchange.

THEY MARRIED ADVENTURE

PROLOGUE

On a cool November morning in 1917, a young Kansas couple sailed into the South Pacific dawn from the islet of Vao in the New Hebrides. Their open twenty-eight-foot whale boat, equipped with a small jib and a main sail, flew over the choppy waters, carried along by the early breezes of the arriving rainy season. They sailed northwest into the Bougainville Strait, with the northern head of the island of Malekula off the port bow.[1] As they rounded Malekula, the sun rose above the water and gave a golden tint to the thick mist that hung in the high forested valleys of the island.

Martin Johnson had just turned thirty-three, and his wife Osa was twenty-three. He was tall, towering six feet, one inch; she barely reached five feet, two inches. He had seen this island once before in 1908 when he sailed past it with Jack and Charmian London on the *Snark*. Now, after several months of filming and photographing in the Solomon Islands, he and Osa were determined to obtain pictures of the isolated and warlike Big Nambas people who lived in the highland forests of northwestern Malekula.[2] There was little sense of anthropological mission in their endeavor. Products of the vaudeville circuit, they were traveling for adventure and profit, making films to entertain, educate, and amuse the American public.

Martin and Osa sat on the thwart of the small boat. Their crew of five Melanesian men, who were naked except for a covering over their genitals, squatted in front of them. They sailed up and down the swells, sweeping by the small coves and bays along the rocky coast of northern Malekula. As the sun rose higher above the horizon, the great banks of mist that had clothed the mountains began to disappear, revealing the high green valleys of the Big Nambas.[3] The early morning light transformed the black and gray shades of dawn into vibrant color. A landscape of blue sky and sea, green forests and great white beaches unfolded before them, all enveloped by currents of air that were clear and pure. It seemed an untouched corner of creation where nature brought the elements together with both drama and grace. Yet the beauty of this place did not cast a magical spell of tranquility over those who lived here. For fear and brutality were as constant as the sea breezes and the gentle rolling of the waves.

In midmorning, they landed on a beach above Espiegle Bay on the northwest coast of the island. They had sailed past other beaches before reaching this point, where frightened and naked Malekulan men darted into the dense cover of the forest that rose up like a green wall above the white sands. Melanesian distrust of Westerners was anchored in decades of exploitation by labor recruiters who carried men and boys off as virtual slaves to the sugar fields of Queensland and Fiji. Traders, whalers, and plantation owners, pursuing their own selfish interests, had played on Melanesian tribal xenophobia and saturated the islands with guns. Armed with "Snyder" and Winchester rifles, the Melanesians intensified the scale and violence of their internecine warfare and also began to use the weapons against outside intruders.[4]

Martin and Osa stepped ashore on a beach considered "safe" by traders and labor recruiters. Leaving their small boat anchored in the bay, they walked a mile into the bush where in a "friendly" Big Nambas village they hired three guides who were willing to take them up into the highlands of the Big Nambas country.

Back in their small boat, they sailed down the coast, where in Espiegle Bay they sighted a small labor-recruiting schooner. The French owner strongly advised them against sailing toward their destination, Tenmarou Bay. However, their Big Nambas guides assured them they would be safe. Ever the risk-takers, Martin and Osa headed for Tenmarou Bay, unmindful of the violent events of the previous year.

In 1916 a plantation owner by the name of Bridges forcibly recruited laborers from among the Dirak people on the northeast coast near Bushman's Bay. In revenge, the aggrieved Malekulans made a surprise attack on Bridges's house as he and his four children were eating lunch. Bridges's Melanesian wife was away with relatives. However, the son of another planter, Corlette, was visiting. Bridges and his four children were hacked to death. The Corlette boy ran through the mangrove swamps trying to reach Bridges's canoe in the bay. As he waded through the shallow waters, he was overtaken and bludgeoned to death. The Diraks took the boy's body back to their village, where it was cut up and cooked. Pieces were then sent to chiefs in the northern highlands, initiating a wave of killings and cannibalism among the islanders. Recipients were obliged to return the gift in kind.

Since the actual killers could not be identified, the British and French, who jointly governed the New Hebrides, decided to punish the Melanesians indiscriminately. The H.M.S. *Torch* was brought in from Sydney with a hundred Australian marines and a platoon of New Guinea native police. They were joined by the British and French Condominium constabulary and the French cruiser *Kersaint*. The British and the French resident commissioners headed the expedition that consisted of a formidable force of 260 armed men in addition to guides and porters. The Malekulans, who traditionally ambushed their enemies in the densely forested mountains, had a significant advantage and managed to kill two European soldiers and five Melanesian policemen in two days of fighting. But forty-four Malekulans were killed and many more wounded. The warships' bombardment of the forested mountain peaks created more noise than damage, but the power of the guns of these man-o-wars, as the Malekulans called them, left an indelible impression on the Big Nambas.[5]

Tenmarou Bay spread out beyond the prow of the Johnsons' boat as a placid vista of calm blue water, white beach, and cool green forest. The scents of the forest drifted on the sea air. The only sounds along the beach were the gentle tumbling of the small waves and the songs of birds in the nearby trees. The beach was deserted, but Martin and Osa had an uneasy feeling that their every move was being watched from the shadows of the forest wall. They pulled the boat up on the shore, scanned the forest for openings to trails, and looked for movement among the trees. Suddenly, a figure came out of the forest and slowly walked down the sloping beach. He was completely naked except for a bark waist belt and a sheath of pandanus fibers wrapped around his penis. His hands were folded over his stomach, and as he got closer he began to speak in *bêche-de-mer*,[6] the lingua franca of the New Hebrides: "My word, master, belly belong me walk around too much."[7] Seizing the moment, Martin offered the man four cascara tablets from his kit. As the man gulped the tablets down, twenty-five Big Nambas emerged from the forest. Martin described them "as terrible as our first visitor."[8] Many wore bark belts and pandanus fiber penis sheaths, and some had bones or sticks inserted through the cartilages of their noses. He set up his hand-cranked Universal motion picture camera and ground out several hundred feet of film. The Big Nambas had never seen a motion picture camera before, and Martin later wrote, "as is often the way with savages, after a first casual inspection, they showed a real or pretended indifference."[9]

The Big Nambas were renowned for their guile and had on several occasions lured visiting Europeans into the bush with initial overtures of friendliness. None of these Europeans ever emerged alive.[10] By peacefully posing for the cameras, the Big Nambas achieved their objective. They said their chief, Nihapat, was a short distance away in the bush and invited Martin and Osa to visit him.[11] Martin had heard of Nihapat, the powerful chief of Tenmarou village who had thirty wives, and decided to see and film him. He and Osa eagerly plunged into the forest, followed by three assistants carrying their camera equipment. The Big Nambas had the upper hand now that Martin and Osa had stepped into the forest. None of the Big Nambas accompanied them and instead delegated a small boy to guide them to Nihapat. This should have aroused suspicion, but Martin's dogged determination to film Nihapat swept common sense aside. As Martin and Osa started up the trail to Nihapat's village, the Big Nambas on the beach quietly disappeared into the forest.[12]

Martin and Osa moved into terrain ideal for the Big Nambas' favorite strategy of an ambush at close quarters in thick forest. The trail cut through dense forest, up steep slopes, and across patches of tall cane grass. Panting and struggling up the steep slopes, they finally arrived on a high ridge, a thousand feet above the beach below. From where they stood, they could see their whale boat anchored offshore like a small dot on the blue of the ocean.[13] It had grown hot and, except for the calls of birds, the forest was silent. On distant peaks, thin columns of white smoke from cooking fires rose up above the trees.

As they stood on the ridge looking at the sea below, they heard a noise, and turning around "saw standing in the trail four armed savages, with their guns aimed at us."[14] Martin had come a long way for pictures of these people, but now the risk had grown too great, and he started down the trail. However, the Big Nambas intercepted them with threatening gestures, foreclosing escape.[15] One of the four Big Nambas climbed on top of a boulder and gave out a high-pitched call. After a few minutes, an answering call came from a nearby peak. The exchange of calls continued every few minutes, the response growing louder each time.

Nihapat, who had been returning the calls, suddenly burst into view on the top of a ridge. He was a magnificent sight—six feet tall with bushy hair, a full beard, and a stick through the cartilage of his nose. Martin described him as "the most frightful, yet finest type of savage I have ever seen."[16] As Nihapat strode over to the Johnsons, Martin moved forward with a package containing red-colored calico, sticks of tobacco, matches, and other trade goods. Nihapat ignored the presents and instead fixed his gaze on Osa, who was terrified. Attempting to take Nihapat's attention away from Osa, Martin began cranking his Universal motion picture camera. Despite the hum of the camera, Nihapat kept his eyes on Osa. Martin continued to film for fifteen minutes as Nihapat stared at her.

Finally, sensing growing danger and having gotten better footage than he had ever hoped for, Martin prepared to leave. After packing up his gear, he went up to Nihapat, shook his hand, and told Osa to do the same. Unfamiliar with the social meaning of the gesture, Nihapat refused to release Osa's hand. He touched her cheeks, rubbed the skin of her arm with cane grass, pinched and probed her, and pulled her hair.[17]

Nihapat's release of Osa was sudden and unexpected. He shouted to the scores of men peering through the cane grass, and they disappeared into the forest. Seeing an opportunity for escape, Martin ordered his guides to pick up the tripods and cameras and began backing down the trail with Osa. They had only gone a few feet when they were seized from behind by Nihapat's men. Martin later wrote, "as I looked at the ring of black, merciless faces, and saw my wife sagging, half-swooning, in the arms of her cannibal captors, my heart almost stopped its beating."[18] Both Martin and Osa carried revolvers, but wisely decided against using them since they were clearly so outnumbered. Nihapat's men forced them back up the ridge. Martin and Osa found this sudden release and just as sudden recapture inexplicable. Whether Nihapat had changed his mind or whether he was toying with them, as Osa later speculated, is unclear.[19]

Nihapat's men picked up the Johnsons' gear and escorted them and their guides across the ridge. As they did so, they suddenly stopped, and glancing at the bay below shouted "man-o-war, man-o-war, man-o-war." There, rounding the point, was the British patrol boat, the *Euphrosine*. It sailed into the bay, anchored, and lowered a small boat that made for shore.[20] Martin saw his chance and gestured to Nihapat that the boat was coming for them. Nihapat then ordered their guides to pick up the loads and let Martin and Osa leave.[21]

Although the beach was only three miles away, the terrain in between was treacherous and steep. Martin and Osa began running as soon as they entered the cover of the forest. They slid down muddy trails, jumped over creepers and vines, and pushed their way through fields of cane grass. The sun was dipping toward the horizon as they "struggled through the jungle in a nightmare of fear."[22] Halfway down to the beach, they came to an open ridge. In the fading light, they could see the elongated silhouette of the *Euphrosine* moving out of the bay. As it did, the deep roaring of conch shell horns rolled across the hills above them, interpreted by Martin as "a message to the savages on the beach to intercept us."[23] On the high slopes above them, Nihapat's men started down in pursuit.

Martin and Osa fled for their lives, hoping to emerge on a stretch of beach free of Big Nambas. The fearsome b-o-o-o b-o-o-o of the conch shells grew louder. Cut and lacerated by thorns and vines, they finally reached the edge of the forest wall. As they scanned the beach, they realized that they had luckily lost their way and had arrived at a point several hundred yards away from where the main trail to Tenmarou village met the beach. At the very end of that main trail, they could

see thirty armed Big Nambas sitting around a fire. In the jungle above
them, Martin and Osa could hear the jungle foliage slapping against
the bodies of the Big Nambas, who were rushing down the hillsides
after them.[24]

The crew of the whale boat, fearing the Big Nambas, had pulled
the vessel off the sand and anchored it in the shallows. Martin and Osa
and their guides raced across the beach for the boat, their feet sinking
into the soft sand. The Big Nambas on the beach caught sight of them
and gave chase. The desperate travelers reached the surf and waded in
toward the whale boat as their crew furiously poled closer to them.
Just as the crew pulled them over the gunwales, the Big Nambas on
the beach reached the water's edge. The sail was hoisted quickly and
the evening breeze carried them out into the safety of the bay.[25]

Martin and Osa eventually sailed back to Vao with success safely
packed away in their film canisters. In seeking out the Big Nambas,
they were leading the adventurous life they wanted while fulfilling the
hopes of their backers, film distributors, and theater-goers. The Johnsons' film distributors and investors were not interested in expository
documentaries sensitively crafted to foster a better understanding of
alien peoples. Rather, they wanted movies that presented the South
Pacific islanders as wild creatures whose lives were governed by a
terrifying yet fascinating irrationality. Their preference was for films
that packed the theaters and left audiences gaping with amazement.
The combination of the exotic, dangerous savages, and courageous
Midwesterners filled the bill perfectly, and for the rest of their lives,
Martin and Osa played the parts they first created for themselves in
their New Hebrides adventure.

CHAPTER ONE

GROWING UP IN KANSAS

Martin Elmer Johnson grew up in Lincoln, Kansas, on the raw edge of a wilderness that was being tamed by plows and railways, and by people whose goal was to settle, civilize, and reshape the face of the land. The last Indians had been driven out by the army and settlers, the buffalo herds had been hunted to extinction, and the railway was being inexorably pushed across the plains.[1] As a child in Lincoln, Martin would have seen only remnants of untouched prairie whose grasses and wildflowers had once blown endlessly toward the horizons under the spring breeze. He would have thrived in the Kansas wilderness that had so recently disappeared. But that wilderness had now been replaced by a world not to his liking.[2] Fulfillment lay beyond the tilled prairie in places he could only imagine as a young boy, but where as a man he would spend most of his life.

Martin was born on October 9, 1884, in Rockford, Illinois. His father, John Alfred Johnson, who was then a foreman in the stem-winding department of the Rockford Watch Company, was born in Jonkoping, Sweden, in 1851 and came to the United States while still an infant.[3] Martin's mother, Lucinda Constant, born in Chillicothe, Missouri, on February 18, 1858, was descended from John Constant, who first settled in Virginia in the late eighteenth century. Some of the Constants steadily moved westward with the frontier to Ohio, Illinois, and then to Missouri. Lucinda was the third of eight children of William Frame Constant and Cecilia Martin; her mother's surname became Martin's first name.[4]

John Johnson's immigrant parents settled in Rockford, Illinois. His father died when he was young, and his mother eventually married Peter Hakanson, who became a strict stepfather to John. As a young teenager, John left home to work as a newsboy in Chicago and New

York, and then moved west to the area of the Black Hills where he became a mule-team driver. Initially he hauled buffalo hides and later supplies for General George Armstrong Custer's army. He eventually enlisted in the army, attracted by the prospects for better meals. John married Lucinda in 1880 and returned to his hometown. After five years in Rockford, they were attracted farther west by advertisements for Lincoln, Kansas.[5]

Lincoln was a frontier prairie town, newly built on the Saline River in north-central Kansas. In 1872 it became the county seat of Lincoln County.[6] The early settlers of Lincoln, anxious to increase the town's size and improve its economy, aggressively promoted its virtues in advertisements in eastern city newspapers. These portraits of Lincoln as a healthy place of idyllic beauty and wealth were successful; Lincoln's population rose from 250 in 1878 to close to 2,000 in 1886.[7]

For John and Lucinda Johnson, this town seemed to offer great opportunities. A railway link to the Union Pacific in 1886 promised further growth for Lincoln and brightened the prospects for the success of the jewelry store John planned to open.[8] The Johnsons relocated there in the spring of 1885, when Martin was several months old. The town itself was nothing but a mass of unpainted wooden buildings and dusty streets. However, beyond the town's limits stretched rich farmland, once the preserve of Indians and herds of buffalo, but now covered to the horizons with stands of wheat. The economic health of Lincoln rested on good weather, good crops, and stable markets. John shared in the town's success in these early years. He rented a store next to the Saline Valley Bank on the town's main street, Lincoln Avenue, and later secured a small wooden frame house for his family on South Second Street.[9]

Life in Lincoln for young Martin was uneventful until he went off to school as a four-year-old. Lincoln's success in attracting new settlers meant an overflowing schoolhouse. Martin found himself in a single room, crammed with ninety pupils in all grades and one beleaguered teacher, Miss Emma J. Lewis.[10] School for youngsters in Lincoln was a dreary affair of repetitive drills and recitations augmented by strong discipline. However effective such pedagogy may have been for herd teaching, it quickly smothered all enthusiasm for learning in a child like Martin.

Martin grew into a boy who was eager to learn about the world around him in his own fashion. It was inevitable that his individuality would collide with routine and discipline both at school and at home. Martin dealt with these conflicts by becoming a chronic truant from school and a runaway from home.[11] The railroad was his usual route of escape, and he rode the rails to the Midwestern towns where his mother's relatives lived. There he found sympathetic listeners who had already heard a good deal from Lucinda about John's hard-driving and authoritarian ways. As sympathetic as they were to Martin's plight, these relatives always sent him back—to yet another round of punishment, rebellion, and flight.[12]

Osa consistently characterizes "Father Johnson" as a benevolent, kind man in *I Married Adventure*.[13] This appears to be a valid picture of an older and mellowed John Johnson after his son had achieved distinction sailing on the *Snark* with Jack and Charmian London. However, before that, John spoke of Martin as an "ungrateful scamp." Far from being benevolent and kind, John was a shrewd and stingy businessman viewed by his own wife and daughter as a slave driver.[14] It is significant that John, who had resorted to running away to escape from his own rough-handed stepfather, had now become so much like him.

The loving center of the Johnson household was Martin's mother, Lucinda. A Christian Scientist, she did all she could to cushion Martin from his father's wrath and eventually succeeded in softening John's attitude toward his son. Martin's sister, Freda, who was born when he was ten years old, joined their mother in later years in supporting his regular attempts at personal independence. As Martin saw it, he could solve his troubles only through escape. Unfortunately, it created further acrimony between him and his father. After many years of prodding from his wife and daughter, John finally came to accept Martin's need for freedom. In letting Martin go in his own unusual direction, he came to terms with the disappointing reality that his thriving business, which he had worked so hard to build, would not pass to his son.

Martin found happiness in Lincoln in the company of his friends Bennie Marshall, the Everett boys, and Elias, Howard, and Jack Rees. The Rees family owned the large, yellow, stone grain elevator and mill that stood on the banks of the Saline River next to a dam and a gentle cascade. The boys would sit under the willows on the sloping riverbank, casting their fishing lines into a calm curve in the river.[15] In this world of the mill and the river, Martin was at peace with himself and free of teachers, parents, and routines. The solitude in the dark cool mill, the flow of the river, and the diversity of nature that unfolded along its banks soothed his spirit and captured his imagination. Martin's love of the natural world was also expressed in the great interest he showed in animals. Squirrels, dogs, snakes, turtles, birds, and many others found their way into his life, and after their death, into the Johnson garden.[16]

The idealized values of late nineteenth-century America permeated life in Lincoln. For young boys, it was a wholesome world of school, church, swimming, fishing, and close friendships. They learned responsibility and contributed to the family's welfare by doing household chores and odd jobs. The strict but understanding guardians of this world were parents and kin, teachers, clergy, and neighbors, whose aim was to lead young boys into manhood. This national ideal of boyhood was given powerful expression in John Greenleaf Whittier's poem *The Barefoot Boy*.[17] However, even Whittier's lines allow for boyhood freedom and escape from adult constraints. The concept that boys will be boys was an integral part of this American ideal. Reasonable allowances were made for missing school, running away, and engaging in high-spirited pranks. These expected and tolerated departures from good behavior were brought to life in Mark Twain's *The Adventures of Tom Sawyer* and *The Adventures of Huckleberry Finn*.[18]

The young Martin described by Osa is a Horatio Alger hero.[19] All his misdeeds are represented as essential preparation for seeking adventure. The young Martin Johnson of Osa's portrait held great appeal for adult readers of the 1940s because he reflected their values, created nostalgia for the simpler times of their youth, and met their expectations of a hero's beginnings.

Osa's account is less than convincing today because it is so patently idealized and draws so obviously on popular literary images of youth. The observations of Martin's contemporaries clearly show how far he departed from the ideal boy of the late nineteenth century.[20] He was completely indifferent to church and school, and shirked everyday chores. Deleted from Osa's portrait is Martin's acrimonious relationship with his father, a facial tic that worsened whenever he became nervous, and the real magnitude of his truancy and flights from home.

In the early 1890s a prolonged drought seriously crippled Lincoln's economy, and John Johnson realized that it would take years for the area to recover. Therefore, in the spring of 1896, he sold his business in Lincoln and moved to Independence, Kansas, in the southeastern corner of the state.[21] A few years before, natural gas and large oil deposits had been discovered in Independence, which assured a healthy local economy for the future. John opened a combination jewelry store and book shop. As he had done in Lincoln, he shrewdly chose a site for his store next door to the principal bank, the Citizens National Bank, that was on the corner of North Pennsylvania Avenue and Myrtle Street in the heart of the town.[22] The façade of the two-story building was accented by a large clock that stood in front atop a tall pole and by the striped awnings, which in summer covered the storefront and the three windows above. This prime location and the town's prosperity soon made John's store one of the most successful in the state.

Although John found success and happiness in Independence, Martin did not. He had lost his friends, the mill, and the river; he suffered the trials of the new boy on the block; and school was no better than in Lincoln. However, John's new line of business was to have a major influence on the course of Martin's life. As he expanded his business to include a variety store, he acquired a franchise to sell Eastman-Kodaks and film.[23] Martin's passion for the cameras and film was immediate and intense, a turn of events which John encouraged, even to the point of building a darkroom for his son in the rear of the store. Martin's new interest gave his father hope that he might turn out all right after all and eventually join him in business. Martin was now a young teenager and more assertive about expressing his independence. Yet his father better tolerated this spiritedness and the boy's ever-worsening faults because of the hope sparked by his new love of photography. John not only indulged Martin with more film than was sold to customers, but also provided him with up-to-date books on photography.[24] While catering to his son's interest, he also tried to teach him to repair clocks and watches, to engrave and sell rings.[25] For Martin, the jewelry side of it was unpleasant medicine mixed into a tasty syrup of cameras and photography. John did not realize that Martin had set his heart not only on the cameras and film, but also on the freedom they could provide. That freedom seemed to be in those faraway exotic places evoked by the overseas shipments he unpacked in the store. It was not just the Venetian glass and Swiss clocks that stirred his imagination, but also the newspapers in which they were wrapped.[26] It was one thing to learn about these distant places in school, but quite another to touch things that had actually been there.

Life for Martin as a teenager settled into a regular routine of school and work in his father's store. Classrooms and a jeweler's eyepiece largely confined him to the small world of Independence, but his daydreams kept his hopes for freedom alive. As he moved into his later teenage years, he was able to achieve a degree of freedom by traveling beyond Independence with his parents' consent. Around this time, he announced to his family that he was "going to travel and make money doing it." This declaration encapsulated the two major aims of his entire life. He would fulfill his dreams of freedom while also pleasing his father, who measured success primarily in business terms.

The life of an itinerant photographer offered Martin his first chance to achieve both goals. In the summer of 1901, equipped with a camera and tripod and a tent for a darkroom, he set off in an old buckboard pulled by a pony named Socks. He borrowed photographic supplies from his father's store and purchased others on credit from a portrait studio in Independence.[27] Socks pulled him across the hot rolling prairies of southeastern Kansas to nearby Altoona, Odesha, and Coffeyville. He quickly discovered that the penny pictures of a roving photographer could not compete with established local studios, even if he undercut their prices. He had barely enough money to cover expenses and soon saw the salvation of his business enterprise in towns without photographers. Someone told him that nearby Chanute lacked a photographer, and so he decided to go there in the late summer and set up a studio.[28]

In the August heat, Chanute did not look much differ nt from Independence. It was approximately the same size, had a main street flanked by rows of wooden buildings and church spires that seemed to dance in the heat waves. Martin rented a small cluttered storeroom above Williams' Opera House on Main Street. Its skylight, essential for portrait photography, let in as much heat as sunshine. Yet Martin endured the heat, pastured Socks on the edge of town, and sent out announcements to Chanute's residents that he was in business.[29]

One of those who heard of Martin's studio was seven-year-old Osa Helen Leighty, who lived with her parents, grandmother, and three-year-old brother Vaughn in a small stone cottage on Malcolm Avenue and Seventh Street, a dozen blocks away. Her closest friend, Babe Halloran, had had her baby brother photographed in the room on top of Williams' Opera House, and Osa was intent on doing the same with Vaughn. The roving photographer from Independence was offering ten-cent portraits, supposedly of much higher quality than his usual penny prints. Osa's father, William Sherman Leighty, was skeptical. Ten cents was a steep price for a portrait by an itinerant photographer who was still in high school. However, Osa's insistence proved persuasive and eventually he agreed.

With the ten-cent piece clutched in her hand, Osa pulled a reluctant and uncooperative Vaughn through the hot dusty streets to the opera house. Vaughn's heavy copper-toed shoes, the long walk, and the heat pushed his patience to the limit. By the time they arrived at the top of the long flight of stairs to the studio, his face was tear-streaked and smudged. The young photographer was not only curt, but also opinionated as to how Vaughn should appear. As an angry Osa watched, he took off Vaughn's white embroidered collar and deliberately messed up his smoothed-out hair. Despite Osa's protests, the photographer took the picture of Vaughn as he thought he should look. The portrait that emerged from the developing tray later that day was not the prim and proper little boy Osa had envisioned, but a grinning urchin with tousled hair. Osa left in silent rage, never forgetting the experience. It would be another eight years before she and the young photographer, whose name she did not know, would meet again.[30]

Martin left Chanute the next day to return to Independence and the start of what would prove to be his last year of school. Neither he nor Osa could have known then that they would eventually spend an unusual lifetime together in exotic places across the seas. Chanute, like Independence, was a quiet prairie town, and Osa fully expected that she would marry there, settle down, and raise a family as had her parents.[31]

In sharp contrast to Martin, Osa grew up a happy child who delighted in collecting colored rocks and in hunting rabbits in the winter with her father. He taught her to shoot, to fish in the nearby Neosho River, to coax the backyard garden into bloom, and to take pleasure in life at home. Like Martin's father, he was the son of immigrants. His parents, Peter Leighty and Ellin Varns, had come to the United States from Austria. After a brief stay in Pennsylvania, they moved to Camden County in central Missouri, where William was born in 1867.[32] He first started to work for the Sante Fe Railroad as a brakeman, and later became an engineer.[33]

Osa's mother, Ruby Isabelle Holman, known to her family and friends as Belle, was descended from pioneer stock. She was understanding, loving, and kind. Under her tender teaching, Osa learned to sew and cook, bake bread, and be resourceful. As a child, Osa was also guided by her maternal grandmother, Nancy Ann Taylor, who lived with the family, and by a maternal aunt, Minnie Thomas. Belle and Grandma Taylor highly valued domesticity and instilled Osa with a respect for it. By the time Osa was a young teenager, her sights were firmly set on a home of her own in Chanute. She and her closest high school friend, Gail Perigo, even entered into a pact to have their weddings on the same day.

Even if teenage Osa wanted an ordinary settled life, her knowledge of her grandmother and aunt's adventures and of her mother's early life allowed her to think about other kinds of lives for women. Her grandmother, who trekked into Kansas from Arkansas next to a covered wagon, married several times and moved around a great deal.[34] She entered the prairie while the Indians and buffalo herds were still there. It was a world of hardship, danger, and sorrow, and not at all the life Osa envisioned for herself. Nonetheless, Osa's grandmother overcame enormous obstacles and was living proof that frontier women were capable of remarkable feats.[35] Belle, who broke with convention by being one of the sharpest card players in the county, married William in 1891 when she was only fifteen years old. She was a very young bride, even for post-frontier Kansas. Osa, their first child, was born on March 14, 1894, when Belle was seventeen years old.[36] Osa could easily see in the lives of both her mother and grandmother that domesticity was not at all incompatible with unconventional behavior. For Osa, however, her mother's half-sister, Aunt Minnie, represented a complete break with those conventions of society that cast the ideal woman as a homemaker and obedient marriage partner.

Minnie Thomas was a cigar-smoking circus performer who for many years worked as a bareback rider. Young Osa greatly admired her and was captivated by the exciting life she led.[37] Minnie represented a different kind of woman, one who had given up baking bread and sewing quilts for the life of a roving entertainer. The significance of Minnie for Osa was not so much what she did, but the fact that she did something so utterly different from most women of her day. That her occupation placed her on the margins of society mattered less to young Osa than to Belle.[38]

There was "something of Minnie in Osa," Belle often said. Osa was a born performer but an indifferent student. She preferred singing solos to schoolwork and especially enjoyed playing the piano for students as they marched out of an assembly. Graced with good looks, big brown eyes, curly flaxen hair, a soprano voice, and spunk leavened with a sweet disposition, she was a regular star at school entertainments.

Osa may have set her heart on a small frame house, a garden, and a family, yet the lives of her own close women relatives spoke of other choices. It was the possibility of defining her life in different terms that partially determined her elopement with Martin. In making this choice, she continued to cherish the domestic values and skills so carefully cultivated by her mother and grandmother. Unlike her Aunt Minnie, she did not discard them as she grew older. They were so much a part of her that they helped define her persona even when she became a celebrity. The Osa that the public came to know was a woman who planted Kansas sunflowers on the slopes of an African mountain and who baked apple pies the same afternoon she made an epic flight over the jungles of Borneo. In transporting her Kansas homestead to far-flung corners of the world, Osa was not engaging in a publicity stunt by dramatizing contrast. Rather, she was being true to herself.

———

Back in Independence, wiser but not richer, Martin returned to school and to work in his father's store. He continued to perfect his photographic skills through trial and error, and as H. C. Ingraham, his friend, observed, "delighted in trick composite photography." He would "take the head of some girl and put it on the body of a sow, a tiger, or a hound pup."[39]

These forays into trick photography were an early expression of a lifelong character trait. Martin was prone to modify reality on film and in his writings in order to meet what he thought were the preferences of his audience. In so doing, he frequently missed documenting the reality that was there. His insistence on photographing the toddler Vaughn stripped of his lace collar and with messed-up hair revealed this trait. Charmian London summed it up in commenting on Martin's book, *Through the South Seas with Jack London*: "Even when the actual truth would be more thrilling than the whopper, he'd rather tell the whopper."[40]

It was Martin's interest in trick photography that led to his expulsion from high school.[41] Using photographs he had taken at a school outing, he made composites of faculty members that showed them in romantic poses. He eagerly distributed these to his fellow students, who spent a hilarious morning looking at them in the halls and cloakrooms. For a few hours, Martin was the star of Montgomery County High School. However, prints eventually fell into the hands of the principal, who, much to Martin's surprise, saw them as indecent. He ordered Martin to collect all the prints he had given out and to bring them to his office. After tearing up the photographs, the principal expelled Martin with the rebuke that his father had "an idle, mischievous wastrel for a son."[42]

This punishment was not as arbitrary as Osa makes it appear nor as harsh as some writers have concluded.[43] The contrived photographs infringed on the morality and conventions of the times. That they had been created and distributed by a problem student whose record included chronic truancy and poor grades made dismissal almost inevitable.

There was more embarrassment than regret in Martin's reaction to his expulsion. According to Osa, the next day he left in shame for Chicago, determined to show his parents and former teachers that he could achieve success on his own terms. He obtained a job as a bellhop at the La Salle Hotel and later worked as an engraver for a leading Chicago engraving firm. Osa recounts that he soon left for Europe, having wagered with his fellow employees that he could make it to London and back on $4.25. Martin then supposedly sailed to Liverpool as an assistant veterinarian in charge of a hundred mules, had his clothes stolen on board, and despite four bloody fights with sailors to recover them landed almost naked. Working at odd jobs such as loading cargo and washing dishes, he moved across Europe to London, Brussels, Brest, Stockholm, and finally to Paris, where he arrived in 1903 when he was in his twentieth year.[44]

On Bastille Day, Martin went to visit Luna Park, where he found that the carousel had broken down, much to the disappointment of the crowds waiting to ride it and of the proprietor who stood to lose a peak day's business. The operator-mechanic was not up to the job of repairing the machinery, and so Martin pushed his way through the crowds, and without being asked, fixed the carousel. This account in *I Married Adventure* finishes in the best Horatio Alger tradition: the grateful proprietor rewarded Martin with a job as engineer. Saving enough money but steadily growing homesick for his mother and sister, he decided to return to Kansas.[45]

A later version of these events has Martin traveling to Europe on the 1906 wager in charge of twenty-eight horses, and returning to the United States as a stowaway.[46] Ingraham presents yet a third version linked to events in his own life. It is at significant variance with Osa's account. He writes that, when he returned to Independence from military school for Christmas vacation in 1902, he went to the Johnson store. There, John greeted him "with a sour face" and said "your friend Martin Johnson is not here. He's stranded in England, the ungrateful scamp. He is no longer a son of mine. A rolling stone never gathers any moss!" Lucinda and Freda told Ingraham that "Martin got a job taking some horses from the Mulhall Ranch in Oklahoma to England. He only got his passage and no return, so now he's over there hungry and penniless." Ingraham then records Lucinda's characterization of John as a stingy slave driver and relates that she was "so glad to tell her troubles to a sympathetic listener that she didn't stop until she was out of breath." Lucinda said that she was going to cable money to Martin later that day from the few savings she had been able to set aside.[47]

According to Ingraham, Martin later attended his friend's graduation from military school in June 1903, a period during which Osa places him in Europe. Ingraham then went to work at his summer job as a stenographer with the Forepaugh-Sells Circus in Columbus, Ohio. Martin accompanied him there and worked at the circus for several weeks as a roustabout. Ingraham adds that later that year Martin worked as a broncobuster at the Zack Mulhall Ranch in Oklahoma, where "Martin liked the cowboys and the general environment of the Mulhall Ranch, but what he sought most was lacking—adventure in far-away places."[48]

In writing to Jack London from Independence on November 5, 1906, Martin claimed that he had been to Europe twice, "once with cattle and once with horses—the last trip I made I left Chicago with $6.00—was gone nine weeks, visited Ireland, Scotland, England and Belgium, and returned to Chicago with twenty-five cents—the first trip I stowed away from Southampton, England to Antwerp, Belgium."[49]

It appears that elements from the two trips were merged into one in *I Married Adventure* and significantly modified to create an exciting human-interest story. In Osa's account, a bold and almost reckless Martin impulsively takes off for Europe from Chicago, and, equipped with little more than determination, forges ahead into the unknown. In reality, the trips were carefully arranged, with Martin traveling as a livestock hand. He certainly had the requisite skills and the personal contacts, having worked on the Mulhall Ranch. His stowing away from Southampton to Antwerp was a bold stroke. However, it was carried off by a youth who had years of experience riding the rails in the Midwest. Home and hearth were always there when he ran into trouble or needed the return trans-Atlantic fare. Thus, the real Martin of this period was not the overly confident and independent risk-taker portrayed by Osa. Rather, he was a determined young man who, buttressed by a dependable family, was able to take measured risks in search of his dreams.[50]

Martin's life between early 1902 and late 1906 amounted to a series of attempts to achieve independence and personal fulfillment in travel to distant places. By his own reckoning, he failed to attain either of these goals and regularly returned home to his parents' patience and generosity. But each return meant facing the unwelcome possibility of a permanent life in the store in Independence. The pattern of flight to Chicago, Europe, Oklahoma, any place but Kansas, speaks of his determination to escape this fate. A precise chronology of his travels at this time is less significant than an awareness that his behavior was being molded by strong emotional and psychological forces.

One can empathize with a father whose twenty-one-year-old son had become something of an aimless rover. John had mustered all that was in his power to offer, and trusted that time and maturity would settle his son down. He continued to see the solution to Martin's problems close at hand in a partnership in the store. That he did so reveals his incomprehension of the driving force behind Martin's behavior. Martin had no doubts about what he wanted, and saw that it lay far away from the store and well beyond the prairie horizon.

CHAPTER TWO

THE URGE TO WANDER

In the spring of 1906, Martin was working with a leading Chicago engraving firm. His father, who arranged the position for him, hoped that a stay in Chicago would cure him of the wanderlust and help him acquire skills he could put to good use in the jewelry store. Martin eventually became an expert engraver, much to his father's delight, but the urge to travel remained as strong as ever. Proximity to the stockyards and previous experiences at the Mulhall Ranch enabled him to get a temporary job as a livestock hand accompanying a shipment of horses to England. His father was dismayed by this turn of events, but could do little to stop him since Martin was a determined twenty-one-year-old somewhat beyond arm's reach.

After delivering the horses, Martin roamed through England, Scotland, Ireland, and Belgium for a few weeks before returning from Liverpool on the White Star steamer *Bovic*. He arrived in Chicago with only twenty-five cents in his pocket but with very firm ideas about future trips hewn by his European experiences. He scorned Cook's Tours, which he said "go over the same well-beaten paths year by year until the places would seem as stage scenery and the people actors." And he both laid out his future travel plans and made a powerful declaration of his life's agenda when he wrote: "I want to see things and places other people don't see."[1]

Martin soon returned to Independence and to the routine of his father's jewelry store. There was little commitment in this return since he planned to start traveling around the world in March of the following year. Setting out east from New York, he hoped to work or bum his way through Europe and Asia, returning to the West Coast via the Pacific. His plans were very vague and imprecise, which of course made it all the more of an adventure. But all this talk of circling the globe gave his parents fits of anxiety and they did their best to discourage him. As they had done in the past, they tried to direct him toward the comfort and security of home and routine. But Martin's feelings relentlessly drove him into a horizon of the unexpected and the unusual with a force that was almost beyond his control.

During the fall of 1906, Martin's vague daydreams of world travel took on a tangible form. He checked into sailing schedules and livestock shipments and laid out a general but imprecise itinerary. Never an avid reader, he seems to have derived his images of the far away from an imagination that was fed more by occasional newspaper and magazine articles than by a steady diet of serious adventure and travel books. However, exotic places that had already been well described no longer took his fancy. The fact that they had already been documented deprived him of the discoverer-interpreter role he sought for himself. He preferred to sail off into the unknown, ever hopeful that he would fall upon some untouched corners of the earth. Eventually he would modify this almost childlike fantasy when faced with the reality that most places had already been seen and described. However, in making this compromise, he never deviated from seeking out the exotic and the unusual and from communicating his own interpretations to large audiences.

While Martin was making plans for this trip, a famous American writer and his wife were about to embark on a seven-year trip around the world, sailing west from San Francisco. Jack London had achieved international fame as a writer three years before with the publication of his book *The Call of the Wild*. Although he was only twenty-seven years old when the book was first published, he had already led a fascinating life full of dramatic contrasts. There were important parallels in his early life and Martin's, which gave fate a hand in bringing the two men together. They were different in many ways, but their differences were complementary and suited their commonalities of impulse and desire. For Martin, Jack became both hero and model.

Jack was born in 1874 to an enterprising and free-thinking mother who embraced women's suffrage, astrology, and spiritualism, and to an egotistical astrologer who abandoned his wife when she became pregnant. Almost three years after his birth, Jack's mother married a widower, John London, whose alcoholism and fecklessness doomed them to poverty and debt. As is sometimes the case in families where one parent is an alcoholic, Jack developed a heightened sense of responsibility for his family's welfare and worked at a variety of jobs to help support them while still a schoolboy. His enthusiasm for this drudgery was fueled by high purpose and solaced by the escape provided by magazines and books in public libraries. Unlike Martin, he was an avid reader of adventure stories and counted the African traveler Paul du Chaillu among his heroes. But he shared Martin's youthful hopes of becoming an explorer who would someday discover unknown parts of the world. His readings served as the inspiration for the adventures he later undertook, and the risks and experiences in these became the substance of much of his writing. The appeal of the wilderness and elemental struggles for survival prominently figure in many of his stories. In his own autobiographical works, he struggles against these awesome powers with nothing more than his own physical strength, endurance, and will to succeed.

Jack avidly read many of Horatio Alger's stories and was strongly influenced by them. Like Martin, he sought the exotic and far away, but to this was added the lure of rags-to-riches success. Jack achieved these objectives through sheer drive, ability, and a willingness to take risks, traits that were present in Martin's character as well.

The road to success for Jack was a difficult one spanning many years. The newspaper boy became an oyster pirate and then a merchant seaman on a three-masted sealing schooner that took him into the North Pacific and to Japan. He became a tramp riding the rails across the United States, a janitor, a laundry worker, and a gold miner in the Klondike. In between, he worked short stints in a jute mill and as a boiler coal shoveler. In all of these settings, he struggled against either nature or social injustice—enduring themes that had a universal appeal when he transformed them into fiction or adventure stories.

His struggles to be a writer were no easier; it took years for him to improve his syntax and to break through the barrier of rejection slips. Jack finally got into print in 1898, when the *Overland Monthly* published one of his Alaskan stories, "To the Man on Trail." However, his literary reputation was not established until the *Atlantic Monthly* published his "An Odyssey of the North" in 1900 and Houghton Mifflin a book of his stories, *The Son of the Wolf,* the same year. His writings brought him international fame in his lifetime. To many readers, though, he was more than just a writer: he was a truly American folk hero, the self-made man.[2]

Jack joined the Socialist Labor Party in 1896 and rapidly became one of its leading spokesmen. But he was also a firm believer in Anglo-Saxon racial superiority. His racial attitudes were forged first in his youth at home, where his mother freely gave vent to her own racial prejudices, and later in the San Francisco Bay area, where recent immigrants were viewed as a threat by earlier Anglo-Saxon settlers.[3] At the time racism was effortlessly expressed by newspapers, writers, and intellectuals, and was an accepted part of the social landscape for most white Americans. Jack's racial views prominently figure in a number of his writings whose themes and characters not only exalt white superiority, but often his own and often contradictory beliefs in atheism, determinism, evolution, and individualism. His racial views were to have an important influence on Martin, who looked up to him as the paradigm for some of the things he wanted to be and achieve.

Jack married Bess Maddern in 1900, the same year that his first book of stories, *The Son of the Wolf*, was published. They had two daughters, Joan, born in 1901, and Bess, born in 1902. However, by 1903, Jack's marriage was breaking up as he became involved with Charmian Kittredge, an upper-middle-class woman, five years older than himself, who had been raised by an aunt who espoused spiritualism, free love, and vegetarianism. Charmian defied the social conventions of the day, worked in an office as a secretary-typist—then a man's occupation—and viewed herself as an emancipated woman. They were married in November 1905, after Jack divorced Bess, and sought to establish a unique marital partnership in which he was Mate-Man, she Mate-Woman, and both of them comrades. This nomenclature of equality, borrowed from sailing and socialism, defined a new kind of relationship between man and woman, which they hoped would be emulated by others.

Achieving this kind of partnership was no easy task, especially in the early years of Jack and Charmian's marriage. Jack was endowed with a powerful ego, plagued by alcoholism and illness, and susceptible to extramarital affairs. Charmian was accommodating and faithful, in robust health, and graced with poise, style, and cultivated manners. But she was also highly independent, willing to take risks, and athletically inclined. She was extremely well educated in the arts and humanities, but naive about the social and political issues that consumed her husband. However, over time she adopted his views and eventually achieved prominence in the socialist movement. Some of her contemporaries regarded her as a new breed of woman worthy of imitation, while others saw her as childlike in her self-absorption, and took offense at her reckless expressions of opinion on any subject she turned to.[4]

That the Londons' marriage proved successful surprised many, given their differences. But their love and the progressive confluence of their interests overcame these differences. Charmian, who had gained some editing experience while working in the offices of the *Overland Monthly*, greatly contributed to Jack's later success by serving as editor, critic, typist, and consultant. She not only polished his manuscripts, but also served as the model for many of his female characters. While Jack's work and interests served to bind them together, they did not submerge her own individuality nor relegate her to an inferior position in their relationship.

Although women's magazines and some leading newspapers gave high praise to the Londons' declaration of equality, their unusual relationship did not go down well with society at large. Their bohemian friends in the Bay Area—the group of poets, artists, writers, and

others who came to be known as the Crowd to both themselves and
the press—were equally disapproving. The prominent members of
this group were George Sterling, the poet; Jim Whitaker, a writer;
Xavier Martinez, a painter who shocked even this group when he married Jim Whitaker's daughter Elsie, who was half his age; Blanche
Partington, a drama and opera critic for the *San Francisco Call*; and
Arnold Genthe, who eventually became a successful portrait photographer. Although the members of this group espoused a number of
unconventional views, male-female equality was not one of them.
They not only concurred with the prevailing societal belief in separate
roles for men and women, but also considered women as subservient
and, in their capacities as wives, mistresses, or friends, were there to
help men achieve success through the exercise of male creativity.[5]

On October 18, 1905, Jack and Charmian left California on a lecture tour sponsored by the Intercollegiate Socialist Society of which
he had been elected president the month before. Upton Sinclair, who
was a major force in the founding of the society, and the others who
guided it saw Jack's role as one of public relations. His stature as a
leading man of letters insured that the socialists' message would reach
audiences that might otherwise turn a deaf ear to the speeches of ordinary revolutionaries.[6] Prior to leaving on the trip, which was to carry
them through the Midwest and the East, Jack purchased a 129-acre
ranch near Glen Ellen in Sonoma County, thus fulfilling one of his
fondest dreams. At the same time, he and Charmian also made a firm
decision to build their own boat and sail around the world. The idea
for this trip actually occurred to Jack in 1900 after he read Joshua
Slocum's book *Sailing Alone Around the World*.[7] Slocum's three-year
voyage on his small boat between 1895 and 1898 had captured the
public imagination and his book, published in 1900, became a huge
success. Jack was adept at getting ideas from others, and Slocum's feat
appealed to his appetite for physical challenges. His initial plan was to
sail through the South Seas, but over the ensuing years this evolved
into a larger scheme of circumnavigating the globe. Initially, he gave
his newly acquired ranch first priority and thought of building the
boat over a five-year period. However, Charmian urged him to reverse his priorities and undertake the trip while they were still relatively young, healthy, and full of enthusiasm.

Jack, who knew nothing about shipbuilding, designed the boat himself and created a two-masted ketch that had a larger sail forward. It
was to be 45 feet long at the water line and 57 by 15 feet overall. He
could have hired professionals to design the boat or else bought a finished craft. But such an easy solution would have deprived him of the
pleasure and challenge of imposing the imprint of his personality on
the vessel. By both building the boat and making the trip, he could
exult once again: "The things I like constitute my set of values. The

thing I like most of all is personal achievement . . . achievement for my own delight. It is the old 'I did it! I did it! With my own hands I did it!'"[8]

The building of the boat began in earnest in early 1906 at the H. P. Anderson shipyard in San Francisco. From the very beginning the project was plagued by a series of construction problems, delays, and enormous cost overruns. Some of these, but not all, were due to the fact that Jack had hired Roscoe Eames to oversee the project. Roscoe, who was married to Charmian's Aunt Netta, was a bright but eccentric man who had absolutely no substantial experience in shipbuilding—or sailing, for that matter. He had achieved some distinction for inventing a system of shorthand, but his work experiences were thinly spread over such diverse areas as teaching secretarial courses, serving as captain of a commuter ferry in San Francisco Bay, and being the business manager of the *Overland Monthly*, the literary magazine that had given Jack his first break.

When construction began, Jack and Charmian were living at Wake Robin Lodge, a property Roscoe and Netta had developed with rental cabins for vacationing families. The couples regularly saw each other and even took their meals with them. Jack always preferred to have close friends and relatives perform all sorts of jobs for him: he believed that they too could meet any challenge if they tried. Roscoe was clearly not up to the task, but his vanity stopped him from admitting it. In fairness, however, only the most experienced shipbuilder could have done better, considering that there were forty-seven unions and over a hundred firms involved in the building of the boat.

As construction progressed, it became clear to Jack and Charmian that Roscoe was incapable of detecting inferior materials and slipshod workmanship and was easily duped by unprincipled suppliers who viewed the wealthy author of *The Call of the Wild* as fair game. Although Jack had ordered the finest lumber and the best metal fittings, lumberyard rejects began to shape the ship's form. When finally detected, the defective materials had to be removed and the work redone. The initial projected cost of $7,000 ultimately rose to $30,000.[9]

Not all the delays were due to poor workmanship, shoddy construction materials, and Roscoe's incompetence. On April 18, 1906, San Francisco was rocked by a devastating earthquake followed by a massive fire. The reconstruction effort immediately created acute scarcities of building supplies and skilled workers. Matters were further complicated for the Londons by emergency municipal regulations that prohibited the use of building materials for anything but homes and businesses.

Even the naming of the boat became embroiled in argument. The publishers of *Cosmopolitan* initially offered to help defray the costs of construction if Jack named the boat *Cosmopolitan Magazine*. He agreed at first, but then changed his mind. However, he did sign contracts with *Cosmopolitan* and also with *Woman's Home Companion* to provide articles about places they would stop at during the voyage.[10] Members of the Crowd and others offered suggestions for naming the vessel, while reporters, sailors, and even some of Jack's socialist associates disparagingly called it "London's Folly." Jack eventually settled on calling it the *Snark*, after the strange creature in Lewis Carroll's poem *The Hunting of the Snark*. In a letter to a magazine editor, he argued that "boats, like horses and dogs, should have names of one syllable. Good, sharp names that can never be misheard." Yet ever the pragmatist, he offered to change the name if the magazine paid for the full costs of the ship and gave it to him as an "out-and-out present."[11]

Jack's unorthodox design and approach to construction were matched by his methods for choosing the crew. He chose Roscoe as conavigator based on the fact that he was a relative who claimed that he could teach himself navigation. That he had absolutely no ocean-going navigational experience did not seem to trouble Jack in the least. As the other conavigator, Jack was equally ignorant of the use of the sextant, compass, and logarithms. His choice of engineer was Herbert Rowell Stolz, a twenty-year-old Stanford University student who was an excellent swimmer and football player.[12] Although Bert had taken engineering courses at Stanford, he knew absolutely nothing about repairing engines. However, Jack, who had met him at Wake Robin Lodge, liked him and assumed that he would rise to the occasion and teach himself engine repair. The choice of a cabin boy was somewhat more rational. Paul H. Tochigi, a young Japanese who had recently arrived in the United States, had become the London's valet a short time before and was willing to make the voyage.

Toward the end of 1906 all of the crew members had been chosen except for one. Extensive newspaper coverage of the proposed trip had already produced a steady stream of letters from hopeful applicants. When Jack and Charmian let it be known that they planned to complete their crew with one of these applicants, the stream turned into a deluge. The applicants included lawyers, bankers, tramps, and millionaires, those who required a salary and those who were willing to serve for free.[13] Many of Jack's decisions were based on impulse and intuition driven by strong feelings of like or dislike. There was no chance that the stacks of applications would be methodically scrutinized and the applicants' claims substantiated by background checks. The choice would be made more on the basis of how Jack felt about the applicant and less on what he knew about them.

On a cool autumn evening, Martin Johnson returned home from the jewelry store and after dinner picked up his sister's copy of the November issue of the *Woman's Home Companion*.[14] There he saw Jack's three-page letter to the magazine's editor describing the proposed *Snark* trip. The letter and three photographs occupied a full page under the title "A Preliminary Letter from Jack London Who Is Going Round the World for the Woman's Home Companion." Jack described the trip in some detail. "We plan to go up the Seine to Paris; up the Thames to London, up the Danube . . . up the Amazon. . . . We expect to spend months on the Canals of China, a summer at Venice, a winter at Naples. . . . Expect to fool around a lot in the South Seas."[15]

In the article, Jack boasted about his skill as a photographer. "I am myself taking along only four cameras, and I know how to use them, too." He also made a point of saying that he was no Cook's tourist. "I've got to see things myself in my own way." He did not ask for volunteers nor encourage people to write directly to him about the trip, probably because by this time he had already received numerous requests from hopefuls.

Martin's response to this letter was immediate and visceral. He later said: "Instantly, I was all aglow with enthusiasm, and before I had finished the article I had mapped out a plan of action. If that boat made a trip such as described, I was going to be on that boat. It is needless to say that the letter I immediately wrote to Mr. Jack London was as strong as I could make it. . . . I did my best to convince Mr. London that I was the man he needed."[16]

On November 5, 1906, Martin wrote a six-page letter to Jack accompanied by a half-page postscript and a photograph of himself. In the letter, he said:

> . . . am writing you with the forlorn hope of you needing an extra man. I'm aware that you will certainly be worried with many similar requests but here goes anyway.
>
> I had already made plans for a two year trip around the world and intended to start the first of March—as it would not then be too cold to 'sleep under the trees' but to get to make such a trip as you intend to make I would undergo any hardship.
>
> Now my proposition is that I go with you as any kind of help you may need and I'm certainly willing to work—you to give me employment; I will expect only my passage and will pay my own expenses while in port—no wages.

You mention being 'there' at photography—well
I'm rather conceited about my ability in that line too. I
have just received a new No. 3 a.1. Kodak with a Plas-
tigmat lens and as we handle Eastman products I can
get credit at any Kodak repository in the world.

I have been to Europe twice—once with cattle and
once with horses—the last trip I left Chicago with
$6.00—was gone nine weeks, visited Ireland, Scot-
land, England and Belgium and returned to Chicago
with twenty-five cents—the first trip I stowed away
from Southampton, England to Antwerp, Belgium; I
only mention this so you will not think I have been on
Cooks excursions. . . . They go over the same well
beaten paths year by year until the places would seem
as stage scenery and the people actors. I want to see
things and places other people don't. . . .

Mr. London I would certainly like to make this trip
with you—could leave any time.

But if you think you could not use me I hope to run
across you in some part of the world.

In his postscript, Martin added: "Forgot to mention my age which is
23—but I think I have seen more of this world in that time than very
few can boast of—guess I'm a regular rolling stone—they say "A rolling stone gathers no moss" but "A rolling stone never gets to be a moss
back."[17]

Martin's letter was a bold and determined plea. He crafted it so as
to present his accomplishments, skills, and attitudes in a way that
would impress the seasoned adventurer. He emphasized that, like
Jack, he disliked Cook's Tours and wanted to see things for himself
and in his own way. And the postscript, with its twist on the proverb
that Martin's father so often used to put down his son's wanderlust,
would have pleased a fellow adventurer.

There was a powerful sincerity and simplicity to this letter and
much in it that would appeal to Jack and Charmian. Martin obviously
had pluck as exemplified by his cattleboat voyages to Europe and his
plans now to take on the world. He had proven his adaptability, was
enterprising and able to put up with hardship. That he was adept at
photography but had difficulty composing a compound sentence were
also in his favor. Jack needed to finance both the construction of the
Snark and the voyage with earnings from his writings; therefore, he
was not about to take a potential writer on board. Yet this was the
Golden Era of the Magazine in the United States and editors increasingly wanted their stories well illustrated with photographs. Although
Bert Stolz was originally taken on to handle both the boat's engines

and the trip's photographic needs, Jack obviously saw in Martin someone else who could not only manage the photography but also obtain
credit with Kodak suppliers anywhere in the world.

While the content of the letter stressed that Martin and Jack were of
like mind on a number of things, the form was meant to convince on
other grounds. It is significant that Martin wrote this letter on his
father's stationery, which listed Kodak cameras and supplies among
the products carried. The letterhead not only confirmed Martin's professed skills with cameras and photography, but also established that
he was the son of a responsible businessman. Leaving as little as possible to chance, Martin also enclosed a photograph of himself. As it
turned out, the photograph became critical in Jack's final decision.[18]

Martin's letter and photograph were added to the pile of supplica-
tions that were coming in to Glen Ellen from all over the country. Jack
and Charmian packed them up and went down to Carmel to visit
George Sterling, who had settled there along with most of the San
Francisco Bay Area bohemian set. Among those who were visiting
with George Sterling that day was Elsie Whitaker Martinez, who left
an oral account of what happened next.

> Carrie Sterling asked us to come over to her place—
> Jack was bringing a bundle of letters from the boys
> who answered his published appeal for a cabin boy for
> the *Snark*, and we were to share the excitement of
> choosing the winner. It did not take long to reduce the
> bundle to two letters—one from Martin Johnson and
> the other, an intelligent, eager lad whose name I've
> forgotten because he was turned down.
>
> Carrie, George, Jack and Marty argued back and
> forth, but I had not declared myself yet. Carrie called
> out, "Elsie, your turn!" I was scanning the photograph
> of the husky, beaming young Johnson. I insisted that
> young Johnson seemed to have all the qualities befit-
> ting a cabin boy. Jack agreed. So Carrie, George and
> Marty gave in and Martin Johnson was accepted to
> have the thrilling honor of crossing the Pacific on the
> *Snark*.[19]

This account, recorded when Elsie Whitaker Martinez was well on
in years, appears accurate in general but is suspect with regard to
some details. The Londons had already chosen their valet, Paul H.
Tochigi, to be cabin boy. Elsie's subsequent paragraph of reminiscences about Martin are clearly inaccurate. She recounts that Jack
fired Martin in Tahiti for speaking with a *New York Times* reporter
about the trip and that Martin then obtained a position with an

anthropological expedition as a photographer even though he knew little about photography. Although Jack may have temporarily fired Martin in a moment of anger, he obviously must have rehired him right away. However, there is no documented evidence that he ever fired Martin, who by this stage of the voyage was in charge of the engines and photography. There were constant changes in the crew of the *Snark* and Elsie could easily have confused Martin with someone else, especially since she was recalling secondhand information after a lapse of many years.

Unlike some of Jack's other choices, the selection process was neither arbitrary nor capricious. While Jack sought the opinions of his friends from the Crowd, his approval of their choice was critical. Everyone saw that Martin's attributes and accomplishments matched what was needed, and he became their choice and Jack's. Jack's decision, reached at Carmel, was fired off to Martin from Oakland on November 12 in the form of a telegram:

> CAPACITY OF COOK ALSO DO TRICK AT WHEEL TWENTY FIVE
> DOLLARS PER MONTH CAN YOU COOK? WHAT'S YOUR WEIGHT?
> TELEGRAPH REPLY   JACK LONDON[20]

The telegram arrived late in the evening and was delivered to Martin as he stood in front of his father's jewelry store. He later wrote: "The instant I saw the little yellow envelope, something told me that this was the turning point of my life. With trembling hands I tore it open, my heart beating wildly with excitement. It was Jack London's reply, the fateful slip of paper that was to dictate my acts for several years to come."[21]

For Martin it was a stroke of luck right out of Horatio Alger and it was fitting that it was the creation of a man whose own life had been greatly influenced by Alger's writings and who symbolized adventure. Although Martin could not cook, he was not going to allow this opportunity to slip him by. Like Jack, he believed he could do anything he put his mind to and predictably shot back a reply.

> SIX MONTHS EXPERIENCE AS COOK WILL DO TRICK AT WHEEL
> WEIGHT 156 LETTER FOLLOWS   MARTIN E. JOHNSON[22]

In a three-page letter he sent Jack that same day, Martin stated that he had worked as a second cook in a restaurant in Kansas City, Missouri, for six months. But he added a caveat: "Did not cook any fancy dishes—all plain food; for the customers were all laboring men." Leaving nothing to chance, he reiterated his other assets: "Roughed it the best part of my life from necessity but to see the country . . . and I can also take a good bit of the work off your hands in developing and finishing for I certainly claim to be an expert in that line."[23] His darkroom skills were good news for Jack and Charmian, who were already having doubts that Bert would make an effective photographic assistant.

John Johnson, who had always discouraged his son's wanderlust, appreciated the significance of the London proposition. While Martin's solo wanderings seemed ridiculous to him, this voyage with one of America's most famous folk heroes was another matter. He was already bursting with pride over a son who had previously brought him so much embarrassment, and was keenly aware of the fame and status that the trip would bring not only to Martin but also to the whole family. He now added his voice in the hopes of securing Martin's position on the *Snark*. This gesture represented a major turning point in his relationship with his son. In a one-page letter he enclosed with Martin's, he wrote to Jack saying: "I am aware that it will be a rough trip as well as a dangerous one and don't much like the idea of letting him go, but then if I was young and footloose as he is, nothing could hold me back if I had the chance of going. So if you want him we will not object. He is strong and healthy, a fair cook, a first class photographer and I will personally guarantee his honesty and integrity."[24]

John Johnson not only gave his paternal blessing to Martin's joining the *Snark* cruise, but also became a party to the white lie that Martin could cook. Since the projected sailing date of the *Snark* was only a month away, Martin had little time to learn even the rudiments of cooking. He and his father negotiated with Jess Utz, the cook at the nearby White Front Quick Lunch Room, who readily agreed to teach Martin all he knew. Martin threw himself into the task of learning to bake bread, make cakes, fry, broil, and marinate. He read cookbooks, made extensive notes, memorized recipes, and took a constant interest in the things his mother did over the kitchen stove. Jess Utz remained skeptical, but within a few weeks, Martin's determination enabled him to master the basics of cooking. To be sure, he was a mediocre cook and he harbored constant fears that the Londons might send him back to Independence in disgrace if he failed them prior to the *Snark*'s sailing.[25]

On November 23, Martin received a lengthy letter from Jack outlining the trip, describing the crew, and laying down the law as to what was expected of everyone. It contained a mixture of levity— "Oh, if you have a bad temper, don't come," and barking orders: "It must be thoroughly understood that when we are on duty, the relations existing will be that of Captain and crew. Off duty is another matter. . . . You've had enough experience knocking about to know what that means." Jack also made it clear that while he welcomed Martin's help with photography and developing, he did not want Martin or anyone else taking pictures of him, Charmian, and the boat for use in magazines without his first seeing them and giving permission. His reasons were very explicit: "I have contracts with certain magazines and it would scarcely be the fair thing for those contracts to be violated by those who go along with me."[26]

There were further letters between Martin and the Londons about clothing, passport requirements, and Martin's wish to stay in Independence as long as possible to engrave souvenir spoons for the Christmas trade. The need to engrave souvenir spoons was really a pretext to buy more time in which to learn cooking with Jess Utz. However, Jack said he wanted Martin in Oakland by December 10 because he claimed he had set the 15th as the sailing date. However, the *Snark* was far from completion and could not have possibly sailed then. Jack's own pretext, spawned by second thoughts, was intended to bring Martin to Oakland well in advance of the sailing date so that he could be more closely scrutinized.

Martin's friend, H. C. Ingraham, obtained $100 from a Wichita newspaperman, Victor Murdock, to help with traveling costs to which Ingraham's father added another $100. John Johnson, overcoming his own stinginess, "opened his old-fashioned snap pocketbook and matched the $100 gifts." With $300 in his pocket, a small satchel of clothes, and one camera, Martin boarded the train and headed for California. His friend Ingraham, who was taking up a job as a timekeeper and commissary car clerk with the Atchison, Topeka and Santa Fe Railway, traveled with him as far as Arizona.[27]

One can easily imagine Martin's emotions the night he arrived in Oakland in a torrential rainstorm. This first meeting with Jack was the high point of his life so far. It was Charmian who greeted him first. "When I rapped at the door a neat little woman opened it, and grabbing my hand, almost wrung it off."[28]

For Charmian the meeting was not as momentous as it was for Martin. In her account of it she says that the house was full of Crowd members when Martin arrived. "While we wives of 'the boys' were entertaining ourselves at my newly acquired Steinway 'B' grand, there arrived, from Kansas, in a drenching southeasterner, Martin Johnson, who was destined to be the only unshaken unit in the *Snark*'s crew. After partially drying himself, he sat down at the game of hearts."[29]

Martin did not notice the others present, only Jack, who walked toward the door to meet him. His description of Jack and of their first meeting was vivid:

A striking young man of thirty, with very broad shoulders, a mass of wavy auburn hair, and a general atmosphere of boyishness . . .

We gripped. And that is how I met Jack London, traveller, novelist, and social reformer; and that is how for the first time, I really ran shoulder to shoulder with Adventure, which I had been pursuing all my years.[30]

CHAPTER THREE

APPRENTICE TO
ADVENTURE

Jack and Charmian London invited Martin to be their guest in their Oakland home until the sailing date, now rescheduled for January 12, 1907, Jack's thirty-first birthday. The gesture reflected not only their generosity, but also Jack's pragmatism. After all, Martin was the only stranger in the crew at this point, and Jack and Charmian needed to get to know him better before making a final decision about taking him aboard. They quickly assessed him as a genial, energetic, and eager-to-please young man, full of enthusiasm for adventure. Fortunately for Martin, and characteristic of the Londons, their strong liking for him as a person obscured any objective assessment of what he was hired to do, namely cook. In this regard, they treated him as they did everyone else in the crew.

Prior to the *Snark*'s sailing, Martin got to know the Londons extremely well as proposed sailing dates came and went. Roscoe's incompetence and the scarcity of labor and supplies were only partially to blame for the postponements. Jack kept modifying the ship's design as it was being built and making last-minute changes that took weeks to implement. As a result of all these delays, Martin eventually spent three months in the London home. The impressions he formed of them at that time were reinforced during the trip. He saw them as the ideal adventure couple, and Jack as the model for some of the things he wanted to achieve. Of course, he had no aspirations of being a writer, but he did want a life of adventure, and for this Jack was mentor and he apprentice. His early recorded impressions of Jack and Charmian are noteworthy because they emphasize those characteristics he admired in each of them and in their relationship: "Jack is like a big schoolboy, good-natured, frank, generous, and Mrs. London is just a grown-up school girl. They are good comrades, always helping each other in their work. Mrs. London I found to be as full of grit as any of us—as we were later to discover, there was hardly a thing on board that any of the men could do that she couldn't do."[1]

Martin, who was never a great reader, now pored enthusiastically over Jack's works. He read *The Sea Wolf* and *The People of the Abyss*, and strongly identified with the latter, which he said "read almost like a passage out of my own life."[2] Martin had spent several days in the slums of London on one of his European trips, and knew firsthand the horrors of life there so vividly portrayed by Jack in this book. He also watched a disciplined Jack write approximately four thousand words a day in longhand, and sometimes served as a sounding board as Jack read passages aloud.

In March 1907 the *Snark* slid down the ways and was towed to Oakland where electricians, plumbers, and carpenters finished the work. Because of the considerable risk of vandalism, Martin and Bert took turns sleeping on deck. One night when Martin was aboard, a severe storm buffeted ships in the bay and wrecked a number of them. However, his quick thinking over the four-hour period of the storm saved the *Snark* from being smashed against a wharf. The engine had been dismantled by the machinists for cleaning, and he had to reassemble it first during the storm before maneuvering the *Snark* into the safety of the bay.[3]

Martin proved his worth to the Londons that night, not as a cook, but as a man who was enterprising, quick thinking, and in possession of unique mechanical skills learned as a watchmaker's son. He may have previously begrudged his years of apprenticeship, fixing everything from grandfather clocks to wristwatches, but from this point on, he regularly used all the skills his father and others had taught him.

The *Snark* was graced with finishing touches in Oakland as Jack was deeply involved in writing *The Road*, his book of tramp reminiscences. The incongruous temporal association of these two events again underscored the contradictions in Jack's life and beliefs. While he penned descriptions of the down-and-out and promoted socialism, the *Snark* was fitted with a deluxe bathroom, teak hatches, bronze propellers, galvanized anchors, a five-horsepower engine, two lifeboats, a dynamo, and several appliances, including electric fans. In the end, the *Snark* became a floating palace. Yet its hull leaked so badly that it once sank into the mud of the bay. Now nearly finished, it weighed ten tons and was very much a reflection of the man who had created it. Like him, it embodied both defects and unusual strengths and was of a unique design that did not neatly fit into any established nautical category.

By March the galley was functional and Martin practiced making bread and cakes for the workmen, whose resounding approbation gave him increased confidence.[4] Although he was the cook, Roscoe and

Charmian actually made the key decisions about provisioning the ship. As might have been expected, most of the food was tinned, but Roscoe saw to it that a good deal of it was of the variety he regularly ate. Because so much of the ship's larder was taken up with tinned food, Martin's job as cook ultimately turned out to be an easy one, since he had little to do but heat things up.

The provisioning of the ship took several days as dray after dray brought supplies down to the wharf. Charmian directed the entire operation, and as Martin later said, "showed a knowledge of stevedoring that astonished us."[5] Among the supplies brought on board were food, clothing, furnishings from the London home, fishing tackle, harpoons, guns, pistols, hundreds of reams of writing and typing paper, five hundred books, and hundreds of phonograph records and photographic supplies packaged in tin against tropical heat and humidity. By this time, Martin had four cameras and his own supply of film and developing solutions.

The packing of so many goods aboard the *Snark* delayed the projected departure date until April 21. However, the day before, as Bert and Martin were packing things away, a U.S. marshall arrived and "pasted a little five-by-seven slip of paper to one of the masts." It was an attachment to the *Snark* from a ship chandler, L. H. Sellers, to whom Jack owed $250. Jack had intended to pay the bill that day, and since it was a weekend, it was impossible to get the attachment legally removed, even after Sellers was paid.

April 23, 1907, dawned as a bright, sunny day. The Oakland wharf where the *Snark* gently bobbed up and down was filled with thousands of spectators, among whom were newspapermen and photographers who were there to record what they thought was their last view of the Londons and their crew. Among the spectators were members of the Crowd and other personal friends of the Londons, as well as friends of Tochigi, Bert, and Roscoe. None of Martin's friends were there, but he did receive many telegrams from Independence, and a delegation of the Oakland and San Francisco Elks came to see him off.[6]

The last farewells were finally said, and the *Snark* left the wharf "with hundreds of whistles tooting us a farewell salute." It headed for the Golden Gate straits and then out into the Pacific Ocean. As the ship sailed into the sea, Martin's feelings were mixed.

> I sat in the stern looking gloomily toward the land.
> . . . I was thinking of the friends and the home I was
> leaving, and wondering if we were really bound for
> the bottom of the sea as so many had foretold. . . . But
> on the *Snark* I was, and on the *Snark* I must remain.
> Gloomy dreams soon ended, and we settled down to
> life on the high seas.

So it was that we put forth into the wide Pacific, in a mere cork of a boat, without a navigator, with no engineer, no sailors, and for that matter, no cook.[7]

As night fell, the *Snark* carried them out beyond sight of land, and "rose and fell rhythmically, the sport of every wave."[8] It also carried Martin off into his horizons of high adventure about which he had dreamed for so many years. Yet there was foreboding and little joy in this, the first major step in a life of adventure seeking. Martin had finally realized that adventure and risk were intertwined, and that the joy given by one could be spoiled by fear of the other. Although he had lingering concerns as the *Snark* sailed southwest into the darkness, he no longer looked back toward land and the security it represented. He came to terms with risk and knew that he had to put thoughts of it aside if he were to enjoy the pleasures of adventure.

Martin's family had many misgivings about the trip and would spend anxious months worrying about what was happening to the *Snark*. The absence of radio contact meant that the *Snark*'s fate could only be known when it put into port or by chance sailed near a large vessel. Even Freda, Martin's young sister, worried about him despite Jack London's assurances: "It is true I have stolen your brother away from you; but then he wanted to be so stolen, and to go on the long journey to behold the Fire People and the Tree People, and the various strange things in the Great Forest, the Great Swamp, and the Great Sea. Believe me, he will be well cared for, and if he be not eaten by the cannibals, he'll return safely home."[9]

Once out into the open ocean, the *Snark* displayed what was to be its chief asset—it could race before the wind at tremendous speed. Jack was flushed with pride and satisfaction, but all of this was short-lived as the ship's major defects became increasingly apparent. To make matters worse, everyone except Jack became seasick. Martin graphically described what happened during the first several days aboard the ship:

> The boat was leaking like a sieve. . . . The sides leaked, the bottom leaked; we were flooded. . . . Our gasoline . . . began to filter out, so that we hardly dared to strike a match. . . . The engine in the launch was out of order and . . . our cherished lifeboat leaked. . . . The floors of the stateroom and galley were slushy with water. . . . The galley floor burst from the pressure of the water. . . . For days I wore thigh-high boots in cooking. . . . The bathroom had long since gone out of commission. The first day out, the big iron levers that controlled the sea-valves and the bath pumps broke into splinters.[10]

The little *Snark* continued to race with the wind, despite every effort to slow it down. However, more significantly, the ship would not heave to, a maneuver in which a sailing vessel can maintain its position when headed into the wind. Instead, it remained in the trough of the wave with tons of water looming above it. The *Snark*'s inability to heave to meant that during a storm the crew could not go below deck and leave the ship to steer itself. Fortunately, a number of calm days, pumps that bailed out the flooded hull, and Charmian's abilities as a sailor worked to keep the *Snark* afloat and on course. Charmian rapidly won the respect of all the crew members: there was no task they performed that she would not undertake herself. No less important, she kept Jack's spirits up when he became depressed about the *Snark*'s defects, especially by its inability to heave to. Despite all the stresses of seasickness, and being on a ship that leaked like a sieve, the crew did find time to enjoy themselves. They fished, played cards, and listened to some of the hundreds of phonograph records Jack had brought on board. Below deck, a disciplined Jack wrote two hours every day in his stateroom, and Charmian typed up his materials on her portable Remington.

Roscoe, whose abilities as navigator increasingly became suspect, believed that the earth was concave and that they were sailing inside of the earth's surface. He had picked up this theory from the writings of Cyrus R. Teed, who claimed that humankind lived inside of a hollow sphere. Jack knew that Roscoe's navigational abilities were slim when he hired him as conavigator and that he espoused Teed's unusual cosmology; however, he wrongly assumed that Roscoe could teach himself navigation prior to the time of sailing. Now, after several days on the Pacific, it became clear to Jack that Roscoe had absolutely no idea of where they were, or where they were headed, for that matter. He was more angered than troubled by this, and since he was a conavigator who himself had not yet studied navigation, was less than severe with Roscoe. However, he set about studying logarithms and how to use the sextant and compass with the help of the books he had brought aboard. Within a week, he claimed he was able to navigate by the sun, moon, and stars.[11]

By all measures, the *Snark* should have been a sailing disaster. Not only was it navigated by a seasick crew, most of whom were incompetent at their assigned tasks, but it also had a leaking hull filled with seawater and gasoline fumes. The two navigators, who were both quick studies, fancied themselves to be sailing on opposite sides of the earth's crust. While Jack's supreme confidence kept up morale, the prevailing tradewinds held the *Snark* on course while the pumps kept it afloat. The interpersonal stresses among the crew were understandable, and it was miraculous that no serious confrontations erupted among them. Bert, Martin, and Tochigi had absolutely no privacy, sharing a small room with bunks that measured 5 feet, 5 inches in length, 7 inches shorter than Martin's 6-foot frame. Sanitary conditions were deplorable, since the bathroom malfunctioned and the crew had to wash themselves and their clothes in the ocean. Yet, despite all of these hardships and defying all odds, the *Snark* sailed into Honolulu harbor on May 20, 1907, twenty-seven days after leaving San Francisco. The press, which had reasonably given the *Snark* up for lost, were amazed as the little ship made for a wharf in Pearl Harbor. For Martin, Hawaii was paradise, not just because of the beauty of the islands, but because it was "land at last."[12]

The *Snark* was something of a wreck when it arrived in Hawaii. Yet Jack was determined to sail on and spared no expense in repairing it. During the five months the Londons remained in Hawaii, the *Snark* was refurbished and given a thorough overhaul. It was not only the ship that had been stretched to the limit by the journey out, but some of the crew as well. Tochigi, who had been severely afflicted by seasickness most of the time, voluntarily resigned and returned to California, where he eventually became a minister. Roscoe and Bert also left. Their departures became grist for the newspapers, which claimed that they had been badly bullied by Jack. On returning to San Francisco, neither Roscoe nor Bert said anything to dispel these rumors.[13] In fact, they gave credence to them through press interviews in which their anger and disappointment were apparent. Roscoe was dismissed by Jack on the obvious grounds that he was incompetent and insubordinate. The parting with Bert seems to have been mutually agreeable, but more so on the side of the Londons.[14]

Thus, of the original crew, only Martin remained. That he had survived the rigors of the trip and was willing to go on speaks for his determination and courage. He stood high in the Londons' esteem—despite his poor cooking—because he was loyal, conscientious, and personable, adept with machines and cameras, and held up well under stress. Jack promoted him to engineer and placed him in charge of film developing.[15] He then hired new crew members, some of whom were fired before the *Snark* left Hawaii. Among these was Gene Fenelon, a circus-manager friend of George Sterling's, and Captain Andy Rosehill, who was a perpetually angry buccaneer whose swearing and rough handling of the crew would almost lead to mass resignations.[16] Rosehill especially singled out Martin for verbal abuse and did all he could to get him fired. In the end, Jack fired Rosehill not only because of his abusiveness to the crew, but also because he kept telling people that he might not stay on the *Snark* very long.[17]

While Jack and Charmian toured the islands and Jack wrote and gave lectures on socialism and the Revolution, Martin remained with the *Snark*, keeping an eye on the repairs and working with the new crewmen. Hawaii was his first exposure to a multiracial society, and his impressions of it, as recorded in his book *Through the South Seas with Jack London*, reveal facile expressions of American racial attitudes of the times. Of the population of Hilo, he said: "The white people . . . live mostly . . . on plantations and the brown population sleeps through most of the day."[18] He vividly encapsulated the race attitudes of whites in Hawaii in describing those of the engineer of the small train that ran between Pearl Harbor and Honolulu: "He didn't care whether 'the cattle'—referring to my fellow passengers—got anywhere or not. . . . As he explained, nothing but Japs and Kanakas (Hawaiians), and Chinamen rode on it, and he didn't care anything about them. As for us, when we rode he absolutely refused to collect any fare."[19]

It was while Jack was in Honolulu that he began writing *Martin Eden*, an autobiographical novel that is considered by many to be among his best works.[20] Over the years, a number of Jack London's biographers have erroneously stated that he began the novel on the outward trip from California to Hawaii.[21] However, Charmian and Martin provide corroborative testimony that he began it in Hawaii.[22] But Martin's claim that part of the protagonist's name was derived from his own has subsequently been challenged.[23]

On October 7, 1907, the *Snark* sailed out of Hilo on the island of Hawaii and headed for Tahiti via the Marquesas Islands.[24] People on the wharf predicted that the ship would never make the 2,000-mile-long traverse to the Marquesas. No sailing ship to their knowledge had ever attempted this crossing because of conflicting currents, unfavorable winds, and unpredictable calms. However, none of this deterred Jack and Charmian, who again looked forward to doing what people said was impossible. Charmian was jubilant. On October 6 she wrote in her diary: "Tomorrow we sail for the Marquesas Islands, and it seems too good to be true."[25]

Except for Martin, there was a new crew on board consisting of Captain James Langhorne Warren, a paroled murderer; Herrmann de Visser, a young Dutch sailor; Yoshimatsu Nakata, an eighteen-year-old Japanese who hoped to work his way back to Japan as a valet; and Wada, a Japanese cook. The Londons first met Warren on the island of Maui the previous July and hired him almost on impulse and in response to flattery.[26] Jack liked Warren so much that in the ensuing weeks after he met him he made a personal appeal to the governor of Oregon, who eventually granted Warren a pardon. Although he was an experienced seaman and appeared to be competent, in contrast to Roscoe, in time his personality defects became only too apparent.[27]

The *Snark* had favorable winds for the first three weeks, and then, for the next three weeks, the engines were used for a few hours a day to augment the occasional breezes. Despite the five hundred books on board, the record player, and the card games, the crew did not have a very enjoyable time. Heat and sunburn, grease, weevils and beetles in the food, and occasional storms sorely tried them. Warren soon showed his dark side and began to strike Hermann and Wada over trivial grievances. As they drifted through the stifling heat of the doldrums, their water supply ran dangerously low, due to both bad luck and incompetence.[28] They encountered favorable winds in the Variables which carried them toward the Marquesas. Finally, almost two months out of Hilo and after zigzagging 4,000 miles, they spotted Ua Huka, one of the Marquesas' volcanic cones. Although luck more than skill had brought them into yet another safe harbor, Martin still felt like a conquering hero and said: "But all things come to those who dare. We had dared mightily. And mightily we reaped of our sowing. We did the impossible."[29]

Martin accompanied the Londons as they made a pilgrimage to Typee Valley on the island of Nuku Hiva, already made immortal by Herman Melville in his book *Typee*. The valley was still a Garden of Eden, but imported European diseases such as tuberculosis had decimated the population, leaving only a small remnant of native peoples. They visited the home of Robert Louis Stevenson, hiked through the lush tropical valleys, and participated in a Marquesan feast. The beauty of the Marquesas and their peoples made a deep impression on Martin.[30]

Jack and Charmian were keen collectors and eventually sent several crates of what are now considered rare Marquesan artifacts back to San Francisco. Martin did his share of collecting as well. Starting in Hawaii, he regularly sent shipments of art and artifacts back to his family in Independence and had them ship back "junk jewelry" with which to trade.[31] Neither he nor the Londons collected the art for the purpose of making a financial profit through resale. In fact, Martin gave away most of what he collected to family and friends.

After twelve days in the Marquesas, the *Snark* set sail for Tahiti and the Society Islands, which lay 800 miles to the southwest. It took seventeen days to navigate through the dangerous atolls of the Tuamoto Archipelago. On December 26, 1907, they sailed into Papeete harbor, close to the anchored U.S. cruiser *Annapolis*, whose several hundred sailors cheered them from the rails as they passed. Jack and Charmian's first impressions of Papeete's idyllic beauty were quickly overshadowed by the bad news that awaited them in the mail. A panic on Wall Street a short time before had left them in serious financial difficulty because of declining magazine and book sales. In addition, Netta Eames, who had been looking after Jack's affairs, had been selling his writings at low prices and was managing his earnings ineptly. There were only six dollars left in their bank account and piles of bounced checks from Hawaii. Furthermore, the bank that held the mortgage on Jack's mother's home had foreclosed on the basis of rumors that the *Snark* had gone down at sea. Jack and Charmian had no choice but to return to California to straighten out their affairs. With no money to pay for their passage, they cabled George Brett of Macmillan who advanced the funds for two round-trip tickets on the *Mariposa*, due to sail from Papeete in a few days.[32]

Martin and the rest of the crew settled down to what would be a three-and-a-half month stay in Tahiti. He and Captain Warren rented a bungalow on the outskirts of Papeete and soon acquired women companions. Martin devotes many pages of his book *Through the South Seas with Jack London* to Helene of Raiatea, whom he characterizes as "the most prominent personage in these islands."[33] Such hyperbole is understandable in a young man who had recently fallen in love. Yet Martin, conscious of his own racial attitudes and those of his readers, never admits to loving Helene. To justify his adulation of her, he unconvincingly tries to depict her as a powerful political figure, which she was not. Although he camouflages his strong feelings toward her, he often lapses into transparent language that shows he was deeply in love with her:

> Hers was the greatest power, though it was not a vested one. She seemed a true South Sea queen. . . . I had ample opportunity to study her—her every mood and whim. . . . Helene had no royal blood, nor was she of chieftain stock, but many a chief or king had less power than she. . . . She had been born with more energy than the average Kanaka, and a constant mingling with the white people had given her ideas above her class. . . . Her figure was admirable. Her skin was a light olive colour; she had two perfect rows of teeth and a brain that never seemed to be still. We had heard of her in the Marquesas Islands and I was anxious to make her acquaintance.[34]

Martin may have indeed heard of Helene in the Marquesas, but not for the reasons he states. She picked him up in the market square the first evening he went ashore in Papeete and remained with him throughout his stay. Captain Warren also picked up a companion by the name of Taaroa. On her return to Papeete, Charmian made some observations about this *ménage à quatre* in the bungalow on the edge of town. Warren, who was given to binge drinking and outbursts of violent behavior, had a fight with Martin on March 10 and then "sicked his big *wahine* (woman) onto Martin's little one, who is *enceinte*."[35] Whether or not Helene was pregnant by Martin remains somewhat unclear from the entries in Charmian's diary. However, it is possible that she was carrying Martin's child since they had been together for two-and-a-half months.

Jack completed the writing of *Martin Eden* when he returned to Papeete, and then on April 4, 1908, sailed the *Snark* to Raiatea, Helene's home.[36] Hermann de Visser had been fired some time before, and in his place Jack hired an eighteen-year-old French sailor, Ernest, who had deserted the bark *Elizabeth*. However, he only remained with the crew for a short time before being dismissed and replaced by Henry, a 6-foot Polynesian sailor whom they later met in Pago Pago. On Raiatea, Jack hired Tehei, a Polynesian navigator, who later proved invaluable.

The *Snark* crew remained on Raiatea for four days and were feted by Helene's family. Martin visited Helene's mountain home and made the following observations about her family. "Her father . . . was an ordinary Kanaka. Her mother was a typical Tahitian. So I have never been able to understand why Helene should be so far above her class. Her environment had been no better; it must have been some strength of character, some intrinsic worth, that elevated her in station and in mind."[37]

There is a tinge of disappointment in his finding her parents to be ordinary Polynesians. It is almost as if he had expected to find a super-race of Raiateans. In pointing out her unseen inner worth, he in effect justifies why she is fit to be his companion. In this regard, Martin was a faithful student of his mentor Jack, who by this time had come to admire racial mixing even though he still adhered to a belief in social Darwinism. Martin also shared Jack's belief in the latter philosophy, which held that the races should remain separate and that the white race would inevitably dominate because of its inherent superiority. Neither Jack nor Martin seemed to have been troubled by the contradictions between a belief in social Darwinism and an admiration for racial mixing.[38] However, the racial mixing they had in mind was selective, of whites and Polynesians, not of whites and Melanesians. Jack wrote of the exquisite beauty of those of mixed European and Polynesian ancestry in his Hawaiian stories, and he obviously approved of Martin's fraternizing with Helene.

Despite his belief in social Darwinism, Jack did not shrink from caustic condemnation of the white Hawaiian elite who had so ruthlessly dispossessed the indigenous population nor those whites who had destroyed the magnificent culture of Typee Valley. Yet Martin only rarely rises to this higher ground in his written description of the *Snark* cruise. Occasionally, he shows admiration for individual islanders such as Helene, Henry, and Tehei. However, the many labor recruiters, plantation managers, and traders who had inflicted enormous harm on the indigenous populations and their cultures usually escape criticism and receive praise. This is not surprising since Martin relied on them as interpreters of the islands and as facilitators for achieving his photographic objectives. Only some missionaries come under attack, in part because they provided the local peoples with Western clothing, thereby transforming them into less attractive photographic opportunities. This is slim cause for condemnation, something Martin must have known since he unconvincingly states that "as soon as the native puts on white man's clothes, he begins to imitate the white man, and to imitate the white man in that part of the world is bad policy."[39] Martin never explains why it is bad policy, but he does describe the converts of one missionary as "mean, thieving little beggars."[40] Although Jack modified his own brand of social Darwinism during the *Snark* cruise, his firm belief in white racial superiority prevailed and made a deep impression on Martin who, in describing the people of the island of Tanna in the New Hebrides, said, "I can describe these people at no greater length and no better than to say, as Jack said, that they were worse than naked."[41] At this time, Martin even remained true to his prejudices when it came to photographs of the people of Tanna. He said that they could not be printed in a volume intended for popular circulation since the people were "only one degree removed from the animals."[42]

Martin and Helene parted company in Raiatea when the *Snark* left for Pago Pago. Stopping at small ports on the way, the group reached Pago Pago in early May and then sailed on to Fiji. It was during this time that Captain Warren's incompetence became most apparent. They were lost for several days among the atolls and lagoons of the Ringgold Islands, and it was only thanks to the skills of Henry and Tehei that the *Snark* did not run aground. Warren, who had no idea of where they were, reverted to drinking and striking the two Japanese members of the crew, Nakata and Wada. He broke Wada's nose in one outburst and would have seriously injured Nakata in another had Charmian not intervened. Thanks to Jack's navigation and the sailing skills of Henry and Tehei, the *Snark* safely sailed into Suva, Fiji, in late May.

During the short stay in Fiji, Jack fired Captain Warren, much to the relief of the remainder of the crew.[43] With Warren gone, it fell to Jack to navigate the *Snark* on to the New Hebrides (now Vanuatu) and the Solomon Islands. He sailed the ship out of Suva, Fiji, on June 6, 1908, and headed southwest for Port Resolution on the island of Tanna in the New Hebrides, where they arrived five days later. The *Snark* now entered the heart of Melanesia, whose peoples were very different in many ways from those of Polynesia. While the Polynesians had already been Christianized, Westernized, and subjugated into full colonial status, the Melanesians were waging what would eventually prove to be a losing battle to preserve their traditional way of life and their ancestral culture. Long abused and exploited by sandalwood traders, copra plantation managers, labor recruiters, and others, they had resorted to heightened levels of violence in order to protect their interests. It was inevitable that this escalation in confrontation with Europeans would also spill over into their ongoing internecine conflicts.

Martin and the Londons carried into Melanesia fond memories of the "civilized" Polynesians with whom they had spent so many happy months, the racial prejudices of their time and preconceptions about the Melanesians fostered by both European and Polynesian clichés. Jack was able to see through the prejudices and preconceptions at times, and he strongly attacked white supremacy in stories such as "The Terrible Solomons" while being the guest of the very white men he was criticizing.[44] Yet as he was condemning white supremacists, he also expressed his belief in white superiority.[45]

There was much about Melanesian societies that roused Martin's and Charmian's disgust. While contact with Europeans had resulted in increased violence, Melanesians still adhered to indigenous cultural traditions that included infanticide, cannibalism, the brutal killing of children and enemies, and headhunting. The Londons and Martin saw the white traders, plantation managers, and labor recruiters as lonely and brave forces of good, combating indigenous practices that were evil and repugnant to their Western values. That the activities of these white men intensified indigenous violence escaped their notice because this was scarcely apparent to casual visitors. They saw the Melanesians through the eyes of the men who were their hosts—men who viewed these island people as inherently violent, brutal, and savage. Labor recruiters and traders did not allow for the possibility that circumstances spanning many centuries had shaped Melanesian values and customs, some of which were repulsive to Europeans. For them, the brutality of these people was somehow genetic and permanent.

The *Snark* arrived in Port Resolution on the volcanic island of Tanna on June 11, 1908, and was warmly greeted by Trader Wiley who along with his partner, Stanton, eked out a meager living trading cheap sticks of tobacco for coconuts. Wiley and the local missionary, the Reverend Watt, were not on good terms since their interests were frequently in direct conflict. Wiley was there to exploit their copra while Watt wanted to save their souls. Martin's sympathies were with Wiley even though he used Watt's darkroom on several occasions. While Wiley gave the local people rifles in order to win their confidence and turned a blind eye to the practice of cannibalism, Watt preached against their "heathen ways" and dressed them up in Western clothing, thus also ruining good photographic opportunities.

Throughout his travels in Melanesia, Martin freely used the words heathen, animal, and savage to describe the indigenous peoples he met.[46] His views and attitudes were neither original nor unique since they merely reflected the prejudices of his time.[47] They were validated by missionaries who were there to save souls, and by traders and labor recruiters driven by the profit motive. He made no attempt to understand the Melanesians, but rather saw them and their customs as bizarre and strange, and judged them against the standards of his own culture. Like Martin, Charmian gave free rein to her racial prejudices in describing the people of Tanna.

> He is quite the nearest to a chimpanzee that I've ever seen. . . . Another old baboon is titillating in a hysterical rising-and-falling squat. . . . The women were deadly unfeminine—nearly resembling the men in face and voice, ageless, sexless, dirty; and they and their men displayed an ungracious inhospitality that made us think vividly and lovingly of the Societies and the Samoans. . . . They were so uneasy, so shifting—lying down, getting up, moving here and there and back again, like a band of monkeys.[48]

Jack and Martin spent an hour on the last afternoon they were on Tanna trading with the local people for their bows, arrows, and spears, which were shipped back to California and Kansas. In exchange, they gave the people tobacco, cheap jewelry sent out from Independence, candy, and red cloth, which was highly prized on the islands. The two men viewed the curios not as sensitively made artistic creations, but as violent expressions of irrational savagery.

Leaving Tanna, they then sailed on to Port Vila on the island of Efate, which was the capital of the New Hebrides. After spending a few days there and without going into the interior of the island, they headed for the Solomon Islands, which lay to the northwest. The Solomons, like the New Hebrides, had been brutally exploited by copra plantation managers, traders, and labor recruiters (known in both places as blackbirders). These European recruiters induced or duped large numbers of Solomon Islanders to board ships that eventually took them to work under virtual slave conditions on sugar plantations in Queensland, Australia, in Fiji, and on copra plantations on other islands. This exploitation, involving as it did gift exchanges of rifles to local chiefs, gave the islanders more destructive weapons with which to settle disputes and blood feuds. It created greatly unsettled political conditions within Solomon Island society, which in turn escalated the indigenous violence that had long been there.

The Solomon Islands that the crew of the *Snark* were to see in 1908 were extremely dangerous and unhealthy. The population was seriously afflicted with malaria, yaws, tropical ulcers, filariasis, and a variety of intestinal parasites. Whites had contributed their own deadly diseases: smallpox, measles, and tuberculosis. Violence, blood feuds, and headhunting were widespread on some islands. Resentment over labor recruitment was strong and frequently led to attacks on recruiting vessels and traders. However, the roots of hatred for Europeans lay in the desire of the islanders for Western manufactures. The poor resources of the islands forced people to trade labor for goods instead of products for goods, giving rise to an endless cycle of exploitation and violence. This in turn profoundly weakened the islanders' own social and political structures and the local economy. Young men who were traded to recruiters by their chiefs were placed in conditions of virtual slavery from which they received little material gain. Yet when they returned, they brought with them new ideas and changed attitudes that destabilized local political authority and disrupted existing social relationships.

In 1896 the British launched a serious attempt to pacify the islands in order to protect the interests of European traders, recruiters, and plantation owners. Paradoxically, their efforts reduced the wealth and hence the political power of many local chiefs, which in turn contributed to more internal instability. The protection of European economic interests came at a high price for the indigenous population. On some islands, blood feuds and violence dominated peoples' lives until the 1930s.[49]

On June 28, 1908, the *Snark* came in sight of Santa Ana, a small island at the southeastern end of the Solomons. After dropping anchor, the ship was surrounded, as Martin said, by "a hundred canoeloads of savages. . . . They started aboard, but with guns we kept them back."[50] The people of Santa Ana circled the *Snark*, waving spears and clubs and shouting a welcome. However, Martin and the others saw hidden danger in these gestures of friendliness. This was not unreasonable since they had been warned that expressions of friendliness were often a prefatory ruse to violence and murder. However, the people of Santa Ana proved genuinely friendly and hospitable despite their appearance, which so frightened Martin and the others. Even when one of them, a Christian named Peter, came forth and spoke in halting English and *bêche-de-mer*, Martin judged him on his looks: "A big, naked savage, uglier than the rest . . . smiled an ugly, ghastly smile that made us shudder."[51]

Martin and the Londons felt justified in their suspicions of Peter when a broken-down trader by the name of Tom Butler sailed into their anchorage and told them to be wary of him. Peter, he said, had tried to spear a European recruiter six months before. That Peter may have had good reason for doing this was never given much consideration. Thanks to him, the people of Santa Ana provisioned the *Snark* with yams, bananas, pumpkins, pigeons, shellfish, and a suckling pig.

Yet this was all taken for granted as a sort of entitlement and never judged as an expression of hospitality.

Jack let it be known that he was willing to trade stick tobacco, beads, cheap jewelry, and red handkerchiefs for curios. He and Charmian sat on a couch on the deck of the *Snark* and spent an entire day trading as lines of canoes came out with the island's artistic patrimony. Anxious to keep prices uniform, Jack traded for Martin and purchased on his behalf.[52]

Charmian vividly described the scene on the ship's deck: "All day they have clambered over the side, eager, avaricious, bringing treasure undreamed. . . . Many a curio we bought right off its wearer, this lending an added value in our eyes."[53] The people of Santa Ana might equally well have described Charmian, Jack, and Martin in the same terms—eager and avaricious—as they were, in effect, stripping the island of its artistic treasures.

Several days later, on July 4, they dropped anchor at Ugi Island, which lies near the much larger island of San Cristobal (now known as Makira). The villages of Ugi had been burned to the ground in 1878 by the crew of the HMS *Beagle* in retaliation for the murder of a copra trader.[54] During the ensuing years, missionaries had made many converts, and most of the people were fairly peaceful. However, Jack and Charmian brought out their arsenal of weapons including Mausers, automatic rifles, Colt pistols, Smith and Wesson revolvers, and gave the people of Ugi a dramatic and intimidating demonstration of target practice. Charmian, who was a crack shot, now regularly carried a .22 automatic and kept a Colt pistol strapped to her waist. This was scarcely necessary on Ugi, but was a wise precaution on islands like Malaita. She shot at birds and other targets just to let the local people know that she was "taboo from any 'monkeying.'" Her marksmanship also helped to establish her position as an equal in the all-male company of the crew and among the Europeans of the islands who had little respect for women.

Mansel Hammond, an Australian trader who had been on the island for about a month, and a Mr. Drew of the Melanesian Missionary Society, facilitated the *London's* contact with the local chief, Ramana. His village had a magnificent canoe house supported by eight tall sculpted posts, which the Londons promptly purchased. One of these posts was purchased for Martin, who later used the upper-sculpted 5½-foot section in his vaudeville act.[55]

In early July they arrived at Penduffryn, a 500-acre copra plantation on the island of Guadalcanal that was owned by Thomas Harding and George Derbishire and managed by an Australian-Frenchman by the name of Bernays. Since Mrs. Harding was away, Charmian was given her quarters, which were spacious and extremely comfortable compared to those on the *Snark*. Despite the comfort, peace, and quiet that enabled Jack to get much writing done, they were told to be always on guard against possible attack from either the local population or the laborers on the plantation. Charmian slept in a room with a rack full of loaded rifles and was told by Harding and Derbishire to keep her revolver loaded and ready to shoot at all times. So great was the risk of attack that no islanders, except the servants, were permitted to set foot on the porches of the houses. As the Londons settled into Penduffryn, Martin and the remainder of the *Snark* crew took the ship to Tulagi, the capital of the islands some 35 miles away, where it was cleaned and repaired.

Life at Penduffryn was a soporific experience for the Londons and their crew, who returned after a week's stay in Tulagi. Surrounded by many creature comforts, large numbers of servants, and doting hosts who were starved for visitors, they settled into a routine of rest, relaxation, and partying. Yet danger was ever-present in the form of unpredictable attacks by the islanders, and from diseases that were now beginning to challenge the ability of the crew to go on. Before reaching Ugi, Martin had already developed a large tropical ulcer on his right lower shin, which did not respond to treatment with a variety of remedies including corrosive sublimate (a mercury compound). The Londons and most of the crew also developed these ulcers, which they thought were symptoms of yaws, but which in all probability were tropical ulcers due to bacteria. They were all racked by regular bouts of malaria despite dosing themselves with quinine, and Tehei developed blackwater fever, a malarial complication secondary to the drug's regular use. Despite ulcers, fever, and chills, Jack and Charmian decided to travel with Captain Jansen of the blackbirder yacht *Minota* to the island of Malaita on a recruiting expedition. Malaita was perhaps the most dangerous of the Solomon Islands at the time because life there was dominated by blood feuds and warrior-leaders known as *ramo* who functioned as hired assassins. *Ramo* engaged in revenge killings, often on behalf of an entire group that raised the necessary bounty in the form of pigs and other valuables. This internal violence easily spilled over toward the white traders and labor recruiters, whose activities were often provocative.[56]

During the trip, the *Minota* grounded on a reef, and the local villagers, hopeful of seizing its bounty of rifles and stick tobacco, menaced the crew and passengers for almost three days until the ship was pulled off to safety. The canoe-loads of shouting and threatening Malaitans who surrounded the *Minota* had intentions far from those of the hospitable people of Santa Ana. During this harrowing experience when the Londons were under real and serious threat, they opted not to fire at the local people as was the usual custom. Instead, they resorted to a variety of other stratagems for diverting the canoes filled with armed men.[57]

But there were lighter moments for the *Snark* crew in the Solomons, as, for example, when Harding and Derbishire invited traders and planters from other stations to Penduffryn for a celebration in the Londons' honor.[58] They drank, played cards, and held a masquerade ball during which Derbishire dressed as an English woman and Martin served as his dance partner. The week-long party ended with everyone agreeing to take marijuana. Derbishire, who was the first to take it, seems to have been high on it for several days. Jack "went clear off his head, acted so wild that Mrs. London was frightened." After that, no one took it, according to Martin, whose turn to try it was the following day.[59]

Jack decided to visit the northwesternmost point of the Solomon Islands, the atolls of Ontong Java, inhabited by people of Polynesian descent. During this trip, his health deteriorated markedly. In addition to malaria, skin ulcers, dysentery, and dental problems, he developed blood in his stools. However, worst of all, his hands and feet became extremely swollen and the skin on them hard, thick, and pigmented. He was irritable, unsteady on his feet, and had difficulty concentrating. No other members of the crew developed this disease, which made it all the more perplexing.

Jack was extremely ill when they arrived back at Penduffryn. Still, he hoped that the relative comforts of Penduffryn would help him recover and enable him to continue the voyage. Harding and Derbishire did all they could to make him comfortable, but they, like everyone else, were baffled by this disease.[60]

During their absence, a Pathé Frères film crew from Paris had come to Penduffryn to make motion pictures of "cannibals." This crew—an Italian, a Frenchman, and an Austrian—had been incapacitated with malaria, and as a result had not yet gone into the interior of Guadalcanal as planned. They were also unprepared for the deterioration of their developing solutions in the hot, humid climate. Martin came to their rescue with his own stock of still picture chemicals. Several days after the return of the *Snark*, the film crew went 6 miles inland into Guadalcanal to the village of a former Penduffryn plantation worker. Grateful to Martin for his help with the developing solutions, and pleased to have additional help, they took him along.[61]

This brief experience represented an important turning point for Martin because it was the first time he participated in the production of motion pictures. Before this, he had thought only in terms of still pictures, an interest valued by Jack, whose magazine editors demanded illustrated articles. His work with the Pathé crew made him keenly aware that these islands and their peoples held a vast potential for motion picture production. It was not only that such films could be made, but also that they could be successfully marketed in the United States and Europe. Martin's help with the shooting and developing of the Pathé film gave him something of a moral claim to it, which he later exercised.

In early November, Jack, Charmian, and Martin left the Solomons on the steamer *Makambo* for Sydney, Australia, where they arrived twelve days later on November 14, 1908. The *Snark* was left behind in the Solomons since they planned to resume the trip after they had undergone medical treatment. Jack was hospitalized at St. Malo Hospital in North Sydney, while Martin became an inpatient at the Sydney Homeopathic Hospital. While Jack's intestinal fistula, malaria, and skin ulcers were successfully treated, his strange skin condition puzzled the Australian doctors who treated him. Even the most eminent dermatologist in Australia was unable to make a diagnosis, something which is difficult to comprehend since Jack clearly had pellagra, a nutritional deficiency disease due to inadequate amounts of niacin. This inability to diagnose a disease which at that time was well known in many other parts of the world, gave Jack no other option than to follow the advice of his Australian doctors, which was that he return to his own climate. In fairness to them, however, they must have given thought to a nutritional deficiency disease since Martin states that they told Jack that he needed fresh fruits, vegetables, and meats, not the canned foods and salted meats that he ate on the *Snark*.[62]

Martin's tropical ulcer was effectively treated with caustic potash, then a standard treatment. However, the swelling in his left testicle continued despite an operation in which the venous drainage to it was cut. On December 6, he wrote to Jack about his ailment: "He [the doctor] examined me and says that when I was operated on before that the doctors had cut the veins to the left testicle and that it was not in working order, and is afraid if he cuts the other side he'll kill the other one—(then I'd be eligible to work in a Turkish harem)."[63] As it turned out, Martin's right testicle was spared an operation, but the surgical procedure on the left one may have rendered him sterile.[64]

Jack, who was understandably concerned about his own health, needed little prodding from the Australian doctors to abandon the cruise and return to California. He wrote Martin from his bed in St. Malo hospital in North Sydney and told him of his decision. Charmian, who had held on to the hope that the cruise could be resumed, was in the same hospital room with Jack, recovering from her latest bout of malaria. When Martin visited them, it was clear that they could not go on. Jack's hands were so swollen that he was unable to write, and as he told Martin, "There are many chances to see the world." But he had only one pair of hands, which were crucial to his livelihood. Martin was crestfallen by the decision. His dream of sailing the world as apprentice to the man who symbolized adventure was abruptly being brought to an end. He had scarcely given any thought to what he would do after the voyage because that seemed so far in the future. He now had to face that uncertain future while coping with the terrible reality that the cruise of the *Snark* was over.

The *Snark*, which was still in the Solomons, had to be brought back to Sydney, which Martin and a Captain Charles Reed did on March 9, 1909. Jack put the ship up for auction and eventually sold it for $3,000, a fraction of its original cost. The crew of the *Snark* now broke up. Henry returned to Pago Pago, Tehei to Raiatea, and Wada to Hawaii. Nakata remained with Jack and Charmian, who returned to California via Tasmania, Ecuador, and Panama, arriving in Glen Ellen in July 1909. Martin was determined to circumnavigate the world and left Sydney on March 31 on the *Asturias* bound for Naples. In writing to Martin's father a few days later, Jack reported:

> I cannot begin to tell you how deep was our regret at parting with Martin. He was the only one who sailed with us from San Francisco who was with us at the finish. And he proved himself a darned fine boy. . . . I don't know who was cut up the worst at our parting—Martin, Mrs. London, or myself. . . . The voyage has done Martin good, has made a man out of him. . . . The trip he is taking all the way around, cannot fail to do him further good. I think it will take some of the wandering out of his blood, and that he will be better fitted to settle down.[65]

The trip may have made a man out of Martin, but it had hardly satiated his desire for adventure.[66] It had shown him that he could travel to the far corners of the globe and accomplish with film what Jack did with words. His timing for this could not have been better, since motion pictures were fast becoming a major form of entertainment. Martin had spent two years with Jack and Charmian, closely living with them under often trying physical and emotional conditions. He viewed them as the ideal adventure couple and knew what made their lives and careers successful. Jack was determined, disciplined, and hard-working, and courted risk and adventure, which he enjoyed to the fullest. Charmian was the perfect partner, brave, enterprising, and a crack shot, but also sweet, considerate, and feminine. She was the ideal sort of woman for traveling to the wild ends of the earth. These impressions and observations helped Martin create a formula for his own future, which he now carried with him as he sailed westward over the Indian Ocean.

CHAPTER FOUR

VAUDEVILLE

Martin arrived home in Independence in the late summer of 1909 after an absence of almost three years. His parents and the Londons assumed that he had been matured by his travels and would now settle down into a conventional way of life. However, he had different immediate plans, being consumed with a fierce determination to achieve both personal and financial success by capitalizing on the *Snark* voyage. He must have given considerable thought to this on his trip home, in view of the speed with which he put his plans into effect. That the *Snark* voyage was a popular subject with the public had already been amply proven by Jack, whose numerous magazine articles were widely read, and by the excellent reception given to Martin's published letters home.[1] Martin correctly reasoned that he could tap into this avid interest in his own unique way by using the medium of photography at which he was expert.

Travelogue lectures illustrated with lantern slides were then extremely popular in the United States. Some lecturers, such as Burton Holmes, had become national celebrities because of their travelogues about exotic and faraway places. In order to be successful, lecturers had to link up with either theater or vaudeville circuits, which measured quality in terms of box office receipts. Travelogue lectures were frequently made more appealing by the addition of motion picture sequences, a feature first introduced by Burton Holmes in 1897.[2] Artifacts collected during a speaker's travels were also displayed and sometimes passed around to the audience.

Martin's objective at this time was to become a travelogue lecturer. However, he lacked public-speaking experience, suffered from stage fright, was only superficially knowledgeable about many of the places he had visited, and possessed a limited number of black-and-white pictures. To be truly competitive in the major theater circuits required motion picture footage and a large variety of lantern slides that had to be hand-colored to make them more appealing. In addition, he needed some start-up capital. His father, who enjoyed basking in the glory of his son's *Snark* odyssey, saw the marketing of his travels as a sound investment. But the panic of 1907 had seriously weakened his financial position, and he was unable to put up any money to get Martin started. As for Martin himself, he was in debt to the Londons for $487.63, had no money of his own, and was being supported by his father.[3]

Martin's goal was finally put within reach by Charles (Charley) H. Kerr, the owner of the Central Drug Store in Independence. Charley felt that Martin's experiences could be translated into successful entertainment. This, together with his own unfulfilled hopes of being an entertainer and the prospects of financial profit, led him into a partnership with Martin. Charley closed his drugstore and converted it into the 340-seat *Snark* Theater, whose interior was made to look like a ship. He put up all of the capital for remodeling the building and for running the theater, with the understanding that Martin would later buy into the partnership with his profits from the show.

The *Snark* Theater opened to a packed house and featured Martin E. Johnson's Travelogues and Charles H. Kerr's Chalk Talks. Martin narrated his travels with hand-colored lantern slides made from his black-and-white negatives, while Charley used chalk to present fast cartoon lectures. Charley also lectured on some of Martin's slides. Although neither of them had ever been in show business before, they displayed an incredible ability to lure audiences. Besides using sensationalistic publicity, Martin shrewdly decided to present his travels not in one lecture, but in a sequential series. Audiences were taken as far as Hawaii during the first lecture, and in subsequent shows all the way out to Fiji. In the early weeks, this was as far as he could take them since the remainder of his photographs were with the Londons, who knew nothing about the theater.

Martin had purposely not told Jack and Charmian about his enterprise, fearful that they would voice strong objection to it. Jack had made it explicitly clear to him when he signed on the *Snark* that no member of the crew could publish or write anything about the trip unless Jack had first seen and approved it. Martin had obviously violated the spirit of this understanding, albeit in a way the Londons could not have foreseen. Eventually, the Londons had to be told, and so on November 25, he wrote them a sheepish letter expressing the hope that they would not object. While appearing somewhat contrite, he was also skillful in maneuvering them into his corner. He took great pains to say that Jack's books were being read in every household in the area because of his show. In addition, he predicted that more copies of the *Pacific Monthly* carrying Jack's articles would be sold in this part of the country than anywhere else in the United States. These somewhat exaggerated claims found an easy mark in Jack, who was vulnerable to flattery and willing to believe them. Martin was also successful in begging off at this time from paying anything on the debt he owed the Londons, claiming that he had to first give Charley Kerr $700 before he could become a full partner. He predicted that once he was a full partner, he would begin to liquidate his debt.[4]

The Johnson-London relationship had already entered a new and more complicated phase. Martin no longer thought of himself as an employee whose fate was tied to an ability to please, but rather as a friend on somewhat of an equal footing. For Jack and Charmian, he was a favored protégé whom they indulged like a spoiled son. This friendship between Martin and the Londons had the power that comes from being forged under life-and-death circumstances. As a result, its foundations ran very deep, and it was able to sustain significant strains. That Martin often defined this friendship in utilitarian terms did not escape the Londons, and at times it irritated them. He summed up his true feelings when in 1910 he wrote that "Jack London is my only stock of trade."[5] He often justified his continued exploitation of the *Snark* voyage to them by claiming that his shows promoted Jack's name and hence his writings. The Londons, who were always strapped for money, reasoned that he might be right, and in any event could do no harm. Another practical reason for not objecting was that it provided Martin with the only income with which he could pay off his debt to them.

Over the next few months, the *Snark* Theater did so well that Charley and Martin opened a 275-seat *Snark* No. 2 in Independence, and an 800-seat *Snark* No. 3 in Cherryvale. In order to keep people coming back, Martin constantly added new material and changed his lecture routine. He obtained still pictures of the islands from a photographer in Tasmania, retrieved his own negatives from the Londons, and in an incremental fashion badgered Jack and Charmian into giving him some of their own negatives of the trip. By March of 1910 he had a total of five hundred slides and was awaiting the arrival from Australia of two short motion picture films made by the Pathé Frères photographers on Guadalcanal: *Dynamiting Fish in the Solomons* and *Making Missionaries Out of Cannibals*. He did not hesitate to present photographs made by others in places he had never visited. In addition, with the help of some twenty books on the Pacific, he acquired the additional knowledge he needed to speak authoritatively to his audiences. Although he had overcome stage fright, his voice still had a nasal quality and his grammar was atrocious. This did not matter so much in Independence and later on in rural Kansas, where he next took his show. However, he knew that he had to overcome these deficiencies if he were to get on the national circuits.[6]

Martin came to see himself as a "travelogue man," to use his own words. The *Snark* theaters and his early visits to nearby towns became a testing ground for refining the show and for raising it to a standard that would make it attractive to the circuit managers. With this objective in mind, he even contemplated making a quick trip to the Solomon Islands or to the New Hebrides during the slow summer season with the help of a backer. There he planned to select ten or twelve "old cannibals," as he told Jack, preferably ones who could dance and sing, and bring them back to the United States, where he felt they would be a sensation when exhibited.[7] While none of these schemes came to fruition, they demonstrate his rapid transformation into an enterprising showman. The lure of travel to exotic places was still powerful, but now it was intimately linked to prospects of making a handsome financial profit in the travelogue business.

Although attendance at the theaters held up well during the winter months, by spring it began to decline, despite Martin's introduction of new pictures and changes in his routine. In order to meet the $220 weekly operating costs, he took his lectures to nearby towns, including Chanute, where Osa Leighty was then a sixteen-year-old high school student. Osa and her friends regularly packed the Roof Garden Theater on Saturday afternoons to see the latest film melodramas and to hear their friend Gail Perigo sing. Gail was Osa's closest friend, but she had dropped out of school to take a regular job at the theater. Gail's boyfriend, Dick Hamilton, who worked as a slide operator for the *Snark* theaters, suggested that Martin listen to her singing in Chanute with the hope that he would hire her. Martin was very impressed with her singing and promptly offered her a job at the *Snark* No. 2 Theater. Gail had hardly been in Independence a week when she and Dick were married on the stage of the theater. Osa was shocked by the site of the ceremony, as well as angered that Gail had broken their pledge of marrying at the same time.

Osa was not left to nurse her injured feelings for very long. Gail promptly wrote her a soothing letter, inviting her to visit Independence and offering to serve as chaperone. It is obvious that Gail, who admired Martin, had more in mind than a mere visit. It was during this weekend visit that Osa and Martin met. They were instantly drawn to one another despite the fact that Osa found Martin's lecture repulsive. With Gail and Dick acting as chaperones, they went to nearby Coffeyville for lunch, and then spent time at a roller rink. In an attempt to impress Martin, Osa volunteered to participate in a chariot race on the skating rink which ignominiously ended with her being flung over the railing into the first row of seats. Martin's expressions of concern were little comfort to her teenage sense of lost dignity, and she left Independence that night in a huff.[8]

In May 1910 Martin invited Osa to Independence to substitute for Gail Hamilton, who, because of a sore throat, could not perform.

Despite her parents' misgivings, Osa accepted and throughout Saturday evening, May 14, her beautiful soprano voice filled the *Snark* No. 2 Theater. Osa was greatly taken with Martin. To a teenager aspiring to be an actress, he was the ideal man. Tall and handsome with gray-green eyes, he was an acclaimed world traveler who exuded appealing country boy manners. Those country boy manners and the values they expressed were very important to Osa because they gave Martin's personality a familiar look. Her feelings were given additional security by the similarity of Martin's family to her own and by her instant liking for them. They spoke of Martin's comfortable future running the jewelry store, which appealed to Osa, who longed for a small house with a garden and children. Yet there were other longings within her, such as acting, which spoke of a different kind of life.[9]

Martin's attraction to Osa was intense and immediate. She embodied all that he wanted in a wife—beauty, charm, a sweet disposition, and a willingness to take risks while cherishing wholesome home and hearth values. Comparisons with Charmian London were inevitable since he viewed her as the paradigm for a wife. Osa was far more beautiful than Charmian but, like her, had a spirit that could readily adapt to changing circumstances. What made Osa most like Charmian was her willingness to assume a role in her husband's work and to allow this work to bind them together. However, Martin appreciated that Osa, unlike Charmian, did not aspire to equality in their relationship. Thus he was selective in his choice of attributes for a future wife, rejecting those that challenged the dominant role of a husband.

On Sunday, May 15, 1910, after Osa had finished her performance at the *Snark* No. 2 Theater, Martin eloped with "the sweetest, prettiest, and nicest little girl in the world."[10] That they were both deeply in love with one another did not alone account for the elopement. He scorned some conventions, and would never have agreed to a traditional wedding. Even if Osa had wanted one, she was comfortable with elopement because justice-of-the-peace weddings and teenage brides had been the norm in her family. Martin and Osa's elopement was both a mutual risk and a common statement about the life they intended to lead. It would be a life in which they would choose their own course, despite the opinions of family and friends.

They quickly took the midnight train for Kansas City, Missouri. There, Martin arranged for a second ceremony to foreclose possible annulment attempts by Osa's parents, since she was under age according to Kansas law. They finally sent telegrams to their parents announcing their elopement, and then telephoned them. Osa's father was intensely angry with what he saw as Martin's manipulation of his little girl. Using language that was both graphic and threatening, he said to Martin over the phone: "Young man, when I meet you, I will kick your ass in so hard that your spine will stick out of the top of your head like a flagpole." However, her mother received the news with equanimity. "After all," she later said, "how could I object. I was married so young myself."[11]

When Mr. Leighty's anger had spent itself, they took the train to Chanute, and after a day's visit returned to Independence, on May 18, where the *Snark* theaters had been "decorated with baby shoes and by banners reading 'Been Around the World and Found a Girl to Marry Him at Last.'" That night, they got up on the stage and in performing together declared that they were now a team.[12]

By early summer, the *Snark* theaters were failing financially despite the addition of motion pictures and other types of performances. Martin had known for some time that he had to take his show on the road in order to achieve financial success. Yet Osa had different plans. When not singing at the theater, she busied herself keeping house in their rented apartment atop a row of stores and making plans for building a frame house on Poplar Street. Martin, however, was writing to a hundred theater managers throughout the Midwest and West, trying to book his show. By then he was in possession of another reel of motion picture film made by the Pathé Frères cameramen, had a thousand colored lantern slides, and had obtained a half-dozen Hawaiian songs from Honolulu for Osa to sing. Osa's Hawaiian pronunciation left much to be desired, but her Hawaiian costume and good singing voice more than compensated for this and enabled her to get "away fine," as Martin said.[13]

Martin made meticulous plans for taking his travelogue on the road. He had a year's supply of banners, colored lithographs, and title posters printed, as well as postcards for sale to collectors. He persuaded the City of Independence to give him a small subsidy, but was unsuccessful in getting "something out of the Eastman Kodak Co. to advertise for them." The curios were packed in a mammoth-sized trunk, and he hoped to exhibit them in empty buildings in towns that lacked theaters. Ever the enterprising showman, he hired "a young negro boy with a mop of hair and dressed him in a lava lava. . . . I will use him to peddle bills in the day time and blow a conch horn in front of the theater at show time."[14]

Martin left no stone unturned in maximizing box office receipts. Using pictures of nude women and describing the sexual mores of New Hebrides men, he prepared "For Men Only" shows, which he assured Jack London were in good taste since several preachers had attended them.[15]

Osa had little say in this decision to take the show on the theater circuit. It dashed her hopes for a small house and garden in Independence, but appealed to her desire for a stage career. Selling their wedding presents and furniture was difficult for her.[16] Yet she knew that it was a necessity given Martin's debts and the costs of taking the travelogue across the country. Although Martin saw the sale as a means of raising capital, he was also glad to be rid of material possessions that symbolized a settled way of life.

In the late summer of 1910, after being home for almost a year, Martin handed over his interests in the *Snark* theaters to Charley Kerr. In order to finance the theaters, he had borrowed a few thousand dollars from the First National Bank of Independence, which held his father responsible for the loan. This was in addition to his several hundred dollar debt to the Londons, about which Osa and his father did not know for a long time. He was incredibly confident that he could not only liquidate these debts, but also make a sizable profit once he started out on the theater circuit.[17]

Traveling with a thousand pounds of baggage, they headed for nearby Humbolt, Kansas, where their box office receipts would total only eight dollars.[18] Not the least discouraged, they moved on to western Kansas, where Martin started to draw upon Jack's novel *Adventure*, whose principal characters appeared in the Pathé Frères film of Guadalcanal. Their daily receipts ranged from twenty to sixty dollars, but advertising, living, and travel costs left them with only ten dollars in profits. Still, they were able to send John Johnson an average of fifty dollars a week to pay off the bank loan.

The road show enabled Martin to prove his worth to his father in concrete financial terms. As he put it, "I set to work to get him out of debt and then I could breathe easier."[19] While he demonstrated admirable filial loyalty and a great sense of responsibility in paying off the loan with his travelogue receipts, the debt in a sense became a rationale for continuing the show. But paying off the loan played only a small part in motivating him. Writing from Denver, Colorado, on December 8, 1910, to Jack London, he described in graphic terms the forces that were driving him:

> Since I have returned I have studied hard and thought of how Jack London . . . if he could get ahead of the crowd—why shouldn't I? And I have studied what the people want and with nine months' training I have made up my mind to get up and do something big—I'm going to keep at it until some day I'm going to be as big a man in my way as Jack London is in his. . . . Now Jack, you remember your early struggles to get a start—I am having the same time only harder for I have a bunch of debts hanging over me that keep me from making my Travelogues what I would like to. . . . I know that I give a better show than Burton Holmes . . . and all I need now is the reputation.[20]

This determination to achieve success by giving audiences what he thought they wanted eventually shaped Martin's entire career. One could argue that he had little choice since his success was usually judged by box office receipts. Yet some contemporary filmmakers created a demand for their visions, something he never did. Martin's statements not only reflect a steely resolve but also Jack London's philosophy that people can achieve whatever they set their minds to. As he saw it, only debts and the lack of a reputation prevented him from besting Burton Holmes, the foremost travelogue lecturer of the time.

In December 1910 Martin signed up with the Sullivan-Consedine vaudeville circuit for $100 per week plus travel expenses. For the next few months, he and Osa traveled to small towns all over Colorado, Wyoming, Utah, and the Northwest, where the travelogues were frequently received with lukewarm enthusiasm. Osa's repertoire of pseudo-Hawaiian songs, presented as part of the show, received a slightly better response. In April 1911, the circuit offered Martin a second contract, whose financial terms were less generous at $80 per week. However, he was provided with two advance men and a lantern slide projectionist who traveled with a projector.[21] They spent their first wedding anniversary in May in Calgary, and by October had performed in 204 towns and cities in Canada.[22] By staying in cheap hotels and eating skimpy meals, they were able to maximize their savings. The income from the Canadian tour put Martin in a position to pay off a good portion of the debts he had incurred with the *Snark* theaters. He proudly wrote to Jack and Charmian about it and also about his plans for getting on the Orpheum Vaudeville Circuit in Chicago. Still, he had no intention of paying off his debt to them until his father was "clean from the clutches of the bank." He was obviously torn between his sense of loyalty to his father and his obligation to the Londons: "I feel mean every time I think of what I owe you. You must know that my first duty is to my father. Of course another way to look at it, I would never have the advantages that I have if it had not been for you."[23]

Charmian, however, was persistent. "Really, Martin," she wrote back on October 28, 1911, "Jack is in sore need of money. . . . Can't you do something?"[24] Martin, who was so absorbeu with getting ahead, responded with flattery, excuses, and promises. He had by then signed up with the Orpheum Vaudeville Circuit in Chicago for an eighteen-month period at $100 per week plus travel expenses. He reminded the Londons that his travelogues were good advertising for Jack in towns that had never heard of him before. Having flattered them, he went on to present his excuses, which included the need to make new glass slides and purchase additional pictures and film footage. Finally, he promised, as he had done in the past, to begin payments in a few months. At the same time, he boldly asked them to send him "all the negatives that we made on the trip, all the pictures that you have of the New Hebrides natives and of leprosy." When Charmian put him off on the grounds that the photos were pasted and the films stored out of easy reach, he responded by sending a $25 payment on the debt.[25]

Charles Edward Bray, who was the general booking manager for the Orpheum Circuit, signed Martin on in Chicago in October 1911. A skilled vaudeville manager, he made out Martin's contract for $150 per week but required a kickback of $50 as insurance against the show's poor performance. Bray first booked Martin in small towns in the Midwest in order to assess the show's box office potential. Osa auditioned with the Orpheum Circuit for a separate act, but was unsuccessful. Her singing remained a part of Martin's travelogues for a time and she frequently helped with the projection of the lantern slides. Bray billed Martin's show as "Martin Johnson's Wonderful South Sea Island Travelogues" along with the subtitles "Scenes and Pictures of Savage Life in the Far-Off South Sea Islands" and "An Arabian Night of the Tropics." Individual sequences of about fifty hand-colored slides were given such titles as "Cannibals, Their Wars, Worship and Tribal Life," "Dances of the Head Hunters," "Leprosy and Elephantiasis," "Missionaries among the Cannibals," and "Midgets of Borneo." Martin created close to forty groups of slides, each of which constituted a separate show. These shows played on consecutive days in a given theater for about a week. The Orpheum Circuit claimed that the photographic record presented was made by Martin himself on his travels, although in fact much of the material was from other sources.[26]

Martin knew that the route to the big-city theaters lay in having truly sensational slides and films. He had some of these already, but not nearly enough. In addition to his own pictures and those that the Londons had given him thus far, he had procured pictures of people with leprosy from a leprosarium in Mandalay, which he had never visited, and pictures of the Solomon Islands and New Hebrides from the captain of the cargo steamer *Moresby* whom he had met during the voyage. However, he obviously preferred having as many of the Londons' photographs as possible, given that he was present when they were taken and the prestige they gave his show. As he embarked on his first Orpheum tour, he knew that his show had to be improved with the addition of new and better photographs of the kind the Londons had made during the trip. In February 1912 he once again leaned on their friendship: "I will make you a proposition and keep to it, if you will send me all the New Hebrides pictures you have, and all the Solomon Island pictures that would do for men only, and a few leprosy pictures. . . . I will send you $20.00 a week (every week) until I have paid you up and the interest on the money. By doing this, I can put on a men only show in every town and make a little on the side."[27]

The Londons did not jump at this proposition, having been lured into similar ones before by the promise of payments. However, they eventually relented in August 1912, when Martin and Osa arrived in California on their tour. The reunion was a pleasant one considering the stresses to which Martin had subjected the friendship. Jack and Charmian held no grudges against Martin despite his stream of requests and the unpaid debt. They genuinely liked Martin and Osa, and wanted them to succeed. Besides, Jack's three books based on the trip, *Adventure*, *The Cruise of the Snark*, and *South Sea Tales*, had been published in 1911, and Martin and Osa were providing good publicity, which could only increase sales.[28]

In September, Bray sent Martin and Osa back through the Midwest via Denver, where Martin went to a school for public speaking in an attempt to rid himself of "nasal tones . . . and bad grammar," for which he had been harshly criticized in newspaper reviews. He continued taking these lessons as he traveled, at times hiring special instructors to work with him at the theaters.[29] He and Osa put on shows in Omaha, Des Moines, St. Louis, and Kansas City, and in December they were playing in Indiana and Kentucky.[30] While they were in Indianapolis during the third week of December they met Ralph D. Harrison, a bank employee who was also an aspiring writer, editor of the local socialist newspaper, and an admirer of Jack London.

Harrison had been corresponding with Jack since 1911, when he had become involved in the estate of a local manuscript collector who had purchased a number of Jack's original handwritten drafts.[31] Harrison eventually returned most of these, but Jack allowed him to hold on to a few in exchange for some Indian curios. Martin described Harrison as "a second Jack London . . . and . . . the greatest Jack London booster I have ever seen."[32] Unknown to Jack, he and Martin agreed to collaborate on the writing of a book about the *Snark* voyage. At the same time, Bray promised Martin a New York engagement and a new contract at $150 per week, 5 percent of the profits, and 50 percent of the "For Men Only" show profits. The Orpheum also gave him $500 to purchase new film footage.

A New York engagement was the hope of every vaudeville performer, and Martin was no exception. Knowing that his future rode on the outcome of his performances there, he made his greatest request of the Londons as he began collaborating with Harrison on the book:

> I want you to send me every South Sea negative we made since the Snark was built, also the album of Samoan girls (nude studies). . . . Now if you dislike to send these pictures to me, just think what a big thing it means to me and I believe you will let me have them. . . . If I can't get them it will seriously cripple

my show. . . . I can't fake so much in New York for
someone is liable to catch me and I have got to have
everything strictly South Sea Island. . . . Another way
you can figure it out . . . every show is an advertisement for Jack.[33]

In early January 1913, Bray brought Martin and Osa to New York,
where they met Martin Beck, one of the greatest vaudeville impresarios and the manager of the Orpheum Circuit.[34] Although Bray was
the general booking manager for the circuit, he was also Beck's private
secretary, which boosted the Johnsons' prospects. Beck decided to
send Martin and Osa over to London first, before booking them in
New York. Their show, "Wonders of the South Seas," opened as a
matinee at the Victoria Palace the second week of March and included
material from New Guinea, Borneo, Sumatra, and Java, which the
Snark had never visited. Martin was delighted with his two-hour
show, which included lantern slides and 6,000 feet of movie film,
most of it hand-colored. He proudly confessed to Jack that he had
taken out "all fake pictures" and was "running a good straight South
Sea show."[35]

While in London, Martin purchased 2,000 feet of film of Samoa,
Fiji, Java, and Tahiti but refused to pay the Londons anything on his
debt since he was still helping his father pay off the bank loans on the
Snark theaters. "I would steal . . . if I thought I could get away with
it—in order to straighten him out," he told them. At the same time,
he said he valued their friendship more than anything on earth and
that it hurt him to have them think he was intentionally trying to
cheat them out of their money.[36] Still, he continued to take advantage
of their friendship.

Martin and Osa left London on March 26 and opened their show at
the Criterion Theatre on Broadway in New York on June 16. Although the show was little changed in terms of content from the London performance, Al Woods, the Orpheum impresario who staged it,
billed it as "Jack London's Adventures in the South Sea Islands."
Martin had consistently used Jack's name in his descriptive literature,
but in deference to Jack's wishes had been careful not to incorporate it
into the title of the show. The Londons were extremely angry when
they learned of the new title, and a profusely apologetic Martin explained that Al Woods had done it without his knowledge. Martin
offered to change the title, but reminded Jack and Charmian that "it is
giving you a lot of good advertising."[37] As usual, the Londons gave in,
and the show ran with its new title. Beck, Bray, and Woods had obviously decided, perhaps with Martin's prior agreement, that the show
could only make it on Broadway by maximizing the use of Jack London's name.

The *New York Sun* gave Martin's travelogue high marks, as did *Variety*, which identified it as an A. H. Woods film presentation and only mentioned Martin in passing as the photographer. The *Variety* reviewer cogently observed that the audience saw little of Jack London in the films but failed to realize that most of the footage had not been shot during the *Snark* cruise.[38] A unique feature of Martin's travelogue was that it was the Criterion Theatre's first showing of motion pictures. There were two shows daily, a matinee at 2:30 P.M. and an evening show at 8:30 P.M. The reasonable admission price of fifty cents for adults (Burton Holmes charged two dollars) and twenty-five cents for children helped keep attendance up despite the summer heat. However, by the fourth week, with the mercury soaring, attendance fell so low that Bray, Beck, and Woods closed the show.[39]

Bray almost immediately booked Martin and Osa through New England under the terms of a new contract which paid them $110 per week plus travel expenses. After this tour, they headed for the Midwest and Canada in the fall, opening in Madison, Wisconsin, on October 5. By January 1914 they were in California, and after once again performing in the Midwest ended the tour in New Orleans in April. While they were in San Francisco, Osa underwent abdominal surgery, which was performed by the Londons' surgeon, Dr. William Surber Porter. The exact nature of this surgery is never mentioned in the extensive London-Johnson correspondence of the period. However, frequent mention is made of the scar and Osa's long postoperative recovery.[40]

On November 21, 1913, Martin presented the Londons with yet another surprise. This time, it was a copy of his book *Through the South Seas with Jack London*, which he had written with the help of Ralph D. Harrison. The day after he mailed the book he sent the Londons an after-the-fact letter of explanation from Minneapolis, where he was on tour.[41]

Charmian was furious. Martin had blatantly violated his agreement with them, but more importantly, he had exploited their generosity to advance his own career. The publication of this book prior to the completion of Charmian's, *The Log of the Snark* (1916), also fueled her anger.[42] Finally, she found the book full of inaccuracies and gross distortions. In 1915 she wrote to Harrison about this: "Some of the stuff in his book was really amazing for its distortion of fact. He meant well . . . he always means well, but he simply cannot stick to the facts, even when they pay. He hears this at first hand from me . . . so I am not telling on him."[43] Martin's lengthy dedication on the flyleaf, acknowledging that they had "made the writing of this book possible, and . . . everything I have done since then," failed to soothe her.[44] Jack, who was recovering from an appendectomy and the shock of seeing his new home, Wolf House, destroyed by arson, let Charmian express their combined anger at Martin.

April 1914 found Martin and Osa in Omaha, Nebraska. They were seasoned vaudevillians by this time and had shared billings with Will Rogers, Chic Sale, and Harry Lauder. They became especially close to Chic Sale and his family, forming a friendship that lasted a lifetime. Osa's role in the travelogues diminished as time went on. Writing to Jack and Charmian on April 2, 1914, she referred to the show as Martin's, described all he was doing to fix up the curio exhibit, and sadly said that she spent a great deal of her time in the hotel room reading. Whenever possible she tried to create a semblance of normal home life during their one-week stands by cooking small meals and sewing. The itinerant life forced upon her by Martin's work was a terribly lonely one, and she had few friends and no family to help her through the episodes of homesickness and depression that became more frequent.[45] Even though they traveled together, Martin often left Osa alone while he worked at the theaters. He dealt with her unhappiness by buying her fancy clothes or by giving her lump sums of money to spend on herself. This behavior on his part continued throughout their entire married life. In later years, he rewarded her with clothes and spending sprees for having put up with difficult conditions in Africa, Borneo, and the South Seas.[46] While this gave Osa some ephemeral happiness, which she vividly describes in her own writings, it was no substitute for love and friendship.

Martin and Osa finished the tour in New Orleans at the end of April. From there, Bray had planned to send them to South America. However, at the last minute, he called the tour off because of its expense and brought them back to New York. Although Martin was still having a hard time meeting his financial obligations, he managed to send the Londons twenty-five dollars in June and another twenty in September.

The summer was usually a slow time in vaudeville because the public preferred outdoor recreations to hot theaters. As a result, Martin was out of work for three months. Finally, Bray, whose friendship for Martin and Osa had grown over the years, put Martin in charge of developing a weekly film travelogue, the Orpheum Travel Weekly. Martin received a salary of $35 per week plus 5 percent of the profits. This was scarcely enough to get by on in New York, and so Osa took in boarders in their four-room apartment at 300 West 49th Street to supplement their income.[47] The Orpheum Travel Weekly was popular, but the profits too slim to get Martin out of debt. Thanks to Bray, Martin's role was expanded to filmmaking, and during that summer of 1914 he made several reels for the circuit, one of which was shot in Boston at a cost of $400. He then shot several reels of New York City and also a reel at Martin Beck's home, which housed rare book and art collections.[48] While he earned little money from these experiences, they gave him a familiarity with motion picture cameras which would greatly enhance his career.

In the summer of 1914 Martin was still in debt to the Londons for $305 and to the First National Bank of Independence for $200. He also owed George Kleine, his slide maker in Chicago, $117 and the grocer $55. He had pawned Osa's furs and silverware and his two cameras for $65.[49] Hard put to make ends meet, he even contemplated suing Bray and Beck for a bigger share of the $3,200 profit the travel weekly had made so far. As he saw it, he had originated the idea in the first place, purchased the films, made up the titles in a workroom in his apartment, and set up the theater routes. Although Jack referred Martin to his lawyer in New York, Martin eventually dropped the idea and later admitted he had been rash in his judgment of Bray.[50]

In January 1915 Martin sent Jack $50, and again he and Osa went on the road, starting out in Illinois and ending in Arkansas. Writing to the Londons on May 26, 1915, from Hot Springs, Arkansas, he praised Osa, saying that except for Charmian, he had never seen anyone who could undergo the discomforts and hardships of traveling as she could. He added: "She is as wiry and nervy as can be and never whimpers at anything. I tell you I was mighty lucky."[51] If he knew of her feelings of loneliness and depression, he never wrote of them to the Londons.

Martin and Osa continued with the Orpheum Circuit for the next two years, where Martin devoted most of his time to the travel weekly and to making films. With Bray's help, he eventually paid off his debt to the Londons shortly before Jack died on November 22, 1916. Jack's death marked the end of an era for Martin, whose life had revolved around his mentor for almost a decade. Writing to Charmian, he and Osa said: "We will not attempt to offer condolences in a loss so irreparable as yours but want you to understand we grieve with you and for you. If we can serve you in any possible capacity—command us."[52]

Jack's death also coincided with Martin's emergence as a talented cinematographer. This, coupled with his knowledge of the South Seas, made him attractive to a group of Boston investors, who, in the spring of 1917, offered to put up $7,000 to send him to the Solomon Islands and the New Hebrides to make a motion picture. With Jack gone, Martin turned to Charmian for help, asking her to send a letter of recommendation to the group's leader, Earl A. Bishop of Watertown, Massachusetts. He also asked her help in getting articles rewritten and published and tried to induce her to help him with publicity by agreeing to receive a series of chatty letters from him from the South Seas: "You might doctor them up and sell them to one of the magazines. I would want nothing out of them, for the publicity would be invaluable. . . . You might get a little money for the articles . . . with your name attached would surely make readable articles, and I should think you would be able to place them."[53]

Charmian obliged by sending Bishop a letter of recommendation but declined the rest of the request in a letter that was remarkably cordial. She included a mild rebuke by suggesting that he get Ralph D. Harrison to rewrite his articles; Martin had, after all, used Harrison to rewrite his book. Why then did he need her now to rewrite his letters? They both knew that the reason was the magic of the London name. Charmian did not allow herself to be drawn into Martin's schemes as Jack had done, and jokingly but firmly wrote: "I would love to do something with your stuff; but it is quite out of the question. Don't you tease now. . . . I simply cannot do it."[54]

During seven years of marriage, Osa assumed the expected role of dutiful wife. Although her domain was the vaudeville circuit and not a small frame house, her identity was very much bound to Martin. Her dreams of an acting career never materialized. Even her singing in Martin's shows came to an end when the travelogues were restructured with motion pictures.

The South Seas venture, however, which Osa was about to undertake, set her apart from the women of her time. Like Charmian, she would find herself in circumstances that were exotic and liberating and be given the opportunity to establish a new relationship with her husband. But while Charmian was a new breed of woman, independent and freethinking, Osa was dependent and faithful to her husband's wishes. Charmian challenged the values of her time; Osa cherished them. The dangers and hardships of travel in the South Seas galvanized the equality inherent in the London partnership. These same forces were to strengthen the already existing traditional roles in the Johnson marriage. Their shared experiences of adventure and success eventually added another dimension to their relationship. They became active professional partners. However, it was a collaboration that became known to the public as Mr. and Mrs. Martin Johnson, not as Martin and Osa Johnson.

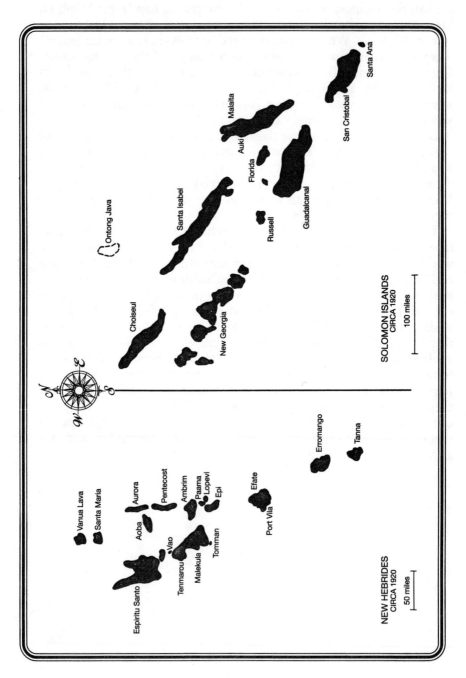

SOLOMON ISLANDS
CIRCA 1920

100 miles

Ontong Java

Choiseul

Santa Isabel

New Georgia

Russell

Florida

Malaita

Auki

Guadalcanal

San Cristobal

Santa Ana

NEW HEBRIDES
CIRCA 1920

50 miles

Vanua Lava

Santa Maria

Aoba

Aurora

Pentecost

Ambrim

Paama

Lopevi

Epi

Espiritu Santo

Vao

Tenmarou

Malekula

Tomman

Efate

Port Vila

Erromango

Tanna

MAP DRAWN BY DOUGLAS DUNN/JOAN SIMPSON

CHAPTER FIVE

SAILING THE SOLOMONS

Once Earl A. Bishop and his fellow investors came up with seven thousand dollars and formed The Martin Johnson Film Co., Martin and Osa quickly made plans to visit the Solomon Islands and the New Hebrides. Martin had regularly kept up his contacts with people there and knew that access to the local populations could be easily facilitated through traders, plantation managers, government officials, and missionaries. The couple left New York in May 1917, visiting Chanute and Independence en route to San Francisco. Osa's mother was appalled by the thought of her daughter traveling among headhunters and cannibals. However, Martin assured her that Osa would be left within the secure confines of mission stations while he traveled around taking pictures. Osa, however, had no intention of being confined in these enclaves, and protested Martin's plan all the way to Australia.[1]

There was a tearful reunion with recently widowed Charmian London in Glen Ellen. She insisted that they take Jack's 30-30 Marlin rifle to augment their two automatic revolvers, and saw them off at the pier when they set sail for Australia aboard the *Sonoma* on June 5. Martin recorded Charmian's goodbye on film with his hand-cranked Universal camera, and later it became the opening scene in his film *Among the Cannibal Isles of the South Pacific*. Aside from the publicity advantage this scene gave the film, it also served to symbolize Charmian's approbation of the endeavor.

Martin's and Osa's determination to shoot the best motion picture ever made in the South Pacific was hardly matched by their photographic equipment. Their Universal camera was but a fragile link to their dreams, vulnerable to mechanical failure, damage, and loss. They were hardly better off with regard to still cameras, taking along only two, a 5 × 7 and a 4 × 5 Graflex.[2] But the 40,000 feet of unexposed movie film that they carried in their canisters, the specially made film storage boxes, and the paraffin for sealing against humidity spoke of an unbridled optimism.

The *Sonoma* stopped in Hawaii and American Samoa before arriving in Sydney on June 26. There, Martin made arrangements to send strips of exposed movie film from the Solomons to Ernest Higgins, who operated one of the finest photographic laboratories in the country. In this way, he was able to verify his results continuously and assess the functioning of his camera in the field. Martin, who had been unable to obtain life insurance in the United States because of where he was traveling, unsuccessfully tried again in Australia. Osa's mother recalled that the insurance companies were concerned that he might purposely disappear to the leisurely life of a beachcomber and Osa would later make a false claim of death.[3] While in Sydney, Martin made a last attempt to get Osa to agree to stay with missionaries, which she adamantly refused to do.

Travel to and from the Solomons was then controlled by the major trading concerns of which Burns Philp and Company was one of the largest. Burns Philp had branched out from trading into copra production and, along with Levers Pacific Plantations Limited, was a major landholder in the islands. Martin and Osa sailed for the Solomons on the Burns Philp steamer *Mindini* in the company of twenty missionaries and some plantation workers.[4] On arriving in Tulagi (Tulaghi), then the administrative capital of the Solomons, they were given a warm welcome by the European officials, some of whom knew Martin from the days of the *Snark* voyage. One of those who was not pleased to see the Johnsons and their cameras was Walter Henry Lucas, who had helped build up the Burns Philp plantation empire. Solomon Island laborers were routinely beaten on most plantations, and Lucas was bent on preventing Martin from filming this and other forms of brutality.[5]

Within a few days of arriving, Martin and Osa met up with Harold Markham, a trader and planter from the Polynesian-populated island of Luanguia in the Ontong Java Atoll.[6] Martin had first met Markham during the *Snark* cruise and promptly hired him and his small 40-foot ketch, the *Lily*. With Markham providing both transportation and services as a facilitator and guide, they sailed 50 miles to the government station of Auki on the island of Malaita. Conditions on Malaita had not changed since Martin and the Londons had visited there in 1908. It was still a violent society where murder was commonplace. There were many peaceful islands where excellent pictures could have been obtained; but Martin opted for Malaita, precisely because it was dangerous, had a reputation for fierce savagery, and offered the best prospects for filming a cannibal feast.

The colonial official in charge of Malaita was William Robert Bell, a middle-aged, teetotaling bachelor who had by then gained a reputation as strict administrator. Uncharacteristic of colonial officials, he vigorously enforced the labor laws, championed the rights of the islanders, and discouraged them from working on plantations for low wages. His by-the-book approach put him in disfavor with some of his superiors and brought him into confrontation with plantation managers who viewed him as both a threat and an eccentric.[7] A powerfully built man with a maimed right hand, he did not shun sharp verbal and written confrontations with the planters, but showed great tact in avoiding violence with the Malaitans. Although he was deeply concerned about the welfare of the islanders, he was also keenly aware that Malaita was a very dangerous place. His clearing at Auki was constantly patrolled by armed sentries, hedges were kept to below knee height to minimize ambush, and he never moved off the station without an armed guard. He gladly gave his permission for Martin and Osa to visit, and proved to be a dutiful but at times taciturn and aloof host. Osa thought him a woman-hater since he ignored her except when upbraiding her for wandering off the station in search of birds and flowers. His house was Spartan and clean; Osa's eye registered his mismatched china, battered silverware, the gramophone on which he played Gilbert and Sullivan scores, and his barefoot servant who wore a freshly pressed white suit, a stiff collar, and tie.[8]

Bell's unequivocal aim was to promote the well-being of the islanders. Unlike Lucas of Burns Philp, he had no concerns that Martin might focus on the conditions of plantation workers and thus arouse outside indignation and intervention. In fact, films depicting plantation overseer brutality could only advance his own crusade. Thus, while Bell gave Martin full access to the islanders, Lucas instructed his managers and overseers to prevent him from filming on the plantations.

Martin and Osa were not social reformers, despite Jack London's example, and the exposure of labor law violations was not high on their documentary agenda. Still, the acting resident commissioner, J. C. Barley, took no chances and diplomatically told them that the administration's help was contingent on their not filming labor conditions and cannibalism. The latter was extremely rare by then, but the fact that it still occurred was an embarrassment to the local colonial government. Martin and Osa were determined to film a cannibal feast and could not remain indifferent to the plight of plantation laborers. While agreeing to Barley's requests at Tulagi, they knew that once away from the seat of government they would have a fairly free hand to film as they pleased.[9]

Martin and Osa spent an agreeable month with Bell on Malaita, although at times his almost missionarylike rectitude made them slightly uncomfortable. Under armed guard, he took them up into highland villages, to local markets, and to the artificial man-made islands of Langa Langa lagoon.[10] With his help, Martin made some superb still photographs and shot thousands of feet of motion picture film. There was nothing staged or contrived in this film record, and today it constitutes an important part of the cultural heritage of the Solomon Islands nation.[11] However, Martin's editing and titles later distorted the true meanings of many of these visual images and infused them with numerous racial comments, some of which were masked as humor. In his film *Across the World with Mr. and Mrs. Martin Johnson*, for example, he claimed that it would be a hundred years before the Solomon Islands were civilized. During a sequence depicting men in Malekula in the New Hebrides—valuable today because it documents modes of dress and body adornment—he commented that one looked like the missing link and a cross between the ape and man. He further appealed to interest in the so-called "missing link" by inaccurately characterizing a group of Malekulans as "monkey people" and claimed that they had abandoned their villages for life in the trees. He commented that the practice of head elongation on the island of Tomman did not affect intelligence because these people had none to begin with.

While on Malaita, Martin concluded that Osa's true value lay in front of the camera's objective, and not behind the viewfinder. She eagerly posed and pantomimed with the islanders, and the resulting screen images of a petite flaxen-haired American woman surrounded by cannibals and headhunters later jarred audiences and drew them to the box office. From one perspective, these islands became Osa's stage set and enabled her to realize her ambitions of being an actress. For beginning on Malaita and continuing for the rest of her career, she was always a star in Martin's films. But her role in his films extended beyond that of being a star. She possessed an open and genuine manner that had universal appeal. This, coupled with her linguistic ability with *bêche-de-mer* in the South Pacific and, later, Swahili in Africa, quickly disarmed people of their apprehensions about being filmed and photographed. On Malaita and other islands, she was able to coax the "Marys," as the women were called, to pose for Martin's cameras. As a result, he obtained many fine pictures that otherwise would have eluded him. Osa's insistence on not being packed off to a mission station and her performance on Malaita also gave a new dimension to her relationship with Martin. He now knew that she was a significant contributor to his creative work and no longer viewed her as playing the limited role that had characterized their vaudeville years.

In describing the peoples of the South Pacific fifteen years later, Osa reflected the racism that was such an accepted part of the white American and European cultural landscapes. She described the chief of a Malaitan village as having toes like those of an ape and as being as black as a gorilla.[12] These simian analogies, so common in Osa and Martin's writings and films, expressed and reinforced prevailing racial attitudes, and fed the beliefs of those who held that dark-skinned peoples were examples of genetically determined racial inferiority. Such beliefs were very widespread at the time among Europeans in the Solomon Islands. J. C. Barley, the acting resident commissioner at the time of Martin's and Osa's visit, wrote several years later that, except for the missionaries, 90 percent of the Europeans on the islands regarded the indigenous population as a necessary evil and as unclean and inferior creatures.[13]

In early August, Markham returned to Auki on the *Lily* as prearranged in order to take Martin and Osa to his island of Luanguia in the Ontong Java Atoll, 250 miles to the north. Much to Martin's surprise, Barley arrived on the *Lily* and announced his plans of sailing with them, claiming he had government business to conduct on Luanguia. While this was true, he also wanted to keep Martin and Osa under government surveillance a bit longer to calm planter fears that they might film conditions on the plantations.

Although Martin and Osa remained at Luanguia for only a week, their stay coincided with the annual coconut harvest and a number of ceremonials associated with it. The Polynesian population of the island received especially high praise from Osa, who extolled their physical beauty and who saw intelligence and character in their high foreheads, strong chins, and thin lips. She contrasted their narrow noses with the flat ones of the Melanesians, and was pleased that their hair was curly rather than kinky.[14] Markham's young wife, Lily, after whom his boat was named, was deaf, but Osa admired her not least of all because she regularly showered with soap and water and washed her clothes.[15] Both Martin and Osa placed great store on personal cleanliness, and he, in some of his writings, presents it as an outward manifestation of inner moral worth.

Many of the customs of Ontong Java are unique in the Solomons, and Martin recorded a number of them for posterity on film and in still pictures. He filmed tattooing, which is still widely practiced there, and ceremonies that made use of large sculpted poles, which he inaccurately characterized as "devil devils." The priests (*makua*) who supervised the ceremonies were similarly called "devil devil men." He also made some excellent pictures of Ontong Java's unusual cemeteries with their carved wooden and coral headstones. While he filmed and shot still pictures, Barley conducted government business with the local people, their chiefs, and the handful of planters and traders who lived there.

After a week on Ontong Java, Markham transported Martin and Osa back to Tulagi. As she had done before, Osa took tricks at the wheel, slept on the *Lily*'s hard deck, and did the cooking. In Martin's eyes, she had measured up to Charmian London, and in some ways had even surpassed her. Although he had clearly obtained some remarkable film footage thus far, he was bitterly disappointed in not being able to film people eating human flesh.[16] He reluctantly concluded that missionaries, government control, and contact with traders and planters had pushed the custom into extinction. Traders advised him to stage a few cannibal feasts, but he refused. In later years, however, he freely staged a number of shots, as did most documentary filmmakers. Staging this type of scene was very risky because the resulting film would inevitably come under intense scrutiny. A charge of fraud would have ruined both his reputation and finances.

In late August, Martin and Osa sailed over to the Burns Philp plantation, Mberande, on the island of Guadalcanal. In 1908 Martin and the Londons had been graciously entertained at this plantation by its managers, George Derbishire and Thomas Harding, when it was known as Penduffryn. However, in 1909 Derbishire and Harding's financial backer, Justus Scharff, sold the plantation to Burns Philp, and in the intervening years much had changed.[17] Derbishire had died in 1914, Harding had left, and the pleasant houses and gardens had disappeared.[18] The new managers, who ran a highly efficient commercial operation, had been forewarned by Lucas not to help the Johnsons; but they eventually cooperated when it became obvious that Martin was not very interested in filming labor conditions.[19]

Martin and Osa went up into the interior of Guadalcanal, where Martin had had his first experience in filmmaking nine years earlier. As Charmian had done, Osa shot pigeons for the pot, and together they filmed village life. Still, Martin was not satisfied, given that the people had acquired Western manufactured goods and that some even wore clothes. After less than a week on Guadalcanal, the Johnsons returned to Tulagi, met up with Markham, and then sailed to Makira (San Cristobal) and Santa Ana. They stopped at the small island of Ugi off the coast of Makira, where Martin had obtained his sculpted house post years before, and then dropped anchor at Santa Ana, where in 1908 he had met the trader Tom Butler and a local guide, Peter. Butler was dying and unable to recognize his visitors, but Peter remembered the visit of the *Snark*, and again was of assistance. Martin made some remarkable pictures on Makira and Santa Ana, which today are of great ethnographic importance.

Martin and Osa left Tulagi on the Burns Philp steamer *Mindini* for Sydney in early October. During their three months in the Solomons, they had shot close to 20,000 feet of film. This was quickly developed by Martin and Ernest Higgins and proved to be excellent. Although it contained wonderful scenes of island life, ceremonies, and portraits of people, it did not capture the one elusive custom Martin wanted— cannibalism.

In pursuit of cannibals, Martin and Osa sailed on the *Pacifique* for Vila, the capital of the New Hebrides, shortly after arriving in Sydney. They spent a few days in Noumea on New Caledonia before reaching Vila on October 26. There they anchored next to the *Snark*, which had just been raised after being two months under water. Martin mournfully described to Charmian how the ship had been gutted both above and below deck, and its stern crushed into an ugly shape.[20]

At the suggestion of local traders and planters, they went on to Vao and Malekula via Espiritu Santo. Vao is a small island, only two miles across, which lies off the northeast coast of Malekula. Roman Catholic missionaries had been working on Vao since the late nineteenth century, and it was a relatively secure place, although living conditions were still very harsh.[21] On Vao, Martin and Osa were given a warm reception by Father Prin, the other missionaries, and the local trader. The traditional culture of Vao was fairly intact at the time of their visit, and Martin was able to document much of it. Despite the influence of missionaries and traders, local customs remained strong, including the unappealing one of burying alive those close to death.

Martin set his sights on nearby northern Malekula and the country of the Big Nambas. Despite a warning from the British resident commissioner, Merton King, he and Osa decided to sail to Tenmarou Bay in a trader's small whale boat. From there, they planned to climb up to the village of Tenmarou whose chief, Nihapat, was one of the most powerful among the Big Nambas. They eventually found Nihapat and his people, but became alarmed when the Big Nambas refused to let them leave. Only the arrival of the British gunboat the *Euphrosine* induced Nihapat to let them go. It is unlikely that Nihapat intended to harm them; however, the Big Nambas' country was a violent place of blood feuds and unpredictable murder, and anything was possible.

Following their return to Vao, Martin was prohibited by the authorities from revisiting Tenmarou. He knew, though, that he had found the very people he had been looking for all these months. Untouched by missionaries and little affected by traders, the Big Nambas represented his best hope of filming cannibalism and headhunting. He left with a determination to visit them again at some time in the future.

By late December, Martin and Osa had shot close to 20,000 feet of film in the New Hebrides. This, plus the Solomon Islands footage, filled forty reels and was more than enough to satisfy those who had invested in the project and to produce a successful feature film.[22] After developing their film in Sydney, they sailed on January 10, 1918, for San Francisco, where they arrived in early February after an absence of almost nine months.[23] Martin suffered from recurrent bouts of malaria on the trip back to the United States and for some time afterward. Sturdy Osa, however, remained healthy but was very glad to be home.

When Martin arrived in New York City, he presented his financial backers with 40,000 feet of excellent film. Although exhibitors were impressed with it, they preferred cutting it into several single reel (ten-minute) shorts. Earl Bishop and the other investors, bowing to the wisdom of exhibitors and looking for a sure and fast return on their investment, pushed for this option. Martin, however, refused to agree, and, while he held out, even took to shooting a few short films in New York City in order to earn money.[24]

Martin's film was technically superb, highly educational, and had required as much effort to make as some entertainment features. But early documentaries such as this were, as Brownlow cogently states, "considered an inferior species, rather like the people they depicted."[25] Reviewers tended to dismiss them with one-line comments, and exhibitors used them as fillers with the entertainment features preferred by the audiences.

There was only one man at the time in New York who could have helped Martin put his film out as a full-length feature. Samuel Lionel Rothafel, the leading motion picture theater manager in the country, had gained both a reputation and success by being a bold innovator.[26] Martin's film represented an opportunity for innovation, and Rothafel quickly seized upon it. There was no recklessness in his decision, because he presented the film according to an old and tried formula, the lantern slide lecture, at which Martin was an expert. At the same time, every effort was made to infuse the film with the recognizable characteristics of an entertainment feature. Entitled *Among the Cannibal Isles of the South Pacific*, it opened as a lecture film of one hour and five minutes in duration at the Rivoli on Sunday, July 21, 1918, and ran for a week.[27] Martin and Osa made three daily appearances, and on one day, when Martin was confined to bed with malaria, Osa successfully lectured alone.[28]

Rothafel's bold stroke drew the attention of the press to Martin's film. Unlike many other films of this genre, it received immediate and widespread acclaim in both the popular press and in trade publications. There was hardly a major New York City newspaper that did not give it glowing reviews. The *New York Telegraph* called the film "a distinct novelty" and characterized it as of "unquestioned educational value." Its reviewer, D. G. Watts, identified one of the major reasons for the film's appeal when he said that it was "a rare combination of entertainment and instruction."[29] Yet the entertainment value, so critical to successful marketing, was achieved at the price of frequently distorting the meaning of what was actually being shown.

The *New York Times*, which gave the film a lengthy rave review, as did *Variety*, said the following of Osa: "Mrs. Johnson appears in many of the scenes, her presence adding an element of striking contrast, and it may be remarked that when she gets tired of following her husband into wild places, she can probably get a mighty good job as a screen star."[30] Reviews in motion picture trade publications were extremely important then since they influenced the selection decisions of theater exhibitors. The film received exceptional reviews in all the leading publications of this kind, including *Motion Picture News*, which said: "These are remarkable pictures and probably the most unusual that have ever been taken. . . . There is plenty of humor brought in to relieve the danger elements."[31] For Martin, one of the most important reviews was a private one from Charmian London. She wrote to him saying: "It is the sheer perfection of your films. . . . Truly, Martin, never have I seen such magnificent moving pictures, such splendid photography. . . . I am quite overwhelmed . . . deeply impressed."[32] These comments not only conveyed her impressions of his film but also recognized his success as a film artist. Jack had lived his adventures and later wrote about them, achieving success with words. Martin, his protégé, had followed this formula and had now achieved success with film. As with Jack's success, it was one that was molded by a combination of talent, sheer determination, a love of adventure, and a willingness to take risks.

The Rivoli film did not include any titles because Martin and Osa provided a running oral commentary before the audience. After the show closed, Martin obtained an additional $500 from his backers to have the silent film titled and new tinted prints made at the Lyman Howe Laboratories in Wilkes-Barre, Pennsylvania. He chose Thomas McNamara, a famous cartoonist, to title the film along the lines of the lecture narrative. McNamara laced the titles with humor, which greatly increased the film's entertainment value and maximized its market potential. The new titling and the improved prints induced Robertson Cole, then a major film distributor for independent filmmakers, to market the film under a contract that gave Martin 75 percent of the profits.[33] In order to tap into the demands of those exhibitors who preferred shorts of this type of subject matter, the footage was also cut into ten one-reel educational pictures, which Robertson-Cole distributed under the collective heading *On the Borderland of Civilization*. These included *Tulagi—A White Spot in a Black Land*, *Through the Isles of the New Hebrides*, *Lonely South Pacific Missions*, and *Recruiting in the Solomons*. This latter footage did not please some of the Johnsons' former hosts in the Solomon Islands. As brief as this film was (ten minutes), it aroused an awareness of European abuses in the Solomon Islands and demonstrated that Martin and Osa were not indifferent to them.[34]

Martin's triumphant success gave him a place among recognized filmmakers. As a result, he no longer stood in Jack London's shadow, nor was he dependent on him. Yet Jack's powerful influence on him would be lifelong.

Martin had no difficulty finding investors willing to put their money into his limited stock company, The Martin Johnson Film Company, of which he was president.[35] Charmian had agreed with him that his fortune would be assured if he succeeded in capturing cannibalism on film. He believed that his only chances for obtaining this footage lay on the forested slopes of Malekula where Nihapat ruled. He and Osa had once fled for their lives from this imposing ruler, but now they were determined to visit him again.

CHAPTER SIX

RETURN TO MELANESIA

The financial success of *Among the Cannibal Isles of the South Pacific* and its variants drew investors to The Martin Johnson Film Company. These monies, together with Martin and Osa's own profits, made possible a second and more elaborate film expedition to the South Pacific. On April 8, 1919, they sailed out of San Francisco on the *Ventura*, bound for Sydney, Australia. A meticulous organizer, Martin had written and cabled ahead to traders, plantation managers, and government officials in the New Hebrides in order to prepare for his planned march through the island of Malekula from north to south. He carried along with him not only newer and better cameras, but also a Pathescope motion picture projector with which to show his last movie to Nihapat and the Big Nambas. Showing the film to the Big Nambas would not only impress them with the white man's power, but would also provide an opportunity for filming their reactions, which could entertain moviegoers at home.[1]

After a six-week stay in Sydney at the home of Ernest Higgins, where Martin tested his equipment and set up a darkroom, they sailed on the nineteen-hundred-ton steamer *Pacifique* for the New Hebrides. They stopped briefly in Noumea, New Caledonia, where they showed their film at a local theater and where they met Merton King, the British resident commissioner for the New Hebrides. King had disappointing news. He was unable to provide a government escort for the planned march down the length of Malekula. Ever resourceful, Martin quickly changed plans and chartered three recruiting schooners he had met up with in Espiritu Santo. Each had large armed crews, and their owners agreed to accompany him and Osa up to Nihapat's village. The *Pacifique* sailed fifty miles off course to drop them off at Vao, where the local population gave them a warm welcome and carried

their sixty-five trunks, boxes, and crates from the beach to Father
Prin's stone cottage.[2]

Four hundred Melanesians were living on Vao, and although they
had regular contact with missionaries and recruiters, they tenaciously
held on to their traditional beliefs and practices. This, coupled with
the regular visits of Big Nambas from nearby Malekula, made both
Martin and Osa somewhat uneasy for their personal safety. Yet the
people of Vao treated them with whatever hospitality they could mus-
ter and carefully guarded their possessions whenever they left for
brief trips elsewhere. While Martin and Osa remarked on their honesty, they attributed it to gifts of stick tobacco.[3] Their writings and
films show no grasp of the complexity of the cultures on Vao and
Malekula. While the Melanesians they met were endowed with honesty, goodwill, and a sense of humor, they were also given to brutal
violence in defense of their lives, property, and territory. Martin and
Osa fell in with the local European expectations of violence and
treachery; and it was easy to misinterpret friendliness and honesty as a
ruse. The Johnsons' continuous exercise of caution, though certainly
wise, was sometimes carried to extremes and prevented them from
seeing the Melanesians' true humanity or empathizing with their suffering. They apparently were not acquainted with any of the Europeans there, who had this broader view and deeper feeling for the
islanders. These more sensitive observers—some missionaries and anthropologists like John W. Layard, who worked in the area in 1914–
1915, and A. Bernard Deacon, who followed him ten years later—
saw the reasons behind the savage revenge killing and the blood feuds,
and recognized the social disruption caused by European interference.[4]
European-introduced diseases such as tuberculosis, whooping cough,
measles, and influenza took a terrible toll on the poorly fed people
with no immunity. Deacon was astounded by the level of depopula-
tion caused by these diseases and the subsequent disappearance of
entire cultures.[5] Survivors barely eked out a living, given the decline
in the numbers able to farm. As a result, they were all the more
vulnerable to the ravages of subsequent epidemics because of poor
nutrition.

A few weeks after their arrival in Vao, Paul Mazouyer, a French
recruiter and plantation owner, dropped anchor at Vao. He was one
of the schooner owners who had agreed to accompany them into the
Big Nambas country. Martin described Mazouyer as "a two-fisted adventurer of the old type" who "had a contempt for the local natives
that has resulted fatally for many a white man."[6] His words were
prophetic; a number of years later, Mazouyer was killed by the Big
Nambas while on a recruiting trip.[7]

Leaving most of their possessions in Father Prin's house on Vao in
the care of their local servants, they sailed with Mazouyer to Ten-

marou Bay, where they met up with the two other schooners, one owned by Perrole, a Frenchman, and the other captained by a young English-Samoan named Stephens. Backed by twenty-six well-armed Melanesians from the three schooners, and equipped with supplies to last a week, they landed on the beach. Nihapat emerged from the jungle as a "fade in," as Martin later said, and welcomed them in *bêche-de-mer*. Osa, in her striped coveralls, slouch hat, and white sneakers, caught his attention almost at once, and during the rest of the visit he regularly sent her gifts of yams, fruits, and sugar cane. Martin feared Nihapat was wooing her and might try to abduct her. The suspicion that governed Martin's actions and those of his party was not returned by Nihapat and his men. So trusting in fact was Nihapat that he came on board Mazouyer's schooner one night and slept on the boards of the engine room. This was an impressive gesture, given the brutal treatment of the Big Nambas by recruiters from these very ships. Martin wrongly but understandably interpreted this as an act of fear-lessness instead of one of friendship and trust, and viewed Nihapat's subsequent actions as strongly influenced by the presence of an armed guard.[8] At no time did he give Nihapat credit for expressing genuine friendship despite the fact that Nihapat fully cooperated with him, treated his party very well, and extended all the hospitality of which he and his people were capable. Nihapat even went so far as to accompany Osa in singing a song as she played the ukulele.[9]

While Martin was unable to understand fully Nihapat's character, he came to admire Osa's all the more. He said that she had all the qualities that went into making an ideal traveling companion for an explorer, "pluck, endurance, cheerfulness under discomfort." Osa herself tried very hard to measure up to Martin's ideal, Charmian London. By the time they reached Borneo several months later, she felt she had.[10] The crucial role she played in facilitating his filmmaking, and her meeting the standards set by Charmian, made her a true partner. Yet neither she nor Martin saw it as a partnership of peers. The purpose of the expedition was cinematography and photography, and everyone saw that as "men's work." Osa's work was still cast in the traditional woman's role of supporting and encouraging projects devised and run by men.

Osa moved freely among the Big Nambas on the beach, put on makeup for the filming that was taking place, and made snapshots with her own Kodak camera. Her easy manner, friendly gestures, and reassuring words in *bêche-de-mer* contrasted with Martin's suspicion and reserve, and did much to win Nihapat over. Nihapat finally invited them to visit his village, where the entire population turned out to greet them, including the women and children. The women were dressed in purple-dyed pandanus grass skirts and head veils that fell over their backs. Martin said that the skirts were matted with filth and that the children were scrawny little wretches.[11] That the skirts were covered with dirt was to be expected, since the women did the gardening, and parasites and malnutrition afflicted the children. Although Martin was aware of this, he never expressed sympathetic understanding, only scornful condemnation. He saw these people as filthy, savage, treacherous, and scowling, even as they presented the party with water to drink, cooked yams and fruit, and put on a spectacular sing-sing celebration using their great carved upright gongs.

Once the visit was over, Nihapat accompanied them on the arduous eight-mile trip back down to the beach. There, Martin set up his portable generator, projector, and movie screen and showed several reels of film to the Big Nambas, including those he had made of them in 1917. Osa reassured Nihapat and his men by sitting among them on the sand during the performance. With the help of radium flares, Martin obtained pictures of "cannibals at the movies" which later entertained audiences in Europe and America.

Back on Vao, Martin and Osa spent long hours developing the still pictures they had made on Malekula. Martin was less than satisfied with the action shots he had obtained of Big Nambas ceremonies and engaged Captain Charles Moran and his schooner, the *Amour*, to take him and Osa back to Tenmarou Bay. Moran had only a few armed men, and Martin's choice of so slim an escort indicates that his earlier visit had persuaded him that Nihapat posed little danger, and that a large force was unnecessary. In his book *Cannibal-Land*, he relates that he had come to the conclusion that the only whites who had been killed or seriously threatened by the Melanesians were those who had grievously abused them. Despite Martin's accurate insights and Nihapat's continued expressions of sincere friendship, he refused to let Osa accompany him into the interior. Nihapat's renewed gestures of kindness toward Osa aroused not only Martin's baseless concerns that he might abduct her, but also jealousy.[12]

The following day, Nihapat insisted that Osa travel inland with them as far as the first stream, where he said his wives were waiting with gifts. Again, Martin suspected treachery, even though Nihapat explained that it was taboo for his most recent wife to look at the sea. When they arrived at the stream, the wives were waiting with gifts of sugar cane, yams, and a new pandanus grass skirt. Seeing this, Martin frankly admitted that his distrust of Nihapat was again unjustified, but he never went the next step and conceded that Nihapat's overall behavior was sincere.[13] He had come to believe the worst of these people and was unable to reconcile the sordid tales of recruiters and traders with his own peaceable experiences. And why not: in part, because gentle savages were not good box office material. Nihapat and his people were presented to moviegoers as fierce, filthy savages whose lives were governed by irrational violence and senseless customs. Their physical appearance on the screen easily lent itself to such an interpretation by unquestioning audiences. Unfortunately, the Big Nambas were not in a position to contest a traveler's tale.

Nihapat's neighbors to the south in Lambumbu Bay were described in somewhat different terms, but in equally derogatory or distorted fashion. Because they made wise use of platforms in banyan trees, Osa dubbed them "monkey people" and Martin concocted an apocryphal yarn that they were war-displaced nomads living their entire lives in trees. According to him, "They were nearer monkeys than men. They had enormous flat feet, with the great toe separated from the other toes and turned in. They could grasp a branch with their feet as easily as I could with my hands."[14] Years later, Osa described one of the old men in much the same terms Martin had two decades before: ". . . was nearer to a monkey than any human being I have ever seen before or since. . . . An alert, nervous, monkey-like expression; quick, sure, monkey-like movements."[15] The curiosity of these people about a white woman—they rubbed Osa's skin and felt her hair—confirmed for Martin that they were "the nearest thing to the missing link there is on earth." He found them mild and spiritless, took their hospitality for granted, and left them because they clearly did not practice cannibalism.

The *Amour* sailed on to Southwest Bay and the island of Tomman, where the heads of male children were purposely elongated through the use of tight bindings. Martin was still "in search of cannibals," as he said, and disappointed that he had not yet found any.[16] On Tomman he was able to film and photograph the sacred men's clubhouse (*amel*), where magnificent clay and wood effigies of the dead (*rambaramp*) were kept along with the cured heads of both ancestors and enemies. These effigies contain the skulls of the deceased over which clay is carefully sculpted in order to reproduce lifelike features. Martin's photographs and films of these *rambaramp* in situ are among the earliest and the best ever made.[17] To his credit, he accurately interpreted them to theater audiences and in his book *Cannibal-Land*. While on Tomman, he was also able to film and photograph the actual process of ancestral head-curing. These films and photographs have since become extremely valuable ethnographic documents.

From Tomman they sailed on to Port Sandwich in southeast Malekula, where they met up with Merton King, the British resident commissioner. Leaving Captain Moran and the *Amour*, they boarded the resident's gunboat, the *Euphrosine*, for a quick side trip to see the eruption of the Lopevi volcano. King later dropped them at Api for a few days, and eventually the *Pacifique* arrived and took them back to Vao. They spent two days developing plates and film in the crude laboratory in Father Prin's house, and then waited for a schooner to take them to Vila, the capital of the New Hebrides.[18] Shortly thereafter, a good-natured Tongan trader named Powler arrived and agreed to take them to Espiritu Santo. The people of Vao, among whom they had lived for so long and who had been of great help to them, showed real regret at their departure. However, Martin thought them incapable of such feelings. As he saw it, they were merely disappointed that they would never again receive so much stick tobacco for so little work.[19]

Ever on the prowl for freaks, cannibals, and headhunters, they sailed to Espiritu Santo, where Martin had been told by traders that dwarfs lived in the hills. With Powler and his fifteen armed Tongan guards trudging along, they hiked for three hours into the interior. The people they found may have been short, but they were certainly not the dwarfs Martin would later try to make them appear.[20] Walking farther on into the heart of the island, they heard the sound of a drum and chanting. Carefully creeping through the grass, they came upon a group of men dancing around a fire over which some pieces of meat were suspended from a spit. Martin suspected and indeed hoped that the meat was "long-pig"—human flesh. What happened next is told by Martin and Osa in four different accounts—his in *Cannibal-Land* and hers in *I Married Adventure, Bride in the Solomons,* and an article in *Life* magazine.[21] Osa's *I Married Adventure* account parallels Martin's, but her other accounts are at slight variance with them. Through their binoculars and telephoto camera lens, they saw what appeared to be a foot and human spleen hanging from the spit over the fire. Since neither of them had ever taken a course in human anatomy, it is unlikely that they could have recognized a partially cooked spleen, especially from such a distance. After Martin had obtained enough long shots of the scene, he gave one of Powler's men a radium flare and told him to put it on the fire. The alleged cannibals continued to eat the meat until the flare actually went off and frightened them into the bush. Given government prohibitions and punishments for cannibalism, it is unlikely that these men would have continued to eat human flesh while an armed stranger walked into the clearing and put a radium flare on the fire.

Once the men had fled, Martin raced into the clearing, hoping to film and photograph partially eaten human flesh. But his hopes were dashed when he found that the men had run off with all the meat. However, he found a charred human head on the fire with rolled leaves plugging the eye sockets. The men who had been dancing and eating soon returned and readily posed for the camera "as innocent children." Although the evidence was unconvincing, Martin would later claim that he had, for the first time in history, filmed a cannibal feast.

On November 9, 1919, Martin and Osa arrived back in Sydney with 25,000 feet of movie film and a thousand stills. Martin quickly wrote Charmian the same day, telling her that they had witnessed human heads being smoked, found the monkey people, and came upon "the remains of a human head, cooked, and still hot on the fire, although the natives fled."[22] This latter statement referred to what he and Osa later billed as the cannibal feast. Yet it is significant that Martin did not describe it as such to Charmian. She had written to him the year before saying that his fortune would be "assured" if he could "succeed in convincing the public of what they were actually beholding—the real, raw cannibal savage."[23] If Martin truly believed that he had filmed a cannibal feast on Espiritu Santo, Charmian would have been among the first to hear of it. Instead, what he described to her was a head-curing ceremony, similar to those he had filmed on Tomman. The decision to characterize this ceremony as a cannibal feast was made at a later date, closer to the time of the film's commercial release. Once this myth was created on film, it was easily reproduced in both Martin's and Osa's writings. Theater audiences and readers never questioned this claim, nor allowed for the possibility that the head of a deceased relative was being ceremoniously cured and that the meat was pork.

Despite Martin and Osa's significant photographic accomplishments in the New Hebrides, the directors of The Martin Johnson Film Company and Robertson-Cole, the film distributor for independent producers, were finding it difficult to market pictures of "savages."[24] They advised them to secure pictures of wild animals, as theater audiences had developed a liking for them. Assured of continued investor support, and after consulting with a number of people in Australia, they decided to go to North Borneo. It was close by, had plenty of wild animals, and its inhabitants were reputed to be headhunters. Martin and Osa did not foresee that the jungles of Borneo were far different from the forests of the New Hebrides. The rain was almost incessant and the sun rarely pierced the thick canopy of trees, creating conditions sure to defeat even the best of photographers.

CHAPTER SEVEN

JUNGLE ADVENTURES

Martin and Osa remained in Sydney, Australia, for three months, until February 1920. During that time, Martin not only developed their films and plates at the home of Ernest Higgins, but also made arrangements for their trip to North Borneo.[1] Osa had mixed feelings about going to Borneo. She missed her family and friends, and was left to spend many days alone while Martin worked in the laboratory with Higgins. Her mother worried about her complaints of loneliness and depression, but felt powerless to do anything about them. Her concerns were fueled in part by the knowledge that Osa's brother, Vaughn, then in France, had already developed a problem with alcohol.[2] Unknown to her mother, Osa had begun to seek solace in alcohol as well. This occasional dependency slowly developed over the years into a pattern of periodic binge drinking.[3]

Martin and Osa had never been to British North Borneo before nor had they ever attempted wildlife photography. Filming animals in the wild required skills and techniques quite different from those they had used in Melanesia. Yet Martin's drive and self-confidence were sufficient to propel them into a veritable unknown. Although wildlife photography was still in its infancy, a number of filmmakers had already produced movies that had become great commercial successes. Foremost among these was *Paul Rainey's African Hunt*, which opened in New York in 1912, where it ran for fifteen months. The film was a "staggering success," as Brownlow has stated, and Martin was well aware that it had earned a half-million dollars for its producers and distributors.[4]

British North Borneo was then administered by a private company of which Sir Joseph West Ridgeway, an experienced soldier and administrator, was president.[5] He placed all of the facilities of the company at the Johnsons' disposal, and provided them with an interpreter, police escort, and government launch. Since there were no roads in the territory, Martin and Osa had to travel up rivers and streams to reach the jungle interior and its wildlife. Following preliminary trips around Sandakan, the administrative capital, they sailed up the largest river in North Borneo, the Kinabatangan, as it afforded the quickest access to the interior. They sailed in a fleet of thirteen *gobongs* (canoes) and were accompanied by Mr. Holmes, the resident commissioner of Lamang, assistants, and an armed guard.

Once upriver, they were greatly assisted by El Hadji Mohammed Nur, the local chief of the Kinabatangan district, who traveled with them to the river's headwaters, the home of the Tenggara people. The Tenggara once had a reputation as fierce headhunters but had largely abandoned the practice, not least of all because a stiff prison term of seven years was imposed on anyone found in possession of a head. Although the Tenggara had abandoned headhunting, they still adhered to their other centuries-old customs. Thanks to El Hadji Mohammed Nur's intervention, Martin was able to obtain some splendid film footage and photographs of the Tenggara, which have since become important ethnographic documents.[6]

While Martin and Osa were in the village of Sungei Iyau, they saw a baby gibbon tied to a chain outside of a dilapidated hut. This small ball of fluff was so endearing that they immediately fell in love with her and promptly paid the three dollars the owners asked. They named her Kalowatt, and for the next several years she became their constant companion, sharing their hotel rooms, ship cabins, and dining room table. Kalowatt defined the Johnsons as "the people with the ape" and associated them in the public mind with the wildlife portrayed in their films and writings. From the time they acquired her, they always traveled with animals in tow and were rarely seen without them. Kalowatt, however, occupied a special place in their lives. She became the child they never had, and they lavished on her both extraordinary affection and care.[7]

Martin and Osa traveled up the Kinabatangan for 420 miles before returning downstream. Once below the river's rapids, they constructed a comfortable houseboat which freed them from the narrow confines of their *gobong*.[8] Up to this point, Martin had obtained little in the way of wildlife sequences, the primary objective of the trip. Early on their way up the Kinabatangan, he had come to the conclusion that he would have to arrange for the capture of animals, which he would then film in natural settings. While at El Hadji Mohammed Nur's village of Pandassan, he had circulated a price list for various species and was pleased to find a number of animals waiting for him on his return. Staging of this kind was common among travel filmmakers of

the time. Martin had an innate aversion to it, but he was left with little
choice, given the poor lighting in the dense jungle canopy.[9]

Returning to Sandakan and the coastal lowlands, they photographed wild water buffalo and elephant with the help of a young
American named Richardson and a Mr. Van Cuylenburg of a nearby
rubber estate. Because their cameras had short focal-length lenses,
they were forced to get very close to the elephant. On July 2 they
walked 16 miles through the jungle in search of a herd, and on finding
one were promptly charged as Martin was setting up his camera. He
fired at the lead elephant with Jack London's 30-30 rifle, but it was a
bullet from the gun of their Malaysian guard that saved their lives.
This encounter, the first in which their lives were placed in jeopardy
by wild animals, taught them an important lesson that served them
well in future years. From that time on, they never approached potentially dangerous game without being covered by a proven marksman.[10]

Shortly before leaving North Borneo, they learned of Martin's
mother's death. The news was devastating for Martin, and as Osa's
mother recalled many years later, "He was so broken up over it that
he cried like a child." He had always remained close to his mother
despite his travels, and regularly wrote to her, as did Osa. However,
he engaged in considerable self-recrimination after her death, telling
Osa that he would give half his lifetime to have her back.[11]

During the third week of July 1920, Martin and Osa left Sandakan
for Singapore, where they spent three weeks filming and photographing. From Singapore, they planned to go on to Cape Town, South
Africa, and travel up the continent for six months by train, canoe,
steamer, and on foot, until they reached the headwaters of the Nile
and Cairo. Just as they were getting ready to set off on this trip, they
received word that the investors in The Martin Johnson Film Company wanted them and their fifty thousand feet of Borneo wildlife film
back as soon as possible, and were unwilling to advance further funds
without seeing some results. Thus they had no choice but to cancel
their projected trip through Africa. Sailing west, they stopped for
several days in Penang, Colombo, and Port Said, where Martin shot
extensive film footage that was later used in a number of educational
short films. By November they were once again in New York, after an
absence of twenty months and after having circumnavigated the
globe.[12]

By the time Martin and Osa returned to the United States, Borneo
was somewhat tired copy. The previous July, the Universal Film
Company, headed by Carl Laemmle, had released *Shipwrecked Among
Cannibals*, parts of which had been shot in Dutch Borneo by cameraman William Alder and by Laemmle's nephew Edward Laemmle. Although the film received excellent reviews, it was not a box office
bonanza.[13] These facts were not lost on the directors of The Martin

Johnson Film Company. As usual, they pushed for releasing the film as educational one-reelers, which were certain at least to return their investment, plus a little profit. Not unexpectedly, Martin argued instead for releasing two full-length features, one utilizing the film shot in the New Hebrides, and the other, the film shot in Borneo.

By early 1921 Martin was still deadlocked with his investors over this issue. However, matters were soon resolved when Alexander Beyfuss and another group of investors formed a film distributing company called the Exceptional Pictures Corporation and purchased the controlling interest in The Martin Johnson Film Company. They successfully marketed Martin's Borneo film, which premiered in New York City at the Capitol Theater on Broadway on September 11, 1921, under the title *Jungle Adventures*.[14] At the time, the Capitol was the largest motion picture theater in the city and was run by the Johnsons' old friend and supporter, Samuel Rothafel.

Rothafel, the acknowledged king of film exhibitors, left no stone unturned in promoting *Jungle Adventures*. Beginning a week before the opening, he placed half-page advertisements in all of the city's daily newspapers, using different copy and graphics for each ad. He also hung cages with live jabbering tropical birds from the theater marquee and in the lobby, and arranged to have oil paintings of Martin's still photographs displayed in shop windows for blocks around the theater. As a final marketing ploy, he induced several department stores to run tie-in ads for sporting apparel. Rothafel was an innovator and given to bold strokes. Still, the *Exhibitors Trade Review* thought it very daring of him to exhibit this type of picture at the head of the program for an entire week. Rothafel may have been a risk-taker, but he was no fool. He was fairly confident that Martin's exquisite footage of exotic nature would appeal to audiences wearied by the competition's offerings. He was also willing to take significant risks at this point in his own career because he was in contract negotiations with the Capitol Theater owners, and a quick box office success was certain to strengthen his bargaining position.[15] Fortunately for him and the Johnsons, his instincts proved correct. Newspaper and trade publications rushed to give the film rave reviews, and people flocked to see it.

Jungle Adventures is a silent film that belongs to the documentary genre, although at the time of its release this was not a widely recognized category. Contemporaries saw it as a travel film whose central theme was the Johnsons' trip up the Kinabatangan River. The film consists of five reels, is 5,245 feet in length, and has a running time of about an hour. It begins with a prologue showing Martin and Osa entertaining guests with an account of their trip. The domestic setting of the prologue sharply contrasts with the subsequent scenes of street life in Sandakan, as well as those of the actual river journey by launch and *gobong*. Interspersed are shots of various animals, not presented in the actual sequence in which they were filmed. Thrills abound: shooting of the river's rapids, the charge of water buffalos, and a visit to the haunts of Malay river pirates. The return trip down the river in the houseboat is then shown, and the picture ends with the safe arrival of the party in Sandakan.[16]

Although this theme and the scenes that carry it along may sound tame to audiences now, *Jungle Adventures* caused a sensation at the time. There were several reasons for this. Technically, the quality of the film was superb. Martin was an acknowledged genius when it came to composition, lighting, and editing, and virtually every reviewer used superlatives to describe these characteristics of the film. People were also drawn to the film by its depiction of the faraway and exotic, and by a chance to see the beauty and grandeur of nature. In addition, as Suzanne Sexton of the *Morning Telegraph* observed, the film was not only "a masterpiece . . . but also a welcome relief from the overstuffed furniture and velvet carpets of society drama."[17]

The *New York Times* summed up the view of many reviewers in saying: "Some of the pictures are amazing, considering the difficulties under which they must have been made, and all of them are entertaining. . . . The spectator with imagination cannot feel that he is being instructed. Unconsciously, he feels entertained. . . . It seems honest. Its subtitles do not make things appear as they obviously are not."[18] The *Times's* reviewer did take exception to the humorous titles, and suggested that the "puns ought to be thrown to the wild beasts."

The titles, intended to increase the entertainment value so crucial to the film's commercial success, were written by Arthur Hoerl, a veteran screenwriter, who also did much of the editing. To his credit, Hoerl did not distort the meanings of the visual images with the sort of misleading titles so often used at the time. This gave the film a genuine character to which both reviewers and audiences obviously responded.[19]

There was but one dissenting voice among the critics, whose review appeared in *Variety*: "The actual jungle scenes are somewhat meager for the length of the film. . . . More is made of the picture in the lobby than on the screen."[20]

Catering to the market for one-reel educational shorts, Martin produced over twenty single-reel short films derived from the footage he shot in Borneo, the New Hebrides, and at some of the other places he and Osa visited during their twenty-month trip. These were collectively marketed as *Martin Johnson's Voyages*, and later as *Martin Johnson South Sea Films*. In addition, he produced a three-reel film about Singapore entitled *Traveling East of Suez* (sometimes called *East of Suez*). These films were released in 1921 and 1922, and were still being widely shown in motion picture theaters in the mid-1920s.[21]

Although Martin spent the early months of 1921 preparing *Jungle*

Adventures for release, he also wrote a series of five articles on Borneo and the New Hebrides for *Asia* magazine. The articles dealing with the New Hebrides segment of the trip were later combined with other unpublished materials to produce his book *Cannibal-Land*, which was published in late 1922.[22] The book was widely reviewed, and the *New York Times* gave it a half page of coverage in its Sunday, December 24, 1922, Book Review section. The *Times*'s reviewer said: "He is not primarily a writer, and perhaps this very fact has rendered the book more graphic. . . . The simplicity of Mr. Johnson's narrative is part of its charm; he does not attempt to be authoritative in an ethnological sense. He merely describes what he sees and he does it with an innate sense of values that, perhaps, reveals the showman but does not destroy the charm."[23] The *New Statesman* commented that "he is neither sentimental about (the savages) nor foolishly censorious. . . . His book is well worth reading." The *Boston Evening Transcript* added that "the narrative, plainly written, with no attempt at rhetorical effect, is followed by the reader often with exciting interest."[24]

As with his first book, *Through the South Seas with Jack London*, reviewers took note of Martin's woefully deficient knowledge of grammar and sentence structure. Martin wrote as he spoke, in language freighted with idioms, slang, and grammatical errors. His spelling was atrocious, and he knew little about punctuation. This was the legacy of his childhood scorn of school, and it plagued him all his life. The public speaking lessons he took during his vaudeville years partially corrected his egregious errors of pronunciation but did little to improve his command of the language. In narrating his later sound films, he always spoke from scripts prepared by others. These narrations have a stilted and deliberate quality, reflecting an intense struggle to pronounce every word correctly.

He was keenly aware that the letters he typed himself contained many grammatical and spelling errors; therefore he often offered excuses to addressees, placing the fault with the typewriter, sluggish ribbons, heat, humidity, and fatigue. In later years, secretaries edited and rewrote his letters as they typed them, and these are dramatically different from those he wrote himself. He never claimed to be a writer and fully expected magazine and book editors to correct his copy. Yet he saw the ultimate literary products as uniquely his own, and the role of editors as mere facilitators for refining his prose. He was furious when, on two occasions, *World's Work* published unedited extracts from his diaries. He thought that the articles were "absolutely rotten" and fired off angry letters to 'officials at the American Museum of Natural History and at *World's Work*.[25] His editors had to tread a fine line as they struggled to meet his demands to preserve as much of his original copy as possible.

Martin felt an enormous need to be in control and to place his own unique interpretations on people, places, and events even when he expressed himself in writing, for which he had so little natural talent. Osa, on the other hand, had no such need and was quite willing to have literary ghosts write her major books. In reading her books for adults, one is never sure whether the feelings and opinions expressed are really her own or those imposed by others to conform to public expectations of a heroine at that time. By contrast, no such doubts exist about Martin's writings; he simply did not allow the editorial process to modify his strong attitudes and opinions, which he hoped audiences would adopt as their own.

During early 1921, Martin also edited a silent feature film about their trip to the New Hebrides. Featuring Nihapat, it was called *Head Hunters of the South Seas*.[26] The story line, like that in *Jungle Adventures*, consists of the travel sequence, which in this case included Vao, Malekula, Tomman, Espiritu Santo, and the Lopevi volcano. Nihapat and the Big Nambas are shown watching a version of the Johnsons' first South Seas film, *Captured by Cannibals*, and looking at large posters advertising the film which were hung from the trees.

Arthur Hoerl, who had written the titles for *Jungle Adventures*, also wrote them for this film and served as editor. Unlike the titles in *Jungle Adventures*, those in this film often misrepresent what is really being shown in order to maximize thrills and excitement. While audiences could not be misled about Borneo honey bears and deer, they were prepared to believe anything they were told concerning the Melanesians, about whom they knew virtually nothing.

Head Hunters of the South Seas was finally released in October 1922, while Martin and Osa were completing their first trip to East Africa. Since Exceptional Pictures had become bankrupt the previous spring, it was released through another distributor, Associated Exhibitors, whose president, Arthur S. Kane, presented it both as a feature and as a five-part series. Despite some early aggressive advertising in trade publications, few exhibitors booked it and overall it was far less successful than *Among the Cannibal Isles of the South Pacific*.[27]

In 1921 Martin was invited to become a member of the Explorers Club. However, an invitation was not extended to Osa, since women were not then eligible for membership. It was at the club that they first met Carl Akeley of the American Museum of Natural History in New York.[28] Akeley was by then the veteran of four extensive trips to Africa and a leading expert on its wildlife. He was also an extraordinary man of many talents who had achieved international recognition as a sculptor, taxidermist, and inventor. He and other scientists at the museum had concluded that the great wild herds of Africa were doomed to extinction. Not unreasonably, they based this belief on the sad fate of North American wildlife, particularly the bison, and the extinction of wildlife in most areas of southern Africa through overhunting by Europeans. As they saw it, there was little hope that

African wildlife would survive roads, farms, and fences, and the unrelenting onslaught of sportsmen. Thus they made it their mission to document this soon-to-be-lost heritage in dioramas in a planned African Hall.

Martin and Osa had originally planned to travel from the Cape to Cairo following their trip to Borneo. On their return to New York, they made this proposal once again. However, the publishers of *Asia* magazine, who had serialized the Johnsons' adventures, proposed that Martin become the official photographer for the museum's Central Asiatic Expedition. This expedition was to be headed by the popular paleontologist Roy Chapman Andrews. Akeley, who was greatly impressed with the superb quality of the footage that was later to appear in *Jungle Adventures*, discouraged Martin from contracting with *Asia*, which was sponsoring the expedition. Instead, in what was a partially self-serving move, he convinced the Johnsons to visit the spectacular plains and forests of East Africa which he knew so well. There, he reasoned, they could fulfill the needs of financial backers, simultaneously contribute to the museum's scientific objective of documenting vanishing wildlife, and most importantly, help him raise private monies for the new hall by popularizing Africa.[29]

The commercial success of *Jungle Adventures* made it easy for Martin to find investors for his projected film of African wildlife. He changed the name of his production company to Martin Johnson African Films and sent out a prospectus to potential investors. His father, now a widower, sold his jewelry store in Independence and offered to invest in the new venture. This, together with Martin's own investment of profits from *Jungle Adventures*, was sufficient to fund almost 75 percent of the costs.

Carl Akeley not only provided Martin and Osa with valuable advice about working in East Africa, but also put them into contact with potential investors who had connections to either the Explorers Club or the museum. By the summer of 1921, Martin and Osa had secured the remaining 25 percent they needed. A part of this was invested by H. Morton Merriman, a leading textile manufacturer and a member of the Explorers Club, and by the stock brokerage firm of Dominick and Dominick.[30]

In the summer of 1921, as *Jungle Adventures* was being readied for release on Broadway, Martin and Osa prepared to sail for East Africa. At the last minute, John Johnson decided to travel with them as part of a grand tour around the world. By accompanying his son, he also made a symbolic gesture of complete approbation of his work, something Martin had sought for so many years. Their companionship on the ocean voyage over to Africa ushered in a new stage in their relationship, and one which Osa would remember best for the rest of her life.[31]

CHAPTER EIGHT

SEMPER ALIQUID NOVI

When Martin and Osa arrived in Kenya in 1921, it was with little knowledge of the country and even less about photographing African wildlife. With few exceptions, most photographs and films of wildlife in East Africa had been made by professional hunters and sportsmen. Their ranks swelled as the upper classes of Europe and America discovered the joys of the hunting safari. The camera became a natural extension of the gun because it documented both the hunt and its results. In time, some of these sportsmen focused their camera lenses on living animals as well. However, their lack of expertise and the limitations of equipment and films generally produced poor results.

During the first decade of the twentieth century, sportsmen continued to be the principal interpreters of African wildlife. It was they, after all, who had the most contact with it, and their reports of encounters with "dangerous brutes" and "cunning killers" usually went unchallenged. Some of their exaggerations can be laid to simple boasting: the fiercer the beast, the greater the hunter's glory at the kill. But the distortions also emerged from the nature of the encounter itself. Hunters rarely observed animals except over the sight of a gun. To them, the ferocious charge of a big game animal was seen as its usual behavior, not as a desperate defense against a threat to its life. Not surprisingly, both the authors and the readers of early twentieth-century safari accounts came to see the big game animals of Africa as violent, vicious, and prone to senseless aggression.

There were few lessons in the amateur experiences of hunter-photographers that Martin and Osa could draw upon. However, there were also some serious photographers who had taken both still and motion pictures that were superlative. Among the most noteworthy of these was a German, C. G. Schillings, who combined photography with hunting and specimen collecting. Like Akeley, he was appalled by the magnitude of the slaughter by unbridled European and American 'hunters and decided to preserve wildlife on film. Through trial and error, he perfected both his techniques and equipment and, during several trips to German East Africa (now Tanzania), produced some pictures that were remarkable for his day. Using live animals such as cows for bait, he was able to photograph predators by means of magnesium flashes, a technique that Martin and Osa were to modify and improve. Schillings, however, was first and foremost a hunter and specimen collector who derived his financial support from German zoos and furriers. Although he had moved the art of African wildlife photography forward, he was limited by the cameras and lenses of the time, and it would fall to future photographers to improve upon his accomplishments.[1]

Still photography of African wildlife was advanced primarily by two photographers, A. Radclyffe Dugmore and Cherry Kearton. Both men were prompted to turn their talents to East Africa by Theodore Roosevelt's celebrated hunting and collecting safari.[2] Dugmore was aware that Roosevelt's expedition would receive enormous publicity and intensify public interest in African wildlife photographs. Familiar with the writings of Schillings, he arrived in Kenya in January, 1909, a few months before Roosevelt, with a contract from *Collier's Magazine* for a series of articles. As his assistant he took along James L. Clark, a young taxidermist from the American Museum of Natural History, who paid his own way. Clark agreed to cover Dugmore with a rifle when they closely approached dangerous game such as lion, buffalo, and rhino.

Dugmore, like Martin, was poorly educated, having been raised by a father who roamed the Atlantic and Mediterranean on a yacht, hoping that something would turn up. Despite the paucity of his formal education, he studied painting in Naples and Rome, and ornithology in the United States under W.E.D. Scott, one of the most eminent ornithologists of the time. He soon became a well-known artist whose drawings and paintings were used to illustrate a number of natural history books. His interest in photography was an outgrowth of his desire to use photographs as well as paintings to illustrate books about wildlife. Most of his early photographs were made in North America, where he experimented with cameras made to his specifications and where he photographed a wide variety of animals in their natural surroundings.

Dugmore and Clark traveled through some of the finest game country in Africa, where with the use of telephoto lenses they were able to obtain some excellent photographs of a large variety of animals. Dugmore used electric cables connected to flashes in order to photograph lions on kills at night from a blind. This was an improvement on

Schillings's technique, which Martin and Osa further refined. In four months, Dugmore and Clark walked fifteen hundred miles and secured photographs of twenty-four species that appeared in his book *Camera Adventures in the African Wilds.* Published in 1910, this volume received rave reviews, and Dugmore was praised in the press not only for the excellent quality of his photographs, but also because he only killed animals "when it was necessary for protection or for food." This minimal degree of killing rapidly became a publicly accepted standard for wildlife photographers such as Martin and Osa, and was not repudiated until the conservation ethic grew even stronger in the 1960s. Dugmore's book made him the foremost photographer of African wildlife at the time, a position he was to hold until Cherry Kearton and the Johnsons began their work in earnest.[3]

Kearton also came to Kenya in 1909, certain that the surge of public interest in the Roosevelt expedition would make it easy to market African wildlife films and photographs.[4] Roosevelt was a great admirer of Kearton and his brothers, John and Richard, who had gained wide recognition in the late nineteenth century for their superb photographs of birds in Great Britain. Although Kearton had an abiding interest in still photography, his main objective on this trip was to produce motion pictures of wildlife. He filmed the vast herds of the Athi Plains near Nairobi, and made some spectacular sequences of a pride of lions from a distance of only thirty yards. He also met Roosevelt in Kenya and was given permission to film his safari. Kearton's subsequent wildlife film was so successful in Europe and the United States that he returned to Kenya in 1911 to do more filming. While there, he met up with Colonel Charles "Buffalo" Jones and his two New Mexican cowboys, Loveless and Mears, whose objective was to lasso game, including rhino, giraffe, and even a lioness, feats that Kearton captured on film.[5]

However, Kearton's greatest accomplishment on this trip was filming Maasai spearmen killing a lion. The spearing of lions was then part of the rite of passage for young Maasai *moran* (warriors), and the young men of neighboring groups such as the Kipsigis (Lumbwa) and the Nandi. Theodore Roosevelt had arranged for such a hunt by the Nandi in 1909, but was unsuccessful in obtaining motion pictures of it. Kearton's motion picture camera was a heavy wooden box mounted on an even heavier tripod and not easily moved to capture the quick action of a Maasai lion hunt. However, after a few failures, he was finally able to film this dramatic scene, which drew millions to the movie theaters.[6]

In 1913 Adolph Zukor, then the head of the Famous Players Film Production Company but later the president of Paramount Pictures, distributed Kearton's African films after a premiere at New York's

Playhouse Theater that was introduced by Theodore Roosevelt. The former president praised the lion-spearing sequence for its excellent quality and authenticity. He took the occasion to note that there was a great temptation to fake wildlife sequences, something Kearton had not done. This was a not-so-oblique reference to Colonel Selig's *Hunting Big Game in Africa* (1909), which had been filmed in a Chicago studio. While not explicitly claiming to be a documentary of Roosevelt's African trip, the film was thought by many to be precisely that, and as a result, Selig profited handsomely. Roosevelt was furious over this film, and particularly appalled by the killing of a captive lion during a faked charge.

Dugmore and Kearton represent the beginnings of a new phase in African wildlife photography, one dominated by professional craftsmen and artists intent on capturing genuine images.[7] The viewing public, ever more sensitive to the message of conservationists, were repulsed by scenes of slaughter, and increasingly became more sophisticated in their taste for authentic films made in the wild by talented cinematographers. This left little place for those wealthy sportsmen who had combined hunting with picture taking, except as patrons of professional photographers.

Many sportsmen themselves were appalled by the specter of wildlife extinction, and converted to shooting with cameras for their own pleasure. Among these was Edward North Buxton, who became a leader of the conservation movement in Great Britain. In the United States, Theodore Roosevelt, an avid hunter, became the leading political force behind the conservation movement. Yet he and many other sportsmen held a view of conservation that included responsible hunting, a position that brought them into conflict with preservationists in the movement. Roosevelt saw no inherent contradictions in his view, since he believed that wise conservation measures together with regulated hunting offered the sportsman and all who enjoyed the wilderness the best hope for the future.

Although Dugmore and Kearton ushered in a new phase in African wildlife photography, a few hunter-photographers still continued to make notable contributions as the transition got underway. Foremost among these was Paul J. Rainey, a wealthy six-foot-four American coal heir, who successfully combined sport in East Africa with producing widely acclaimed wildlife films. Of all the Americans who went on shooting safaris in Africa in the early twentieth century, Rainey comes closest to H. Rider Haggard's fictional character, Allan Quartermain, the heroic white hunter of such books as *King Solomon's Mines*. Haggard detailed the exploits of this hero in several novels beginning in 1885. Quartermain is courageous, sportsmanlike, respectful of game, and endowed with endurance, resourcefulness, and physical strength. He is the ideal gentleman hunter who transports the ethics of the English hunt to the African bush. While Quartermain's conduct reinforced the standards of the hunt for Victorian and Edwardian boys, his exploits also mesmerized them and later drew some of them to the great landscapes of Africa.[8]

Hunting and riding were very much part of Rainey's patrician upbringing; in later life he distinguished himself as a yachtsman, polo player, hunter, and athlete. He owned a racing stable on Long Island for several years and was prominent in the social colonies there and in Newport. He also owned a 10,000-acre hunting preserve and cotton plantation known as Tippah Lodge near Cotton Plant, Mississippi, where he reared and trained packs of fox and bear hounds. Following a successful trip to the Arctic in 1910 and inspired by Theodore Roosevelt's safari, he set out for East Africa in 1911. He intended to hunt big game while on horseback, use bear hounds to bring lions to bay, capture animals and bring them back alive to the United States, and make a film record of both wildlife and his adventures while on safari. Hunting lions while on horseback was already an established part of the sportsman's ethic in East Africa when he arrived. However, no one had ever used trained dogs to bring African game to bay. This innovation did not go down well with many in the horse-and-hound set in Great Britain, but others saw nothing wrong with it.

Rainey was accompanied on this trip by ER M. Shelley, his dog trainer; John C. Hemment, a cinematographer; Edmund A. Heller, a taxidermist from the Smithsonian Institute who had been on the Roosevelt safari; and white hunters Alan Black and George Outram. In Nairobi, Rainey secured the services of Herbert K. "Pop" Binks, the leading local photographer who filmed alongside Hemment.

Rainey's bag of twenty-seven lions in thirty-five days shocked some local government officials and eventually led to a tightening of regulations governing the size of such kills. Yet, the aim of many of Rainey's hunts was the live capture of animals in traps for later taming and training. Hemment and Binks filmed the various hunts and also took extensive pictures of wildlife. Through the use of blinds and the carcasses of dead animals, they were able to film predators at fairly close range. However, the film sequences that most impressed Martin were those taken from blinds at water holes in the arid north of Kenya at Laisamis. Schillings, Dugmore, and Kearton had all photographed from blinds. However, Rainey used this technique at water holes in semidesert where game was forced to congregate in large numbers in the dry season. Martin viewed the films shot by Rainey at Laisamis as the finest African wildlife footage he had ever seen. Even before he arrived in Kenya, he was determined to improve upon Rainey's results by using the same approach of blinds at water holes in an arid region.

On returning to New York, Rainey produced a silent film, *Paul J. Rainey's African Hunt*. Most of it used the 100,000 feet shot by Hemment and Binks, but it also included some footage shot by Akeley, who was financially hard-pressed at the time. He sold Rainey some of the footage he had made in East Africa in 1909–1910, and this was incorporated into the film. Rainey's film was distributed by Carl Laemmle and released on April 14, 1912. It created a sensation, and eventually grossed a half-million dollars.

Rainey returned to East Africa in 1912. He produced a second film called *Rainey's African Hunt*, which was released on June 22, 1914, and which also received critical acclaim.[9] From the footage shot and purchased, he also produced several short films, including *Common Beasts of Africa* (1914) and *Military Drill of the Kikuyu Tribes and Other Native Ceremonies* (1914). The Kikuyu footage was shot by Akeley, who is credited as the film's author.[10] Rainey eventually used his African films for philanthropic purposes, giving numerous benefit lectures illustrated by them.

Rainey became the beau ideal for many young men who were increasingly more influenced by what they saw on the silver screen than by what they read in books. Even though Dugmore and Kearton produced pictures and films of equal quality, they did not inspire viewers the way Rainey did. Rainey's personality, his courage, athletic prowess, and a love of adventure were all prominently featured in his films. Dugmore and Kearton remained behind the viewfinder and only rarely appeared in front of the camera's lens.[11] While all three men produced accurate documentaries of animals in the wild, Rainey also gave the public a vivid and thrilling pictorial account of his own travels and narrow escapes.

Of all those who had produced wildlife films in Africa, Martin admired Rainey most. In discussing early wildlife photography, he said: "The real beginning was with *Paul Rainey's African Hunt*, which was followed by an imitative succession of pictures, good and bad."[12] Martin's praise extended to Rainey the man as well: "News has come to me of Paul J. Rainey's death. I should like here to add my tribute to the many that have been paid him; for he was a thorough sportsman and left behind him in Africa a clean and splendid record."[13] And Martin was tremendously excited when he finally reached Laisamis and found the water hole that he thought was the site of Rainey's blind: "I saw again in imagination the rhinos and the elephants of which he had told the story. It seemed strange that I was there, where he had been, ready to write the next chapter of the picture-record of animals."[14]

Martin very much wanted to follow in Rainey's footsteps. Although Rainey was neither a cinematographer nor a photographer, he had succeeded brilliantly in capturing his personal adventures and a genuine picture of Africa on film—a combination that had to remind Martin of his own formula for travelogue films. For Martin, Rainey was an idol, a bold and resourceful innovator whose perseverance and risk-taking had been rewarded by both public acclaim and commercial success. As Martin saw it, Rainey had accomplished in Africa with film what Jack London had with words in Alaska and the South Seas. Not surprisingly, when he and Osa arrived in East Africa, they traveled like pilgrims to "the places where Paul Rainey had camped."[15]

The East Africa that Martin and Osa saw in 1921 was still a frontier wilderness where settlers, hunters, men of God, and men of the bottle mingled in the swirl of pioneering that bound aristocrats and the low-born together in common cause. The need to survive and the will to succeed formed the social cement that held them together, producing a unique era analogous to that of the American West a half-century earlier and Amazonia in the late twentieth century. The frontier spirit could not, however, overcome the deep cleavages in this society of transplanted Europeans. British settlers established farms and ranches, and in the process sometimes swept aside the rights of local Africans. The settlers clashed almost continuously with colonial administrators over the rights of the indigenous peoples and the regulation of the settlers' activities. There were social cleavages as well, as the younger sons of British aristocrats sought their fortunes in this new land next to those who had emigrated out of Great Britain's industrial slums. In time, the white settler community took on the hierarchical character of its counterpart in Great Britain, albeit with distinctive local modifications. Many who farmed became "white hunters" on the side, responding to a demand from the Anglo-Saxon elite for hunting safaris. So successful were they at hunting that some took it up as a full-time profession. While white settlers competed for land, Roman Catholic and Protestant missionaries vied for the souls of Africans, some of whom, such as the Kikuyu, were confined to reserves, reminiscent of the reservations for American Indians in the United States.[16]

The battle lines were drawn very early on with regard to wildlife. Some of the white settler-farmers, whose agricultural interests came into direct conflict with game, believed that the game had to go in the interests of economic development and progress. The majority of settlers, however, wished to see the game preserved, provided it did not jeopardize their economic interests. The colonial government's position came down firmly on the side of game preservation. This derived in part from a sense of moral obligation, strengthened by the dreadful examples of the rapid destruction of game in North America and in southern Africa by European hunters and farming interests. The government's stand was buttressed by constant pressure from conservationists in Great Britain and by the significant revenues earned from hunting licenses and the monies spent by visiting sportsmen. The government's side was also strengthened by those farmers who became part-time hunters and guides for wealthy European and American sportsmen. They received significant income from this work, and over time became strong advocates for game preservation.[17]

Game preservation efforts in the British East Africa Protectorate (which became Kenya Colony and Protectorate in 1920) began two decades before Martin and Osa arrived there. While the Game Department was not formally established until 1907, a ranger for game preservation was appointed in 1901 by Sir Charles Elliot, the high commissioner. The person chosen for this position was Arthur Blayney Percival, a highly respected naturalist who had already achieved distinction for the ornithological specimens he had collected in the Arabian peninsula. Blayney, as he was known to his friends, was a staunch advocate of game preservation, and it was primarily through his efforts that the Game Ordinances of 1906 were drafted and passed into law, and the northern and southern game reserves established. Despite the colonial administration's commitment to game preservation, the Game Department was staffed by only a few officers. Blayney rose to the rank of senior assistant ranger in 1910, and in 1919 was appointed chief game warden, a title he was to carry until his retirement in 1923.[18]

Although others served in administrative positions above him in the Game Department over the years, it was Blayney's name that became synonymous with game preservation in East Africa. He brought to his work not only the knowledge and skills of a superb field naturalist, but also a sense of mission. He quickly won the respect and admiration of visiting naturalists, including Theodore Roosevelt and Carl Akeley, who sought him out for advice. Akeley and Blayney developed a warm friendship based on mutual respect and their common interest in game preservation. It was because of this friendship that Martin and Osa were brought into contact with Blayney when they arrived in Kenya.[19]

Akeley set forth a new agenda for Martin and Osa: he wanted them to make authentic films of wildlife in its natural state, devoid of contrivances and fakery. This sharply conflicted with the demands of the entertainment industry with which they had been so long associated. Martin's superb skills had never before been mustered in the interests of science and posterity. His entire career up to then had been molded by the standards of entrepreneurs who had inherited Barnum's mantle. The outlets for his work had been vaudeville and motion picture theaters, and his intimate professional associates were promoters and managers who catered to market forces. In urging Martin to become a first-rate wildlife photographer, Akeley was in effect asking him to make something of a break with his past. He knew that such a transformation had to be gradual and might never be complete. However, he was optimistic that Martin could rise to the challenge and allow his work to be more influenced by the needs of science than by those of theater impresarios. In order to give Martin and Osa every chance for success in this new mission, he enlisted the help of the one man in Kenya who most shared his vision of documenting wildlife on film. Blayney willingly agreed to Akeley's request and did all in his power to assist Martin and Osa in producing films that met the standard that both he and Akeley valued.

On arriving in Nairobi, the capital of Kenya, Martin, Osa, and John Johnson checked into the Norfolk Hotel, which by then had become legendary as the meeting place of white hunters and visiting sportsmen. However, after three days there, they rented an eight-room bungalow, twenty minutes from the center of the city. Set on an acre of land, surrounded by tall trees, the house was ideal for Osa, who promptly planted a vegetable garden and large oval beds of flowers. She enjoyed keeping house and Martin remarked that it was a real joy for her to do so in Nairobi. The three Johnsons lived in three of the eight rooms, used one for storing their safari supplies, and converted the rest of the house into a laboratory. Martin considered it the best field laboratory he ever had up to that time, as did a number of other people, including Dugmore; Sir Edward Northey, the governor of Kenya; Sir William Northrup McMillan, a prominent leader among the white settlers; and Akeley, who later used it to develop the first motion pictures of gorillas ever made in the wild.[20]

Martin and Osa received encouragement on all sides. However, it was Blayney who advised them on the hundreds of details concerning safari life, the habits of wildlife, and the best ways for obtaining photographs.[21] Neither one of them had ever driven an automobile before, and had to take driving lessons when it became obvious that safari Fords were indispensable. Osa, who had done some shooting in the Solomon Islands, now became a crack shot. With help from Blayney and Stanley Taylor of the Bureau of Native Affairs, they hired an African staff consisting of household servants and a headman, Jerramani, who was from Tanganyika (now Tanzania). Jerramani was an M'Nyamwezi, an ethnic group which had long excelled at safari work. He had been with the Roosevelt expedition, and this alone was recommendation enough. He was assisted by Ferraragi, who was from Nyasaland (now Malawi), and who also acted as Osa's gun bearer.

In marked contrast to their attitudes toward Melanesians, Martin and Osa had a real affection for their African employees and treated them extremely well. Their relationship with them also contrasted sharply with the way many other whites treated Africans; in Kenya, Europeans favored beatings with the *kiboko* (rhino or hippo hide) whip for insubordination and inefficient labor. Martin developed a reputation among their African staff as being *pole pole*, a Swahili expression conveying the sense of being gentle and kind. Although he and Osa filtered their perspective through the prevailing European views of the time and were often paternalistic and patronizing, they nonetheless came to a revised understanding of people of color. In Melanesia, their contacts with local people were distanced by fear and misunderstanding. However, in East Africa, they were thrust into immediate and intimate contact with Africans, and this enabled them to see their humanity. This better understanding jarred the racial prejudices they had acquired in their youth, reinforced in Melanesia, and never discarded. Neither Martin nor Osa ever successfully resolved this conflict, and were at times confounded by the contradictions between the racial realities they knew and the racial preconceptions they retained. In depicting Africans on film, they frequently catered to popular white American racial prejudices, and reinforced them in response to market forces. Yet, in their public and private writings, they often described individual Africans with a respect and understanding unusual for their times.

Martin and Osa followed Blayney's advice and limited their initial safaris to the Athi Plains close to Nairobi. Because Fords were then viewed as vehicles that could go anywhere on the plains, they purchased one from Newton Ltd., the Nairobi-based safari outfitters, purchased a secondhand one from a hunter, and rented a Ford truck to carry supplies. In preparing for their first trip, they were greatly helped by a twenty-year-old American, Bud Cottar, who was to act as Martin's assistant during most of their stay. Cottar was the oldest son of Charles Cottar, who had first come to East Africa in 1911, inspired by the Roosevelt trip. The elder Cottar, who had moved a great deal across Texas, Oklahoma, and Colorado, became the first American big game hunter in East Africa, a life that suited his rugged individualism and independent spirit. His son Bud, whose real name was Charles Cottar, Jr., was born in Oklahoma on January 26, 1901, and arrived in East Africa in 1915 with the rest of the family. He was a superb mechanic and hunter who honed his skills under his father's constant tutelage. When Martin hired him in 1921, he was widely respected as an excellent marksman.[22]

Although Martin and Osa mention Cottar in passing in their writings as having helped them organize their field trips and for driving the Ford truck that carried their supplies, he actually played a much larger role. He covered them with a rifle whenever they got close to dangerous game, and shot game animals to provide their African staff with the government-mandated ration of meat. While Osa was frequently filmed covering Martin with a rifle as rhino, lion, and elephant charged, it was Cottar who provided the actual cover—but out of the camera's range.[23] In later years, others provided this kind of protection even though Osa was a crack shot. Martin never relied solely on her in case of a charge, as they implied in their writings and as depicted in their films. Although Osa's bullets sometimes saved Martin and his equipment from a rhino's horn or the claws and fangs of a lion, it was just as frequently a shot from someone else that effected the rescue.[24]

True to Akeley's advice, Martin set out to obtain films of wildlife in its natural state. However, he also wanted to get thrill-packed footage that would make the scientifically valid sequences acceptable to exhibitors and audiences. It was all well and good to film rhino browsing and trotting across the plains, but such scenes were no substitute for a rhino charging the cameraman. Martin already knew that the successful formula consisted of combining both types of footage and of placing pretty Osa before the camera lenses. In order to get action shots, animals had to be provoked, much the same way as sportsmen did. Osa was routinely sent out with rifle in hand to provoke rhino, elephant, and even lion as Martin cranked the camera. Her own skill with a gun, and the stand-by sharpshooter behind the camera notwithstanding, this was a highly risky maneuver. Yet, it is one she eagerly engaged in and clearly enjoyed. Silver screen images of diminutive Osa chasing elephants or being charged by lions and rhino became a hallmark of Martin's African films and greatly contributed to their success.

The first trip to the Athi River produced pictures that in Martin's words were "worthless."[25] Herds took off at their approach and attempts to drive the animals from behind toward the camera were usually unsuccessful. Their second try at photographing game on the Athi Plains included a colorful character by the name of John Walsh, who drove out from his tin shanty to shoot game for the African meat market in Nairobi.[26] For five dollars a day, Walsh promised to get Martin close to the herds. He delivered on this promise, driving Martin across the plains in his beat-up Ford at breakneck speeds right into the middle of grazing herds of antelope and zebra. By the time the dust cleared and Martin set up his camera, the animals had vanished. Following the advice of others who had photographed wildlife, he built a series of blinds along the Athi River and at scattered water holes fifteen miles from Walsh's shanty. The animals, aware of these new structures, avoided these water holes and stretches of the river. Martin learned from this that animals would only congregate at a water hole with a blind if the next available source of water were five or more miles away. Martin and Osa were further limited by the fact that their longest lens was a 425-mm telephoto. This compared poorly to lenses of 1,000 mm and more routinely used by later generations of African wildlife photographers. Human daring and risk had to compensate for technology's inadequacies. To get the pictures they wanted, Martin and Osa had to move in close to the wary animals. Despite all the problems encountered on the Athi Plains, Martin did obtain some excellent film footage, particularly of wart hog. These results and their new field experience convinced Blayney that they were ready for a major safari, and suggested the Ithanga Hills.[27]

They set out with their Fords, ox wagons, and 110 men, just as the short rains were beginning. It would not be an easy expedition. The game of the Ithanga Hills, like that of the Athi Plains, had been extensively hunted, and as a result was wary. The heavily forested slopes and ravines afforded excellent cover for the animals, especially buffalo, which abounded in the area. Much to the chagrin of their headman, Jerramani, the Johnsons panicked and ran up the side of a ravine when they thought a herd of buffalo was about to charge. The Africans who accompanied hunting safaris viewed such flight as cowardice, and Jerramani felt disgraced. There was nothing worse for a headman than to have a *bwana* (master) who fled. However, in time, Martin and Osa stood their ground, shot two buffalo when they charged, and in so doing displayed a courage that elevated them in the eyes of their African staff. However, it was Osa's shooting of a male lion that truly won them the respect of their staff. Thereafter, the Africans affectionately called Osa *Memsahib Kidogo* (Little Missus) and Martin *Bwana Piccer* (Master Picture), names by which they came to be known during all their years in East Africa.[28]

Over the next several months, Martin and Osa went on a number of other photographic safaris to game areas to the north, south, and west of Nairobi. The precise chronological sequence of these trips is difficult to ascertain because the itineraries presented in their writings conflict with both documentation provided by others and events they themselves describe. In *Camera Trails in Africa*, Martin states that they went to the Southern Game Reserve, then to the Loita Plains, and finally up north to the Chobe Hills (Shaba Hills) and Mount Marsabit. This sequence is an idealized one, and neatly fits in with Martin's account that Blayney wanted them to first visit areas closer to Nairobi in order to acquire the experience necessary for the arduous trip to the north. Documentation from others, however, places Martin and Osa in the north before they went to the Southern Game Reserve. On February 23, 1922, Dugmore met them at the Guaso Nyiro River in the north, and several days later used the blinds they had built at Laisamis a few weeks before.[29] They were in Nairobi in March during a demonstration and strike caused by the arrest of the African nationalist Harry Thuku. Martin, Osa, and John Johnson went into Nairobi at the height of the demonstration, and later Martin wrote accounts of it in his book *Camera Trails in Africa*, and in a letter to Akeley.[30] In his book, he states that they had just returned from the Southern Game Reserve when the demonstration occurred in Nairobi and that it had interrupted their preparations for a trip to the Loita Plains. Following this trip, Martin has them going up north to search for a lost lake that Blayney had told them about. It appears that they went up north to Marsabit for the first time in late 1921, where they spent three months and then returned to Nairobi in early March, after which they visited the Southern Game Reserve and the Loita Plains. In late March 1922 they went up north again, this time to the Shaba Hills, where they spent two months.

Soon after they first met Blayney, he told them about a crater lake in the north of Kenya where wildlife abounded, especially elephant. Martin claimed that Blayney showed them a "quaint old book" written by a Scottish missionary who had allegedly discovered the lake which no one else knew anything about, and which did not appear on any maps.[31] He and Osa were determined to find this undisturbed wildlife paradise, which lay somewhere in the vast arid stretches of northern Kenya. Their quest for this long-lost lake, which Osa later named Lake Paradise, represents the climax of Martin's book *Camera Trails in Africa*, and is a major highlight of several of their other books, including *Safari*, *I Married Adventure*, and *Four Years in Paradise*.

In reality, Martin and Osa's claims that the lake was lost are fabrications that have long irritated many people familiar with Kenya and the history of its early exploration. The lake in question lies in a crater at the top of Mount Marsabit, a forest-covered volcanic mountain (altitude 5,584 feet), 330 miles north of Nairobi. The lake was a familiar feature of the landscape to the Boran, Gabbra, Rendille, and Samburu pastoralists who herded throughout the region. The first white person to visit Marsabit was the American physician-explorer Arthur Donaldson Smith, who arrived at the lake on September 9, 1895. Smith, a superb scientific observer, had traveled from Berbera in Somaliland over to Lake Rudolf, and was en route to the Tana River when he encountered Mount Marsabit. He said the following of Marsabit: "Nothing could be more charming than this Marsabit. Surrounded by a large forest and lying at the top of the mountain is a lake a mile square, clear, and deep. The jagged walls of a crater form a semi-circle about it, while from another side, a broad road leads out from the forest to the open meadow beyond."[32]

Eighteen years later, in 1913, Geoffrey Archer, a British administrator who set up the first government post on Marsabit, wrote the following tribute to Smith in *The Geographical Journal*: "To Dr. Donaldson Smith is due the credit of having been the first scientific explorer to penetrate inland from the east coast of Rudolf and locate Marsabit; and the position he assigned to the Crater Lake in the year 1895 serves as a good example of the high degree of accuracy he maintained in the survey of his route."[33] Archer also had some acid comments to make about Martin's alleged rediscovery of the lake: "Many years later Martin Johnson, that great photographer, described his hunting for the lost lake. . . . But Marsabit was known even before this century."[34]

Following Smith's mapping of the lake, a number of visitors went to Marsabit. In 1907 the Boma Trading Company built a station on a ridge overlooking the lake, a site that was taken over by Archer for a government post (*boma*) in 1909. This post was moved to the northwestern side of the mountain in 1915, where the town of Marsabit has since developed.[35]

By 1921, when Martin and Osa arrived in Kenya, a good many Europeans had visited the lake, and Archer and Lieutenant-Colonel J. H. Patterson had published pictures of it. Patterson reported that the local Samburu pastoralists called the lake Angara Sabuk (Great Water); he described the lake as "glistening like a sheet of burnished gold in the brilliant sunshine."[36]

Given this historical record and Blayney's obvious familiarity with the Northern Game Reserve in which Marsabit was located, it is unlikely that he would have characterized the lake as lost. Similarly, since no Scottish missionary was ever involved in the early exploration of northern Kenya, this part of the story is also pure fiction. One can understand Martin and Osa's desire to keep the location of the lake a secret from sportsmen whose hunting would have scattered the game and made serious photography impossible. Even Johnson backers such as George Eastman, who later visited the lake, were purposely imprecise in their descriptions of its location so as to hinder sportsmen's access to it. One of those who visited the lake in 1926 with George Eastman was his physician, Dr. Audley D. Stewart. In response to a 1961 inquiry about the lake's location, he wrote:

> There is no Paradise Lake in Africa. When Martin and Osa Johnson wanted to get someplace to be alone, they went to Lake Rudolph on the Kisut desert just below the Ethiopian border and built their hideaway on its banks—a beautiful spot. It is accessible but *rough* going from Nairobi. We spent a week with them there in 1926, but since they are both gone for several years, I doubt if there is much left of their campsite. I trust this will aid you in your search.[37]

Although thirty-four years had elapsed since Martin and Osa had left Lake Paradise, Stewart was still trying to keep its location a secret, even from someone who merely wanted to see it. He created the fiction that the Johnsons' campsite was on the shores of Lake Rudolf, denied Lake Paradise's existence, and discouraged efforts to find it by characterizing the journey as tough going, so strongly did he respect Martin and Osa's desire to preserve Lake Paradise's wildlife and beauty. The colony's hunting ordinances in the 1920s were then so weak that several waves of sportsmen could have quickly decimated the mountain's wildlife populations. These fears were well founded, as sadly demonstrated in the 1970s, when most of Marsabit's elephants were killed by poachers.[38] A more immediate reason for the Johnsons' keeping the place a secret was a strictly practical one. Once hunters entered an area, the animals fled and scattered, making photography practically impossible. The showman in Martin insisted on embellishing the truth and adding the spice of adventure to their trip.[39]

The Northern Frontier District (NFD) in which Marsabit was located was still on the margins of administrative control in 1921 when Martin and Osa entered it. Ethiopian raiders from across the border regularly poached elephant, stole livestock, and even abducted people. This, combined with highly independent and at times warlike nomadic populations who scorned colonial rule, made the area a dangerous and insecure one. In late 1921, just as Martin and Osa headed north into the district, a military administration was put in place under Major T. S. Muirhead of the Fifth King's African Rifles (KAR).[40] This military administration replaced the civilian one, which had been increasingly unable to deal with Ethiopian incursions and local unrest.

Trekking up to Marsabit in those days was no easy matter, even though the 172-mile road north from Archer's Post on the Guaso Nyiro River was in a good state of repair.[41] The administrative post at Marsabit was a very small one, consisting of a handful of individuals and a battalion of the KAR. Thus, anyone who, like the Johnsons, planned a stay of several weeks, had to be completely self-sufficient once they entered the district, a situation that pertained even until the early 1960s. Government regulations required that a porter's load not exceed sixty pounds. And so for two weeks, Martin, Osa, and Cottar supervised the packing of their tents, clothing, food, and photographic equipment into sixty-pound loads. Each man had to be given a daily ration of ground cornmeal, known in Swahili as *posho*, supplemented by a half-pound of meat a day. Since *posho* was generally unavailable in the NFD, a sufficient supply had to be taken up by ox wagon.

Cottar, who guided Martin and Osa to Marsabit, supervised the trucking of their supplies to Thika, 32 miles from Nairobi; from there, they were transferred to four wagons pulled by teams of twelve oxen each. Once the supplies were in Thika, Osa, Martin, John Johnson, Cottar, and a few of their African staff left Nairobi in the three Fords. They drove to Meru, situated on the northeastern flanks of Mount Kenya, where they recruited seventy porters for the march up to Marsabit. With the four ox wagons and seventy porters slowly following them, they drove down the Timau Escarpment to Isiolo, then a veterinary quarantine station. The veterinarian in charge of the station, Dr. McDonough, was extremely hospitable and suggested they remain to celebrate Christmas with him and the station staff. Their Christmas celebrations included a rhino hunt, in which John Johnson had a narrow escape while trying to dodge behind a tree.[42] Seven miles from Isiolo was the camp of an eccentric freelancer by the name of Rattray, who captured and tamed wild animals. He had had great success taming Grevy zebra, which he believed could be put to harness in the government's transport system. Martin and Osa developed a genuine fondness for Rattray, who eventually became a very close friend. It was he who suggested that they visit the soda springs in the Shaba Hills where they later obtained some of the finest wildlife pictures of the trip.[43]

Martin and Osa soon set off for Archer's Post, a small conglomeration of huts clinging to a bluff overlooking the Guaso Nyiro River. This post had been set up a dozen years before by Geoffrey Archer, and between it and Marsabit lay nothing but wilderness. Although there are seasonal rivers to the north such as the Milgis and the Merille, the Guaso Nyiro is the only permanent river in this part of Kenya. The country to the north of it was considered extremely treacherous because permanent water holes were few and scattered at great distances. Moving a small army of porters across a landscape, which at times takes on a lunar appearance, was an enormous and dangerous undertaking. The desert crossing to Marsabit frightened a number of the Meru porters, and several soon deserted. Martin then had to send to Meru for replacements before they could start out.

Because this journey was so arduous, John Johnson stayed at Archer's Post with a cache of supplies to be used on the return trip to Nairobi.[44] The porters and a single ox wagon were given a two-day start before Martin, Osa, and Cottar started out in the Fords for Marsabit. With Cottar guiding them, they moved on to the Wells, Karo, the Merille River, and finally Laisamis, where Paul Rainey and his party had photographed wildlife. They built blinds at the Laisamis water holes, but had little success using them, since the animals avoided them out of fear. Dugmore, who used these same blinds several weeks later after the animals had become accustomed to them, remarked that Martin "had made the 'blinds' of stone, so that they looked like houses, with roofs of palm leaves. They were very comfortable, but were too conspicuous and artificial in appearance. No self-respecting animal could be expected to approach such elaborate structures, at least not until it had become accustomed to seeing them."[45]

Once across the Kaisoot Desert, they entered the foothills of 5,000-foot-high Mount Marsabit, which then abounded with game, especially rhino and elephant. A few more miles brought them to the Marsabit government post, where they were welcomed by the officers of the KAR. While they were at the Marsabit post, they met a small, thin man with a lopsided jaw whose name was Boculy (Bakuli).[46]

Boculy, who had been working as a guide for the KAR, was an expert at tracking game, especially elephant. Martin and Osa were keen on hiring him, which they did with the agreement of the KAR officers. Boculy was among the Africans for whom Martin and Osa expressed unreserved admiration. Because of his skills in tracking elephant, they fondly called him "the Little Half-Brother of the Elephants." It was he who guided them over the elephant trails that laced the forest and led them to the Crater Lake on one of the mountain's summits. As they emerged from the forest toward the wooded 200-foot-high cliffs that surround the lake, Osa exclaimed, "It's paradise, Martin!" And thus the lake that had been known as Crater Lake since Smith had first seen it a quarter of a century before was given the name Lake Paradise, by which it is still known today.[47]

Marsabit is a broad, verdant mountain endowed with cool springs, deep pools, and spectacular ravines. African olive trees cover its higher slopes with their large twisted trunks and gray-green leaves. The trees are festooned with large masses of Old Man's Beard moss, whose light green color and filigreed texture shift in the shafts of sunlight that fall from the canopy above. The twisted tree trunks and the dangling moss give the forest that enchanted look reminiscent of illustrations in a tale from the Brothers Grimm. There is often a haunting silence in this forest, broken only by the tolling of a far-off dove, and a calm made uneasy by the knowledge that lion, buffalo, and leopard lurk in the hidden ravines. Deep forest smells drift on the early morning breeze and thousands of butterflies hover above the lake and around the numerous pools. It is the sun and the breeze that carry off the early morning mists, revealing both the verdant slopes and the desert browns that lie beyond. The somber shade of the forest is broken at one of the mountain's highest summits by an extinct volcanic crater the Africans call Gof Sokorte Guda. It is in the center of this high crater that Lake Paradise nestles, surrounded by broad green meadows that stretch to the forest wall. From the crater's rim one can see the Kaisoot Desert stretching off to the south and the jagged purple and gray slopes of the Ndoto Mountains to the west. Great white puffs of clouds drift over the crater's rim and cast broad shadows on the blue surface of the lake. The clouds and the breeze are intoxicating and create the feeling of being on the roof of the world.

Marsabit was, as now, far from the usual safari routes. As a result, few white hunters had ever fired their guns in this ancient forest. The undisturbed wildlife, together with the lake's water supply so necessary for developing film, and the proximity to the desert with its water-hole-dependent game, made Marsabit the ideal place at which to secure a permanent film record of African wildlife. Martin and Osa quickly realized that Blayney was right about Marsabit. Even before they left the mountain's slopes, they resolved that they would return to shoot the kinds of films that overhunting made increasingly difficult to obtain elsewhere in East Africa.

Despite Marsabit's beauty, it can also be a dangerous place; buffalo, rhino, and elephant roam its dark trails almost unseen. On one of their last days on the mountain, Martin was almost killed by a charging elephant he had aimed at, not with a camera, but with a gun. Although his bullet found its mark, the elephant charged; Osa cranked the camera until, at the last possible moment, she snatched her rifle and fired. The elephant knocked the camera over and fell dead six feet from Martin, who almost collapsed from fright.

Martin and Osa reluctantly left Marsabit in February 1922. There then followed a trip to the Southern Game Reserve with Cottar, after which they moved on to the Shaba Hills, where they made some of their finest wildlife pictures. By late 1922, they had shot 100,000 feet of movie film and hundreds of still pictures. With Osa helping him, Martin developed these in his Nairobi laboratory, which had by then become a meeting place for wildlife photographers and those interested in conservation. Dugmore and Akeley developed their motion pictures there, and Northey and McMillan were regular visitors.

A year and a half of intense experience in the African bush had successfully transformed Martin and Osa into first-rate wildlife photographers. With help and advice from Blayney and Cottar, and encouragement and guidance from Akeley, they had produced films that were truly unique and spectacular for their times. These films were to amaze and thrill audiences, impress naturalists and scientists, and prove that the ancient Greeks were correct when they said: "There is always something new out of Africa."[48]

CHAPTER NINE

MEN OF

HIGH PURPOSE

Martin and Osa returned from Africa in early 1923 and immediately set to work marketing their film and obtaining backing for an elaborate expedition to East Africa. These two objectives were related since the film's success or failure was bound to influence investor interest in the proposed expedition. Unlike the situation in the past, their production and marketing activities were affected by the scientific standards set by Carl Akeley and the American Museum of Natural History. While trying to adhere to them, they came under intense pressure from motion picture distributors who pushed for thrills and sensationalism in order to insure the film's success. Distributor arguments were given added weight by the release of a competing film on January 18, 1923, entitled *Hunting Big Game in Africa with Gun and Camera*. This full-length feature was produced by H. A. Snow and his son Sydney in southern Africa between 1919 and 1922. Financially supported by wealthy citizens of Oakland, California, through their natural history museum, the Snow film became a spectacular commercial success at the Lyric Theater in New York and throughout the country.[1] However, Akeley was horrified by it. Writing to George Eastman, the head of the Eastman Kodak Company, he characterized the Snow film as the last word in misrepresenting Africa, and specifically its wildlife. He later told prospective investors in the Johnsons' proposed return expedition that the Snow film was largely faked, misleading, and brutal from the standpoint of the sportsman.[2] Nonetheless, the Snow film was an enormous success, and boasted two hundred and fifty first-run bookings within twelve days of its release. This was a reality that neither the Johnsons nor their promoters could ignore.

That Martin, the expert showman, ultimately came down on the side of the museum might seem surprising at first glance. However, a combination of commitment to Akeley's ideals and his own self-interest induced him to avoid editorial fakery. A year in East Africa and an association with people such as Akeley and Blayney Percival had rallied his nobler instincts in the interests of their conservation mission, to which he now subscribed. The shrewd and manipulative side of his character enabled him to see that his film would lose little popularity if it were kept authentic. His cinematography was far superior to the Snows', and images of Osa chasing elephants or being charged by rhinos held greater appeal than their faked animal scenes. In return for this editorial purity, he obtained unprecedented official endorsement of the film by the museum, an enormous asset that was later fully exploited by promoters. Chief among these promoters was the Johnsons' old friend, Samuel Rothafel, director of productions of the Capitol Theater, whom Akeley won over to his point of view. Akeley, who wrote Rothafel at Martin's request, emphasized that the film merited greater success than any African picture ever made, and that it was "full of beauty and thrills."[3] Ever the innovator, Rothafel was willing to forgo a little faking for the sake of the museum's endorsement, which had never before been given to a commercial motion picture. In return, Akeley and the museum achieved their goal of popularizing their vision of Africa through the Johnsons' film. They hoped that this would lead to support for the new African Hall at the museum.

Martin and Osa had originally planned to call their feature *Safari*, but later changed it to *Trailing African Wild Animals*. A silent film, consisting of seven reels and 6,000 feet, it was titled by Terry Ramsaye and edited by him and Martin. Ramsaye, a native of Kansas, was a former journalist who later became one of the movie industry's most respected writers. He cleared the titles with Akeley and showed the film to him and to Henry Fairfield Osborn, president of the museum, before its release. Leon Victor of the Metro Picture Corporation distributed the film but provided it with far less publicity than Universal gave the Snow picture. The film premiered in Baltimore on April 15, was released on April 23, and opened at Rothafel's Capitol Theater on May 20.[4]

Although Metro had not given the film the level of promotion Martin and Osa wanted, Rothafel did his best to make the Capitol opening a stunning success. He himself introduced the evening's program, whose format contained many vaudevillian elements. There was an orchestral prelude; a short travel film, *Capri*; newsreels; impressions of Verdi's *Il Trovatore* by the Capitol orchestra; an hour of featured artists; and finally the film, which was shown at 9:00 P.M. The preserved head of the elephant that Osa had shot so dramatically at Lake Paradise was exhibited in the lobby along with various skins, trophies, and photo displays. Rothafel and Metro sent out press kits that included a powerful quote from Akeley: "The picture is, by far, the finest thing in wildlife pictures that has come out of Africa, or any other place for that matter. It is accurate and truthful, chuck full of beauty and thrills. It is the most thrilling picture I have ever seen." Governor Gifford Pinchot of Pennsylvania, a prominent figure in the conservation movement, added his praise: "The picture is by far the finest big game picture I have ever seen."[5]

Trailing African Wild Animals follows Martin and Osa's safari in search of the "lost" lake. Scenes of encounters with animals in other areas are added in as integral elements of the journey. The press release made a point of stating that animals were killed only when necessary, and the titles point out that a hundred and twenty rhino were filmed, but only four were shot. This was an obvious effort to silence potential condemnation from an increasingly conservation-minded public. However, audiences of the early 1920s were not sophisticated enough to realize that the animals killed had virtually all been provoked into violence by Martin and Osa. Before an animal was killed, Martin, Osa, and their staff staged scenes of themselves standing in mortal danger, surrounded by rhinos intent on charging them, stalked by leopards, pursued by killer lions, and threatened by elephants. The fact that these distortions were crafted into the film reflects some degree of compromise on the part of Akeley and Osborn, who certainly knew them for what they were.

The climax of the film, the elephant charge at Lake Paradise, made audiences gasp every time. Cutaways, obviously filmed later, show a horrified Osa cranking the camera as the elephant bears down on Martin. Finally, in another cutaway, she lifts her Winchester rifle and fires, saving Martin's life.

Trailing African Wild Animals received immediate rave reviews in both the popular press and trade publications. It was described in newspaper reviews as "awe-inspiring and chilling," "ever so exciting," "one of the finest and most authentic pictures," "magnificent," "a real thrill," "a wonderful source of entertainment and education."[6] While the close-ups of animals and Martin and Osa's cinematography were given high praise, it was Osa's presence in the most thrilling scenes that caught the attention of most moviegoers. *Women's Wear* accurately observed that "Mrs. Johnson shares equal honors with her husband in the making of the film."[7] Most other reviewers said much the same, marveling at diminutive Osa staring down a charging rhino and confronting a leopard. The *New York World* summed up the value of these scenes:

> Of course, one of the reasons for the film's attractiveness is the presence . . . of Mrs. Johnson herself. She is seen in various positions unbecoming a timid

lady, and she appears not to have the slightest objection to the tickle of a lion's whiskers across her cheek. . . . Her distinctly feminine personality forms a striking contrast with the barbaric and quite evidently dangerous surroundings. . . . The young lady not only takes a very active part in the proceedings, and proves herself possessed of courage and no little skill with the rifle.[8]

The *Evening World* reinforced this view with the comment: "Don't overlook the 'Mrs.' in the title. The mere fact that a woman was so prominent in so many thrilling and dangerous situations adds a great deal of interest to this animal feature."[9]

The inescapable conclusion is that, without Osa, this film, like the previous ones, would not have attained the same level of success. The public had some interest in authentic wildlife films, but wanted something more. Thrills and spills helped, but the theme of beauty and the beast was always certain to succeed. Martin's appearances in this film, as in his other features, are few, in part because he was most often behind the camera, but also because of his facial tic.[10]

Comparisons with the competing Snow film were inevitable.[11] The Johnsons' film received praise for its greater authenticity and technical superiority, while the Snow film was credited for its better subtitles. That many of the subtitles in the Snow film were misleading and sensational bothered Akeley, but entertained and pleased unknowing audiences and reviewers.[12] Martin's and Osa's personal appearances at the Capitol Theater run during the evening and the 2:00 P.M. and 4:00 P.M. matinee performances were a decided asset. Martin narrated the film in calm, measured tones, debunking popular myths about the dangers of Africa. Yet the powerful images on the screen only reinforced prevailing beliefs and led many reviewers to conclude that the Johnsons were extremely reckless or else very courageous. Osa created a sensation at the end of the performances when she appeared on stage. Audiences admired her beauty, charm, and elegance, and marveled that beneath it all lay incredible prowess and courage. And she brought the house down when she confided to audiences that she longed for the wilds of Africa because she was afraid of the dangers of the city, especially taxicabs.[13]

Martin renewed the effort of dispelling many popular misconceptions about Africa through a series of articles in *Asia* magazine.[14] These articles, published in 1923, formed the basis of his book *Camera Trails in Africa*, which appeared a year later. Reviewers were quick to strike at Martin's Achilles' heel, characterizing his writing as "not particularly distinguished" and as written in a chatty style that "makes no impression on the reader."[15] Despite such acerbic remarks, the book received some excellent reviews, which also reveal much about contemporary American values. Public rejection of tales of the hunt are evident in a *Booklist* review: "There is no glorifying in insensate killing; no killing for the sake of killing. For that reason alone, the book should appeal to sportsmen." However, firmly held clichés about Africa were scarcely dislodged by Martin's new vision of a land of tranquility, bright sunshine, and beauty: "The writer so thoroughly dismisses the notion that Africa is dark and dank and infested with savage tribes and ferocious beasts, and so ably pictures a new Elysium that the book invites the tourist rather than the daring, and it is difficult to believe that Africa, even now, has been so tamed."[16]

Martin and Osa briefly traveled the lecture circuit with their film in the spring of 1923, and then visited their families in Kansas. Ever since their return, they had devoted much of their energies to obtaining financial backing for a five-year expedition to East Africa. Such an ambitious plan was not likely to draw investors who wanted a quick return on their money. Also, according to Martin's own preliminary estimates, the amount of money needed was staggering. He projected a total capital need of $150,000, of which $60,000 was required for the first year.[17] These amounts dwarfed those he and Osa had used to finance their previous trips. In the late spring, they traveled to Rochester, New York, and tried to induce George Eastman of Eastman Kodak to invest in their proposition. Eastman refused. This refusal, and lack of interest on the part of others they approached, convinced them that they had to link up to the American Museum of Natural History.

The timing could not have been better, since the museum's leadership and scientific staff saw themselves in a race to record and collect specimens doomed to disappear in the wild. Henry Fairfield Osborn, the museum's president, summed up this belief in his 1922 annual report: "The reason that certain of our expeditions are being pressed so hard at the present time . . . is that the natural life and beauty of the world are vanishing with almost incredible rapidity. . . . Unless we secure the records of these native races now, our future exhibition halls of Asia, Australia, and certain parts of Africa will be incomplete."[18]

Akeley's greatest dream was to build the African Hall, which would contain dioramas of various species in replicas of their natural habitats. He was not only in charge of designing the hall, but also largely responsible for raising the private funds needed to build it. He saw a definitive film record of African wildlife as an important complement to the hall. However, he also viewed popular films about Africa as a sure means of raising money to build it. As he saw it, private donors who were better educated about Africa were more likely to support his cause. In addition, he hoped that a sizable financial investment by the museum in the Johnsons' expedition would enable it to share in subsequent film profits that could support the hall's construction.

George H. Sherwood, then the museum's executive secretary, and later its director, shared Akeley's views. He and Akeley became the Johnsons' internal advocates at the museum and successfully brought Osborn over to their side. Osborn needed little convincing. A man of enormous vision, he was a renowned paleontologist who, as president of the museum since 1908, had transformed it into the leading institution of its kind in the country. The Board of Trustees with which he surrounded himself was largely comprised of men of great wealth—bankers, industrialists, and businessmen—men who firmly believed in the museum's educational and scientific missions. Thus, from the very outset, even if the museum did not directly sponsor Martin and Osa, Osborn's support of the idea would have facilitated access to people of means who had an interest in wildlife conservation.

Akeley and Sherwood at first tried to induce the museum's Board of Trustees to underwrite the costs of the expedition. With this in mind, Martin wrote Osborn on June 6, 1923, outlining his plans, giving cost estimates, and asking for either financial support or nonfinancial sponsorship that would facilitate attracting investors. He described his plans for building a permanent camp at Lake Paradise, from where he hoped to produce three features within as many years: *Songa: The Tale Bearer*, *African Babies*, and a comprehensive film of African wildlife. *African Babies* was to be "a story of native children, and young wild animals." Once it and the story of Songa were completed, he would finish the main picture, which was to be the story of Africa's wildlife.[19] Martin's request was strengthened by the fact that Arthur Page, the editor of *World's Work*, had agreed to publish a series of his articles and pictures and have them syndicated in newspapers around the country, thus creating a demand for the subsequent films. Martin, Akeley, and Sherwood were further encouraged by Eastman's renewed interest, a fact bound to impress the trustees. On July 25, Eastman sent one of his executives, George Blair, to New York City to meet with Akeley, who firmly convinced him of Martin's unusual talents and of the enormous value to science of his proposal. The following day, Akeley wrote Eastman a long letter in which he outlined the need for making a film record of African wildlife before it was too late, praised the authenticity of the film *Trailing African Wild Animals*, and described Martin's arrangement with *World's Work*. He heaped superlatives on Martin: "He has no superior in wildlife cinematography. Technically, his work is unsurpassed, and in composition, lighting, and so forth, he is a master. He is ingenious and resourceful and blessed with physical strength and unlimited energy. . . . It seems to us that he has all the necessary equipment including a partner, Mrs. Johnson, who is everything that a partner in such an undertaking should be. In short, we believe in Martin Johnson."[20] Osborn endorsed the letter with a brief paragraph, and on July 27 it was sent to Eastman, who promptly promised to invest $10,000. This, combined with $15,000 from other sources, made a total of $25,000, leaving the museum with some $125,000 to raise.[21]

It is of more than a little interest that, in all of the voluminous correspondence between those concerned with this project, Osa is rarely mentioned. Akeley includes her in the same breath as the equipment, underscoring what a man's world she moved in. Thus, despite Osa's prominent role in filming, developing, and setting up shots, she was still perceived as were most women, as unequal and subservient partners to their husbands. Yet Osa's beauty and charm played a critical role in the complex business negotiations that followed. Eastman and the others who supported the expedition all fell under her spell and found it difficult to refuse her requests.

In August, Akeley wrote to Martin in Chanute telling him that everything was on course and that there could be "no possibility of a hitch anywhere as far as museum cooperation and affiliation is concerned." He ended his letter with "best wishes to the three of you," thereby including Kalowatt. This was characteristic of Akeley, whose own pet simian at home was considered a member of his family. Martin promptly replied, telling Akeley that "Kalowatt and I are having a fine time in the watermelon patches. I think we are both part negro for we eat little else but melons." He also told Akeley that five thousand members of the Ku Klux Klan had marched through Chanute with a fiery cross and that as a consequence "all the negroes and poor white trash had left."[22]

Before leaving for Kansas in the summer, Martin had been introduced to F. Trubee Davison, a museum trustee and lawyer who had inherited a $4.5 million endowment from his banker father. Davison, who later became the museum's president, in turn introduced Martin to Daniel E. Pomeroy, a prominent banker who had been a director and vice-president of the Banker's Trust Company. Pomeroy, who would later serve as a museum trustee for many years, had a keen interest in the scientific and educational missions of the museum. He was not particularly interested in Martin's plan as a commercial venture per se, but told Osborn that he would help raise the necessary $125,000 if the Johnson proposal were something the museum really wanted.[23]

Meanwhile, the slow deliberations of the Board of Trustees dragged on through the late summer and early fall, with the matter being shuttled between the board's Executive Committee and a special Ad Hoc Interim Committee. Some trustees felt that the museum's tax-free status would be jeopardized by its becoming involved in producing

Martin (seated on floor), Jack and Charmian London (seated third and fourth from left) at a masquerade party, Penduffryn, Solomon Islands, 1908 (Jack London Collection, California Department of Parks and Recreation).

Martin and a young Solomon Islander. A photographic study in racial contrasts by Jack London, 1908 (Jack London Collection, California Department of Parks and Recreation).

Martin (center) and Charley Kerr (extreme left) in front of the Snark No. 2 Theater, 1910 (Photograph by Martin Johnson. Negative No. 120358. Courtesy, Department of Library Services, American Museum of Natural History).

Left to right: Jack and Charmian London, Nakata, Osa, and Martin at Glen Ellen, California, 1912 (Jack London Collection, California Department of Parks and Recreation).

Nihapat helping to set up Martin's Pathescope motion picture projector, Malekula, 1919 (Photograph by Martin Johnson. Negative No. 108318. Courtesy, Department of Library Services, American Museum of Natural History).

Osa and Tomman islanders with cured ancestral heads, 1919 (The Museum of Modern Art, Film Stills Archive).

Martin and Osa with the elephant killed at Lake Paradise, 1921 (The Museum of Modern Art, Film Stills Archive).

Lake Paradise as it appeared during the Johnsons' stay in the 1920s (International

Museum of Photography at George Eastman House).

Flashlight photograph of an elephant at a waterhole near Lake Paradise (Photograph by Martin and Osa Johnson. Negative No. 314004. Courtesy, Department of Library Services, American Museum of Natural History).

Martin's most famous flashlight photograph, northern Kenya, mid-1920s (International Museum of Photography at George Eastman House).

A. Blayney Percival (left), Kenya's chief game warden, and John L. F. Boyes (right), a leading Kenya settler, Nairobi, late 1920s (Courtesy of Mrs. Margaret D. Kummerfeldt).

Boculy, "Little Half-Brother of the Elephants" (International Museum of Photography at George Eastman House).

Osa with her companion, Guyato (right), and an unidentified woman on the shore of Lake Paradise, 1925 (International Museum of Photography at George Eastman House).

Osa with recently circumcised Kipsigis (Lumbwa) girls, 1926 (The Museum of Modern Art, Film Stills Archive).

Osa preparing to leave on a camel safari into the N'Doto Hills, 1924 (The Museum of Modern Art, Film Stills Archive).

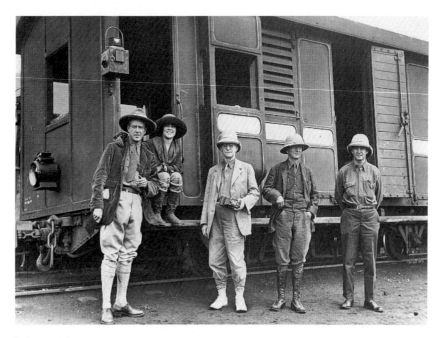

Left to right: Martin, Osa, George Eastman, Daniel E. Pomeroy, and Audley D. Stewart, M.D., Nairobi, 1926 (International Museum of Photography at George Eastman House).

Kipsigis (Lumbwa) men surrounding a speared lion. Left to right in center: Carl E. Akeley, Martin, and white hunters Aubrey Fitzpatrick ("Pat") Ayre and Philip H. Percival, 1926 (International Museum of Photography at George Eastman House).

Martin and Osa celebrating the success of the Kipsigis (Lumbwa) spearmen, 1926 (The Museum of Modern Art, Film Stills Archive).

Martin's portrait of a young Kikuyu man (International Museum of Photography at George Eastman House).

One of Martin's finest lion pictures, Serengeti Plains, 1928 (International Museum of Photography at George Eastman House).

The three Boy Scouts and their African companions on the Serengeti Plains, 1928. Left to right: David R. Martin, Jr., Douglas L. Oliver, and Robert Dick Douglas, Jr. (International Museum of Photography at George Eastman House).

The 1929–1930 Johnson expedition to the Congo. Left to right: Cameraman Richard Maedler, sound technician Lewis Tappan, Osa, Martin, and DeWitt Sage (International Museum of Photography at George Eastman House).

Osa with Mbuti pygmies at Bwana Sura in the eastern Congo, 1930 (International Museum of Photography at George Eastman House).

Osa, DeWitt Sage, and Martin in the eastern Congo, 1930 (International Museum of Photography at George Eastman House).

Part of the crew of the 1933–1934 aerial safari in front of Osa's Ark. *Left to right: Osa, Martin, and Robert Moreno. Pilot Vern Carstens is seated on top. The African members are unidentified (Courtesy of the late Belle Leighty).*

Advertisement for the dance, Congorilla, inspired by the Johnsons' film of the same name (*The Museum of Modern Art, Film Stills Archive*).

Osa's photograph of a man on the Ituri River, the eastern Congo, 1930 (International Museum of Photography at George Eastman House).

The Spirit of Africa *landing at N'Goronit, Kenya, 1933 (International Museum of*

Photography at George Eastman House).

Osa, Martin, and Wah their pet gibbon on their arrival in New York City from Africa, August 9, 1934 (NYT Pictures).

Martin's famous photograph of a proboscis monkey in the wild, North Borneo, 1936 (International Museum of Photography at George Eastman House).

OSA JOHNSON
PRESENTS
MARTIN JOHNSO
LAST PICTURE

**PRODUCED BY
MR. AND MRS. MARTIN JOHNSON**

THE LAST..AND GREAT-EST..ADVENTURE OF THE MAN WHO BROUGHT ADVENTURE TO YOU!

Sights never before seen!

The Isle of the Incredible...where fish climb trees!...snakes fly!...monkeys have "schnozzolas"!...oysters grow on tree-trunks!...head-hunters still lurk! ...Murut men blow death!...and the raging "devil-beast" holds the jungle in a reign of terror!

RELEASED BY 20th CENTURY-FOX

Theater lobby poster for the film Borneo, *1937 (Authors' collection).*

Martin being carried from the wreckage of the Western Air Express plane, January 12, 1937 (AP/Wide World Photos).

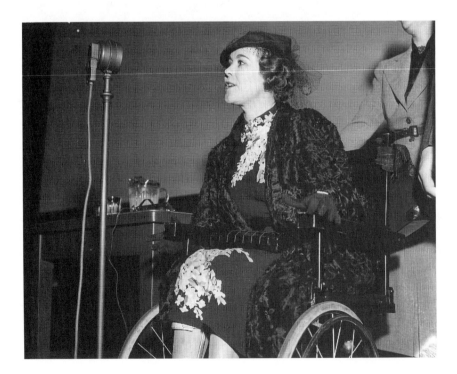

Osa looks on as New York City Mayor Fiorello LaGuardia signs a giant mock-up of I Married Adventure, *1940 (NYT Pictures).*

(Facing page, bottom) Osa speaking from a wheelchair during her lecture tour, Kansas City, March 6, 1937 (AP/Wide World Photos).

Left to right: Osa's mother, Belle Leighty, Pascal James Imperato, and Osa's aunt, Minnie Thomas, in front of Belle's home, Chanute, Kansas, February 1970.

commercial films. Others worried that investors in the Johnsons' expedition would be drawn from the museum's usual supporters, thus siphoning money away from other projects. Finally, a few voiced concern about investing so much money in one man, and one trustee acidly commented that the quality of the Johnsons' films was due to the use of telephoto lenses and not talent. By early fall, it was clear that there was strong trustee support for scientifically endorsing the expedition but not for financing it, either directly or through a subsidiary corporation. The latter idea had been developed by Davison and Pomeroy and presented to the board by A. Perry Osborn, a lawyer and son of the museum's president.

Pomeroy was quick to sense the feelings of the board and realized that a new and imaginative approach had to be devised. He, Davison, and A. Perry Osborn finally came up with the idea of establishing a separate company, the Martin Johnson African Expedition Corporation, of which Pomeroy became president. Davison served as first vice-president, Akeley as second vice-president, and James L. Clark, who had earlier accompanied Dugmore and Kearton in East Africa, as secretary-treasurer. With a banker, a lawyer, and two naturalists as officers, the corporation undertook to finance the Johnsons' expedition through the sale of preferred and common stock.[24] It then entered into a trust agreement with the museum, whereby the latter agreed to supervise the activities of the expedition, in addition to editing and endorsing its commercial films. In return, the corporation agreed to hold the museum legally harmless, and to give it all of the expedition's photographs, films, and trophies once it had completed its commercial exploitation of them. The trust agreement, dated January 2, 1924, was promptly signed by Osborn, who proudly characterized Martin as "a man of real genius, the like of which we have not seen and shall not soon see again."[25] This arrangement fell short of one of Akeley's original objectives, which was to use profits from the Johnsons' films to finance the construction of the African Hall. However, it helped to galvanize men of means, such as Eastman and Pomeroy, around the cause of building the hall. In addition, it promised to result in films that would generate broad public interest in African wildlife and the museum's conservation mission, thus facilitating fund-raising for the hall.

Martin and Osa felt that they had to reach Marsabit before the spring rains or else lose several months waiting for the Guaso Nyiro River to fall. Even as the legal formalities of setting up the corporation were being made, they pushed ahead with preparations for the trip. In November the museum advanced them $37,000 from funds provided by investors in the soon-to-be-established corporation. Osborn wisely believed that the museum needed to obtain some form of collateral from the Johnsons in return for such a large advance. At the same time, he suggested to Pomeroy that the corporation protect itself by insuring the Johnsons' lives and their equipment.[26] At first, Sherwood and Akeley were opposed to asking for collateral, but they soon came around to Osborn's way of thinking. They suggested that Martin donate all of his previous films and photographs to the museum, a form of collateral that was fully acceptable to Osborn. On December 5, 1923, when he was four days out to sea, Martin wrote Osborn a formal letter of donation:

> I take pleasure in hereby presenting to the American Museum of Natural History all of my negatives, both still and motion pictures, to be the permanent property of the Museum. The only condition that I feel it necessary to impose is that during the lifetime of Mrs. Johnson and myself, this material shall not be used except for Museum purposes. . . . After our death, the Museum shall be entirely free to make such use of this material as it may wish.[27]

The same day, Martin also wrote to Lloyds Film Storage in New York City authorizing access to his films by museum officials. Because of space constraints and because the Johnsons still retained distribution rights to the films and photographs during their lifetimes, the materials were not immediately moved to the museum. Osborn announced the gift to the public in January, when the directors of the Martin Johnson African Expedition Corporation were also named.[28]

Martin and Osa sailed out of New York on the *Leviathan* on December 1. Unlike their previous trips that had been undertaken to meet the demands of showmen, this one was supported by men of high purpose who held them to the highest standards yet set for wildlife cinematography. Never before in the museum's history had the energies of so many been focused on the work of one man and his wife. Martin was elated as the ship edged away from the pier. He had reached the highest point of his career, had the official backing of the museum, guaranteed financial support for several years, and enjoyed the genuine friendship of men such as Eastman, Osborn, Pomeroy, and other powerful figures who came from a world he had scarcely known before. Yet, as Osa looked back toward the pier and the ever diminishing figures of her parents, John Johnson, and Martin's sister, Freda, her eyes welled up with tears. Overcome with sadness, she retreated to their stateroom, where she sobbed uncontrollably. Martin's recitation of their good fortune and the large basket of flowers from Eastman did little to console her. Osa later admitted that she found it difficult to understand the reasons for her tears in view of their stunning success and the exciting challenges that lay ahead. Still,

Martin had an inkling of what was wrong when he commented tartly that perhaps she preferred staying behind with her family to living in wild corners of the world.[29]

There was an inner essence in Osa that needed the security of a home and the steady love of family and friends. But she also felt she had to demonstrate to her husband and others that she was up to the hardships of the life he had chosen for them. Osa endured this conflict all her life, and consistently deferred her dream of a home and family in favor of the man she loved. She pleased and reassured Martin by dismissing his barbed surmise that she preferred to remain home in Kansas. No matter how strong her desire for a home of her own, her need for Martin's approval and the public's admiration was even stronger.

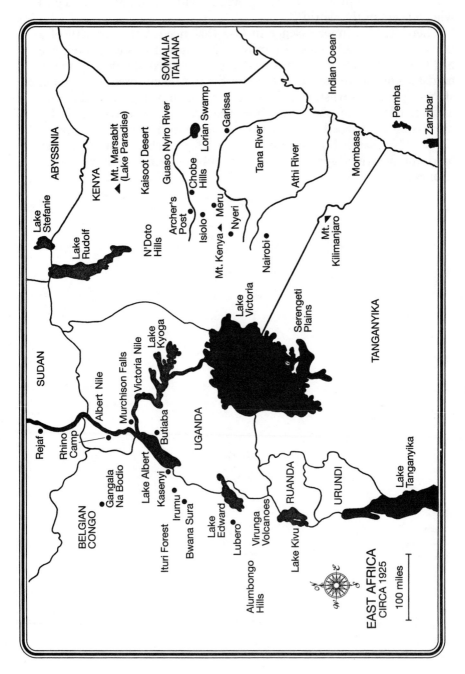

EAST AFRICA
CIRCA 1925

100 miles

MAP DRAWN BY DOUGLAS DUNN/JOAN SIMPSON

SUDAN

ABYSSINIA

Lake
Stefanie

Lake
Rudolf

KENYA

N'Doto
Hills

▲ Mt. Marsabit
(Lake Paradise)

Kaisoot Desert

Guaso Nyiro River

Lorian Swamp

SOMALIA
ITALIANA

• Garissa

Tana River

Athi River

Indian Ocean

Pemba

Zanzibar

Mombasa

Archer's
Post

Isiolo •

• Chobe
Hills

Mt. Kenya ▲ Meru

• Nyeri

Nairobi •

Mt. ▼
Kilimanjaro

Lake
Victoria

Serengeti
Plains

TANGANYIKA

Rejaf •

Rhino
Camp

Albert Nile

Murchison Falls

Victoria Nile

Butiaba •

Lake
Kyoga

UGANDA

BELGIAN
CONGO

Gangala
Na Bodio •

Lake Albert

Kasenyi •

Irumu •

Bwana Sura •

Ituri Forest

Lake
Edward

Lubero •

Virunga
Volcanoes

Alumbongo
Hills

Lake Kivu

RUANDA

URUNDI

Lake
Tanganyika

CHAPTER TEN

BWANA PICCER
AND MEMSAHIB KIDOGO

On the afternoon of April 12, 1924, Martin and Osa stood on the rim
of Marsabit's Gof Sokorte Guda crater and looked down on Lake
Paradise.[1] Behind them lay months of intense preparations in New
York, London, and Nairobi, and an arduous trip through the dry
scrub of Kenya's north. The first thick clouds of the impending rainy
season hung over the mountain but parted now and then, allowing
shafts of sunshine to fall on the surface of the lake. Since leaving
Nairobi several weeks before, they had been racing against the "big
rains," which finally began just as the sun set beyond the crater's rim.

The Johnsons' 1924 expedition to Lake Paradise stands out as one of
the last great safaris of an era that was fast coming to an end. Already,
cars and trucks had largely replaced the scores of porters who once
accompanied hunting parties, resulting in safaris that were both extremely mobile and efficiently able to get by with just a handful of
personnel. Unlike those on an ordinary hunting safari, the Johnsons
had to transport a complex array of photographic equipment and supplies, in addition to many goods and materials needed to build a permanent settlement in a region not easily accessible by automobile. All
this paraphernalia forced them to rely on porterage and on ox and
mule wagons, which by then were already on the wane.

They had brought most of their equipment and supplies from the
United States, not least of all because some of them had been donated
or else purchased at cost in return for product endorsement. All of
the twenty-one cameras were American-made. Included among them
were eleven still and ten motion picture cameras, which were
equipped with custom lenses made by Bausch and Lomb in Rochester, New York, and Dallmeyer in London. Five of the motion picture
cameras were Akeleys; two of them were mounted together, one

taking pictures in slow motion, and the other in regular time. In contrast to the Johnsons' previous trips, their motion picture cameras were equipped with powerful telephoto lenses, the longest being 1,500 mm.[2] Martin and Osa still had to rely on their daring to get in close to animals, since these telephoto lenses did not always produce sharp images. In addition, their large-format still cameras were manufactured with only standard lenses and used glass plates.

During their almost three-week stay in London, they purchased tents and camping equipment from Benjamin Edington, a firm that specialized in outfitting colonial officials and hunting parties bound for the tropics. A Victorian legacy of belief in the evils of tropical sunlight produced not only pith helmets but also Solara khaki outfits containing red and purple weave supposedly effective in blocking out what were then considered the sun's dangerous ultraviolet rays. The Johnsons had their Solara tailored in Nairobi by Tarleton, Whetham and Burman, and also bought long spine pads, which some travelers wore on their backs as added protection against the sun. They wore high boots or puttees, a fashion dictated by then current beliefs in the ever-present dangers of insects, snakes, and noxious plants. Many considered their arsenal of eighteen guns inadequate, but Martin thought it excessive, considering that they were going to Africa to study animals in a free and unmolested state.[3] Most of their weapons were gifts from friends, and as it turned out, their shooting was extremely restrained by the standards of the time.

George H. Sherwood, then the museum's executive secretary, asked that the U.S. Department of State communicate with the British Foreign Office about facilitating the work of the expedition. This was promptly done by the American ambassador in London, Frank B. Kellogg, who sent a note to the Foreign Secretary, Lord Curzon, asking for the full cooperation and assistance of the colonial officials in Kenya and an exemption from customs duties on the expedition's scientific equipment.[4] Although the customs duties were not waived on all the supplies, instructions from London quickly mobilized extraordinary cooperation from Kenya's colonial officials. Martin himself sent letters and telegrams ahead to Kenya in order to prepare for their arrival, and he secured the assistance of their friend, Blayney Percival, who had just retired from the Game Department.[5] Martin and Osa arrived in Mombasa's Kilindini Harbor on the SS *Mantola* on January 24, 1924, after a long voyage from London. Looking out over the ship's railing, they saw the smiling faces of two of their old African staff, M'Pishi, their cook, and Mohammed, their watchman, who had come down to meet them.

Martin and Osa landed with 250 crates, all of which had to be opened and passed by the customs inspectors. Besides the camera equipment, film, guns, and camping gear, the crates contained a

Delco generator, butter churns, Coleman stoves, shovels and spades, flower seeds, film developing solutions, cigars, fishing tackle, drug supplies, canned food, and everything required for setting up a home including rugs, towels, soap, quilts, dishes, and electric fans. By the following day, the crates had passed through customs; most were loaded on freight cars for the trip to Nairobi, but those containing the film were placed in a special refrigerated car which Martin had rented.

A gold rush on the Mara River coinciding with the coffee and sisal seasons created a scarcity of cars and ox wagons. As they temporarily settled into the Percivals' three-room house in the Parklands section of Nairobi, Martin frantically sent out telegrams and runners with letters, trying to line up transport. They also began hiring their staff. Jerramani, their former headman, and his assistant Ferraragi were away in Mozambique, and so on Blayney's advice they hired Bukhari as their head man. He was a superb leader, powerfully built and a better marksman than most white hunters. Martin and Osa greatly admired and respected him and, contrary to the accepted practices of the times, often allowed him to cover them with his rifle as they went in to photograph big game. Their permanent staff included individuals from several different ethnic groups. Suku, a Meru, became their houseboy; N'dundu, a Kamba, their gun bearer; Thu, a Kikuyu, photographic assistant; Jagonga, a Luo, head porter; and Abdulla, a Ugandan, driver and mechanic. Abdulla, Bukhari, and M'Pishi faithfully worked for the Johnsons during their subsequent African trips.

All of the equipment and supplies had to be repacked into the usual sixty-pound loads. What next followed represented the finest in safari logistics. By late February they began to send their equipment and supplies in relays north to Isiolo, where they were looked after by Rattray, whom they also temporarily hired, and by Dr. McDonough, the veterinarian. Five trucks, four gutted Hupmobile cars, and three wagons each pulled by eight mules carried the sixty-pound loads to Isiolo, where they were joined by four ox wagons sent out from Nyeri loaded with four hundred gallons of gasoline and a hundred loads of *posho* (ground cornmeal). Fourteen experienced porters, supervised by Bukhari, accompanied the mule wagons on foot, and forty additional porters made their way from Meru to Isiolo. Martin, Bud Cottar, and Abdulla uncrated and assembled the Willys-Knight cars which arrived from New York via Durban, South Africa.[6]

Before leaving Nairobi on February 21, Martin and Osa gave several showings of their film *Trailing African Wild Animals* to packed houses at the Theatre Royal in Nairobi. The showings, which were arranged by the *East African Standard*, netted two thousand dollars, of which the Johnsons received half. A benefit matinee was later organized for children, with the proceeds going to the Society for the Prevention of Cruelty to Animals. The governor of Kenya, Sir Robert

Coryndon, was high in his praise of the film, as was Blayney, who attended two performances.[7]

With three of the Willys-Knight cars readied, and power of attorney given to their friend Sir William Northrup McMillan, they set off for Isiolo accompanied by Abdulla and Bud Cottar, who drove his own Ford loaded with precious photographic plates and unexposed movie film. Three days of relatively easy driving took them around the western flanks of Mount Kenya and down the Timau Escarpment to Isiolo. Once there, what had thus far been a triumph of safari organization began to go awry. Martin unwisely added camels to his safari even though his men had no experience handling them. This led to inordinate delays as the camels bucked and threw off their loads. In addition, lured by accounts of undisturbed big game in the Mathews Range to the west of the Marsabit road, he opted to try this route, which some officials mistakenly said was shorter. Arriving at the Guaso Nyiro with their vehicles, wagons, camels, and seventy men, they waited for Blayney, who showed up on March 6 in his Ford. Blayney, an experienced traveler in the Northern Frontier, was unconvinced that the mountain route was shorter, but gave in to Martin's determination to film the game there. He and Martin set off looking for passable routes as Cottar returned to Nairobi; Osa remained near the river to supervise the bulk of the safari. During several days of rough travel, they discovered that there indeed was abundant game in the Mathews Range, but that the mountains were impassable for heavily loaded vehicles and wagons. They gave up, returned to the river, and led the safari to the Marsabit road at Archer's Post. There, Martin wisely traded his five camels for *posho* and donkeys, regrouped his seventy men, three vehicles, and mule and ox wagons, and on March 24 headed north toward the Kaisoot Desert.

The mule wagons were given a few days' head start while André Dugand, the most experienced transport officer in the Northern Frontier District,[8] brought up the rear of the column with two ox wagons and some of the porters. Dry river beds full of soft sand were a constant problem. Often, the vehicles and wagons had to be unloaded before being pulled and pushed across the beds over the fronds of dolm palms, which were placed on the track to afford some traction. Lions roared around the camps at night, and rhino frequently charged through the column of porters. The party's moves across the Kaisoot Desert were carefully calculated between known sources of water. However, these were sometimes dry, and one often had to dig down into the sand of dry river beds just to obtain small quantities of water. By late March, the group left the desert and began to move into the undulating foothills of Mount Marsabit. Finally, on April 2, they arrived at the Marsabit *boma* (government station), where they were warmly greeted by Lieutenant Harrison of the King's African Rifles (KAR) and by their old guide Boculy, who was delighted to see them.

Their permanent camp at Lake Paradise was a unique version of American homesteading on an African frontier. There was little question about the best site for the camp, since the Boma Trading Company and the government *boma* had sequentially occupied the top of the low southwestern wall of the crater between 1907 and 1915. This ridge and the land sloping to the south of it had been originally cleared by Ralph Gandolfi Hornyold and Frederick Roy of the Boma Trading Company. They and the government officials after them had built houses, laid out paths and a garden, and widened the elephant trail that led from the lake to the Marsabit road.⁹ Blayney supervised the construction of the permanent buildings on this site by Meru carpenters who placed the logs upright in African fashion. Despite the rains, trees were quickly felled, thatch was cut from the mountain's lower slopes, and buffalo, elephant, and rhino dung were gathered for stucco. The skyscraper of the village was Martin's laboratory. Measuring 12 by 18 feet, its roof was 30 feet high and, like some of the other buildings, had a double roof with an air space in between which kept the room cool in the hot season. Equipped with a darkroom painted black, drying drums for movie film, racks, developing vats, tables, and storage cases, the laboratory was electrified and also had running water, which was filtered through charcoal, sand, and cotton. The Johnsons' personal quarters consisted of a house for sleeping and a 14-by-17-foot sitting room that had a fireplace in the center and a porch overlooking the lake. Osa painted their bathroom with several coats of white paint and plastered a mixture of crushed pink and white rock over the walls of their bedroom. They also built a kitchen, storehouse, garage, workshop, guest room, tool house, carpenter house, a building for the generator, an underground vault for storing film, and several other structures. Below the ridge to the south, Osa laid out a 4-acre vegetable and flower garden, behind which stood the thatch houses of the African staff. Pens were built for the donkeys, chickens, cows, and camels, and the camp and its gardens were enclosed by a 6-foot-high stockade of thornbush. All the resources at hand were used in ingenious ways, such as shaping the wood from packing cases into flooring. And so the Johnsons created a rustic homestead, the first permanent home of their married life. By July 21, the principal buildings of the camp were completed, and to celebrate the event, they killed an ox, held a great feast for their staff, and raised the Stars and Stripes atop a tall pole in front of their sitting room. As Osa later remarked, it was an impressive little village reminiscent of what their great-grandfathers had built on the American frontier. It was also unique in East Africa—no other photographers had ever built such a homestead in order to carry on their work.

Back in New York, Pomeroy devoted large amounts of his time to selling shares in the Martin Johnson African Expedition Corporation from his fourteenth floor office at 30 Church Street. By April 1924 there were a total of twenty-four stockholders whose shares could not be redeemed until 1928.[10] Alice L. Seixas, the corporation's assistant secretary and treasurer, regularly gave stockholders copies of the reports Martin sent in from the field. These reports, often written in the form of long letters to Pomeroy or as diary entries, were also later transformed into articles for *World's Work* and used as the basis for Martin's book *Safari*.

Life for the Johnsons at Marsabit consisted of long periods of predictable hard work during which they spent entire days in waterhole blinds and nights perched in blinds built up in the trees. There were a number of water holes near the lake where game regularly came to drink during the day. They gave some of the holes names such as Wistonia, Lily Pool, Maji M'kubwa, Sunga, Old Lady, Martin Johnson, and Boculy. Wistonia, about an hour's walk from their camp, was their favorite. Surrounded by 50-foot-high rocks, it lay in a deep ravine and gave rise to a stream that cascaded in little rapids down to the valley below.[11] Taking a basket lunch, they would leave camp at five in the morning and go on foot to Wistonia, accompanied by Bukhari and some of their staff. Once there, they would enter their thornbush blind and remain in it all day until 7:00 P.M. They found that the best time for photographing was from nine until eleven in the morning, and from 2:30 to 4:30 in the afternoon. Atmospheric and lighting conditions were ideal then, and large numbers of animals came to drink. At 5:30, the alarm clock would go off in camp, and Suku would send the staff to the waterhole. Standing high up on a nearby rock, they would wait until Martin blew his whistle, indicating they were ready to leave. At night, they often photographed from tree blinds using magnesium powder connected to battery-supplied electric wires. Although the blinds were sturdily built, they were no protection from leopards and rhino, which often came dangerously close, nor from the rain that sometimes left them soaked for hours on end.

They spent long hours in these tree blinds, observing a great variety of animal species. These are especially detailed in Martin's book *Safari*, and reveal what excellent animal behaviorists the Johnsons were for their time. When there was no game in sight, they read, and Martin smoked cigars whose smoke and smell did not seem to disturb the animals in the least. They became intimately familiar with individual animals and gave them affectionate names. Houdini was a bull elephant who disappeared every time they tried to photograph him, and Lady Sweet Potatoes was a female elephant who regularly raided Osa's garden. At the camp, Osa had an assortment of unusual pets including Kalowatt, which the staff considered her *toto* (baby), a cheetah named Marjo given to her by Blayney, two Persian kittens, a mule named Lazy Bones, and a genet cat called Spots.[12]

The animals in northern Kenya migrate according to the seasons, and the Johnsons would often follow them a ways to get photos. The elephants would move between the Mathews Range, the Lorian Swamp, and Marsabit. During the rainy seasons, Martin and Osa often went south to Laisamis, where they photographed and filmed at water holes and along the course of the dry river bed. Intent on getting the best rhino pictures possible, Martin would sometimes abandon the blinds and lie prone on the sand in the night darkness ready to release the flash as rhino approached. They occasionally went down to Nanyuki at the base of Mount Kenya, where Osa fished in the clear streams and sometimes visited Nairobi in order to pick up supplies and attend to business affairs.

In December 1924, they decided to take a camel safari into the N'Doto Hills to the west of Marsabit. They left Marsabit with thirty camels, two mules, fifty porters, six Boran camel men, Boculy, and Arthur Buchanan Sanderson, a whiskey manufacturer who had become a white hunter: Sanderson had replaced Blayney, who left Lake Paradise once most of the camp had been built. He was an excellent shot, experienced in bush craft, and responsible for both running the camp and for providing cover, as Blayney had, whenever Martin and Osa approached dangerous game.

The trip into the N'Doto Hills was an arduous one that lasted until January 17, 1925. In spite of Boculy's remarkable tracking skills, they encountered little game, except for some elephant near Issedan. It was here that a bull elephant charged them while they were filming from a perch atop a large rock. Martin considered that this elephant gave them "the finest elephant pictures" to date.[13] While he used the movie camera, Osa took stills with a Graflex; she obtained excellent shots which were later published, but without giving her due credit. Osa regularly went out on day trips to nearby water holes with Boculy and Bukhari, where she took many pictures to fill in gaps in their record and to relieve her boredom.[14] While Martin confirmed that these were of excellent quality, he only rarely acknowledged that they were hers. Still, he was unstinting in his praise of her hard work, superb marksmanship, and liking for safari life.

Martin, who was obsessed with his work, often closeted himself in his laboratory for days and nights on end. In her book *Four Years in Paradise*, Osa admits that she grew lonely and needed to have more diversion than just gardening. She was fortunate in having with her a young Boran woman companion, Guyato, whose devotion and concern helped alleviate her sense of loneliness. But Guyato's companionship, day-long photographic trips, and walks in the forest in search of orchids and red pom poms were only a partial solution. When not on safari or photographing at water holes, there was really little for Osa to do at Lake Paradise except supervise the household and gardens, which were already cared for by several experienced and dependable servants. Despite the idyllic accounts she wrote at the time[15] and several years later, Osa was sometimes depressed and sought comfort for her loneliness in alcohol. Martin's response to her alcohol abuse was usually one of patient understanding, but on occasion he scolded and threatened her. While he admitted that "she was bound to be lonely at times," he hoped that her love of fishing, hunting, and adventure, and her interest in animal life, would carry her a long way.[16] He supplemented this wishful thinking with the immediate expedient of brief visits to Nairobi, where he hoped she would have her fill of the things women needed.

It was in Martin's self-interest to believe that Osa's needs could be met by this kind of a quick fix and by the spending sprees he encouraged in New York, Paris, and London. To have done .otherwise would have required coming to terms with the reality that Osa's needs were not occasional but continuous, and that her emotional problems could not be addressed as long as they continued the life-style he had chosen for them. Her drinking binges left him angry and exasperated, and he lived in constant fear that she might wander off intoxicated into the forest and be harmed by a wild animal. He made her promise him that she would never go far from camp without N'dundu, their gun bearer. Not stopping there, he also threatened to skin Bukhari alive if he failed to guard her, and he took comfort in the fact that all of the staff were devoted to her.[17]

Osa's mother could do little to help her from such a distance except send frequent letters of encouragement. She was greatly troubled by Osa's descriptions of her loneliness and depression, and tried to help in "a Christian way," as she later described it. She made Osa promise not to drink alcohol and to seek strength in daily inspirational and Bible readings. Osa faithfully kept up her readings, but found that they were of little help in preventing periods of depression.[18]

In 1925 Martin hired as an assistant a seventeen-year-old American boy, Beverly Heckscher Furber, the son of Percy Norman Furber, a major investor in the corporation. The senior Furber, who headed the Trans-Lux Corporation, had made his fortune perfecting a projector for stock quotations. His son, Beverly, the black sheep of the family, had an intense interest in natural history and was a crack shot.[19] Furber's job at Lake Paradise was to assist Sanderson, whose job was to cover the Johnsons with a rifle as well as run the camp. On May 3, 1925, some six months after young Furber's arrival, he and Sanderson unwisely went into some thick brush a quarter of a mile from the lake to track down rhino which Martin and Osa wanted to photograph. They suddenly came onto three of them; one charged and tore into Sanderson's right thigh despite having received two shots from Furber. Martin and Osa, who were three hundred yards away on an anthill, came running to the scene and found that Sanderson was semi-conscious and bleeding profusely.[20] They carried him back on a stretcher to the lake, where they nursed his wounds for an entire month. Sanderson made a slow but steady recovery and was ambulatory by early June, when Martin and Osa decided to go on a visit to Nairobi.[21]

Sanderson, who wanted to return to Nairobi for rehabilitative treatment, resigned, which Martin regretted, since he considered him to be one of the best men in the country. The situation with regard to Furber, however, was quite the opposite. Although Martin wrote to Percy Furber that his son's shots had undoubtedly saved Sanderson's life, he discharged the youth and sent him back to New York.[22] It does not appear that Furber's performance during the rhino charge was the cause for his dismissal. He was, according to some who knew him, an unreliable individual who suffered from alcoholism, grounds enough for Martin to have fired him. In writing to Akeley, who must have already been aware of Furber's problems, Martin said, "I am sending young Furber home . . . draw your own conclusions."[23]

According to his son, Sanderson later died of complications from his wounds.[24] Neither Martin nor Osa ever mention his death in their writings, although Martin briefly describes the accident in *Safari*, and in greater detail in his report to Pomeroy. Many years later, Osa's mother strongly denied that Martin ever lost anyone on his expeditions, even when confronted with Sanderson's death and that of an African staff member who died of tetanus.[25] Besides the obvious censure that fell on expedition leaders whose men were seriously injured or killed while behaving recklessly, as Sanderson and Furber clearly had done, Martin must have had serious concerns about the impact of this accident on investor confidence in his judgment and abilities. He had by his own admission sent the two men into the dense bush after the rhino. Regretting this later, he said, "One might say it was foolish for us to go looking for rhino in the bushes."[26] This serious error of judgment on Martin's part did not, as it turned out, have any long-term consequences for him. The public was never told what really happened, and Pomeroy and the others were led to believe that Sanderson himself was solely at fault.

Pomeroy, Sherwood, and Osborn kept close watch on Martin's and Osa's photographic productivity. In late 1924 Osborn asked museum staff member James L. Clark, who had filmed in Africa with both Cherry Kearton and A. Radclyffe Dugmore, to evaluate their work to date. Clark reasonably concluded that the trip to Lake Paradise and the construction of the camp had consumed many months of their time, but that from this point on they would "be getting results daily."[27] At around the same time, an old friend of Clark's, Alfred J. Klein, who had once worked as a taxidermist at the museum, returned to New York from Kenya with some excellent wildlife footage. Klein, who had gone out to Kenya in 1910 on the heels of the Roosevelt expedition, first worked as a taxidermist but later became a white hunter who made wildlife films as well. Pomeroy was very impressed with Klein's films and expressed an interest in acquiring them since he had by then decided to expand the corporation into a larger nature film production company.[28] It was not until three years later that he acquired the Klein footage for thirty thousand dollars. It included a short sequence showing Maasai spearing lions that was incorporated into the Johnsons' 1928 film *Simba*.

By November 1925, a year and a half after they had arrived at Lake Paradise, Martin and Osa had secured enough footage for a first film, *Wanderings of an Elephant*. They had even projected it in the lightproof grass house they used as a theater, and had shown it to the local Boran, Gabbra, and Samburu people, who were amazed by it. As good as the film was, Martin was not satisfied with it. Writing to Pomeroy, he frankly stated: "It is a great elephant film, but from the public standpoint it has not enough thrills . . . no excitement to it, and I am enough of a showman to know that the public demands thrills and lots of them."[29]

Pomeroy and the other officers of the corporation had already approved Martin's suggestion that this be their first release. This represented a change of plans, since *Songa: The Tale Bearer* was to have been the first picture. But as Martin explained to both Akeley and Pomeroy, Songa, the Meru warrior who had so impressed them a few years before, had deteriorated in both looks and attitude. Besides, while the Meru people lived a few hundred miles to the south, at Lake Paradise elephants wandered into their backyard every day. Although Martin assured both Pomeroy and Sherwood that he was taking extensive footage of indigenous peoples and their customs, he reminded them that his main charge was to film wildlife.[30] Given the enormous scope of this mission and their distance from the Meru people, he and Osa simply did not have enough time to produce an African version of *Nanook of the North*.[31]

When the footage for the elephant film arrived in New York in late 1925, Pomeroy had it carefully examined by Terry Ramsaye, who had titled *Trailing African Wild Animals*. Ramsaye, who by then was a highly respected film producer and editor as well as an experienced showman, was impressed by the superb wildlife sequences. However, he bluntly told Pomeroy that the film stood no chance of being a commercial success. He pushed for more action scenes featuring charging animals and the Johnsons themselves. This was a commonsense business suggestion but one that ran contrary to the entire philosophical essence of the Johnsons' mission. Pomeroy, who was skillful at finding solutions to difficult problems, eventually came up with a compromise. While the Johnsons were to continue obtaining authentic wildlife footage of interest to both science and the public, they would also produce action shots that could be incorporated into commercial films. This was acceptable to the museum, although Sherwood in writing Martin skirted the issue of action shots and instead stressed that he should depict the difficulties they had to overcome in producing the films.[32] Ramsaye was more to the point, requesting both action shots of Martin and Osa and more excitement. Even Akeley put forward the suggestion that Martin obtain action shots by filming Stewart Edward White's bow-and-arrow big-game hunt, using caution in showing the manner of killing, and then only of animals that were "likely to appeal least to public sympathies."[33]

This revision of the production agenda confirmed what Martin and Osa had known all along, that authentic wildlife films devoid of thrills and entertainment would not succeed economically. When it came to investor-supported films, even those sponsored by scientific institutions such as the museum were subject to powerful market forces. As these forces had shaped Martin's and Osa's careers, they now began to alter the museum's own scientific mission. Martin and Osa were skillful enough, however, that they were able to produce both types of films without compromising the integrity of the scientific footage.

Keeping to production schedules, however, was often difficult given unpredictable weather conditions, changing animal migration patterns, and the arrival of visitors. Although Lake Paradise was remote, it soon became a magnet for lonely young colonial and military officials posted to the Northern Frontier. Martin and Osa enjoyed these visits, although on occasion their visitors remained for a few days, preventing them from getting any work done. T. S. Muirhead of the KAR, who was a frequent visitor to the lake, was high in his praise of Martin's work and wrote a complimentary assessment of him to officials in Nairobi:

> Martin Johnson is in residence at the Crater Lake some 12 miles from the Boma. During my time in charge of the N.F.D., I have treated him as a government official. . . . The work he is doing is of great importance to the Empire in general, and Kenya in particular. It is unfortunate that a British subject has not taken on this particular work but there is nothing more to be said. Mr. Martin Johnson has been most hospitable and kind to officials at Marsabit and elsewhere in the Frontier, and will at all times assist the Government in anything requested.[34]

Despite these compliments, there is a slight tinge of disappointment that a British subject was not carrying out this mission. The Johnsons were, after all, Americans who were peripheral to the colonial social hierarchy by which settlers, administrators, and others were defined. Their intruder status and later success mobilized both resentment and jealousy which sometimes found expression in local deprecatory assessments of their work. However, their sincerity, generosity, and kindness to many disarmed much of this prejudice.

Visits from local officials were not the only breaks in the routine. Sir William Northrup McMillan, a leading white settler who weighed three hundred pounds, journeyed up from Nairobi in a convoy of four Cadillac cars fitted with double tires on the rear axles. In late January 1925 they met Prince Youssouf Kamal of Egypt at Longenia, not far from the lake; after leaving him and his hunting party, they traveled to the Guaso Nyiro to meet the Duke and Duchess of York, later King George VI and Queen Elizabeth. Osa presented them with fresh vegetables from her garden, and Martin gave them a package of wildlife photographs. The duke recorded the January 29, 1925, meeting in his diary:

> Left Camp at 5.30 and walked straight to Archer's Post where we found the cars we had left before in an old banda. After breakfast we found the Martin Johnsons on the other side of the Uaso Nyero, and we pulled their cars across for them. We sat and talked to them for some time. Martin Johnson is an American who is out here, up at Marsabit, taking cinema pictures of big game for the American National Museum. The Government have given him every facility, and he is allowed into the Game Reserve. He is a very nice man. His wife, who is smaller than Elizabeth, is also very nice, and they are both very keen on picture making. He has taken some wonderful photographs of every sort of animal in its natural surroundings. He came with us to where we had lunch, and then took a film of us doing various things which I am sure will be very funny. This, of course, is for our own use and will not be used for publication. Then we motored to this camp.[35]

In late July 1925, the Johnsons traveled to Nairobi, visited the Percivals at their farm near Magadi Junction, and then went into the Southern Game Reserve with Blayney and his ten-year-old stepson, J.D.T. Breckenridge (Punch), who was on holiday from boarding school. They photographed wildlife there until August 12. During the ten-day trip, Punch, who was a good shot himself, occasionally acted as gun bearer for Martin and Osa. One day, he was holding Martin's 405 Winchester in his right hand, and one of Osa's rifles in his left, as they were filming a splendid elephant on a river bank. Suddenly, the Winchester discharged on its own, and the elephant fled. Martin later told Blayney that the rifle had discharged on its own twice before. Understandably, Blayney was extremely upset by the incident, as serious injury could have resulted if Punch had not been holding the rifle correctly. He tested the rifle himself several times, but could not get it to discharge on its own. Yet he surmised that there was a defect in the trigger mechanism and advised Martin to get rid of the rifle. When he returned to Lake Paradise, Martin sent Punch a thoughtful letter on the back of a photograph of the elephant that had fled, and a photograph of a rhino that had charged them when they were filming from the top of a termite mound. Such a considerate gesture was typical of Martin, who, despite being shrewd, hard driving, and demanding, was also extremely generous and kind. In signing off in this letter with "Osa and Kalowatt send their Salaams," he once again emphasized the special place this endearing gibbon ape occupied in their lives.[36]

Among the many Africans who visited the Johnsons' Lake Paradise camp was Ali Abdulla Muhammed, a domestic for the KAR, who arrived there with Major Tremaiyne Miles from Ethiopia sometime in 1926. In May 1989 at his home in Marsabit, he gave the following account to the Reverend Paolo Tablino of the Marsabit Catholic Mission, and to Philip Joshua, a schoolteacher.

> A few years after the First World War and before the Gabbra year of Farasade (1926), I accompanied a British officer, Major Mail, and his KAR soldiers from Mega in Ethiopia to Marsabit. We moved on foot from Mega to Moyale and then through Sololo, Turbi, and the Dida Galgalo to Marsabit. At Marsabit we went to the camp of white people at Gof Sokorte Guda where there were houses, many people from down country, and a white woman. The only whites in the camp were the woman and her husband, a man who took pictures. There was an African in the camp from Tanganyika named Bakuli. From the lake we went on to Meru. It took us one month to walk from Mega to Meru.[37]

Muhammed's account, given more than sixty years after the event, is remarkable for its detail and accuracy. The Major Mail he refers to was Major Arthur Tremaiyne Miles, who served with the KAR on the Northern Frontier. At the time, the British maintained a consulate at Mega to deal with constant problems along the border, and Miles made regular visits there. Muhammed's recollection that Boculy was from Tanganyika is correct, a fact that was perhaps well known in the KAR ranks since Boculy had worked for them as a guide. Muhammed also recalled Harry Barron Sharpe, who became the district commissioner at Marsabit in 1927, and Vincent Glenday, who served in the Northern Frontier from 1913 to 1939 and became a legend to both Africans and colonial officials.[38]

In the spring of 1925, Eastman approached Akeley and asked him to accompany him on a hunting trip to Africa. Akeley accepted with the proviso that the trip be connected to the collecting missions of the African Hall. Eastman readily agreed to this, and over the ensuing months, a large collecting expedition was organized. Financed by Eastman, Pomeroy, and Daniel B. Wentz of Philadelphia, the Akeley-Eastman-Pomeroy Expedition (also known as the Eastman-Pomeroy-Akeley Expedition) arrived in Kenya in 1926. It included Akeley and his second wife, Mary L. Jobe; two landscape artists, William R. Leigh and Arthur August Jansson; and two taxidermists, Robert H. Rockwell and Richard C. Raddatz. Leigh and Jansson painted the landscapes, which were later reproduced as backgrounds for the hall's dioramas.

Before the expedition left New York, Martin suggested to Akeley that Osa and Mary Jobe go to Lake Paradise while the men hunted. Expressing what a man's world it was, he told Akeley, "I don't believe the men would be keen on having women on the safari . . . men usually get away on trips of this kind in order to be free for a while and so they can cast off conventions." At forty-eight, Mary Jobe was sixteen years older than Osa. She was an extremely well-educated woman with a degree from Scio College and a master's degree from Columbia University. She was also a highly respected explorer in her own right, having made several expeditions to British Columbia, where she mapped previously unknown areas and studied the Skeena and Peace Indians. In recognition of her explorations in the Rockies, the Canadian government named a peak in her honor, Mt. Jobe. However, for Martin, her education and remarkable accomplishments were not a passport to a man's world. In giving this advice, though, he greatly underestimated both Mary Jobe and Osa. They flatly refused to be packed off to Lake Paradise, and traveled with the men.[39]

Although this expedition did not arouse quite the same level of public interest as Roosevelt's had some seventeen years before, it has since achieved a similar legendary status. This is due to the prominence of those who participated in it, and because it was among the last of the great collecting expeditions sponsored by a major museum. Its participants knew only too well that the East Africa that had been such a sportsman's paradise, largely inaccessible from Europe and America except to the privileged, was on the verge of disappearing.

Eastman, who was to celebrate his seventy-second birthday while on this safari, had become a sportsman late in life. He enjoyed camping and the out-of-doors, and supported the museum's goal of creating a hall to present African wildlife to the public. He not only collected specimens for the hall, but also donated funds to build it. Yet he was not a conservationist in the true sense of the word. Pomeroy, on the other hand, understood the need for conservation and lent his energies and wealth to the museum's efforts in this regard. He was a keen sportsman who had previously hunted in the Sudan. The trip to East Africa provided him with an opportunity to combine sport and philanthropy with a site visit to the field operations of the motion picture company he headed.[40] This was important as far as the investors were concerned, as well as for Terry Ramsaye, the company's consultant, who had been urging the filming of more thrilling sequences. Pomeroy strongly put Ramsaye's views across to Martin and Osa soon after his arrival in the spring of 1926.

Eastman, who was accompanied on this trip by his personal physician, Dr. Audley D. Stewart,[41] spent three months in East Africa between May and September. Pomeroy, on the other hand, remained much longer, until January 7, 1927, securing additional specimens for the African Hall. Eastman's white hunter was Philip Percival, Blayney's younger brother, and Pat Ayre served as Pomeroy's.[42] Martin and Osa, who journeyed down from Marsabit to meet Eastman and Pomeroy in Nairobi, considered the visit the most important of their Lake Paradise stay. In preparation for it, they had worked for weeks building a special 20 × 25-foot log house for Eastman, situated next to a game trail leading to the lake. They accompanied Eastman and Pomeroy on a preliminary trip to the Rift Valley, where the camaraderie of camp life spawned close friendships among them all. Eastman, who enjoyed the company of beautiful women, was also a gourmet cook. Osa's extraordinary skills with recipes and cooking, and her versatility at doing everything from fishing and shooting to driving a car across the plains, quickly won Eastman's admiration. He considered her the life of the camp, and commented that, even though she looked and acted frivolous at times, she was also efficient and just about perfect.[43] While the landscape artists, taxidermists, and the Akeleys traveled to different locations, Eastman and Pomeroy headed north for Lake Paradise, stopping en route to shoot and collect. They arrived at the lake on June 13 and remained there until June 22, when they set out on a camel safari from Laisamis. Their stay at the lake was understandably short since they could do no shooting there. Yet Eastman and Osa busied themselves in the kitchen experimenting with a variety of recipes, including Eliza's foaming sauce and chili con carne.

Before setting out for Africa, Pomeroy planned to see to it that Martin and Osa filmed a lion-spearing sequence on the Serengeti Plains in Tanganyika (Tanzania). In late July, Eastman, Pomeroy, the Johnsons, and the Akeleys arrived in the Serengeti and traveled as far south as the Grumetti River. Maps of the Serengeti were already peppered with a number of camp sites that marked the passage of various hunters. Prominent among these named locales were Bailey's Camp, Klein's Camp, and Simpson's Camp. Klein, the American white hunter, had in fact blazed the oxcart route into the Serengeti from Kenya, and Simpson, a mining engineer from California, was among the first to hunt extensively in the western part of the plains. While in the Serengeti, they went to Simpson's camp and en route met up with two hunting parties, one consisting of Mr. and Mrs. Church of New York who were accompanied by Klein, and the other of Ralph Pulitzer and Paul Daugherty accompanied by Alan Black, who was one of the leading white hunters. On some days, while Pomeroy and Stewart hunted lion, Osa and Eastman remained behind in camp baking bread and Mrs. Kelley's lemon meringue pies. But Eastman was not timid when it came to shooting, bringing down five lions during the short time he was in the Serengeti. Although he bagged most kinds of big game, an elephant with suitable tusks eluded him throughout the trip.

In early August, forty Lumbwa (Kipsigis) men with spears were trucked in from Narok, where they had been recruited by a local trader by the name of Agate. Using their cars, the Johnsons, Akeleys, Pomeroy, and Eastman tried to drive lions into suitable positions for both spearing and filming. Because the *dongas* (ravines) were deep, the lions sought refuge in them, and Martin was unable to film either the lions or the Lumbwa. The party then moved on to Simpson's camp, where the *dongas* were shallower. Here they made several attempts to film the Lumbwa spearing lions, but were unsuccessful until August 9, when a male lion was successfully surrounded in the open and speared, an event which Martin filmed from a car driven by Pat Ayre. Two days later, when the cloudy weather cleared, three more lions were speared, and Martin again obtained extensive footage of the kills. The Akeleys also filmed these sequences, but were at a considerable distance away, and according to Eastman, did not obtain footage as good as Martin's.[44] Eastman, in his account of these killings, made a point of saying that no one in the party had any desire to do it for sport, but only to secure a record for the museum.

The lion-spearing sequences that Martin shot in the Serengeti were the most thrilling he had ever made. He, Akeley, and their patrons used automobiles to block routes of escape and to drive lions into the open, and employed experienced, paid actors who performed on cue. This was justified on the grounds that a permanent film record of a

vanishing custom could only be made through reenactment. However, it was not merely reenactment that was involved, but contrivance as well. The public was never made aware of the scheme when
the films were shown, nor was Martin candid in his book *Safari*, where
he presents the spearings as chance encounters.[45] Only Eastman, who
was always a practical recorder of facts and events, presented what
really occurred, and then only in a privately printed book intended for
a limited readership.

Eastman left Kenya in late September 1926, taking back with him
4,400 feet of Martin's lion-spearing sequences, and six hundred of his
black-and-white still negatives.[46] Martin and Osa remained in the Serengeti a while longer with the Akeleys, while Pomeroy traveled to
other locations in search of specimens for the African Hall. Akeley's
health deteriorated at this time, but he recovered sufficiently to go off
on a trip to the Virunga Volcanos in the Congo (Zaire) to study gorillas. On returning to Nairobi, Pomeroy purchased a three-bedroom
home for Martin and Osa in Muthaiga, a suburb of Nairobi. Set on
four landscaped acres, it was located on Lucania Road (renamed Mu-
tundu Road after Kenya's independence in 1963). It was to remain
their home and base in Nairobi until 1934. They moved into it in mid-
December and, because it was unfurnished, lived in it as if on safari.
They built a photographic laboratory and a garage which were well on
the way to completion by January 1927.[47]

While Pomeroy and Eastman were in Africa, Osborn and Sherwood attempted to prop up investor confidence at home by staging a
showing of the Johnsons' photographs and films in the museum's auditorium. In addition to inviting corporation investors, they opened the
lecture to the museum's membership and were shocked when five
thousand people showed up for the available three thousand seats. As
a result, a number of investors were elbowed out of the auditorium
and responded the following day with irate letters to both Osborn and
Sherwood. To mollify them, a second showing was arranged for the
corporation's stockholders on May 20.[48] Martin and Osa's films met
with an enthusiastic response from both audiences. Ramsaye, however, was less impressed, since the films contained no thrills and
lacked entertainment value. He argued that the reaction of the museum's membership and the corporation's stockholders was not a good
barometer of the general public's interest. Enthusiasm on the part of
self-selected individuals with an avid interest in natural history, like
that of public television audiences to nature films decades later, did
not guarantee popular success in local movie theaters. Sherwood told
Ramsaye, however, that Martin and Osa were getting the thrilling
sequences he wanted and that some of them were already on their way
to New York.

Pomeroy's visit to East Africa convinced him that Martin and Osa had obtained enough footage to produce one major film. While this was two fewer than they had promised, it was sufficient to satisfy the needs of the corporation, whose stockholders had to be paid off by December 31, 1928. Given the time needed for editing, titling, and arranging for distribution, Pomeroy told them that they should return to New York the following spring. Therefore, when they went back to the lake in the fall of 1926, it was with the intention of closing the camp down.[49] This was not an easy decision for them, not only because they had planned on a five-year stay at the lake, but also because they had come to love this place more than any other in the world.

Despite Osa's episodes of depression and loneliness, and Martin's long hours in the laboratory, their days at Lake Paradise were the most idyllic of their careers. High up on one of Marsabit's peaks, surrounded by a great primeval forest that echoed no mechanical sounds except those from their own camp, they were wrapped in extraordinary natural beauty. In the mornings, the mist carried the scent of wild jasmine; at night, the light from the moon silhouetted the domelike forms of elephants near the lake. From their veranda, the afternoons were full of silence, broken only by the breeze drifting through the trees. All around them was a world cut off from hunters, settlements, and trade routes, and from time. It sheltered animals large and small, elephant and rhino, lion and leopard, and gentle bush buck that drank from the mountain streams. They understood how privileged they were to be in this place, and their attachment to it was lifelong. Their greatest creative achievements occurred on these mountain slopes and in the vast desert that spread out below. Like the pioneers on the American frontier who served as their inspiration, they used all their ingenuity and talents, overcame adversity, and through endurance and hard work created their finest hour.

They wanted this place to be their home. Even the name they gave it, Lake Paradise, symbolized their vision of it as the closest thing to heaven they could imagine. Yet they knew that it could never be their home for long if it were to remain undisturbed. Leaving it was difficult for it was here that their intense love of animals and nature was fulfilled and joined with their creativity and desire to succeed. When they did finally leave, the lake remained a sanctuary for the animals and a reminder that their fondest dreams had been achieved.[50]

After closing the Lake Paradise camp in early December 1926, they stopped at Meru, where they learned that Carl Akeley had died in the Virunga mountains on November 17.[51] Akeley's sudden death was a shock to all who knew him, but especially to Martin and Osa, whose photographic mission had been largely shaped by his ideals. It was he who had inspired them to seek a new direction in their photography and who had won them the support of the museum. He had not only been the spiritual leader, so to speak, of the African Hall, but also of their work, and his death left an enormous void.

In January 1927, Martin and Osa traveled up to Meru from where they hoped to climb Mount Kenya.[52] They left Nairobi with two Willys-Knight trucks, some of their regular staff, and John Wilsheusen, a young American driver-mechanic who enjoyed car racing and who had previously worked for Pomeroy and Eastman. At Chogoria, they were assisted by a missionary physician, Dr. Irwine, and his wife in recruiting some seventy Meru porters and obtaining mules for part of the ascent.

They started up the mountain on January 16, and three days later arrived at an elevation of twelve thousand feet. It was so cold here that their wash basins froze and they were forced to wear their overcoats most of the time. The day after arriving at this elevation, Martin, Osa, and some of their men developed severe coughs and slight fevers. That night, however, both Martin and Osa developed high fevers, as did a number of their men. Sensing that some type of serious outbreak was occurring and realizing that they could not get down on their own, Martin offered a handsome reward to any of the men who would race down the mountain and bring Dr. Irwine back up. Several men volunteered, but on reaching the mission found that Dr. Irwine was away. However, the resourceful Wilsheusen gathered a dozen men and drove and pushed one of the Willys-Knight trucks up the motor track that had been cut up to the timberline several years before. He managed to reach them in a day and promptly brought them down the mountain. By the time they arrived at Chogoria, Martin was recovering but Osa was unconscious. Her lips were cyanotic and her breathing labored, symptoms compatible with both influenza pneumonia and high-altitude illness. The persistence of Osa's symptoms after the descent speaks for influenza pneumonia, although some of the initial ones may also have been due to high-altitude illness.

Osa was placed on a comfortable bed in a grass hut. At first, Irwine gave Martin little hope that she would survive. They decided to send for Dr. Gerald V. W. Anderson, one of the most respected physicians in the country.[53] While Anderson was on his way, Irwine sent Wilsheusen down to Nairobi in order to bring up a nurse to care for Osa. After Anderson had examined her, he confirmed that she had pneumonia in both lungs, and was as guarded in his prognosis as Irwine had been. He thought that an ice cap might help her. So, Wilsheusen raced down to Nairobi for an ice machine and returned with it the same day. Two weeks after she had been carried off the mountain, Osa began to show signs of improvement; her convalescence at the mission took another month.[54]

In retrospect, it appears that the Johnsons and their men were the victims of influenza, which was then epidemic in the country. Osa's infection may have been initially complicated by high-altitude illness, and later by a subsequent bacterial pneumonia resulting in a prolonged convalescence. Wilsheusen's quick thinking in removing them both from the mountain probably saved Osa's life. His frantic trips to Nairobi alerted the press about their plight, and an Associated Press reporter quickly filed a story about it. The news shocked officials at the museum in New York, who were still reeling from Akeley's death. There was little they could do from so far away, but the voluminous correspondence between them during the following weeks speaks of both their concern and affection for the Johnsons.

Following their recovery, Martin and Osa left Chogoria for Nairobi, where after a stay of ten days they boarded the train for Mombasa. From there, they took the *Bernardin Saint Pierre* to Marseilles, and after a short time in Paris and London sailed on the *Leviathan*, which arrived in New York on May 16, 1927.[55] They had been away in Africa three and a half years. In that time, they had firmly established themselves as both the leading wildlife photographers of their time, and the principal interpreters of Africa to the American public.

CHAPTER ELEVEN

WITH LIONS AND
BOY SCOUTS
ON THE SERENGETI

When Martin and Osa returned to New York City in the spring of 1927, the era of sound movies had already begun. The previous January, Warner Brothers Pictures had released *The Jazz Singer*, whose Vitaphone talking sequences and sound effects revolutionized filmmaking. Not everyone in the movie industry was convinced that talkies were necessarily the wave of the future, even as the transition got underway. Conversion to sound entailed major capital expenditures, not only at the studios but also in movie theaters. This, coupled with the need to decide between two competing sound systems—disc and film track—and the in-production status of many silent films, delayed conversion decisions for a few years. Yet when the public preference declared itself firmly in favor of the talkies, the silent era quickly came to an end.

The transition from silents to talkies occurred over a two-year period, 1927–1929, just as Martin and Osa prepared their African footage for release. This period was characterized by many hybrid productions that were neither completely silent nor completely sound. Talking dialogues were often added to silents as either prologues or else spaced within the films themselves. Musical scores were also inserted, and some films were released as both silents and with some form of sound.[1]

Martin, Osa, Pomeroy, and Ramsaye confronted this revolutionary change in filmmaking when they began to produce a full-length feature from the 200,000 feet of silent stock shot in Africa. They ultimately opted for the safest course of action, which was to create both a silent version and ones containing various sound elements, including musical scores and a talking introductory. However, when their film *Simba* was released on January 23, 1928, it was the sound versions that proved the most successful.[2] Yet all the sound versions contain the hallmarks of a silent film, including Ramsaye's titles which appear on backgrounds produced by the Hap Hadley Studios. The talking prologue, also written by Ramsaye, depicts Martin in a tuxedo and Osa in formal evening wear standing in an elegant living room. She fusses over him with wifely gestures as he explains their travels in the stilted fashion that often characterizes his monologues. The introductory, which was called a microphonic talk, was followed by a silent recapitulation of the Johnsons' previous travels. Then came a sound sequence: a vocal number, "Song of Safari," composed by Herman Ruby and Sam Stept and sung by Frank Munn, who was a recording star for Brunswick Recording. The song was followed by the main portion of the film, accompanied in the sound versions by various musical scores recorded by the RCA photophone process.[3]

The sound tracks for *Simba* were only one innovation among many. The technical quality of the film surpassed anything Martin and Osa had produced thus far. Decades later, *Simba* still stands out as a superb wildlife film whose technical quality is suffused with grace and beauty. For the first time, Osa was credited as a coproducer and cinematographer, a rare achievement in a male-dominated industry. Another woman, Lillian Seebach, whom Martin had first hired in 1921 and who was to work for him and Osa for close to twenty years, did much of the cutting and editing. Yet neither she nor the Africans shown in cutaways filming with Akeley cameras are acknowledged in the credit listings.[4] Their involvement in the production of the film, however, demonstrates the Johnsons' increasing need for staff to create the kind of films the public wanted. Before producing *Simba*, Martin and Osa pretty much went it alone on the cinematography, relying only on freelance title writers and sometimes on editors. Public demand, technical advances, and the rapid evolution of the filmmaking craft made it clear to them that collaborators and field crews were now indispensable.

While *Simba* contains much that is new in terms of quality and credit sharing, it retains the racial sight gags that characterize most of the Johnsons' previous films and many films of that era. Africans are depicted as either stupid or incompetent: for example, there is a cutaway of an old man trying to open a beer bottle with a can opener he had obviously never used before, set to the popular tune "How Dry I Am." Similarly, the "Queen of the Lumbwa," an elderly woman with her hair shaven off, as was then the custom, is shown smoking one of Martin's cigars. Ramsaye's title reads: "The queen had worn her hair short for years, but this was her first smoke." Other scenes depict an African dwarf dancing, an African woman sitting at Osa's dressing table putting on white face powder, and two scantily dressed girls. The cutaway, mocking not only the Africans but contemporary

American "flappers" as well, bears the title: "The short skirt movement has gone about as far as possible."

The racism inherent in these titles and cutaways appears surprising at first, since the film was produced and released under the auspices of a major scientific research institution, the American Museum of Natural History. But, while the museum insisted on the validity of the wildlife sequences, it gave no thought to fostering a vision of equality among the races. In fact, Osborn, the museum's president and a brilliant paleontologist, was an outspoken champion of Nordic superiority, a proponent of immigration restrictions, a supporter of the eugenics movement, and the author of theories that held that education and environment could not fundamentally alter racial differences. His views, forged within the environment of his times, came into direct conflict with those of the eminent anthropologist Franz Boas, who held that all the races of mankind have the capacity to develop high cultural forms. Boas successfully challenged Osborn's claims that only Nordics are capable of democratic government, and that Raphael, Leonardo da Vinci, and Galileo all had Nordic ancestors.[5] Writing about Osborn, Boas said that it was unfortunate that someone who in his own area of science enjoyed a well-earned reputation permitted himself to follow the lead of uncritical race enthusiasts.[6] Among the latter was Osborn's close friend, Madison Grant, a museum trustee who was also president of the New York Zoological Society. Grant, who did much for conservation, was a prime mover in the eugenics movement, a proponent of immigration restrictions, and the author of a book, *The Passing of the Great Race*, in which he preached against miscegenation and argued for the immutability of both racial bodily characteristics and psychological predispositions.[7]

Grant and Osborn were not unique; but they reflected the views of the many Americans and Europeans who converted eugenics into a movement to protect class interests. That their views did not produce the public outrage they would many years later confirms how widely held they were at the time. Indeed, racist and misogynist jokes were so much an accepted part of American entertainment that their absence would have been much odder than their continuing appearance in the Johnsons' films.[8]

Simba was copyrighted by Pomeroy on January 14, 1928, and three months later he donated to the museum the 200,000 feet of film made by the Johnsons between 1924 and 1927. At his and Martin's insistence, the 2,326 still negatives made during this period were stored at the Eastman Kodak Company, it being fully understood by all the parties concerned that they were the property of the museum.[9] The receipts from *Simba* rolled in at an amazing pace, enabling Pomeroy to quickly pay off investors and give Martin and Osa their $100,000 share. Since Pomeroy owned the film, he was at liberty to modify it, which he did, with the addition of a six-second cutaway of sable antelope filmed by Arthur S. Vernay in Angola.[10]

The story line of *Simba* traces Martin and Osa's journey to Lake Paradise—with numerous extra shots of wildlife and peoples—followed by a second trip to Tanganyika, where Lumbwa cattle herds are allegedly being attacked by lions. The necessity for killing the lions is established through the contrived story that they were attacking Lumbwa villages and cattle, and had in fact killed the "king's" prize bull. The need to kill the lions is further justified during a lengthy series of scenes in which the Lumbwa exhaust all other means for ending the attacks. During this segment, audience anticipation is skillfully built up as the Lumbwa stage their dances and recite incantations to drive the lions away. Recently circumcised young men, erroneously described as priests, are sent into exile after their bags of charms fail to foil the lions. In an attempt to infuse humor and build up suspense, a group of circumcised young women are, equally inaccurately, presented as a new consignment of wives for the beleaguered "king," obviously arriving at an inopportune time. The failure of the dances and incantations, and the inability of the witch doctors to drive the lions off, coupled with the constant prodding of the "queen" who puffs on one of Martin's cigars, leaves the "king" no choice but to summon his warriors. With the stage thus set, the Lumbwa spearmen are sent off into the Serengeti Plains, where in fact they have never lived.

Audiences still move to the edge of their seats as the warriors fan out across the plains in search of *simba*, the lion. Eventually, they surround a magnificent male, and in a truly dramatic sixty-five-second sequence fend off his charges and bring him down with their spears. The next scene consists of Alfred J. Klein's nineteen-second sequence of Maasai spearing a lion at another time and place. Less dramatic than Martin's previous longer sequence, and obviously filmed at a greater distance, it serves to sustain audience excitement, but at a lower pitch.[11] The final scenes of the climax last eighty-five seconds and depict an obviously provoked lion deciding on his prey. Will he choose the Lumbwa, or go after Martin and Osa? Again, the audience's excitement rises, not out of fear for the Lumbwa who have proven their mettle, but for Martin and Osa. Several short cutaways alternate between Osa, poised to shoot, and the slowly advancing lion. Finally, the enraged lion rushes forward, and Osa brings him down with two shots, all shown in well-crafted cutaways, since she did not actually kill this animal. The Lumbwa hail Osa as a heroine and hold the dead lion aloft, paying tribute to a valiant foe—and mollifying animal lovers in the audience.

The next sequence shows Osa back in camp, dressed in an apron and a safari hat, and using a bottle to roll a pie crust. She is assisted by her cook and three small children. The tranquil domestic scene was intended to contrast sharply with what went before. Although the juxtaposition is a contrivance, it does accurately re-create the texture of Osa's life in the wild. She was certainly courageous and a crack shot, but she was also a Kansas housewife who carried her American homespun values with her to the African plains.

While in New York City in the summer of 1927, Martin not only worked with Ramsaye and Seebach preparing *Simba* for release, but also signed a contract with George Palmer Putnam, the head of G. P. Putnam's Sons, for a book about their time at Lake Paradise that was published in 1928 under the title *Safari*. Putnam, an aggressive publicist, built up an impressive list of true-life adventure books authored by daring explorers and aviators such as Knud Rasmussen, Richard Byrd, William Beebe, Amelia Earhart (whom he later married), and Charles Lindbergh. He and the Johnsons met through Pomeroy, who was setting up a new nature film production company, Talking Picture Epics, of which Putnam became a director.

Putnam had perfect timing when it came to publishing books. To insure that his authors would meet deadlines, he often engaged talented literary ghosts and secretarial crews.[12] Among those who ghosted books at Putnam's was Fitzhugh Green, a naval officer and, under his own name, the distinguished author of numerous books; he had been a member of the American Museum of Natural History's Macmillan Expedition to the Arctic in 1913. Green ghosted over forty books; according to Putnam, he was the only man who could produce a book outline one day and a completed manuscript a few days later. Although he ghosted Martin's 1929 book, *Lion*, his role in *Safari* was more that of an editor, since much of its content had already been previously published in magazine articles.[13]

Putnam's genius for marketing books led him to publish a juvenile series of real-life adventures for boys. What set these books apart from others in the field was that most of the authors were often boys who had accompanied expeditions to distant lands. Among them was his own son, David Binney Putnam, whose book, *David Goes to Greenland*, became a classic of the 1920s. There was scarcely a boy in America who could not identify with the lucky few who set off with the heroic explorers of the day. The ever-enterprising Putnam wed his business interests in boys' books to a philanthropic one in the Boy Scouts of America. He provided the funds to send Boy Scouts (chosen by a series of local and national committees) on famous expeditions. Their accounts, quickly written and published after their return, found a ready audience among the 600,000 Scouts in the country as well as among other young boys (and a good many girls, too). Although Putnam's philanthropy provided some boys with the experience of a lifetime, it was also a shrewd business investment, since his company handsomely profited from the sales of the subsequently produced books. These books, while allegedly authored by the boys themselves, were usually ghosted by people like Green.

In the spring of 1928 Putnam released *Safari*, and several months later he published Green's juvenile market biography of Martin, *Martin Johnson: Lion Hunter*. Both rode to quick success on the huge wave of interest generated by the film *Simba*. *Safari* received some excellent reviews, especially because of its photographs. The *New York Herald Tribune* called it "a first-rate book," and said that "the photographs are superb." The *New York Evening Post* was more discerning: the book owed its value "first to the superb photography . . . and . . . to the number of intimate facts it contains in connection with wild animals." It concluded, however, that "from a literary point of view, the book has little merit." The *New York World* came right to the point: "Never did such fine photographs carry such inadequate writing," and the *Springfield Republican* made the cogent observation that "many of the chapters have appeared in magazine articles and it is regretted that . . . Mr. Johnson did not smooth out his narrative by eliminating some of the repetitions."[14] Despite the negative comments, *Safari* was a great commercial success, thanks to *Simba* and Putnam's timing.

With the release of *Simba* in January 1928, Martin and Osa entered the ranks of superstars, and their names became household words across America. However, it was not the film alone that brought about their success, but also their magazine articles, personal lecture tours, and the newspaper and newsreel accounts about them. The press now regularly reported on their arrivals and departures, and even on some of their adventures as they were taking place, thanks to improved communications in Africa and the presence of wire-service reporters in the field.[15] The public focused not only on their travels and adventures, but also on them as personalities. This shift in public focus in turn affected how Martin and Osa presented themselves in films and in print. Ever a deft showman, Martin was skilled at projecting a more glamorous Osa while still exhibiting her long-established image that combined courage with domesticity. The films that followed *Simba* placed a greater emphasis on their own exploits, a shift that helped to make them one of America's leading adventure couples, a distinction they shared with Charles and Anne Morrow Lindbergh.

Osa was glad to be home and was not looking forward to a quick return to Africa. Her spells of depression became less frequent once she entered the warmth and security of her parents' home, and this was a strong force in her decision against going back. For entirely other reasons, Martin was not prepared to launch yet another expedition. With the era of the talkies firmly established, he knew that their future success lay in making sound movies, a technical area in which they had absolutely no expertise. The production of sound movies required not only a mastery of newer skills, but also the purchase of expensive equipment. Martin was confident that, with time, effort, and plenty of capital, they could overcome all of these obstacles. More troubling, though, was the realization that they had reached the limits of their own cinematographic vision of Africa. These limits were not those imposed by the technology of the times, but rather by the temporary exhaustion of their own enthusiasm and creativity. Sound was obviously a new twist that could be exploited. But having shot 200,000 feet of film over a three-year period, it was hard for them to imagine what else they could film and commercially market.

As the Johnsons struggled with these problems, George Eastman was planning a safari to the headwaters of the Nile. There he hoped to shoot a white rhino, even though they were endangered, and an elephant which he had failed to bag on his 1926 safari. When another couple was unable to accompany him, he invited Martin and Osa along as his guests. This offer, from a revered patron, was not one they could easily decline, even though Osa was intensely unhappy about accepting it. Her mother later recalled that there was no trip about which Osa initially felt less enthusiastic than this one, and that during the early part of it she was very depressed.[16] Martin's initial reservations were overcome by a complex arrangement worked out with Putnam, and by the knowledge that his and Osa's participation would help promote their film *Simba* and the book *Safari*. Martin decided that, after parting with Eastman at the Nile headwaters, he and Osa would return to the Serengeti Plains for a stay of several months. He agreed to write a series of letters about the trip to Fitzhugh Green, which Putnam planned to publish in newspapers. The publicity value of these to *Simba* and *Safari* was obvious, and, as in the past, the letters were to be worked up into a book that Putnam planned to publish. With Martin's agreement, Putnam proposed that the Boy Scouts of America choose two boys from among its membership for a summer safari with the Johnsons in Serengeti. He and his son, David Binney Putnam, agreed to pay the travel expenses of these two scouts, and later a third scout was added when David T. Layman, Jr., agreed to donate the necessary travel costs.[17] It was also agreed that the three Boy Scouts would write a book about their experiences to be published by Putnam, and that Green would write a biography of Martin for boys. The most controversial aspect of the Boy Scout arrangement, and the most valuable from a publicity standpoint, was that each of them was to shoot a lion while in Africa. Some conservationists argued against this, but the prevailing view of white hunters that lions were often vermin and wanton killers won the day.[18] It was the prospect of fifteen-year-old Boy Scouts hunting lions that most riveted the attention of the press, and, not surprisingly, Putnam stood his ground against the critics. When Martin and Osa sailed out of

New York harbor on the *Berengaria* on December 14, 1927, it was not only to accompany Eastman, but also to engage in a brief promotional safari that was very much the product of Putnam's genius, and which was financed by the Martin Johnson African Expedition Corporation.

Besides the Johnsons, Eastman was accompanied by a personal physician, Albert David Kaiser, a pediatrician by training who also had an interest in public health.[19] Once the *Berengaria* docked, the party moved with kaleidoscopic speed through Europe, spending Christmas on a train traveling from Paris to Nice. There was a one-day trip to Monte Carlo, where Osa won 560 francs ($25.00) despite Eastman's prediction that she would lose. They then went on to Genoa and boarded the *Italia* for Alexandria, where they arrived on January 2. With stops at Cairo and other places, they traveled by train to Khartoum, their comfort assured by Eastman's meticulous preparations and the dutiful attentions of local colonial officials. These preparations included the leasing of a steamer, the *Dal*, from Thomas Cook's; it was fitted out with new furniture, a General Electric refrigerator, fresh linens, new tableware, a phonograph, and a larder of imported foods. Even Eastman admitted that life on the *Dal* was luxurious. The steamer was accompanied by a supply barge that carried some of the crew, fifteen donkeys, and six goats.[20]

The *Dal* left Khartoum on January 10, 1928, for what would be a two-week trip up the Nile to Rejaf in the Sudan, where Eastman's white hunter, Philip Percival, had two cars and two trucks waiting. It was a leisurely journey, and Osa found it boring at times. She and Martin filled their time reading, photographing, and shooting at occasional crocodiles on the riverbank. A few days after leaving Khartoum, they arrived at Kodok on the west bank of the Nile. The similarity of the name to Kodak was irresistible and induced them all to buy post cards, which were surprisingly available at this remote and tiny administrative post. Eastman, ever the practical inventor, took a strip of canvas from a reclining deck chair and, using dinner and dessert plates and a phonograph record envelope, traced out the lettering for "Kodok," which he then filled in with a carpenter's pencil. The numerous photographs made by Martin of Eastman holding a Kodak at Kodok in front of the sign and surrounded by local people later created a sensation.[21]

After leaving Kodok, they entered the Nile's vast swamp, the Sudd, for a few days and finally arrived at Rejaf on January 25, 1928, two days after *Simba* had its premiere in New York. Good roads built by the colonial administration enabled them to get to Yei in the southern Sudan in a few hours, and from there they went on to Faradje (Ferandje) in the Belgian Congo (Zaire), where the district commissioner, Baron van Zuylen, and his American wife gave them a warm welcome. Osa came down with dysentery during this leg of the journey, but Eastman, who doted on her, saw to it that she was made comfortable. They motored over to Arua in Uganda, and then moved to Rhino camp on the Albert Nile with a safari of a hundred porters, fifteen of whom were assigned to carry cases of Evian water. At times, Eastman traveled through the bush in an improvised sedan chair carried by Africans and equipped with an umbrella for shade.[22] He finally got an opportunity to shoot a white rhino while Martin and Osa were off in another direction trying to photograph them. With the white rhino trophy in hand, Percival's next challenge was to see that Eastman got his elephant. For this purpose, they moved down the Albert Nile to Laropi (Larobi), and then to Dufile. On February 10, Percival sighted a large bull elephant standing sideways in the bush. However, closer inspection with the binoculars revealed that he had only one tusk. The ever-pragmatic Eastman, who had allotted only two more days for this hunt, decided that one tusk was better than none, and shot the elephant. To celebrate this triumph, Osa made mutton stew for dinner, along with dumplings from Eastman's biscuit mixture, and rice pudding.[23]

Martin and Osa accompanied Eastman back to Rejaf and the waiting *Dal*, and as he later wrote, they stood "disconsolate on the dock," when the steamer pulled away. His admiration for Martin and his affection for Osa had grown during the two months they had spent together, and solidified a relationship that was special for all of them.[24]

Martin and Osa took one of the trucks used by Eastman and traveled to the edge of what is now the Garamba National Park in northeastern Zaire, where at Gangala Na Bodio they filmed the twenty-six domesticated elephants then at this special training camp.[25] From there, they went on to Gombari, where for the first time they saw the Mbuti pygmy people of the Ituri Forest. Although they shot considerable film footage of the pygmies, who had been brought together for their benefit by the local district commissioner, they resolved to return again to produce a complete film of them.

They finally arrived at their Nairobi home the second week of March and, after three weeks there, set off on a leisurely safari to the Serengeti. Their plan was to set up a semipermanent camp there that included a garden, chickens, an ice-making machine, and a record player, while they filmed and photographed lions. Although from a certain perspective the Johnsons were more casual travelers on this trip than intrepid explorers, it must be remembered that the Serengeti was a very wild and dangerous place. It is easy to lose sight of this today, when game parks are full of animals completely habituated to humans and automobiles. Hunting on foot with a gun or camera in this region required considerable skills and was not without great risks. The Johnsons' experience certainly lessened the danger but could not entirely eliminate it, as the untimely deaths of numerous white hunters proved.

While Martin and Osa were setting up their camp in Serengeti, the Boy Scouts of America chose Robert Dick Douglas, Jr., of Greensboro, North Carolina; David R. Martin, Jr., of Austin, Minnesota; and Douglas Oliver of Atlanta, Georgia, as the lucky three boys who would join them for a month in Africa. They left New York City on June 10 and arrived in Mombasa on July 9, from where they were accompanied to Nairobi by two East African Boy Scouts. There they were met by Martin and Osa, who quickly whisked them off to the Serengeti two days later.[26]

The spectacle of Serengeti with its vast herds of wild animals and magnificent lion populations made an indelible impression on these fifteen-year-old American boys. Sixty years later, two of them vividly recalled their experiences. As Boy Scouts, trained to be self-sufficient, they found it awkward to have servants. Yet, with so many predators around, they were grateful that Bukhari, the headman, slept on his cot with his gun at night next to the opening of their tent. They took an instant liking to the Johnsons, and were very impressed with their extraordinary hospitality, efficiency, and hard work. Oliver recalled that Osa was a logistical genius who not only kept the camp running efficiently, but who also helped Martin set up the cameras and advised on the shots. She was always with Martin whenever he was photographing, and in Oliver's view, was indispensable to the production of the resulting films and photographs. Martin's dedication to obtaining authentic pictures of undisturbed wildlife greatly impressed the scouts, as did his compassion for animals, which he never killed except for food or self-protection. They recalled that on one occasion, he spent six hours pursuing an eland that had been wounded by a gun bearer and was greatly troubled by the animal's suffering.[27]

The Johnsons went to great pains to see to it that the scouts were kept out of harm's way. Osa gave them firm instructions about drinking only the camp's purified water, and saw to it that they ate well and got a good night's rest. This exercise of motherly instincts was a joy to her, and she later confided to her mother how she wished she had had a son like one of them. But it was not only in camp that she hovered over them, but also out on the plains when they stalked game and hunted lions. In a sense, the visit of the Boy Scouts fulfilled one of Osa's fondest dreams, which was to be a mother, even in the wilds of Africa, which, despite her mixed feelings about it, had become her home. Not surprisingly, both she and Martin felt extremely sad when the scouts left Nairobi on August 16 and headed for home.[28]

Martin and Osa returned to the United States in the fall of 1928. They were especially excited about their lion footage and by the

scenes of the 1928 wildebeest migration they had filmed in the Serengeti.[29] They had shot fifty-two thousand feet of motion picture film,
all of it silent; it was too short for a full-length feature, and too full of
lions for a public that had so recently seen *Simba*. However, Ramsaye
and Pomeroy hit upon the idea of producing a film that recapitulated
the Johnsons' previous travels and ended with the most recent trip
involving the Boy Scouts. Although all of the footage was silent, they
added an RCA Photophone sound track providing a continuous narration by Martin, written by J. Leo Meehan and Ramsaye. This film,
Across the World with Mr. and Mrs. Martin Johnson, was released by
Pomeroy's company, Talking Picture Epics, and premiered on January 20, 1930, at the George M. Cohan Theater in New York City. It
received high praise in the popular press and was an immediate commercial success. *Variety*, however, panned it, calling it "tiresome entertainment for the adult film addict" and noting that the Boy Scouts
had been worked into the last quarter to insure commercial success.
The *Variety* reviewer also took exception to such contrived sequences
as close-ups of a Boy Scout's knees shaking as he allegedly hunted
lions, and the juxtaposition of a golf game and lions dodging golf balls
that were obviously thrown at them. The Johnsons' product endorsement efforts also came under fire. In return for the donation of Willys
trucks, they prominently showed the name of the manufacturer. Similarly, their cook wore an apron bearing bold lettering, Maxwell
House Coffee, in return for the free supply of coffee they had received.[30]

Across the World with Mr. and Mrs. Martin Johnson begins in a drawing room, perhaps a small hotel ballroom, where Martin and Osa are
entertaining guests. Among these, but not identified, is Osa's mother,
who sits beside her. Also there is one of the Boy Scouts, Dick Douglas, who had been part of Putnam's lecture circuit promoting *Three Boy
Scouts in Africa*. Martin proposes to show nine reels of their travels
from a projector in the room, and then begins his narrative, replicat-
ing a format that was then the fashion in travel films. Suspense is built
up by fading in and out of the drawing room scene, where the dialogue and questions from the guests heighten viewer interest. In contrast with their other films, the Johnsons included a lengthy sequence
showing a number of their African staff at work and identifying them
by name.

While this film comes across at first as a talkie, in fact it is a hybrid,
characteristic of the period of transition from silents to sound. The
drawing room dialogue produced in New York City is sound, but the
remainder of the film is a silent to which a sound track was added.
Martin and Osa both knew that this convenient technique of adding
sound to silents was but a temporary measure. The era of sound pictures had, in fact, already entered Africa with Paul L. Hoefler, who

arrived with sound equipment in 1928 to produce *Africa Speaks*. Hoefler, whose film was released by Columbia Pictures on September 15, 1930, traveled to some of the Johnsons' secret haunts, filmed the Nandi spearing lions, and visited the pygmies of the Ituri Forest, recording the sounds of Africa along the way. While many of the sound sequences were recorded in Africa, others were later produced in the United States.[31] Hoefler had barely completed his cross-Africa trip in 1929 when Martin and Osa set out again for Nairobi with a sound crew and state-of-the-art sound equipment, intent on producing the first sound picture made entirely in Africa.

CHAPTER TWELVE

GENTLE GIANTS
AND FOREST PEOPLE

By early 1929, Martin and Osa had firmed up their plans to produce a sound film of the Mbuti pygmies of the Ituri Forest and of the gorillas of the Virunga Range. As in the past, they invested their own funds in the project and then sought additional financial backing. Among those who put money into the scheme was George Bascomb Dryden, a rubber merchant who was married to George Eastman's niece. However, the principal investor was Henry Williams Sage, a New York lumber merchant who was also a trustee of the American Museum of Natural History. With this significant financial investment in hand, they approached the Fox Film Corporation, which finally agreed to invest $26,000 in the production and to provide the services of a sound cinematographer, Richard Maedler, and a sound technician, Lewis Tappan.[1] At the time, Fox had taken the lead with its Movietone sound system, which had been developed in conjunction with General Electric. This system recorded sound on film, whereas Warner Brothers' Vitaphone sound-on-disc process used synchronized phonograph records. Although the sound-on-disc process had ushered in the era of sound movies with *The Jazz Singer* in 1927, it was Fox's system that eventually prevailed.[2]

The Johnsons' arrangement with Fox represented a further evolution in the sponsorship of their motion picture productions. This was the first time that an established motion picture company financed their work and, as a result, had a say in the production. Although Martin and Osa are frequently referred to as independent filmmakers, in point of fact their independence was always fettered to some degree by the wishes of investors, market forces, and, in this case, by direction from a major Hollywood studio. The contract with Fox left them with considerable creative latitude, which was later modified somewhat by the studio's own editors and writers. Fox's provision of a sound crew was not only a necessity, since the Johnsons had absolutely no experience producing talkies, but also gave the studio some control of the production in the field.

As the negotiations with Fox were going on, Martin and Osa went on tour using a silent lecture film, *Adventuring Johnsons*. Drawn from their previous footage, this film recapitulated their travels much as did their later commercial sound film *Across the World with Mr. and Mrs. Martin Johnson*. Their previous film footage and still negatives had grown considerably in quantity, and posed a major storage problem. In April 1929 Martin and his assistant, Lillian Seebach, carried out a complete inventory of the motion picture film. In addition to the 200,000 feet donated to the museum by Pomeroy from the 1923–1927 African trip, they estimated that there were 51,000 feet at the museum and 300,000 feet at Lloyds Film Storage at 130 West 46th Street in New York City, making for a total of 551,000 feet.[3] The still negatives, like the motion picture film, were the legal property of the museum. At Martin's request and with the agreement of the Eastman Kodak Company, they were stored free of charge at the company's Rochester, New York, headquarters, as this facilitated the reproduction of quality prints. Martin deposited albums with numbered prints at the museum, and both he and museum officials used them when placing orders with Kodak.[4] The issue of whether the Johnsons or the museum should pay the storage bills at Lloyds became a thorny one for a while. The fact was that the museum had legal title to the film, but the Johnsons had commercial exploitation rights during their lifetimes. Eventually the museum agreed to pay the costs of storage and the problem was resolved.

Besides lecturing, editing film, and raising money for the Congo expedition, Martin also wrote several magazine articles and, with the help of Fitzhugh Green, completed his book *Lion*, which Putnam published in early 1929. Thanks to Green's ghosting, the writing received a passing grade from most reviewers; the *New York Times* called it, "good journeyman writing, pleasant if not distinctive."[5] Green also produced a juvenile biography, *Martin Johnson: Lion Hunter*, which Putnam brought out late in 1929 at around the same time that he published *Three Boy Scouts in Africa*. This latter book was ghosted by Green, and its senior Boy Scout author, Robert Dick Douglas, Jr., was sent on a nationwide lecture tour.[6] Douglas was also prominently featured in the talking dialogue sequences of *Across the World with Mr. and Mrs. Martin Johnson*, which was released in early 1930. Putnam made a bold and winning stroke by publishing three books about the Johnsons in the year that lay between the release of their two successful films *Simba* and *Across the World with Mr. and Mrs. Martin Johnson*.

The talented and prolific Green, who had made all of this possible, also found time to produce a juvenile biography of Richard E. Byrd, another of Putnam's true-life adventurers, who had recently gone off to Antarctica with another Boy Scout in tow.[7]

Osa, who had written two articles for *Good Housekeeping* before 1929, produced a series of nine articles for the magazine in 1929 and 1930 dealing with African baby animals. These were quickly packaged by Putnam into a book, *Jungle Babies*, published in the fall of 1930. Although the book was very successful, it received lukewarm reviews for its writing style, which the *Saturday Review of Literature* said did not "do justice to the subject matter." The *New York Herald Tribune* was more positive: "Mrs. Johnson writes somewhat as she talks in her husband's talking films—very cutely . . . and that is something to which children and grown-ups can listen indefinitely."[8] The book was illustrated with twenty-one drawings by Margaret Flinsch, and was published with Osa identified as Mrs. Martin Johnson. This was, to some extent, a matter of convention, but it also traded on name recognition. Similarly, the *New York Herald Tribune* reviewer was facile in using the phrase "her husband's talking films" as if Osa had nothing whatsoever to do with their production.

By the late summer of 1929, with the Fox contract secured, the Johnsons made final preparations for their trip to the Belgian Congo. The funds from Fox and the other investors were quickly used to purchase equipment and to cover travel costs, with the remainder being placed in a liquid bank account from which cash could be drawn to cover ongoing expenses. On Tuesday, October 29, 1929, a few days before they were set to sail for Europe, the stock market crashed. Within two days, Fox's stock fell from $119 to a dollar a share.[9] Yet the company's terrible misfortune and the overall market crash had little impact on the expedition, since its assets had been converted into equipment and cash.

Martin and Osa sailed for Europe with their crew in the company of George Dryden and his son, George Eastman Dryden, who were going on a hunting safari for several weeks. In addition to the Fox sound men, they took along with them twenty-six-year-old DeWitt Sage, a son of their principal investor, Henry Williams Sage. Although Sage's father was the leading backer of the expedition, this fact was not the main reason the Johnsons chose to take him along. They had met him in East Africa in 1926, when along with James P. Chapin, the museum's associate curator of birds of the Eastern Hemisphere, he had traveled mostly on foot through the eastern Belgian Congo from Lake Albert to Lake Tanganyika. He was familiar with the Ituri Forest and the Virunga volcanoes and had scaled the nearby Rwenzori Mountains; he spoke French, the official language of the Congo, and was conversant in the local language. As the Johnsons' safari director, he ultimately hired most of the African personnel, settled their disputes, looked after the cars and camera equipment, facilitated contacts with local Belgian officials, guided the safari over terrain new to the Johnsons, and, as Martin said, acted as "Our Gang of Men" because he was capable of doing so much at once.[10]

Martin, Osa, and the Drydens visited London, Paris, and Berlin before boarding the SS *Njassa* for Mombasa. But Osa, despite the good company and Martin's gifts of expensive lingerie and a stunning evening gown, often cried herself to sleep. Once they arrived in Kenya, she busied herself organizing their various safaris, and her mood markedly improved. Her bouts of depression seem to have been particularly severe whenever she left home, which she attributed to being separated from her loved ones. Martin did his best to cheer her up, and her mother and Aunt Minnie sent a constant stream of reassuring letters. Unfortunately, whenever her feelings of anxiety and depression became overwhelming, she sought relief in alcoholic binges. In time, this pattern evolved into one of frequent intoxication, leaving a deleterious effect on her health and placing great strains on her marriage. Martin tried to be patient and understanding, and did all he could to discourage her drinking. At times, though, he became exasperated with her and resorted to threats, which had little effect. In attempting to find a solution to the problem, he and her mother compromised in allowing her to have beer, believing that its alcoholic content was so slight as to pose little risk of her getting very drunk.[11]

Osa tried to fill in the voids in her life by intensifying her relationships with patrons such as George Eastman and Daniel Pomeroy, both of whom greatly admired her. Eastman became Uncle George who sent biscuit flour out to her for Christmas, and Pomeroy similarly sent her both gifts and money, and for several years had new automobiles delivered to her mother on Christmas Eve. These friendships assumed enormous importance for Osa, and she brought her parents into their orbits in order to strengthen them. She regularly encouraged her mother to use her railroad pass to visit both Eastman and Pomeroy, and later even the Drydens in Chicago.[12]

On arriving in Nairobi, Osa enjoyed the task of furnishing their home in Muthaiga. This was the place Pomeroy had helped them buy in 1926, but where they had so far spent little time. She wrote excitedly to her mother about the rooms, the four acres on which the house stood, and the flower and vegetable gardens she planted. The joy she expressed about this home had as much to do with the emotional security and sense of fulfillment it provided as with its physical beauty. She had always wanted a home with a garden, like the one her parents had in Chanute, Kansas. Understandably, the house in Muthaiga assumed great importance for her; after almost twenty years of marriage, it represented a dream come true.[13]

While Osa busied herself with the gardens and furnishing the house, Martin supervised the finishing touches on the 20-by-90-foot laboratory, garages, and an engine room where the Delco electric plant from Lake Paradise was installed. In the rear of the property, not far from the Muthaiga Club, he built an enormous wire cage 70 feet long, 30 feet wide, and 30 feet high, which was later used as a studio to film various animal sequences.[14] For the interior of the house, Dryden presented Martin and Osa with a splendid radio encased in a beautiful cabinet, and it was given a place of honor in the living room.

Although the Mbuti people of the Ituri Forest and the gorillas of the Virunga Volcanoes were the principal objectives of this expedition, Martin and Osa opted to start filming in sound on the Serengeti and in the Northern Frontier. There were several reasons for this decision: the Drydens wanted to hunt lions in Serengeti, some of the equipment was delayed, and there was a need to test out the sound system. However, most important was their desire to capture on sound film the spectacle of the East African plains which they had so laboriously recorded on silent film over the previous decade. Other filmmakers had come to East Africa with sound cameras, and they feared that these newer productions might eclipse their own silent ones. Paul Hoefler had already produced sound portions of *Africa Speaks* in Africa, and his film was due to be released a few months later, on September 15, 1930. In addition, a Metro-Goldwyn-Mayer (MGM) Hollywood film crew, directed by W. S. Van Dyke, had arrived in East Africa to produce *Trader Horn*, which was released in early 1931. This represented the first time that Hollywood had gone on location in Africa with a cast that included Harry Carey, Edwina Booth, Aubrey Smith, and Duncan Renaldo. Van Dyke, who had gained fame for his collaboration with Robert Flaherty in producing *White Shadows in the South Seas* (1927), and who would later produce the first sound film about Tarzan, *Tarzan the Ape Man* (1932), encountered the usual difficulties in filming on location in Africa. Louis B. Mayer, the general manager of MGM, and Irving G. Thalberg, the studio's supervisor of production, were disappointed with some of his African footage. Although much of it was good, it had to be augmented with footage shot on sets in Mexico. This was secretly done so as to hide the fact that the film had not been entirely made on location in Africa. *Trader Horn* was later an enormous commercial success but clearly, like *Africa Speaks*, was not completely filmed on location in Africa.[15]

Martin and Osa's fears that the arrival of Hollywood film crews represented a threat were not unreasonable. For most of the 1920s they had enjoyed a kind of cinematographic monopoly on Africa, not only because of the quality of their work, but also because they had no real competitors. That era had now obviously come to an end. Hoefler, who arrived in Kenya in 1928 to film *Africa Speaks*, quickly went to a number of places where Martin and Osa had made their films. Inspired by the lion-spearing sequences in *Simba*, he brought Nandi men down into the Serengeti, where he filmed the same kind of footage.[16] Van Dyke even tried to get to Lake Paradise but was thwarted by the flooded Guaso Nyiro River. However, he was lavish in his praise of both Martin and Osa:

> If anybody wants to see African game life as it really is, I would advise him to see this picture (*Simba*). . . . I never met Johnson, but would like to go on record as saying that I think his wife is a "peach" and game to the core. Not particularly because she faces the charge of big game, but because she drinks the water, eats the food, and smiles through the bites and annoyances of African bug life. There are few women who would stand for as much of it as she does.
>
> Johnson himself I greatly admire for the infinite amount of patience the man must have. . . . I know for a fact that Martin Johnson and his wife spent five months on one lion location getting lion stuff only. Five months in the African bush represents an inconvenience and monotony that would have made Job look like a piker.[17]

Van Dyke's words only partially characterize what was unique about the Johnsons and their work in Africa. While their films, like many Hollywood productions, portrayed glamor, theater, and melodrama, they were also highly personalized and stylized adventure stories. As a result, Martin and Osa occupied a special place not only in filmmaking, but also in the minds and hearts of Americans. Not surprisingly, Hollywood's coming to Africa had no impact on their continuing success.

They spent the first several months of 1930 making sound movies in the Serengeti and in the Northern Frontier. Although the presence of Maedler and Tappan limited Osa's own camera work, she did take some flash pictures of lions at night, and she was extremely proud of them. Dryden, who traveled to Serengeti with them, was as impressed with her as Eastman had been a few years before. She not only managed the camp and took occasional pictures, but also excelled at hunting and fishing. Frequently, the main course for dinner was what she had either caught or shot earlier in the day.[18]

By late summer, they set off for the Congo with ten tons of equipment loaded into seven cars and two trucks, all of which were shipped on flatbed railroad cars to Tororo in Uganda. The sound equipment alone weighed 350 pounds, and the portable electric generating unit

3,000 pounds. In addition, they carried along 100 cases of food, 150 boxes of petrol, oil and grease for the cars, tents, guns, ammunition, outboard motors, and a host of other supplies. Sage, Maedler, and Tappan traveled with them, as did their headman Bukhari and twenty of their regular East African staff. Never without pets, they took along two Colobus monkeys, Elanor and Tumbu.

It took them two days to reach Tororo and another four days to motor over to Butiaba on Lake Albert, where they took the *Samuel Baker* over to Kasenyi on the Congo side of the lake. There they left most of their staff, cars, and supplies, while they chartered a wood-burning steamer, the *Livingstone*, for a short trip down the Albert Nile to Murchison Falls (now Kabalega Falls) to film hippo, crocodiles, and elephants. The ever-enterprising Martin borrowed one of the *Samuel Baker*'s lifeboats and equipped it with an outboard motor so that he could get close to the river's banks to film the crocodiles. After obtaining some truly splendid sound footage, they returned to Butiaba, where they boarded the *Samuel Baker* for the short trip over to Kasenyi. There they completed formalities with the local Belgian officials and purchased a young chimpanzee, Teddy.

Roads in the Belgian Congo were excellent at the time, but their destination, Irumu, was more difficult to reach because the road west was full of hairpin turns that slowed down their heavily loaded cars and trucks. Their old friend Baron van Zuylen, whom they had met in 1928 at Faradje, was in charge at Irumu, and he greatly facilitated the work of the expedition. Irumu was then an important administrative post in telegraphic contact with the territory's capital, Leopoldville, and through it with Brussels.[19]

Belgian administrative control of the Congo had been achieved in part by the construction of good roads and by forcing the population to live next to them. Although the Mbuti pygmies roamed the Ituri Forest, they had regular contact with the Africans who lived alongside the roads, thus making access to them fairly easy. Setting up a camp 6 miles from Irumu, Martin and Osa drove south along the road to Beni in search of a suitable pygmy band, which they soon found at Bwana Sura's village. There, two Mbuti men, Deelia and his son Salou, agreed to bring their peoples in from the forest to be photographed. With this location secured and the Mbuti rewarded with salt and tobacco, Martin and Osa traveled west through the Ituri Forest to Mambasa. En route they met an Mbuti named Piligbo whose village was soon to be the site of a Protestant mission started by an American missionary, Bill Deans. Piligbo promised to bring in a large number of Mbuti in three days' time, during which Martin and Osa returned to Irumu to register their East African men and obtain hunting licenses.[20]

Piligbo was true to his word, and brought in four hundred Mbuti, who patiently waited until the Johnsons returned. With Bill Deans's help, the film crew spent a day filming Piligbo's people. Martin and Osa quickly came to the conclusion that this site offered the best prospects for in-depth filming of Mbuti life. They therefore asked Deans to supervise the construction of a studio pygmy village next to a stream, which was accomplished with Piligbo's help, in three weeks' time. Meanwhile, the expedition went south to Bwana Sura's village, where they filmed for a week. It was here that Osa was photographed and filmed driving a truck loaded with forty Mbuti. When later shown in theaters and published in articles and books, these images created a sensation.

Once they had exhausted the possibilities of Bwana Sura's village, they returned north to the studio village, which had already been completed. The lure of bananas, rice, palm oil, tobacco, and salt, and Piligbo's efforts, brought some five hundred Mbuti to the site. Martin and Osa and their crew spent three months at the studio village, though they were without sound for three weeks when the cam on the gasoline-powered generator broke. The high humidity of the Ituri Forest caused the sound film to swell, the banks of batteries to deteriorate, the wires and connections to corrode, and mildew to form on the lenses and camera cases.[21]

Martin's role at the studio village was more that of a producer and director than cameraman. Although he occasionally used a silent motion picture camera and took stills, he did not use the sound cameras with which most of the footage was made. Osa, who did little photographic work at this time, spent most of her time assisting in the direction of the film shots and in supervising the camp. Ever concerned about her alcoholism, Martin did not allow any alcohol in the camp, and in Sage's words, "watched her like a hawk." Despite this, she occasionally obtained locally brewed banana beer through their African staff.[22]

Sage's memories of the Ituri Forest camp were still vivid a half-century later. He remembered Martin's determination and hard work, and that his patience was sorely tested because of adverse climatic and lighting conditions. Martin was tense most of the time and gave vent to a fierce temper with a tirade of curses and swearing whenever things went wrong.[23] Sage thought that his health was a factor in these outbursts. Martin had complained of lumbago since 1925 and constantly had indigestion, which he wrongly attributed to a "dropped stomach." This diagnosis had been made by a physician in the United States who obviously still believed in the medical theory of visceroptosis, the displacement of bodily organs, which by then had been discredited. No doubt, Martin's diabetes mellitus had also become manifest, even though it would not be clinically diagnosed for a few more years.[24]

On completing their film record of the Mbuti, Martin and Osa traveled south with their crew to the Ruindi Plains, where they established a camp on the Rutshuru River. They left Maedler and Tappan at this camp to film hippo while they, Bukhari, and Sage went on to the Lulenga Catholic Mission at the foot of Mount Mikeno, arriving there on October 10, 1930. Their objective was to climb up Mikeno, film and photograph gorillas, and visit Carl Akeley's grave at Kabara. Here they acquired two guides who had previously traveled with Chapin and Sage, Jakobo and Magoulo, and 165 porters. Because of his "dropped stomach," Martin took along a sedan chair, since the physician who had made this absurd diagnosis had said the condition would be worsened by walking. The ascent of Mikeno was no easy matter, as Sage already knew and as Martin and Osa were to discover. The air on the mountain was cold and damp, and drizzle and mist covered the slopes for hours on end. Despite these odds, they started up the mountain for what would prove to be a ten-day trip.[25]

When the Johnsons made their visit to the mountain gorillas in 1930, popular views of these animals were still strongly shaped by the tales of nineteenth-century travelers, particularly those of Paul Du Chaillu, and by more recent exaggerations and distortions from glory-seeking hunters. Gorillas were described as vicious and dangerous and given to savage attacks on human beings, including the raping of women. Akeley, who had spent time among the mountain gorillas of the Virunga volcanoes, was convinced that they were gentle creatures.[26] Yet his views were based on fairly limited observations, and he admitted that much remained to be learned about them. While his views were eventually proven correct, at the time they were not bolstered by sufficient field evidence capable of dislodging popular beliefs.

In retrospect, it is clear that just about everything known about gorillas, whether from white hunters, naturalists, or local people, had been learned in situations where humans had threatened the huge primates. Accounts of humans who had been attacked by gorillas filled numerous books, even those of the Akeleys.[27] What was not often described was the degree to which the animals had been provoked. The popular consensus that emerged from all these stories was that gorillas were elusive and unapproachable, prone to vicious and unpredictable attacks, and that just getting near them was a significant accomplishment achieved at the risk of life and limb.

Akeley was among the few who doubted this consensus. While allowing for the fact that gorillas could be bold and aggressive when threatened, he maintained that they were essentially gentle in character. Had he lived, and had he been able to continue his studies of these apes, the world might have learned several decades earlier than it did that they were indeed gentle, and that they could be habituated to human presence and even touched by humans in the wild.[28] As it was, these facts did not emerge for another forty years, until the prolonged field studies of animal behaviorists such as George B. Schaller and Dian Fossey.[29]

Martin's various accounts of gorillas in the wild are markedly contradictory. In an August 30, 1931, *New York Times Magazine* article, he is quoted as saying: "I would not call the gorilla a dangerous animal. . . . Certainly no one ever provoked gorillas more than I did, first and last, in trying to photograph them . . . not one of them ever charged home." Later, in his book *Congorilla*, he refuted the worst distortions about gorillas. Yet he also used hyperbole to describe some of his own personal encounters with them: "Screams of rage, shrieks of surprise, barks of alarm . . . the possibility of a concerted, mass attack upon us by the apes . . . powerful enough to rip a man to shreds."

The exaggerations in the book may have been the result of editorial interventions aimed at spicing up the tale. What is more certain is that the Johnsons found gorillas to be gentle, even though the animals must have been terrified by the efforts to photograph them. Writing ten years later in *I Married Adventure* for a public grown more sophisticated in their knowledge of gorillas, Osa said that Martin felt that the tales about viciousness had to be debunked. Osa's statement, while made from the security of hindsight, was not entirely an attempt to recast Martin's view as more current and acceptable. Rather, she used it to justify their capture of gorillas, since Martin claimed that the distortions could only be discredited by their bringing one of the animals back to the United States.[30]

While Martin, Osa, and Sage came close to many gorilla groups on Mikeno, they had little success in getting good film footage and photographs of them. After a week on the mountain, they began their descent, stopping to visit Akeley's grave at Kabara. They repaired the log stockade around the grave and dutifully draped both the Stars and Stripes and the Explorers Club flag on the tombstone. Mud, leaves, and twigs had blocked up the openings between the logs, causing puddles to form around the grave, a fact Martin later reported in an article in the *New York Times Magazine*. Akeley's widow, Mary Jobe, who was intensely jealous of the Johnsons, especially of Osa, was quick to respond with a stinging letter published two months later. In it, she methodically described the arrangements she had made for the perpetual upkeep of her husband's grave, and supposed that the Johnsons had arrived just before the periodic visit of her caretaker. In a final sentence that dismissed the Johnsons' genuine act of kindness and reflected her strong resentment, she said: "It has not been left for the casual visitor to the place to make alterations and repairs."[31]

After a short stay with the White Fathers at the Lulenga Mission,[32] they went into the Alumbongo Hills to the west of the Virunga Range in order to film gorillas. Martin also wanted to go into this area to capture a live gorilla, for which he had obtained a special permit from the Belgian government with the help of Dr. William M. Mann, then the director of the National Zoological Park in Washington, D.C. Climatic and topographic conditions in the Alumbongo Hills were no better than on Mikeno. Rain, mist, humidity, mud, and moist vegetation, together with the elusive behavior of gorilla groups, made filming practically impossible. On November 8, 1930, they reached Kibondo, a small village slightly to the east of the present-day Parc National de la Maiko. With the permission of the Belgian administrator at Lubero, they secured the help of an African hunter, Chief Pawko, who used dogs to hunt gorillas, a strategy guaranteed to frighten them. Martin did not help the cause of gorilla conservation by offering to buy gorilla skulls. While thirty were offered for sale, he bought only a few, which he later presented to the American Museum of Natural History.

Eventually, Pawko and his men separated two immature gorillas from their group. The frightened animals sought refuge in a tree and were easily captured when the tree was cut down. Tied by their hands and feet to poles, the animals were later caged in one of the trucks. That night, the gorilla group hovered near the camp "calling to the captives." In the camp itself, the Johnsons held a big celebration and rewarded their African staff with tea, sugar, and cigarettes. Although they had a permit to capture only one gorilla, they decided to keep both, since Bukhari had incorrectly concluded that one was male and the other female. The prospects of breeding them in captivity obviously increased their value to science.

En route to Irumu in early December, they purchased a sickly male baby gorilla for $60, and named him Okero. Osa later called this gorilla Snowball, and wrote a children's book about him. In order to take the three gorillas out of the Congo, they had to obtain the permission of the governor of the Belgian Congo in Leopoldville and the Belgian colonial department in Brussels. With the help of their friend Baron van Zuylen, cables were also sent to Brussels, and to the American ambassador there. The $250 cost for sending the cables was well worth it; a week later, they had the necessary permission.[33]

The capture of the two immature gorillas, which were named Congo and Ingagi, and the purchase of Okero solved one of the Johnsons' major cinematographic problems. Rain, mist, and dense vegetation had prevented them from obtaining much useful footage of gorillas in the wild. Now in possession of three gorillas, they created a studio in the large cage on their Muthaiga property, where the animals were filmed and photographed against what passed for a natural wild setting. During the several weeks that this filming was going on, one of the gorillas lost a large tuft of hair from the back of its head. This presented a serious problem since Martin wanted to pass the

animal off as several through skillful film editing. When their veterinarian was unable to cure the problem, they called on their personal
physician, Dr. J. R. Gregory. A half-century later, Gregory vividly
recounted what happened next: "I said I thought it was probably a
vitamin deficiency, but didn't have an idea as to which one. So I told
them to go to the chemists [pharmacists], House McGeorge, and get
all the vitamin pills they could and throw them in the cage. The amazing thing is that the gorillas took only certain ones and left the rest.
The gorilla's hair grew back, and they were able to resume filming,
later passing off one gorilla as many by editing the film."[34]

During the breaks in studio filming created by the gorilla's loss of
hair, Martin and Osa went on short trips to Lake Nakuru to film
flamingos, to Isiolo and the Guaso Nyiro where they visited Rattray,
and to the Aberdere (Nyandarua) Mountains where Osa succeeded in
shooting a bongo. Realizing that there were few action scenes in the
films they had shot thus far, they made numerous attempts to get a
rhino to charge one of their trucks. Gregory, in recalling their frustrated efforts, said: "Martin had a car padded on all sides with old tires
and had Osa walk out in front to provoke the rhino to charge. It was a
courageous thing for her to do, but all of their 83 attempts were unsuccessful."[35]

Between filming and hunting, the Johnsons also socialized in Nairobi and were guests at elegant balls at Government House. Osa always wore one of several beautiful evening gowns to these affairs and,
according to most, looked much younger than her thirty-seven years.
However, her alcoholism marred one of these evenings, according to
Gregory, who was also present: "She had a very serious drinking
problem, and once, at Government House, she got so drunk that she
had to be carried out to the car. Martin was terribly upset at her, and
they argued as she was being placed in the car. She took off one of
her shoes and began hitting him in the face with the heel. He was incredibly patient with her, mothered her, looked after her, and really
tried to keep her on the straight and narrow."[36]

Martin and Osa left Kenya in June and arrived in New York aboard
the *Excalibur* on July 3, 1931, with two African animal keepers, Aussaine, a Mganda from Uganda, and Manuelli from western Kenya.
Their menagerie consisted of three gorillas; a cheetah named Bong;
two chimpanzees, Teddy and Bee Bee; and two monkeys, Elanor and
Kimo. The animals were housed at the Central Park Zoo while the
Johnsons settled into the St. Moritz Hotel.[37] To stay near the animals,
the two animal keepers slept on the floor in the elephant house. Some
black leaders in Harlem protested, but the public at large saw nothing
wrong since, as the newspapers observed, these men had never before
slept on a bed.[38] The press took a great deal of interest in the Africans,
particularly when they visited Harlem and the offices of *The Amster-
dam News*. This coverage reflected racial attitudes that were then such

an integral part of the American cultural canvas.[39] Eventually, the Johnsons moved Aussaine and Manuelli to a rooming house at 109 West 99th Street, in response to the demands of Harlem civic leaders. Even after the Africans left for Africa on October 1, 1931, the *New York Times* ran an absurd story that a Great Dane belonging to a police lieutenant, Cuthbert Behan, had died of a mysterious illness due to a curse inflicted by one of them. Behan, the arsenal precinct desk officer in Central Park, had previously reprimanded the men at Martin's request for getting drunk in Harlem. After the reprimand, one of the men, according to the *Times*, "rolled his eyes like two ivory balls in a jet-black head, fixed them on the lieutenant, and muttered something in a queer, low tone." Behan could not tell which one it was because, as he said, "all Africans look alike to me." However, Martin, who had given him the Great Dane as a gift, said a curse had been placed on him.[40] This story is less important for its details than for the fact that it documents how pervasive racial stereotyping was at the time, and that the public was still gullible enough to believe in such fictions.

On October 10, 1931, the Johnsons began a national lecture tour using a silent film, *Wonders of the Congo*. Starting in Akron, Ohio, they traveled through the Midwest to Seattle, Washington, and to California. They returned east via Tucson, Arizona, and Atlanta, Georgia, and ended the tour on December 19 in Rochester, New York.[41] After their return, they moved into the Essex House, an elegant residential hotel that was to be their New York City home for the next five years.[42]

Since returning to New York City in July 1931, Martin had been extremely busy preparing his book *Congorilla* for publication. It was brought out in January 1932 by George Palmer Putnam, who in August 1930 had joined the publishers Brewer and Warren to form a new company, Brewer, Putnam and Warren.[43] The book received high praise for the quality of its photographs, but not for its writing. The *Boston Transcript* said that "The story is told in a delightfully informal, unliterary manner . . . truly superb illustrations." *Outlook* said much the same. "Mr. Johnson does not write well, but the magnificent photographs and the interesting material have always pulled his books through."[44] Osa was busy at the time writing short stories about African animals, seven of which were published in 1932 in *Good Housekeeping* and later as a book, *Jungle Pets*. Charmian London greatly enjoyed these new stories and wrote to Osa about them. Although Charmian and Osa saw one another infrequently, their friendship was warm and enduring. Osa expressed her feelings for Charmian in a letter written from New York City on March 18, 1932:

> I wish we did not live so far from each other because
> we have so much in common. We would have lots of

fun talking about the things we like to do and have done, and maybe doing some of them.

If you get a chance to come to New York, do let us know. We would dearly love to see you again before we return to Africa. . . .

With lots of love to you, my dear Charmian.[45]

In this same letter, Osa also described her feelings about George Eastman's death by suicide a few days before:

I am in bed after the strain of Mr. Eastman's funeral yesterday in Rochester, coupled with a night on the train and an early 6:45 arrival in New York. I am completely exhausted.

I feel as if somebody had been smashing my heart with a hammer, because of that dear old man's passing and the attendant circumstances. I was terrifically fond of him, and this is the first big shock I have ever had.[46]

Eastman was suffering from multiple myeloma, a painful cancer of the bone marrow, for which there was then no effective treatment. He shot himself through the heart at his Rochester, New York, home in the early afternoon on March 15, 1932, leaving a note: "To my friends: my work is done. Why wait? G.E."

Martin had kept up a continuous correspondence with Charmian, chronicling both his current work and future plans. However, now he reached that point in life when memories begin to assume ascendancy over ambition. His letters to her at this time contain warm reminiscences about the *Snark* voyage: "Your several mentions of the Snark cause me to sit back in my chair and dream over our glorious adventure—the most wonderful time of my life, but kid like, I'm afraid I could not realize it then, at least the full value of it. Of all the adventure I've had since then, and any I may have in the future, nothing will ever equal the Snark voyage."[47] He also recalled his early days with Jack and Charmian with great fondness: "Gosh! When I think of the great time I had living on the Snark at Hunter's Point . . . the things I cooked for my meals—the hours with the old whalers who were then watchmen . . . the poker games with you and Jack, George Sterling and Dick Partington, and the rest of your crowd—that rainy night I arrived in Oakland in the midst of a poker game—and—Oh, Hell! I'm getting to be a sentimental old fool." Thinking back on his own 1906 letter to Jack, he added: "But Charmian, it was all wonderful; a young, healthy fellow—big adventure. And now I must keep a stenographer to answer all the thousands of letters that come from boys (and girls) who want to go adventuring with Osa and me. I answer them all, for I remember it was just such a letter as these boys write to me, that I wrote to you and Jack which made it possible for me to make the Snark voyage. Gosh! How I hate to turn down these youngsters who want the opportunity to do just what I did!"

To deal with the mounting burden of office work, Martin hired a secretary, Helen Joyce, who had previously worked for Lowell Thomas.[48] He interviewed her at his small rented room at Lloyds Film Storage on West 46th Street, where he and Lillian Seebach cut and edited film. Lloyds's cutting rooms and projection theaters were full of rough-speaking men whose technical jargon and profanities were accepted as tools of the trade. Martin himself had acquired these over the years, but was extremely concerned about Joyce's being exposed to the steady din of curses. However, she survived Lloyds's rough and hectic environment, and became not only a superb secretary but also a loyal friend.[49]

By late spring, Martin and Seebach had cut the Congo sound footage into its final form for the film *Congorilla*. Its ultimate story line was greatly influenced by Truman H. Talley, who served as its editorial supervisor. Talley, a leading producer of documentary films, was for many years the executive vice-president of Fox Movietone News.[50] His association with the Johnsons was to be a long one, during which he served as editorial supervisor of two of their subsequent films. Martin was not keen about releasing *Congorilla* during the summer because, as he commented to Charmian, "Summer time is no time to put out a picture."[51] Although audiences generally preferred the beaches to hot theaters, Fox executives thought otherwise, and forced a grand premiere on Martin and Osa at the Winter Garden Theater in New York City on the evening of July 21, 1932.[52] It was their carefully considered opinion that the first sound picture entirely produced in Africa would draw huge crowds at any time of the year.

Martin, Osa, and Osa's mother appeared on stage at the premiere, while floodlights lit up the marquee outside. It was a very satisfied Martin who said to reporters that "all the New York big shots are here." And indeed they were, for this was truly a historic event. Even the title was new and striking, with its ingenious combination of "Congo" and "gorilla." The essential story line of *Congorilla* takes the Johnsons from the preparations for their Congo expedition and the hiring of men, through scenes of wildlife on the African plains and close-ups of the Mbuti people with a contrived marriage ceremony worked in, to the climax: the capture of the two gorillas. Most of the gorilla scenes in the film were actually made in the studio cage in Muthaiga, using the two captured animals and Snowball. The set was so well constructed with trees, vines, and brush that no one detected that the footage was not shot in the wild. Despite these contrivances, there is an enduring value to *Congorilla*: it documents, in sound and sight, Mbuti customs, which have much changed over the ensuing decades, and the spectacle of wildlife in areas where it has since become almost extinct.

Congorilla opens with characteristic vaudevillian humor. An African musician playing a harp is shown seated before Martin and Osa. She motions to a laughing and cigar-smoking Martin, points to the African, and then grimacing, plugs her ears with her fingers. Martin taps the man on the shoulder to stop his playing. In the next scene, they are seated at a table hiring African staff. Although they both spoke excellent Swahili, they feign difficulty in understanding the name of a man from Embu. He clearly pronounces it as Kamayena, repeats it twice in response to their quizzical grimaces, after which the next man also repeats it. "How will I ever write his name down?" Martin asks. "Oh, call him coffee pot and let's go," Osa offhandedly replies, resolving the problem. Audiences roared with laughter during scenes such as this, as they did when two Mbuti tried to light up one of Martin's cigars, and when they blew up a balloon that eventually burst. Laughter also filled the theaters when Osa sang a parody of the hit song "Yes, We Have No Bananas" that went "Yes, we have enough bananas today," while standing next to a mountain of bananas, and when she danced next to a phonograph placed on a drum playing jazz music surrounded by pygmies. Martin's narrative and dialogue sometimes display stock lines from vaudeville. In giving them cigarettes to smoke, he says: "Now smoke your heads off. I hope you get sick." Later on he expresses the racial opinions of some local colonial administrators when speaking of Mbuti babies: "I found them about the same size of a civilized baby when they are born, and they grow until they are about ten years of age. Then all development seems to stop. An old pygmy seventy years of age is still a child of ten, both physically and mentally."

Compared to *Simba* and *Trailing African Wild Animals*, *Congorilla* contains many more racial sight gags and racial put-downs. They are continuously woven into the story line with the obvious purpose of maximizing the film's entertainment value. They are very vaudevillian in character, and in that tradition derive from a pervasive but innocent assumption of superiority. In vaudeville, the Irish, Italians, Jews, Poles, and many other immigrant groups, as well as blacks, were frequently cast as inferiors in order to generate humor. This technique was only successful if the portrayals were done with a degree of affection and a friendly hand. Martin and Osa, who were experienced vaudevillian performers, used this well-established approach when they presented the Mbuti pygmies as ignorant and naive, and placed them in situations guaranteed to produce laughs among white American audiences.

That the racial gags of *Congorilla* were well received is only too clear in its press reviews. The *Herald Tribune* said that "there is nothing in town more hilarious than the efforts of two of the pygmies to light the cigars." The *New York Daily News* reviewer, Irene Thirer, found that the high point of laughs was when the pygmies ate soap, blew up a balloon that burst, and tried to light cigars. "And how those brown midgets go into their dance," she noted, commenting on the Mbuti dancing with Osa to the music of a phonograph record. The *New York Times* observed that the film "formed a good model for the future," and claimed that the Mbuti were "shown with high good humor and a friendly hand,"[53] confirming what good vaudevillians the Johnsons were.

However repellent the racial elements of the Johnsons' films may strike latter-day viewers, it would be unfair to single the Johnsons out for censure. They carried into Africa a white ethnocentric perspective tinged with both innocence and arrogance. The racial superiority they expressed was the rule at that time for their society. As products of this society, they were often true to its norms for literature and film, and usually presented only whites as heroes and heroines. They described the Mbuti and other Africans as either naive or savage, or else depicted them for comic relief. Their racially based comedy techniques received high praise from the entertainment industry as evidenced by a complimentary review of *Congorilla* in *Variety*, which observed that "the business with the pygmies attempting to light cigars was good for a marathon of laughs."[54] In the final analysis, the Johnsons' failure to promote a sympathetic understanding of the peoples of Africa was the result of their being prisoners of attitudes and values which they did not have the ability to fully challenge and which continuously brought them commercial success.

With *Congorilla*, Martin and Osa made the transition to sound. The challenge that now lay before them was not technical but rather creative. They had spent a decade filming the peoples and animals of Africa, and now they wanted to combine their own enthusiasms with what the public wanted. Their long experience told them that other films could still be made in Africa if they had the appeal of novelty. That novelty, as they saw it, now lay in harnessing America's fascination with airplanes and flight, and linking it with the bright Africa they knew so well.

CHAPTER THIRTEEN

AFRICA
FROM THE AIR

By 1932, aviation had become the crucible in which many explorers and adventurers proved their worth. Richard Byrd and Floyd Bennett flew over the North Pole in 1926, Charles Lindbergh across the Atlantic in 1927, and Amelia Earhart across the Atlantic in 1928 with Wilmer Stultz and Louis Gordon. To the American public, Martin and Osa were the quintessential explorers, a perception they themselves had promoted for many years. Yet they had not taken on the challenge of aviation. Thus their decision to launch an aerial safari over Africa was in part motivated by the need to measure up to public expectations. In addition, intense public interest in aerial photography guaranteed the commercial success of films made of Africa from the air.

In the spring of 1932, Martin and Osa traveled to the Sikorsky Aviation Corporation's factory in Bridgeport, Connecticut, and later purchased two amphibians, a Sikorsky S-38BS, which was a twin-engine ten-seater, and a smaller five-seat single-engine Sikorsky S-39CS. Both were powered by Pratt and Whitney Wasp radial engines. The larger plane was painted with zebra stripes and called *Osa's Ark*, while the smaller one was painted with giraffe spots and named *The Spirit of Africa*.[1] Although the Johnsons took flying lessons and obtained licenses, neither of them ever became a skilled pilot. In fact, they never piloted the planes during take-off or landing, and only rarely took the controls during flight. However, their promoters presented a very different picture to the public, enhanced by attractive portraits of them dressed as aviators. This strategy enabled them to advance their image as explorers while they left the flying to skilled pilots.

On December 31, 1932, Martin and Osa sailed from Brooklyn, New York, on the *City of New York*, bound for Cape Town, South

Africa. They traveled with a staff of six men, several tons of equipment, $50,000 worth of lenses, and a pet gibbon ape named Wah.[2] The two airplanes were carefully placed in cradles and lashed to the deck under the careful supervision of the ship's captain, George Wauchope, who later became their close friend and married Martin's secretary, Helen Joyce. Their objective was to fly the length of Africa and to film wildlife and peoples in the regions they knew best. There was little in the way of collective aviation experience for Africa, and given uncertain weather conditions, uncharted terrain, and difficulties in getting rescued, the Johnsons were taking real risks. Martin reduced the risk by bringing along a highly qualified pilot, Vern L. Carstens, who was to remain with them throughout the trip. He helped supervise the construction of the planes and was, as he later said, "delighted to get the job because it was during the depression." Although only thirty-two at the time, he was considered one of the best pilots in the country; he also taught the Johnsons to fly.[3] The Sikorsky plant provided a second pilot, Boris Sergievsky, and a mechanic, Al Moroway, who left once the planes were functioning satisfactorily out of the Nairobi Aerodrome. Despite having purchased expensive aerial maps from London, the pilots found that they had to navigate "by guess and by God" since the maps were so inaccurate.

The production of sound films from the air required not only special camera bases on the aircraft, but also a technical staff capable of handling complex equipment. Martin hired Arthur Sanial as a sound cameraman who was assisted by Robert C. Moreno, the son of the silent film star Antonio Moreno. Martin also took along a former Eagle Boy Scout, Hugh S. Davis, who assisted him with film developing. The Fox Film Corporation, which underwrote some of the costs, estimated that it would take two years for the Johnsons to produce an animal photoplay in sound; the company stipulated this time period in a contract that Martin signed on November 23, 1932.

The Johnsons arrived in Cape Town on January 23, 1933. After assembling the planes, they took off on a 3,500-mile journey to Nairobi, where they arrived ten days later. Sergrevsky and Moroway remained for two months while a hangar was built and the planes underwent test flights. Carstens, who feared that the carpenters had miscalculated the width of the hangar, breathed a sigh of relief when the larger of the two planes, *Osa's Ark*, taxied inside. "There was only a hand's length from the tip of each wing to the wall," he later recalled, "but at least it fit!"[4]

Aviation fuel was available only in a few large towns such as Nairobi, Mombasa, and Kisumu, and supplies were unpredictable. For these reasons, Martin brought in a large supply of fuel from the United States in fifty-gallon drums, which he purchased at a discount from the Shell Eastern Petroleum Company. These drums were

distributed to the various points where a field crew would later build
airstrips. In return for this discounted supply, Shell's name prominently appeared in a number of pictures. Other products were donated or sold at cost in return for endorsements, including Coca Cola,
Maxwell House coffee, Fisk tires, Coleman stoves, and Gold Medal
flour.[5]

During the Congorilla expedition, Martin had come to depend on
controlled studio conditions when his attempts to film gorillas in the
wild failed. He had the studio cage behind the house at Muthaiga
refurbished with trees, vines, and rocks, and he even constructed an
artificial stream with the help of a garden hose. Eventually, he used
this studio setting to film baboons and monkeys, leopard, cheetah,
wart hog, and a lion, most of which were captured by Hugh Stanton,
an animal trapper and big game hunter.[6] Martin was frequently stri-
dent in his condemnation of Hollywood productions that tried to pass
off studio shots as having been made in the wild. He saw nothing
hypocritical in his own use of such artifices, rationalizing that the animals were truly wild and that many were set free again once the filming was completed. Theater audiences were never told that some of
the wildlife sequences were filmed in a backyard studio setting, albeit
in Africa.[7] However, most Nairobi residents knew about this and
many came out to Muthaiga to see both the studio and the animals.[8]
Among them was Ray Nestor, an artist well known for his water-
colors and drawings of Kenya. He lived across the road from the Johnsons in 1933, and recalled: "They ran a miniature zoo in their large
garden, where the animals were housed in fenced-in enclosures.
Among these was a lion, whose roar was very impressive at night."[9]
E. A. Ruben, the head of Express Transport, who regularly transported the Johnsons' goods to and from Mombasa, also visited the
studio: "They had very large animal cages on the Muthaiga property
with trenches constructed such that the animals were separated one
from the other. A leopard was on the bottom when I was there, and
baboons and monkeys on the top. They were able to make close-up
pictures in this studio that had a natural-looking backdrop of trees."[10]

Although Martin filmed in this studio extensively, he continued to
take pictures of animals in the wild. The studio not only served as a
convenient setting for taking close-ups, but also for filming contrived
sequences and reenactments of actually observed events. The contrivances included a fight between a wart hog and a tame leopard, for
which Martin was taken to task by F. Trubee Davison, president of
the American Museum of Natural History: "I regret that you used
dramatic license in the presentation of the 'fight' between the leopard
and the wart hog, which scene is superfluous in an otherwise superb
picture."[11]

From one perspective, Martin and Osa had fallen back under the influence of film distributors and theater managers and the market forces they represented. Akeley, who had played a major role in redirecting their talents toward genuine wildlife photography, had died some seven years before, and the museum's direct involvement with their projects had ended with the 1928 trip to Serengeti. Although newer technology and greater experience enabled them to make better films, it was the needs of the entertainment industry and not those of science that now shaped the content of their productions. While some fakery surfaced in their wildlife sequences, their portrayals of Africans began to display greater sympathy and understanding, reflecting their own genuine feelings about Africans, with whom they had worked so long. Ruben recalled that "they had a knack with the Africans who greatly admired them. They were extremely kind and generous with the Africans, so much so that some local Europeans thought they spoiled them."[12] Their personal physician, J. R. Gregory, corroborated Ruben's observations: "They were very democratic with their African staff, and this did not go down well with some of the European old guard."[13]

This departure on the part of the Johnsons reflects not only their own changing personal attitudes, but also the fact that they were outside the colonial social hierarchy, and therefore free to depart from its norms for race relations. Many of the Europeans who were chagrined by their attitudes simply dismissed the Johnsons as eccentric and mustered as evidence their "flashy" zebra-striped and giraffe-spotted planes. Yet Martin and Osa were not intimidated by this. The respect they developed for Africans had been forged under the harsh and often life-threatening conditions of the bush and was not susceptible to social censure. Also, their extensive years of experience with Africans enabled them to challenge even their own prejudices. It was obviously a wiser Martin who remarked that "mother love among the pygmies of the Ituri is no different from the mother love to which we have grown accustomed here at home." And his comment that the Mbuti pygmies were "very intelligent indeed" was a far cry from his prejudicial characterizations of a few years earlier. He even admitted that European complaints about African body odors were unfair since, as one of his staff said, "To us black people, the white man smells every bit as bad as the black man does to you."[14]

During 1933 and 1934, the Johnsons greatly modified their usual field logistics. The planes enabled them to reach remote areas without an army of porters, and so their African staff was limited to only thirteen men. These men worked under the supervision of Fritz Malewsky, a white hunter who also covered the Johnsons with a gun whenever they filmed big game. Malewsky and the small staff used five trucks to set up supply depots, and they built crude landing strips in various parts of the country.

The Johnsons' first trip was in *The Spirit of Africa*. They flew to Ngoronit, a water hole on the eastern slopes of the N'doto Hills to the west of Laisamis in northern Kenya. Martin was hopeful of filming the elephant herds which at that time followed a multiyear migration route between the Aberdare Mountains (Nyandarua Mountains) to the south, the Lorian Swamp, Mount Marsabit, and the Mathews Range.[15] The elephants did not show up at Ngoronit because they were at that time several hundred miles to the east in the Lorian Swamp, an event the Johnsons would not be aware of until several weeks later. However, Lake Rudolf (Lake Turkana), which was then a very wild place under tenuous administrative control, was nearby, and Martin and Osa were drawn to it by the preliminary reports of the Lake Rudolf–Rift Valley Expedition headed by Vivian Fuchs of Cambridge University. The trip to Lake Rudolf required the larger plane, *Osa's Ark*, and expansion of the Ngoronit air strip to a size of 2,100 by 120 feet. While Carstens returned to Nairobi to bring up the larger plane, the Johnsons and their staff enlarged the strip and named it "Carstens Airdrome." Using *Osa's Ark*, Carstens ferried the party in relays up to Ferguson Gulf on the western shore of the lake, opposite Center Island. There, the local Turkana people helped them build a camp from where they operated for several days.

Lake Rudolf lies in the Rift Valley, and a combination of geographic and climatic conditions create strong winds that blow across its surface with gale force. Carstens was constantly fearful that the plane would suffer serious damage, even at night when parked. "I felt that there was something very eerie about that place," he later said when speaking of the lake. "We just had no business being there." Carstens flew the Johnsons to Center Island, a barren and inhospitable place where Martin was almost bitten by a puff adder. He then piloted them to the southern shores, where they filmed the El Molo people and searched the lake for crocodiles.

The Johnsons' aerial expedition to Lake Rudolf, which took several days, was truly a remarkable achievement. Sir Vivian Fuchs, an eminent explorer and geologist who led expeditions to the lake in the early 1930s for Cambridge University, observed that "they were almost certainly the first to fly over the lake. . . . During my 1930–32 years there was no flying to my knowledge. . . . In 1934, the Royal Air Force landed a plane at Lodwar accompanied by a small Shell Company Gypsy Moth. I flew over northern Lake Turkana in the latter."[16]

Vern Carstens, who was a modest man, never claimed a first for flying over Lake Rudolf, allowing for the possibility that "someone might have strayed up there before we did." What is more certain is that the Johnsons and their party were the first to use an amphibian on the lake.

Once Martin and Osa had completed their photographic work at the lake, Carstens began to ferry the party and their supplies back to Ngoronit. On his last trip to the lake to pick up Moreno, he had the worst mishap of the entire trip when the plane sank into mud and landed on its nose. It took him, Moreno, and the Africans a day to extricate the plane by using split logs as runners. Back in Ngoronit, Martin and Osa anxiously scanned the horizon and were relieved when the plane finally appeared overhead, many hours late.

Sending Malewsky and their ground crew ahead, they prepared for a trip to Garba Tula and the Lorian Swamp. En route, they flew over Lake Paradise but did not attempt a landing because of its small size and the high cliffs surrounding it.[17] Eventually, they flew down the Guaso Nyiro River to the Lorian Swamp, where they found several very large herds of·migrating elephants. While Martin filmed with his Bell & Howell Eyemo movie camera, Davis stood head and shoulders out of the hatch taking stills. Moreno and Sanial took turns holding on to his feet to prevent him from being thrown out of the plane whenever they hit air pockets.[18]

F. Trubee Davison, who became the American Museum's president in 1933, left New York City with his wife, Dorothy, on June 15 to join the Johnsons in Africa.[19] The purpose of their trip was to secure the additional elephant specimens needed for the group that was to be the centerpiece of the Akeley African Hall. George H. Sherwood, the museum's director, sensitive to public opinion about shooting wildlife, emphasized that the elephants that were to be shot were so-called "shamba" (garden) elephants that raided local crops.[20] Yet this was wishful thinking, since the animals the museum needed had to be less than full-grown so they would complement Akeley's own giant bull, which was to dominate the group. Such specific size requirements were not likely to be met among the rare elephants that raided African gardens.

The Davisons flew from Cairo to Kisumu on Lake Victoria on an Imperial Airways flying boat with Pete Quesada, a U.S. Army pilot and close friend. Al Klein, who was then one of Kenya's leading white hunters, supervised their safari of nine motor cars, ten skinners, and a large staff.[21] Klein had chosen the area of the Tana River near Garissa as the best place for securing the specimens. While Davison traveled to Garissa by road, Carstens and Quesada piloted the two planes there with the rest of the party. There, the district commissioner, Harry Barron Sharpe, who was an old friend of the Johnsons from the days when he had served at Marsabit, prepared a rough landing strip.

While Martin and Osa were excellent hosts to the Davisons, they had little stomach for the killing that followed. Martin remarked that "while shooting does not mix well with photography, Osa and I had been asked to go with them and we were glad to be able to do so." Once the hunt got under way, Martin said, "Osa and I cared little enough for all this, for we were passing up literally dozens of excellent opportunities for photographs."[22] Eventually, the Davisons shot a total of five elephants, which now stand as part of the group in the Akeley African Hall.

Once the elephant hunt was over, Carstens flew the Johnsons and the Davisons in *Osa's Ark* to an improvised landing strip that Malewsky had carved out of Serengeti's grasslands. Martin was a man at peace with himself, secure in his accomplishments and more intent on enjoying the wonders of Africa than in taking up its challenges. He was someone who rarely expressed his feelings, but he now poured them out in both his subsequent book and film about this trip. In *Over African Jungles*, he wrote:

> We were merely floating through the clear air, beneath the blue sky and above the endless quiet plains.
> . . . Here, certainly, was Africa as God had made it—to me, at least, the most interesting and thrilling land on earth. . . .
> We seemed to be floating motionless in space—miles above the earth—thousands of miles from the world of men—viewing a world so untouched . . . that it was impossible not to feel that we were closer to the maker of it all. . . . Surely if one can get away from the troubles and problems of economics and civilization, the world is beautiful yet.[23]

As he was lifted high above the great landscapes of Africa, he came closest to reaching what had always been the goal of his life—freedom to do as he pleased, to come and go at will and fully enjoy encounters with the unusual and unforeseen. While narrating their film *Baboona*, he spoke of these feelings with both poetry and conviction: "This wandering life was a wonderful experience—no laws to obey—nowhere in particular to go—and months to get there. Free as the air we were flying and never knowing what we would see from one minute to the next."[24]

The Davisons spent several weeks on the Serengeti, where the Johnsons introduced them to prides of lions that were easy to approach. Using a killed zebra as bait, Martin got the lions to surround the plane with Osa inside. In film sequences that later amused and thrilled movie audiences, she opened the plane's hatch from time to time and quickly closed it as the lions tried to jump in. This was extremely risky as the glass on the hatch was not strong enough to withstand significant force. Finally, she chased the lions away by throwing flour at them. Both Martin and Osa were accustomed to taking these kinds of risks, which even shocked Carstens, who was a test pilot. He recalled an experience with a male lion near Lake Amboseli in Kenya:

> I was driving Martin in an open car with him in the rear with a movie camera. He kept telling me to drive in closer, but each time I did, the lion became very agitated. I had no rifle next to me, and Martin's in the rear was no comfort since he was so preoccupied with his camera that he would not have had time to use it. Still, he ordered me to drive in closer and closer, really oblivious to the danger and to my protests. Finally, the lion charged, and I swung the car around and sped off, almost throwing Martin off his feet. Martin was furious with me, saying that he could have shot the lion in time. I told him that he was a damn fool and that if he wanted to go back he would have to go alone. Later, he apologized.[25]

After a few weeks in the Serengeti, the Johnsons flew the Davisons to Kisumu in *Osa's Ark*; there they boarded the flying boat for the four-day trip to Cairo. More than half a century later, Dorothy Davison recalled their time with the Johnsons with great fondness: "They both managed every move we made. Osa took care of the food and cooked delicious meals over an open fire, and Martin advised and arranged our everyday trips. Consequently we had the best of everything. Due to them we collected the many requests the Museum of Natural History hoped we would bring back. . . . I could tell many a story about these two people who became our friends."[26]

Martin's secretary, Helen Joyce, arrived in Kenya in the fall of 1933, having sailed from New York City on the *City of New York*. After picking her up in Mombasa in *The Spirit of Africa*, they flew her to Nairobi, and shortly thereafter took her with them on a short trip to the Ituri Forest in the eastern Belgian Congo. Martin had sent Malewsky and Moreno ahead to Gombari to build a rough landing strip. Gombari was the place where the Johnsons had first seen the Mbuti pygmies in 1928, and its location on open savanna adjacent to the forest made it ideal for aerial access.

Some twenty Europeans turned out to greet the members of the Johnson party when they landed on the airstrip that had been specially built for them by 150 prisoners. In addition, two hundred Mbuti were on hand, having been brought in by the local administrator. The Johnsons spent only a few days among the Mbuti, during which time they took six of them up into the air at one time for a flight over the forest. Martin was struck by the pygmies' ability to recognize topographic landmarks from the air, and characterized them as "very intelligent."[27]

It took Carstens ten hours to fly *Osa's Ark* back to Nairobi. He next flew the Johnsons in *The Spirit of Africa* to Raymond Hook's Nanyuki farm on the slopes of Mount Kenya. Hook, who had arrived in Kenya in 1908, was also a big-game hunter and helped the Johnsons set up the camp while Malewsky brought in the trucks, staff, and supplies. The American staff was now smaller, as Sanial and Davis had already returned home; they were no longer needed because the bulk of the photographic work had been completed and Martin had become proficient in the use of his motor-driven Wall sound camera.[28] After assessing the changing wind conditions on the mountain, Carstens had three runways built.[29]

While they were on the slopes of Mount Kenya, they discovered a small cave where four baby cheetah had been abandoned. They immediately adopted the cheetah, and then used the cave as a studio where they filmed and photographed other captured animals. Iris Mistry (nee Roberts), whose family had a farm near Nanyuki, frequently saw the Johnsons when they were filming at this location:

> Once the Johnsons were parked at a filling station in Nanyuki and had a leopard on a chain in a crate. They took the animal out and tied it to a post. A crowd of Africans formed and began teasing it. I was twelve at the time, and had always wanted a leopard. I made my way through the crowd and cuddled the leopard. It began to purr and rub its face against mine. Martin filmed a troop of baboons that lived on our farm and told us that he was going to do a film on chameleons, portraying them as [huge] monsters. It was to have a surprise ending in that he would finally show one on Osa's hand. He said that he was going to put this film in a capsule that would not be opened for a hundred years.[30]

Martin and Osa were determined to fly over Mount Kenya's 17,058-foot peak, a goal that had eluded them several years before. No one had yet directly flown over the peak nor photographed it from the air. Thus this attempt, if successful, was to be a first on two accounts. When a clear morning appeared in mid-January 1934, Carstens decided to make a first attempt in *The Spirit of Africa*. Martin was on board, and he did not have the heart to discourage Osa and Moreno from coming, too, though he knew that the added weight would delay their ascent and prevent them from reaching the required altitude before the clouds rolled in. Sure enough, by the time the group flew over the peak, it was heavily cloud-covered. Still, Martin was able to take a few pictures from various angles. On the morning of January 20 Carstens made a second attempt with just Martin aboard, and they rapidly reached an altitude above the still cloudless peak. Carstens later wrote: "The air was perfectly smooth and clear. . . . It was a magnificent sight beyond words of description. . . . The cold was intense. . . . To pilot the ship required no physical effort and I felt no discomfort in the rarefied atmosphere, but the efforts of lifting and manipulating the various aerial and movie cameras left Mr. Johnson verging on exhaustion."[31]

Shortly after leaving the Mount Kenya camp, Osa experienced some unexplained episodes of vaginal bleeding. She was treated by both her personal physician, Dr. J. R. Gregory, and his associate, Dr. C.F.D. McCaldin, who specialized in gynecology. Gregory and McCaldin advised strict bed rest and an early return to the United States for definitive surgical treatment. Osa remained in their Muthaiga home under the care of a full-time nurse, while Martin and Carstens left for a short trip to Mount Kilimanjaro. It was May 1934 when Marthe Barbezat (Barbie Adcock), a Swiss nurse, took up her duties caring for Osa:

> Osa was not very well, but not ill. . . . She agreed to stay in bed until lunch time, and eventually was up the whole day. I . . . enjoyed every moment as Osa was a wonderful young person, friendly, lively and kind. The first morning she asked me whether I would mind her four cheetahs coming in the bedroom for one hour. . . . They were so beautiful, and played with us and admired themselves in the full looking-glass. . . . On the first afternoon, Osa took me to the kitchen door, level with the garden. There appeared a baby elephant which put its head affectionately on Osa's shoulder. They obviously loved each other. Osa told me that a gallon of cream had to be added to cow's milk as elephant's milk is much richer.
>
> One day, Osa told me to walk her in the lovely garden. A monkey suddenly jumped from a tree and took off my uniform cap.
>
> Another time, I came face-to-face with a full-grown leopard on a chain with a keeper.
>
> Osa was so kind to me. She took me to their enormous food store and asked me to take what I fancied for supper. I chose a tin of California peaches which,

with some of the elephant's cream ration, were delicious.

Martin and I only met at mealtimes, so I did not get to know him well. . . . At mealtimes there were two nice young Americans (Carstens and Moreno) discussing details with Martin. Martin was very concerned about Osa's health, and repeatedly asked me to be very firm with her. . . . He was good-looking and very nice, but it was Osa that I got very fond of.

Osa was kind, lovable, and generous. She kindly and thoughtfully gave me several of her lovely dresses which were the envy of the other nurses, and which I wore for years. In 1936 at Easter, I wore one when I set off for Mombasa to get married.

By and by, in the years after, I received letters or cards from Osa . . . and I deeply regret not having kept them forever. The last one was in reply to my letter when Martin died. Osa was heartbroken, as they deeply loved each other. There was such a happy atmosphere round them.[32]

At his camp at Longinya near Lake Amboseli, Martin was kept informed about Osa's condition on a daily basis. Adcock or Osa phoned the local shortwave broadcasting station in Nairobi each day, which in turn relayed the information at 7:15 P.M. to a small portable receiver Martin kept in camp. Carstens flew back and forth to Nairobi, ferrying supplies and using dry lake bottoms near Lake Amboseli as landing strips. He flew Martin around the peak of nearby Mount Kilimanjaro but refused to fly over it, fearing the powerful down drafts.[33]

By the early summer of 1934, the Johnsons had completed their filming and were ready to return to the United States. Martin proudly told the *East African Standard* that "my wife and I are both confident that in this film we have the best picture we have ever made."[34] After filming the peoples and wildlife of Africa for so many years, Martin had temporarily come to the end of his creative visions of the continent. He told Dr. Gregory that he did not plan to return, and for emphasis said, "We've sucked Africa dry."[35] Yet he wrote to Eddie Ruben of Express Transport: "On the eve of leaving Africa for probably two or three years, I want to thank you for all your kindness and courtesies. . . . I want you to know I appreciate it."[36]

The implied intention of returning perplexed Ruben since Martin had sold the Muthaiga property to Phillip Whitemarsh, a gold miner and sportsman, and disposed of their trucks and equipment.[37] Ruben viewed these sales as representing a permanent break with Kenya and a decision not to return. The thought of the Johnsons never returning saddened many, since they had come to occupy a special niche in colonial Kenya and were affectionately regarded. The local press was high in its praise of their work and expressed the hope that they would return.

Martin asked Helen Joyce to travel back to the United States by ship with their menagerie, and hired a Meru man named Twarugoji to serve as an animal keeper. This menagerie included Toto Tembo, the baby elephant, four cheetah, a leopard, and a pet hyena. The Johnsons themselves returned to Europe in *Osa's Ark* with Carstens at the controls, and arranged to have an experienced pilot, M.C.P. Mostert, fly *The Spirit of Africa*. Mostert, who was going home to Great Britain on leave, had been flying for Kenya's Wilson Airways for five years and had already flown the Nairobi-London route fifteen times.

Osa's Ark was fitted with a special bed for Osa, and on July 15, 1934, they left on the first leg of their 6,600-mile flight to London. They flew down the Nile Valley and across North Africa, reaching London twelve days later via Sardinia and France. With the planes safely secured on their cradles on deck, they sailed from Southampton on the SS *Manhattan*, reaching New York City on August 9.[38] They had flown 60,000 miles over Africa and had exposed 160,000 feet of movie film.[39] Martin could not have known then that his break with Africa was indeed permanent, and that he would never see it again.

CHAPTER FOURTEEN

RETURN TO
THE RAIN FOREST

Within a few weeks of arriving in New York City, Osa entered Roosevelt Hospital, where she underwent surgery for the removal of a benign uterine tumor. Her mother, Belle, who had come from Chanute, planned to stay until she was fully recovered. However, on September 7, a week after Osa's operation, they received the tragic news that William Leighty, Belle's husband and Osa's father, had been killed when the passenger train he was driving collided with a lone locomotive at 4:00 A.M. near Grand Summit, Kansas. Osa was extremely distraught on hearing the news, and her emotional state was worsened by the fact that both Belle and Martin had to leave her alone in New York and travel to Chanute. There they learned the terrible details about William's body having been badly burned and trapped under the overturned locomotive for almost ten hours. Their grief was compounded by anger when it became known that the lone locomotive had been traveling on a passenger track through human error.[1]

Following William's funeral in Chanute on September 10, Belle, Martin, and other members of the family faced the harsh financial consequences of this tragedy. William would have been eligible to retire in four months at age sixty-five on an annual pension of $3,000. However, his retirement plan only provided for payments to a surviving spouse if the pension had already begun. Thus, Belle found herself excluded from any pension benefits and without future means of support, despite the fact that her husband had worked for the railroad for fifty years. With Martin's support, she filed a suit against the Atchison, Topeka, and Santa Fe Railway. The court awarded a sizable judgment of $8,000, which Pomeroy invested for her. She soon moved out of her home into Chanute's Tioga Hotel, where she led the life of a grande dame for several years.[2]

A week after the funeral, Martin was back in New York City, "working night and day on the new film," as he told Charmian in a letter. He was actually working on two films, *Baboona*, a commercial feature that was to be released by Fox, and *Wings over Africa*, a silent intended for use during an upcoming lecture tour. He had already booked ten good lecture engagements and was hoping for more. Eventually, he and Osa signed a lecture tour contract with the Radio-Keith-Orpheum Vaudeville Exchange, Inc., for $1,000 a week. Under the terms of the contract, they were required to make three daily appearances on weekdays and four on the weekends. The lecture tour provided them with badly needed capital and helped to carry them over until receipts from the Fox feature began to come in. In fact, they tried to delay the release of *Baboona* because it directly competed with their lectures and was bound to cause cancellations.[3]

On October 20, Osa wrote Charmian from their apartment at the Essex House overlooking Central Park: "It was awfully sweet of you to send me that darling autumn leaf from the ranch. Its coloring is beautiful. I can look out my window over Central Park and all the autumn shades of bronzes, reds, yellows, and very greens, look more like a painting than anything I have ever seen." Osa, however, had more on her mind than the autumn foliage. In a telling paragraph, she wrote Charmian: "I don't mind telling you that our flying over Africa has put a lot of gray hairs on my head, and while I wouldn't have missed it for anything in the world, still it certainly was a strain on my nerves."[4]

These brief phrases succinctly reveal Osa's ambivalence about traveling. Yet, in public, she hid her true feelings beneath rapt descriptions of the places they had already visited and expressed enthusiasm for returning to the jungle. Her exuberant comment to Charmian that "we think we're going to the South Seas . . . and won't it be grand to go back . . . and see our great old friend Nagapate" is suspect, given her strong desire to remain home. She knew only too well that she could never convince Martin to give up foreign travel. So she came up with a compromise solution consisting of brief trips for the purpose of producing lecture films from which she thought they could make "a nice little living." She felt that she could tolerate brief trips abroad, and told Charmian that she had "pleaded with Martin to do no more feature pictures" that required protracted stays in remote and lonely corners of the world. To give her argument added weight, she said:

> Everything has been going out for the last two years and nothing coming in. Both of us are commencing to worry about how the picture will go over with the public. . . . I want us to just make lecture pictures . . . instead of going into these great big productions where

we have to worry about film concerns taking the picture and if they don't like it we have to peddle it
around. Poor darling Martin works every night until
twelve or one o'clock and he looks so tired and worn
out that I want him to go now, without any crew, just
we two, and make a picture and take life a little
breezy.[5]

Osa's proposal that they produce only lecture films was insightful,
since it directly addressed the role that prolonged stays in isolated
areas played in bringing on her moods of depression. In addition, it
was both reasonable and feasible since she and Martin could easily
have made a very comfortable living from such films. Martin, however, could never have accepted this proposal: he viewed himself as an
independent feature film producer and not as the "travelogue man" he
had once been, and he could not settle for a lesser level of professional
attainment. He refused to do this even when his diabetes mellitus had
progressed to the point where his physicians advised him to take daily
insulin injections and to curtail his foreign travel. Instead, he half-
heartedly adhered to a diabetic diet and enthusiastically threw himself
into plans for producing a new feature film in Borneo.

The day before Martin left New York City for his father-in-law's
funeral, the animals he and Osa had collected in Africa arrived by
ship. They were all temporarily housed at the Central Park Zoo,
where they were looked after by their keeper, Twarugoji, who had
accompanied them from Kenya. The press and the public were en-
thralled by the baby elephant, Toto Tembo, whom Osa later referred
to as Pantaloons in her writings. Martin offered to sell Toto Tembo
and the other animals to the Central Park Zoo for $4,500. When the
zoo was unable to raise the money, he agreed to sell the animals to the
St. Louis Zoo for the same amount. On October 11 he, Osa, and
Twarugoji boarded *Osa's Ark* at North Beach Airport in Queens, New
York, and, with Boris Sergievsky at the controls, flew the animals to
St. Louis via Columbus, Ohio. Toto Tembo was given a rousing welcome at the zoo by large numbers of children who had gathered there.
He quickly became the zoo's main attraction, but unfortunately con-
tracted pneumonia and died a short time later.[6]

By late 1934 the Johnsons' commercial film *Baboona* was ready for
release. As part of its pre-premiere promotion, Martin and Osa participated in a one-day round-trip flight between Newark and Miami
aboard an Eastern Air Line transport piloted by the famous aviator
Eddie Rickenbacker. During the trip, which set a new speed record,

the Johnsons projected *Baboona*, which became the first sound movie ever to be shown in flight. Another part of the film's promotional campaign was a nationwide contest for a free round-trip to Africa aboard the *City of New York*, offered by the ship's owners, the Farrell Lines.[7]

Baboona had a gala premiere at the Rialto Theater in New York City on the evening of January 22, 1935. The Johnsons' own guest list included many who were associated with the museum, industrial and financial leaders such as Harry Sinclair, Walter Chrysler, Richard K. Mellon, Henry Williams Sage, and Bayard Colgate, and well-known celebrities, among whom were the boxing champion Gene Tunney, Lowell Thomas, and Eddie Rickenbacker. Both of Carl Akeley's wives were invited—his first wife, Deelia, for whom the Johnsons had great affection, and Mary L. Jobe, with whom they maintained a correct but distant relationship.[8]

The film deservedly received widespread praise. From a technical perspective, it was the best film they had produced to date. The *New York World Telegram* called it "fascinating . . . startling . . . breathtaking," while *Showman's Trade Review* said that it was the "best of big game expedition films." The *New York Times*, although it allowed that the film "possesses fascination," faulted it for devoting an "unconscionable sum of footage to the minor domestic activities of the Johnsons." Richard Watts, Jr., the film critic for the *New York Herald*, wrote an especially acidic review:

> Mrs. Martin Johnson, slightly assisted by her loyal and retiring husband, darts coyly about the continent of Africa . . . making the natives and animals love her. By a fine exercise of restraint, the valiant lady indulges in a minimum of nose-powdering. . . . Most of the time, in fact, you will find her in happy domestic attitudes. . . . The pygmies . . . appear in their customary supporting role, although they are no longer cast for the one-time comedy part . . . that is because Mr. Johnson forgot to bring along the cigars.[9]

Baboona grossed $15,000 during its first week's showing at the Rialto, and $5,500 the second week. These were sizable receipts considering that the country was in the depths of the Great Depression. Theater managers around the country booked it, and their assessment of it was summed up by R. B. Garvin, the manager of the People's Theatre in Fredonia, Kansas, who told the *Motion Picture Herald* that it was "one of the best the Johnsons have produced."[10] In retrospect, it was the high technical quality of the film and the novelty of seeing Africa from the air that primarily carried it to success. The story line was a familiar one, built around the Johnsons' actual trip. Highlights included a rhino spearing sequence and contrived scenes shot in the backyard studio showing a troop of baboons under attack from a leopard. Yet the 6,663 feet of *Baboona*, unlike most of the Johnsons' previous films, contains few racial sight gags. Martin's narration is at times poetic, and, in sharp contrast with his characterizations in the film *Congorilla*, he speaks of the Mbuti pygmies as "old friends" and as "the happiest people in the world." While both Martin and Osa were listed on the credits as coproducers, only Martin was credited with the actual photography. Truman Talley, who had supervised the editing of *Congorilla*, did the same for *Baboona*, assisted by Lew Lehr and Russell Shields.[11]

During the early part of 1935, Martin, who was now fifty years old, completed the manuscript for what would be his last book, *Over African Jungles*. Published by Harcourt Brace and Company in the fall of that year, it is probably the best written of all his books. Ghosting and editorial assistance certainly helped, but the book's strengths also emanated from Martin himself. He was more intent on marveling at the wonders of Africa than in conquering them. He realized that he had in fact achieved his goal of being "as big a man in my way as Jack London is in his."[12] He was comfortably settling into success and middle age, and took more pleasure in reminiscing about the past than in planning new challenges for the future. He considered *Over African Jungles* his literary magnum opus, and expressed his great pride in it one evening to his mother-in-law as he sorted out galleys on the floor of their Essex House apartment. Reviewers thought well of it, too, the *Manchester Guardian* calling it "fascinating" and the *New York Times* "absorbing."[13]

The Johnsons' decision to travel to North Borneo (Sabah) in 1935 did not so much represent a response to challenge as it did a desire to revisit a familiar place where a commercially viable film could be made. In many ways, this trip was less of an expedition in the accepted sense of the times, and more a leisurely visit to a place where there were few real dangers. Martin expressed this notion at a luncheon on August 8 at the Hotel Gotham in New York City, where he told 150 members of the Circus Saints and Sinners Club and the Adventurers Club that the main purpose of the trip was "fun."[14]

The Johnsons left for North Borneo on August 12, 1935, on the Dutch steamer *Kota Pinang*. They took with them an American staff of two, James Laneri, a pilot, and Joseph Tilton, a cameraman who later became a distinguished photojournalist.[15] The smaller of the two

Sikorsky amphibians, renamed *The Spirit of Africa and Borneo*, was placed in a cradle on the deck, and two hundred boxes and crates were put in the hold. The trip to Belawan, Sumatra, via the Suez Canal and the Indian Ocean, took a month. Once there, they reassembled the plane and transferred their cargo to the *Maradu* for the final leg of the voyage to Sandakan, North Borneo. While Laneri piloted the Johnsons via Singapore, Tilton sailed on the *Maradu*. They stayed in Singapore for ten days as guests of the Sultan of Johore and then flew to Kuching in Sarawak, where the British Rajah, Vyner Brooke, gave a dinner in their honor. From there, they went on to the small island of Labuan before flying over the then impenetrable Crocker Range and the rain forest of North Borneo. This was the first flight over the interior of North Borneo, and permission for it was first denied on the grounds that it was too dangerous.

At the time of the Johnsons' arrival, North Borneo was administered by the British North Borneo Company and was a protectorate of the British Crown. There were fewer than a hundred Europeans in this quiet backwater of the world, most of whom were either employees or dependents of employees of the company. Among these was Henry G. Keith, then the conservator of forests and director of agriculture of North Borneo. He and his wife, Agnes Newton Keith, an American by birth and a writer, became close friends of the Johnsons and greatly facilitated their work in the territory. The government provided the Johnsons with an eight-room residence in Sandakan free of charge in return for photographs of the country, its peoples, and the fauna. The Keiths helped them recruit a staff, among whom was Logan, who served as an interpreter, and Saudin bin Labutau, who cared for their captured animals. In sharp contrast with their characterization of alien peoples in earlier works, Osa said of Saudin that "Martin and he became . . . great friends."[16]

In order to film the wildlife of North Borneo, Martin and Osa built a small settlement on the Kinabatangan River near Abai. Covering an area of four city blocks, the site was first cleared of rain forest, after which carpenters sent out from Sandakan built several buildings from bamboo and palm fronds. In addition to personal quarters for themselves, the Johnsons built a house for Laneri and Tilton, a mess hall, a hangar for the plane, quarters for their staff, and a guest house, storeroom, and photographic laboratory. Because of the risk of fire, the buildings were widely separated from one another. In order to deal with heavy rains and flooding, elevated earthen pathways were constructed connecting all of the buildings. While the camp was being built under the supervision of a Filipino named Mendoza who spoke fluent English, the Johnsons flew out each day from Sandakan, a trip that required only an hour, compared to six hours by boat. Their chief carpenter, Ching Wo, a Chinese, not only constructed the buildings but also made all of the furniture. Once the camp was completed, Martin and Osa named it "Johnsonville."

There were striking differences between the Abai camp in Borneo and the Lake Paradise camp in Africa. These differences reflected not only distinct architectural responses to unique environments, but also the purposes of the respective missions. At Lake Paradise, the threat from elephant, rhino, lion, and leopard were constant, creating a need for protective thornbush enclosures and sturdy buildings. At Abai, no such threats existed. The Johnsons' sense of mission and commitment of time also shaped these camps. The sturdy camp at Lake Paradise, with its pens for livestock and its garden, spoke of the seriousness of the mission and a long-term commitment. The lightweight buildings of Abai, on the other hand, reflected that they were intended for a short time. The risks at Abai were also few compared to those at Lake Paradise. In case of serious illness, Abai was but an hour by plane from Sandakan. By contrast, Nairobi was a hard two- to three-day trip by road from Lake Paradise.

To some extent, the Johnsons' own staff at Abai reflected the ethnic diversity of North Borneo. The indigenous population consists of several groups—Murut, Bajau, Dusun, and Kadazan (Dyak), within which there are subdivisions. Immigrant groups include the Chinese, Indians, Malays, and Filipinos. Mendoza, who supervised all the staff, was Filipino, as was John Calero, the airplane mechanic. Feeli, a woman who later starred in their film, was Malayan-Filipino; Saudin, the animal keeper, was a Murut; and Logan, a guide and interpreter, was Indian.

Once the Abai camp was functioning, the Johnsons were able to begin filming wildlife. Martin hired Feeli's father, a Filipino trapper who regularly sold captured animals in Sandakan, to bring in a large number of monkeys, which were placed in a studio cage at the campsite. As he had done in Kenya, Martin filmed and photographed a number of animals in this studio, including deer, civet, wild pigs, and honey bear. Although he occasionally used 300-mm telephoto lenses, Tilton recalled that he preferred working with the shorter focal length lenses that produced sharper images. Having the animals in captivity enabled Martin and Tilton to make close-ups using these shorter lenses. In addition, the two men filmed from blinds near salt licks and water holes.

Over the next several months, Martin, Osa, and their staff made several excursions to different parts of North Borneo. They visited the Tenggara headhunters whom they had first photographed sixteen years before, and filmed the Murut, Dusun, and Kadazan (Dyak) peoples and some of their rituals and customs. In addition, they made a special trip by raft and *gobong* (dugout) up the Kinabatangan in order to obtain the first pictures of proboscis monkeys in the wild.

There was not much to keep Osa occupied at Abai, and humidity, rain, insects, and the hard soil foiled her attempts to create a garden. Contrary to his practice in Africa, Martin allowed alcohol in the camp, but kept a close eye on it. Despite his vigilance, Osa occasionally became intoxicated in the procession of overcast, rainy, and boring days during which she found little to do. Tilton recalled many years later that Osa rarely used a camera during the trip, though she was very much involved in setting up shots.[17] Six months after they had been in North Borneo, she wrote to her mother about the film they were producing: "This climate is the very dickens to deal with. It is so hot that when I put on my makeup for the movies it just melts. . . . We have been getting some very nice movies. . . . This is a very different picture than we have ever made and I do think it will go over great . . . if it doesn't, I will certainly be very blue."[18]

Martin later wrote to Charmian describing their trip up the Kinabatangan by raft:

> I do keep a diary of notes of each day's happenings for reference when I get back and write my new book. . . . Each morning I am up at four o'clock . . . shave, eat breakfast. By daylight, I am ready for the day's work . . . first loading movie and still cameras . . . then we either photograph the river people who collect here at camp . . . go into the jungle after animals or perhaps fly into the interior where we land on rivers and swamps and photograph what we see. . . . We live for days or sometimes weeks on our bamboo raft. This raft has four rooms, our bedroom, a darkroom, a kitchen, and a storeroom. On it we have a kerosine Electrolux refrigerator and a small electric light plant.[19]

Although Martin and Osa were in the depths of the Borneo rain forest, they took along a bit of civilization with them. Their creature comforts on the raft were reminiscent of those George Eastman had taken along on the *Dal* when they sailed up the Nile in 1928. Nonetheless, the interior of North Borneo was a harsh place, where daily rains amounting to 250 inches a year, constant humidity, and insects plagued both the Johnson party and their camera equipment. In addition, no roads had yet pierced the interior, which was still largely impenetrable except by air and river craft. Thus, when they were away from their plane up the narrow affluents of the Kinabatangan, they were indeed completely cut off for days from the outside world.

The unbearable climate, daily frustrations in filming wildlife, and Osa's alcoholic binges placed Martin under enormous stress. On one occasion, he physically assaulted two carpenters who were not performing up to his expectations, and only Harry Keith's intervention prevented him from being put in jail. Visible strains also appeared in his relationship with Osa. She usually became aggressive and argumentative when drunk, and Martin often resorted to slapping her in order to stop her screaming. He told Tilton and Laneri that he was fed up with her drinking, no longer knew what to do with her, and that he was seriously thinking of divorcing her when he returned to the United States.[20] This statement about divorce is more revealing of the stress he was under than of real intent. Agnes Newton Keith observed that Martin's anger was easily aroused and that when dealing with his local staff he would "swear at them and threaten to beat them up at one moment, and write gift checks for them the next."[21] His mercurial expressions of anger over Osa's alcoholism were understandable, especially under the stress of Borneo's hot, humid, and insect-infested jungles.

Yet, it is unlikely that Martin would ever have actually carried out his threat and sought a divorce. It was not just love that cemented his relationship with Osa, but also shared experiences and hardships spanning a quarter of a century. They were not only joined by marriage, but also by a professional partnership that sustained his enormous success. This success was due in large measure to Osa's faithful and understanding support, and a denial of her own hopes for a home and children. She had sacrificed what was most dear to her so that he could lead the life of a wanderer. Although she reaped substitute rewards of wealth and fame, these never gave her the satisfaction she was seeking. Martin was well aware of this, but his own ambitions and the social conventions governing a wife's role prevented him from considering a course that would have placed her needs first. Her claim that alcohol gave her refuge from the anxiety, loneliness, and depression she often felt while on expeditions did not completely ring true since she also drank at home. Still, Martin felt some responsibility for her drinking, and on occasion expressed guilt over not giving her the affection and attention she needed. Yet he could never bring himself to deal with the root causes of her unhappiness, but rather sought temporary solutions molded around their itinerant life-style.[22]

The high point of the trip was the capture of two full-grown male orangutans, one of which, later named Truson, was placed in the Bronx Zoo in New York City. The Johnsons captured seventeen orangutans in all, but most escaped. Osa's written description of the capture of Truson and Martin's later film record of it are shocking to audiences several decades removed from the event. The Johnsons' film editors anticipated possible contemporary objections to the capture by justifying it on the grounds that the animal was terrorizing a native village. So little was known then about these gentle apes that no one publicly challenged this now obvious fiction. In order to make audiences even more unsympathetic, the orangutan was described by Lowell Thomas in the Johnsons' subsequent film *Borneo* as a devil beast, old gloomy face, a brute, the fiercest battler on earth, and as fierce and morose with a somber and scowling face. To facilitate the capture, Martin had Laneri fly the plane over the treetop where the animal had taken refuge. When this failed, he had tear-gas billies fired at the ape, but these too proved unsuccessful. Finally, suffering from thirst and hunger after three days' entrapment in the tree, the animal rushed down toward the ground, only to be caught in nets borrowed from the New York City Fire Department.

This climax of the film *Borneo* thrilled audiences even through the 1950s. Yet several decades later, it is highly offensive to audiences that are fully aware of the gentle nature of these animals, their endangered status, and the brutality of the Johnsons' means of capture. Yet it must be remembered that Martin and Osa, as well as most others who encountered full-grown male orangutans in the wild, considered them extremely dangerous. It required a few more decades and the scientific field work of animal behaviorists to overturn long-established beliefs.

By September 1936 the Johnsons had obtained all of the film footage they required.[23] As they prepared to leave North Borneo, they disposed of their unused supplies by giving them away. The Keiths inherited their refrigerator and canned foods, and thanks to Osa's generosity, Agnes's "dressing table had Fifth Avenue beauty creams and lotions as it had never seen before." The Keiths were not the only recipients of their generosity. They gave their local staff parting cash bonuses and other gifts. This generosity marked their relationships wherever they went, and was regularly extended to everyone from colonial officials to the staff who performed the most menial tasks. Osa in fact upset British colonial standards in North Borneo for master-servant relationships by "showering clothing on the female servants" and by allowing them to iron in the living room. This generosity of theirs is certainly not apparent in their writings because it was censored by their own modesty. Kindness, generosity, and democratic relationships fostered enormous affection for them among their staff in North Borneo. Agnes Newton Keith poignantly described how the Johnsons' former staff came to her in a group when the radio announced Martin's death and whispered over and over, "He was so good to us."[24]

Martin and Osa left Sandakan by ship bound for Singapore, where they picked up the Blue Funnel Line freighter *Myrmidon* bound for New York City via India, Cape Town, and Dakar. They traveled with a large menagerie of animals, including several orangutans and gibbons which were cared for by Saudin aboard the ship. They arrived in New York City on October 25 with 151,000 feet of film and three thousand still photographs.[25]

While the press expressed interest in the Johnsons' film and pictures, it was their three-hundred-pound orangutan who stole the headlines. Bringing fierce animals back alive from the wilds had by then become a necessary achievement for many explorers. Both scientists and the public believed that these animals were extremely dangerous, thus providing living proof of an explorer's prowess and courage. A contemporary of the Johnsons, Frank Buck, achieved fame as an explorer and hunter for the cargoes of wild animals he brought back from Africa and elsewhere. The title of his 1932 film, *Bring 'Em Back Alive*, not only became an aphorism but also created a requirement for those who professed to be explorers.[26] Thus, in capturing animals in Africa and Borneo, the Johnsons were not simply meeting the requests of zoo directors, but, more important, were living up to their public image.

CHAPTER FIFTEEN

1937

In late October, Martin and Osa introduced their three-hundred-pound orangutan to the press. Housed in a specially built cage at the American Museum of Natural History, he was named Truson, the indigenous name for the small streams that cut through the Borneo rain forest. Journalists flocked to see him because he was the largest orangutan ever captured in the wild and brought to the United States, and also because of his presumed viciousness. Despite public preconceptions and Martin's comments that he was dangerous, Truson meekly sat in his cage eating honeydew melon, oblivious to the crowd of onlookers. Truson obviously did not meet journalistic expectations, nor did his keeper, Saudin, who was dubbed the "Wild Boy of Borneo," an obvious play on the popular expression, the "Wild Man of Borneo."[1]

Saudin was an intelligent, perceptive, and sensitive nineteen-year-old who had never been outside of North Borneo. He rapidly adapted to living in New York City's complex environment, and later gave an account of his experiences to Agnes Newton Keith, who published it in the *Atlantic Monthly* in 1938, and in her book, *Land Below the Wind*. Prominent in his story is the great affection he had for Martin and Osa, which he also expressed in letters he wrote later. Martin gave him tours of the city and took him to boxing and wrestling matches while Osa mothered him. They showed him how to use the slot machines at a Horn and Hardart Automat, purchased clothes for him, including nine neckties, and took him on a flight to Connecticut, where they visited their pilot, James Laneri.

While at Laneri's house, Saudin was invited to sit down at the dinner table with all the guests, but was "ashamed to eat with them because I did not know how to eat the food cleverly as they did."

Although he was terrified of descending in elevators, he said nothing, fearing that people might think of him as "just a jungle man." Eventually, Saudin learned to negotiate city traffic and make his way from the hotel to the Central Park Zoo, where he cared for the Johnsons' animals.

Because of immigration regulations and the Johnsons' imminent lecture tour, Saudin had to be sent back to North Borneo. Martin booked passage for him on the Dutch freighter *Kota Djandi*, which was to sail on January 1. "I was very sad to hear this," Saudin later told Keith, "he was very good to me . . . I cried like a child." Even a trip to Times Square on New Year's Eve failed to cheer him up. He cried when Martin said good-bye to him the next day at the hotel and when Osa left him at the ship. Martin and Osa also shed tears, and as her mother later commented, felt as if they were losing a son.[2]

Since returning to New York City, Martin had been busy cutting the Borneo film footage with Lillian Seebach and handling his office work from a room at the American Museum of Natural History. By mid-December, they had put together a silent lecture film, *Jungle Depths of Borneo* (also called *Adventuring through Borneo*), and had begun to cut sound negative for the commercial film *Borneo*, to be released by Twentieth Century-Fox. Martin had always arranged their lecture tours, usually by signing on with one of the vaudeville circuits. However, by the late 1930s, lecture tours were being arranged outside the framework of vaudeville circuits by speakers' bureaus and lecture agencies. Agents had become an indispensable element in these often complex tours, which, if successfully organized, provided an enormous level of exposure.

Martin, who had long resisted using an agent, now realized that they had to employ one if they were to be successful. In the fall of 1936, he hired Clark Hallan Getts, the forty-three-year-old director of Clark H. Getts, Inc., a lecture and radio production bureau that booked both speakers and performing artists. Clark had already managed successful tours for the pianist Jan Paderewski and the writers Theodore Dreiser and Sherwood Anderson. Born in Whitehall, Wisconsin, in 1893, he had received an A.B. degree from the University of Wisconsin in 1914, and an L.L.B. degree from Columbia University in 1916. From 1920 to 1926, he was a journalist in China representing both British and American newspapers. For a three-year period after his return to the United States, he lectured widely on China and Manchuria. Following this, he worked for the National Broadcasting Company promoting lecture tours, and then in 1933 established his own lecture bureau.[3]

Clark was intelligent, sophisticated, and creative. His many interests included art, literature, current events, and history. Although his young company was a small one, he was highly respected in the field, and more important as far as Martin and Osa were concerned, he produced results. By December 1936 he had arranged an $87,000 nationwide lecture and radio tour for the Johnsons that was to begin in Salt Lake City, Utah.

Martin and Osa flew to Salt Lake City, where they presented their lecture to several thousand children gathered in the Mormon Tabernacle. Clark, who did not travel with them, remained in New York City, where he worked at securing additional bookings. On the morning of January 12, 1937, Martin and Osa boarded Western Air Express's flight Number 7 bound for California and Burbank's Union Air Terminal. They had each paid $34.75 for one-way tickets and an additional $17.51 for 103 pounds of excess baggage. The plane, a twin-engine Boeing 247, was piloted by William W. Lewis and copiloted by Clifford P. Owens. After an uneventful flight to Las Vegas, the plane was delayed for thirty-three minutes by Western Air Express's chief dispatcher in Burbank because of uncertain weather conditions. At 9:00 A.M., the dispatcher instructed Lewis to fly to Daggett, California, where he was told he would be given additional instructions. Once over Daggett, Lewis communicated by radio with the Burbank dispatcher, advising him that he would be over Palmdale at 10:40 A.M. and would arrive at Union Air Terminal twenty-five minutes later. Lewis in turn was told that the ceiling at Palmdale was 2,000 feet with light snow, that at Saugus it was 800 feet with light rain, and that at Burbank it was 3,000 feet with a lower stratum of clouds at 1,500 feet around the east hills. Given the low ceiling, Lewis requested and received permission to make an instrument landing at Burbank.

Western Air Express had adopted well-defined procedures for making an instrument approach into Burbank that had been approved by the U.S. Department of Commerce. These included the use of various radio beams and the prompt initiation of de-icing on descent through cloud cover in which ice was apt to form. Arriving near Burbank, Lewis nosed the plane down into the overcast at the 5,500-foot level. As he did so, he instructed copilot Owens to turn on the deicers. For unknown reasons, Owens failed to do so. As ice built up in the carburetors, the plane began to toss and roll, and Lewis had difficulty controlling it. Matters were made worse because Lewis had unwisely turned off the Saugus station beam, a clear violation of established procedures, and was navigating by imprecise average compass readings. During the seventeen-mile trip from Saugus to Burbank, he strayed three miles off course to the east. Thus, as he entered the Newhall Pass, he was three miles closer to the fog-shrouded San Gabriel Mountains than he should have been. Osa later gave a vivid description of this phase of the flight: "We got into very bad weather . . . the plane was doing all sorts of funny things. . . . It was all over the sky. . . . We seemed to be going down in the plane like a dive. . . . He (the pilot) throttled back the motors and was gliding in just a few minutes before, a very few, and I remember praying to God that we would hit the airport."[4]

As they neared Los Pinetos peak, the plane "just sunk," as Lewis later testified, "sunk with what we commonly call a down draft. . . . I looked back to see how much ice there was on the airplane, and what did I see, thorn bushes." The plane crashed into the mountain with a tremendous impact that sheared off the motors and split the fuselage. The sound of the crash was so loud that it was clearly heard by tuberculosis patients at the Olive View Sanitarium four miles away.

Martin and Osa were immediately knocked unconscious by the impact. One of the nine passengers, James A. Braden, president of the Braden-Sutphin Ink Company of Cleveland, was killed instantly and his body thrown on top of Osa. Another passenger, Arthur Robinson of Rochester, New York, managed to crawl out of the wreck and make his way to the sanitarium, despite a fractured ankle. A rescue party of doctors and nurses immediately set out from Olive View, followed by another rescue party dispatched by Sheriff Eugene Biscailuz of Newhall. The group from Newhall made its way up the peak on foot and by using a buckboard pulled by six mules. By the time the rescue teams arrived, most of the survivors had regained consciousness, and their screams were clearly audible for several miles around.

Martin's injuries were extensive and serious, and included multiple bilateral fractures of the jaw, fractures of both legs, a cerebral concussion, and a fractured nose. He quickly became delirious with pain. Osa tried to comfort him and reached over to wipe his brow despite the fact that she could barely move and was in great pain herself from a fractured right knee and back injuries. Finally, when the physicians from the sanitarium arrived in the early afternoon, they gave Martin morphine, which eased his pain. He, Osa, and the other injured passengers were carried to the twenty-square-foot space of the glass-enclosed Los Pinetos Fire Lookout Tower, one hundred yards away. From there, they were later carried on stretchers, five miles down the mountainside to ambulances waiting on U.S. Highway 99. It was dark when they reached the ambulances, which took them to Good Samaritan Hospital in Los Angeles.

Several hours elapsed from the time of the crash until Martin, Osa, and the other passengers were hospitalized and given appropriate treatment. The treatment available then for trauma victims was rudimentary compared to the interventions developed several decades later. Matters were complicated not only by the time delay but also by Martin's untreated diabetes mellitus. Thus, from the very outset, his survival was in doubt.[5]

When they arrived at the hospital, both Martin and Osa were placed under the care of Dr. Sidney Rogers Burnap, a fifty-three-year-old physician who was a 1909 graduate of Columbia University's College of Physicians and Surgeons. Burnap was not a board-certified surgeon, but limited his practice to that specialty.[6] As he and his staff desperately tried to reverse Martin's state of shock, Western Air Express and Olive View Sanitarium sent telegrams to Osa's mother, Belle, assuring her that the Johnsons were not seriously injured. She had set out by train from Chanute for Los Angeles as soon as news of the accident reached her. As her train got closer to Los Angeles, the news became more guarded.

Martin slipped into coma in the early morning hours of January 13. However, Burnap kept this news from Osa out of concern that it might worsen her own condition. As she slept in a heavily sedated state nearby, Martin's breathing grew more labored and his coma more profound. Burnap's efforts proved increasingly futile, and shortly after sunrise Martin died.

The news of Martin's death flashed across the country by radio just as the early morning editions of newspapers were announcing his and Osa's survival in the crash the day before. The outpouring of public grief that followed reflected not only the enormous affection people had for him, but also the fact that he was a gallant national hero who had been prematurely and tragically struck down. A January 14, 1937, *New York Times* editorial best summed up the feelings of most in saying: "Would that he might come back to us from his last adventure—and with his camera."

Belle received the tragic news of Martin's death aboard the train, which did not arrive in Los Angeles until 3:30 P.M. She immediately went to the hospital and agreed with Burnap that Osa not be told yet. Although the world knew of Martin's death, Osa was unaware of it until the following day, when Burnap gently told her, "I have some bad news for you." Osa had already begun suspecting the worst when her requests to see Martin were politely denied. "Oh, I knew it," she exclaimed to Burnap and Belle, "I just knew it." She took the news much better than either Burnap or Belle had anticipated. Yet it was clear to both of them that Osa was devastated by Martin's death, and they constantly worried about its impact on her recovery.[7]

Osa's friends rallied to support her as best they could. In New York, Daniel Pomeroy immediately assumed responsibility for paying the salaries of the Johnsons' staff, which included their secretary, Elizabeth Welsch; an office boy, Philip Shea; their film-editing assistant, Lillian Seebach; and a maid, Grace Bryant. He also advanced $1,000 to cover Osa's medical care. Granton T. Stanford, the general counsel for the Sinclair Oil Corporation, who was a friend from New

York City, contacted his assistant, R. W. Ragland, in Los Angeles and instructed him to give Osa and Belle all the help he could. Ragland was at the Los Angeles train station to meet Belle and assumed all the responsibilities for arranging Martin's funeral. Stanford even advanced $1,008.82 to cover the cost of a casket, burial clothes, and temporary entombment at Forest Lawn Cemetery.

Both Pomeroy and Stanford knew that Martin and Osa had little financial liquidity when they set off on this lecture tour. Most of their funds were tied up in their soon-to-be-released film, *Borneo*. Thus, as Osa lay in her hospital bed recovering from the shock of Martin's death and her own injuries, she was in serious financial difficulty. In addition, she had little experience in business matters, which Martin had always handled, complicated now by the need to settle his estate. The decisions that she faced involved not only finances and Martin's estate, but also her own future life and career. Pomeroy knew her vulnerabilities and recommended that she retain his lawyer, Marshall McLean. McLean in turn engaged Clarence M. Hanson, a Los Angeles attorney, to represent Osa in a planned lawsuit against Western Air Express. Yet neither Pomeroy nor McLean could be of much help with regard to her future because that was something she herself had to decide.

While Pomeroy, Stanford, and McLean tried to assist Osa with financial matters, Charmian London and Agnes Newton Keith came to comfort her in the hospital.[8] Belle, who had arrived the day Martin died, remained with Osa throughout her hospitalization, as did her brother, Vaughn. It was obvious to Clark Getts that he had to go out to Los Angeles, if for no other reason than to receive instructions from Osa about the now temporarily suspended lecture tour. Belle and Vaughn strongly resented his arrival a week after Martin's death. "He just came in and took over," Belle complained years later, "pushing us aside and deciding what was to be done." Clark, however, felt that he had to take a strong hand and rescue Osa from both her mother and Vaughn:

> Vaughn had stocked the closet in Osa's hospital room with enough liquor to open a cash bar. Mrs. Leighty was kind and well intentioned but unable to come to terms with the fact that Osa couldn't manage her affairs on her own. Salvaging the lecture tour was the surest way of making Osa financially secure. Mrs. Leighty and Vaughn obviously didn't trust me nor like me either, and insisted on accompanying the tour. I told them that we couldn't travel across the country with a caravan, incurring added expenses on their account.[9]

Osa was determined from the very outset to resume the tour, and viewed it not only as a tribute to Martin's work and ideals, but also a financial necessity. Thus she needed no convincing from Clark when he arrived. However, they sharply differed about Belle and Vaughn accompanying the tour. Clark was aware of Osa's problem with alcohol and flatly refused to take "a personal bartender along." While he won on this point, he had to compromise regarding Belle, allowing her to travel with them on the initial phases of the tour, which began after Martin's funeral.

On February 23, 1937, Osa left Los Angeles by train and accompanied Martin's body to Chanute for burial. Four days later, two thousand people attended the funeral at the Municipal Auditorium, where the Reverend J. J. McInery of St. Patrick's Roman Catholic Church and a friend of Martin's recalled that air crashes had recently taken the lives of several famous men, including Will Rogers, Knute Rockne, and Wiley Post. Many of Martin's and Osa's friends attended, including F. Trubee Davison and his wife, Thomas Craig of Eastman-Kodak, James Laneri, and Vern Carstens, all of whom served as honorary pallbearers.[10]

Osa's relations with Freda Cripps, Martin's only sister, had now become strained on two accounts. Osa had vetoed Freda's plan for burying Martin in Independence, and Freda for her part was proving uncooperative with regard to her brother's will. Martin's will, which had been drawn up in Chanute on June 10, 1935, was probated in New York City on March 12, some two weeks after the funeral. In it, he bequeathed Freda a 20 percent share in his films, still pictures, and writings, with the remaining 80 percent going to Osa. Osa did not begrudge Freda this amount.[11] However, she and Clark were seriously worried that it would enable Freda to create mischief with regard to lecture tours and future derivative films. And indeed, she was already proving unreasonable, demanding that she receive 20 percent of the proceeds from Osa's lectures in which Martin's films were used. This was unacceptable to Osa, since income from lectures reflected not only the film used, but also her own personal appearances and hard work. Despite this persuasive argument, Freda remained obstinate and hired a lawyer to protect her interests. Her attorney fortunately saw the reasonableness of Osa's position, and convinced her to accept a film rental fee of $25 per lecture day. However, when Osa's second lecture tour got under way in the fall of 1937, Freda once again became obstinate, provoking a rebuke from Osa: "For many years, Martin and I have been sending funds to the Johnson family, often when we did not have them to spare, and ALWAYS with my full consent and approval."[12] Freda eventually agreed to the $25 daily fee, which she was regularly paid as long as Osa gave lectures using Martin's films. These fees, in addition to her 20 percent share in the royalties from the commercial films and books, gave her annual incomes of several thousand dollars in the late 1930s and early 1940s.[13]

Clark had relaunched the lecture tour while Osa was still in the hospital by having Joseph Tilton narrate the film. It opened in Pasadena, California, on February 9, and Osa said a few words to the audience from her hospital bed over a telephone hookup. Following Martin's funeral, she joined Tilton and was on tour in the South and Midwest throughout April and May. During these lectures, Osa said a few words from her wheelchair before turning the program over to Tilton. At first, booking Osa alone was a problem, as Clark later recalled. "The country was so sexist then that many theater managers didn't like the idea of a woman lecturing alone." In addition, theaters and sponsors insisted that she be billed not as Osa Johnson but as Mrs. Martin Johnson, on account of name recognition.

While Osa, Tilton, and Clark were on tour, McLean tried to settle Martin's estate. In March he collected on a $12,000 life insurance policy Martin had taken out with the Sun Life Assurance Society of London. Aside from the life insurance, Martin's estate was valued at only $10,000, consisting of a small amount of cash, the two airplanes stored at United Aircraft Corporation in East Hartford, Connecticut, 400,000 feet of movie film, 10,000 still negatives, several feature films, seven movie cameras, seven still cameras, and eleven trophies, including the head of the elephant shot at Lake Paradise in 1922. In addition to the expected bills, McLean had to deal with three claims against the estate. One of these was made by Lina Pictures Corporation, with which Martin had a contract for the distribution of some of his pictures. This claim was finally defeated in 1940 after it had gone to trial and had been rejected on appeal. A second claim was made by a taxidermist, John Murgatroyd, who had badly prepared some of Martin's trophies several years before. Because of their poor quality, Martin had refused to pay Murgatroyd's bill, and had some of the trophies redone by Jonas Brothers, the well-known taxidermists in Mt. Vernon, New York. This claim was eventually settled for $1,000.[14] The third claim came from a trusted friend, James Laneri.

At Martin's funeral, Osa was, as she later said, "out of my mind" with grief and shock. It was then that Laneri, who was unemployed, persuaded her to hire him. Their agreement called for him to repair the two planes in Connecticut and to be billed for time and materials. Laneri had also proposed that they go barnstorming together in one of the planes in May and June. Osa later said that she never made a firm commitment to Laneri about barnstorming, although it is possible she did at a time of great mental confusion. Such a proposal from a trusted friend would have been very appealing to Osa, who then needed the support of a strong man. However, once Clark's influence had asserted itself, Osa claimed that she had never agreed to the barnstorming proposal. Laneri, however, insisted that she had, and demanded to be compensated because, as a result of their understanding, he had turned down an offer from Pan American Airways.[15] McLean personally met with Laneri, and made allowances for his poor accounting methods. However, he seems to have concluded that Osa's agreement to the barnstorming proposal was firmer than either she or Clark were now willing to admit. As a result, on August 13, 1937, he wrote Osa and enclosed a blank check for her to fill out and sign. While acknowledging that Laneri had already been paid $900, he suggested that he be given $640 to cover recent expenses and be provided with some additional compensation for the cancellation of the barnstorming venture.

Clark, who had already become the new man in Osa's life, seems to have been behind her obstinate refusal to pay Laneri. Instead of filling in an amount and signing the check, she sent it back to McLean with a letter saying that "like many other people, Jim probably has the opinion that I am now quite rich and, being a woman, very 'easy' to persuade in business matters. . . . But for this job, he would have been starving these several months."[16] At the same time that she was writing this to McLean, she was telling others how fortunate she was in having an excellent manager like Clark. It was uncharacteristic of Osa to quibble over a few hundred dollars, especially with someone like Laneri, who was a good friend. While her letters of refusal bore her signature, they were clearly written by Clark, whose intent was not so much accurate accounting, but rather denial of satisfaction to a former admirer. In the end, McLean's wisdom finally prevailed, and Laneri's claim was settled for $1,000.[17]

Seebach spent the early months of 1937 working with Truman Talley at Twentieth Century-Fox, preparing *Borneo* for release. Martin had originally planned to narrate the film, but with his death, Fox hired Lowell Thomas to do so, a task which he completed in April.[18] Seebach, who had worked for months on the film, was extremely upset that Talley omitted her name from the credit title. She wrote to Osa, reminding her that "Mr. Johnson always gave me credit as film cutter on all his pictures." Clark, however, had no intentions of taking the matter up with Talley, since he was negotiating an important contract with Fox for Osa to function as a technical consultant on Darryl F. Zanuck's film *Stanley and Livingstone*. Instead, he had Osa sign a harsh letter to Seebach, rebuking her for not being more efficient in producing the new Borneo lecture film they planned to use in the fall. In the same letter, Osa also took Seebach to task for speaking her mind to Dr. Sidney Burnap, who had treated the Johnsons. Seebach found his bills outrageously exorbitant, which they were, and told him so.[19]

In early June, Osa and Clark flew to Hollywood and signed a contract with Zanuck. Although Zanuck hired Osa as a technical adviser to Otto Brower, who was to shoot parts of the film on location in Africa, Clark was hopeful that the contact would serve to promote a screen career for her. Unfortunately, while Osa had an actress's presence, she had little acting talent. More importantly, on returning from Africa, she was inebriated when she walked into Zanuck's office. Clark, who like Martin kept a close eye on her, recalled that she went to powder her nose, and in the process consumed two miniature bottles of liquor. Whatever hopes he had of advancing Osa's acting career were dashed when she staggered toward Zanuck's desk.[20]

Osa and Clark sailed from New York City on the *Normandie* on June 16, 1937. From London, they took the Imperial Airways flying boat to Kenya. Osa's role during the three months they spent in East Africa was considerable. Brower relied on her advice about locations, recruiting almost a thousand Africans, for filming wildlife sequences and for running a camp with twenty-five whites and several hundred Africans.[21] Forty years later, Clark proudly recalled that Osa was "truly magnificent when out in the bush. She was at her best then and had no equal. She knew the habits of the animals better than anyone and was a master at bush craft."[22]

While Osa and Clark were in Africa, Twentieth Century-Fox released *Borneo*. It opened in New York City on September 3 at the Rialto and initially brought in $8,000 per week.[23] From a technical standpoint, it is by far Martin's finest film. He not only used cinematographic techniques made possible by advanced camera systems, but also demonstrated his own evolving artistry and creativity. The narrative by Lowell Thomas, however, shows the absence of Martin's influence and a regression to the sort of racial sight gags and sensationalism that had characterized the film *Congorilla*. Martin had successfully kept most of these out of *Baboona*, despite pressures from film editors, but they reappear in force in *Borneo*. For example, Thomas describes the Johnsons' workers at Abai as "the laziest people on earth. Work of any kind bores them to tears. Their principal activity is boating, cooking, cock-fighting and gambling."

In the scenes showing the proboscis monkeys, Lew Lehr, a veteran newsreel spoofer, speaks with an affected German accent. He refers to a juvenile monkey as Ludwig and says: "Still papa ain't home yet. He must be out mit der boys again, drinkin' . . . yep, she sees him, on der front step—plastered! Look at dat souse. He just stuck his nose in der Lodge and dey filled it up."[24] These obvious ethnic puns, which were criticized by some, were a holdover from vaudeville, where they were frequently used.[25] Yet they were also prototypical of the ethnic jokes that then littered American film, journalism, and literature.

Borneo received widespread praise. *Film Daily* called it "remarkable," *Variety* (Hollywood) said it was "absorbingly entertaining," and the *New York Herald Tribune* characterized it as "a fitting monument to a brave man." However, others were sharply critical of it. *Variety* said that the film was "never exciting," while the *Christian Science Monitor* found that it was "no great tribute to the memory of the explorer." The *New York Times* reviewer best summed it up in saying: "It is a vivid celluloid account of nature's beauties and marvels which has been edited and spliced into a suitably triumphant travelogue. . . . The familiar pattern of a Johnson film—the scenic backgrounds, the spectacle shots alternating with believe-it-or-not natural freaks, all culminating in the man-against-nature climax."[26]

Borneo was a great commercial success, and by October 1938 Twentieth Century-Fox had paid Osa and Freda Cripps a total of $79,325.86 in royalties.[27] These revenues, plus fees from the lecture tour, placed Osa in a very secure financial position. Unlike Martin, she did not intend to reinvest her monies in another expedition. Rather, she followed the plan she had described to Charmian in 1936, to produce lecture films from which she could make a comfortable living.

While Osa was away in Africa, she remained in the public eye through a series of articles she wrote as a journalist for the *New York Times*.[28] However, gossip columnists provided even greater coverage by accurately speculating that she and Clark were romantically involved and that they planned to marry. Ed Sullivan, the *New York Daily News* columnist, not only wrote about it but also mentioned it in his radio broadcast. Seebach, who had been Martin's loyal assistant for almost two decades, wrote to Clark in Africa and told him what the gossip columnists were saying. She followed this up with a letter to Osa, telling her that Wayne Faunce, the vice-director of the American Museum of Natural History, had asked her if there were any truth to the rumor. Faunce candidly told Seebach that he and others at the museum were very upset at the prospect of Osa marrying Clark.[29] Their objections had nothing to do with Clark himself, whom they hardly knew, but rather with Osa's failure to be the dutiful widow. Seebach's letters did not go down well with either Osa or Clark, whose romantic involvement was also being frowned upon in Kenya by old Johnson friends.[30]

Osa and Clark returned to New York City on the *Queen Mary* on November 15, and almost immediately went on tour with the new Borneo lecture film which Seebach and Fox had cut for them during their absence. Since Martin's death, Seebach had continued to work for Osa from the office at the museum, handling correspondence and managing the accounts. By the spring of 1937, Osa had discharged Martin's secretary, Elizabeth Welsch, and his office boy, Philip Shea. She moved most of the functions of Martin's office to Clark's at the Waldorf Astoria Hotel. This left only Seebach working at the museum office. Seebach was intensely loyal to Martin's memory and was a constant source of inside information for Belle, Aunt Minnie, and others who were increasingly unhappy about Clark's growing influence. Their resentment of him resulted in part from his curtailing the financial favors to which they had become accustomed. Even Martin had grown weary of the incessant requests of some of his relatives. Osa's patience with her family had also grown thin, to the point that when her only niece, Osa Yvonne Leighty, was born, she exclaimed, "Oh no, another mouth to feed!"[31] None of Osa's relatives justified their dislike of Clark on the grounds that he tempered her generosity toward them, but rather invoked his alleged dark motives. They did not fully understand the basis of Osa's relationship with him. She needed affection as well as the strong presence of a reliable man in her life. Clark gave her both.

Seebach, who had worked so intimately with Martin for two decades, tried to maintain his influence and that of relatives and old friends in Osa's new life. In a sense a haunt from the past, she was out of step with the direction of Osa's new career. In addition, through circumstances not of her doing, she had been drawn into a broad range of business matters beyond film cutting. McLean, for example, discussed Osa's business affairs with her as well as with Pomeroy and Davison. On learning this, Osa wrote McLean a letter expressing sharp disapproval. Clark no doubt had a hand in this letter, since his new managerial authority was clearly being challenged. McLean sensed that his discussions with Seebach might have placed her at risk of losing her job. Therefore, he promptly replied to Osa, characterizing Seebach as her trusted representative who had always acted to serve her best interests. Despite this endorsement, Osa fired Seebach on January 24, 1938, on the grounds that her services were no longer needed full time. She cushioned the blow by telling her that she might retain her from time to time on a weekly basis, and provided a hundred-dollar bonus to help her with dental care. Clark was certainly not unhappy to see Seebach go, since he viewed her as the potential agent of those who increasingly wanted to subvert his management of Osa's career.

It was a stronger and more confident Osa who set out on the fall tour. She played to capacity houses everywhere and was extolled in newspaper headlines as a heroine. Clark's intent was to transform her from Mrs. Martin Johnson to Osa Johnson, to define her as a person different from Martin, and to enable her to achieve success on her own. As Clark saw it, that success was not to be found in adventures in Africa, but in herself. It was her beauty and charm as well as her homespun modesty and personal adventures that he tried to draw out from beneath the shadow of Martin's memory. However, this new Osa Johnson, like Mrs. Martin Johnson, was to be the creation of the man in her life.

CHAPTER SIXTEEN

GLAMOROUS OSA

When it became apparent to Osa that Western Air Express was unwilling to come to a settlement, she filed two lawsuits against them, one for $502,539 for Martin's wrongful death, and another for $204,000 for injuries to herself. She waived the right to a jury trial, fearful that jurors hard hit by the Depression would be swayed against her because of her fame and wealth. The airline, however, insisted on a jury trial, which was its right. The trial began in December 1938, and as Carstens recalled, "Osa never had a chance with that jury."[1]

The airline's pilot, William W. Lewis, admitted to the jury that he had not followed the required procedures for making an instrument landing into Burbank, and that his copilot had failed to turn on the de-icers. Western Air Express defended his actions on the absurd grounds that they were appropriate because of an act of God, namely the weather. Osa's attorney correctly pointed out that the procedures in question had been specifically drawn up for instrument landings, which were usually attempted only when visibility was poor due to bad weather conditions. Carstens, who attended the trial, said: "There was no way that jury was going to find in Osa's favor despite the overwhelming evidence that the pilot and copilot had been careless and negligent. They viewed Osa as a wealthy celebrity who didn't need any more money. She sat in the courtroom dressed in clothes that were worth more money than any of them had earned in the previous year."[2] The judge was keenly aware of possible juror prejudice against Osa and carefully instructed them not to consider her earning potential in reaching a verdict. Carstens felt that they ignored this advice, and was not surprised when they returned from their deliberations on the evening of December 29, 1938, and denied Osa damages.

Osa appealed the jury's decision before the California Court of Appeals and requested a new trial. Not surprisingly, the three-judge panel was not inclined to overturn the jury's findings of fact, and on August 28, 1941, denied the motion for a new trial.[3]

In late 1937, Osa moved from the Essex House to an apartment on the thirty-third floor of the Waldorf-Astoria Hotel, close to Clark's office. Once Martin's estate was settled, she dissolved Martin Johnson Films Inc., the corporate entity under which he had functioned, and on Clark's advice formed Osa Johnson Inc. Pomeroy had kept the Martin Johnson African Expedition Corporation alive in order to market *Simba*. However, after Martin's death, he formally dissolved this corporation, which was by then largely inactive.[4]

Clark was well aware of the fact that Osa's future career was very much dependent on their maintaining a good working relationship with the museum. Martin's original bequest of all motion picture film and still photographs produced before 1924 allowed for Osa's commercial exploitation of them during her lifetime. However, she was very much dependent on the museum's good will for access to them and to the films and pictures produced between 1924 and 1928, to which she had no legal rights.

Martin and museum officials had enjoyed a very collegial relationship. They had provided him with a small office in return for access to his pictures and films, which they used for educational purposes. Although the museum's executive leadership saw the value of this arrangement, some in the lower levels of the bureaucracy cooperated only grudgingly. Since space allocations partially defined the importance of programs, few were willing to give up any of their space. The issue became more acute when Martin informally indicated that he eventually intended to present or bequeath to the museum all the still negatives and motion picture film that he and Osa had produced. Writing in 1935 to Roy Chapman Andrews, then the museum's director, Wayne M. Faunce, the vice-director, pointed out that Martin's intended gift "would not be an unqualified blessing because we have no place to store the huge quantity of material involved." Since the motion picture footage was on a flammable nitrate base, it had to be stored in the museum's fireproof vault, which Faunce said was already overcrowded. He suggested either a special off-site storage building, for which Martin or someone else would have to pay the rent or, better still, only selecting those items the museum considered of permanent value. Faunce rightly assumed that the second plan "would probably not satisfy Martin, who wants to keep his stuff together." Because the museum did not come up with an acceptable plan, Martin never donated any of the photographic materials produced after the

1928 trip to Serengeti. Instead, he bequeathed them to Osa and his sister, Freda.[5]

The museum, however, was very much interested in obtaining the films and still pictures from the Johnsons' subsequent expeditions, to which Osa held title. Aware of this, Clark further insured the museum's cooperation by having Osa informally tell them of her wish to bequeath all these materials to them. However, she never entered into a formal legal arrangement with the museum, and ultimately bequeathed her films to her mother. Even after Osa's death, museum officials considered inducing Belle to relinquish her rights to these materials for a nominal sum, something she would never have done because she was deriving some income from them.

The first major test of this cooperative necessity came in early 1938 when Osa asked to borrow footage from *Simba* in order to make a presentation to Columbia Pictures. Clark had approached Columbia about making a film of Martin's life, which was to include footage shot by the Johnsons themselves. Columbia found his proposal appealing, not least of all because the use of preexisting footage meant that the film could be produced on an extremely low budget. While these negotiations were going on, Clark and Osa produced a lecture film, *Jungles Calling*, which served to test the market for the proposed Columbia picture since it was also a recapitulation of the Johnsons' lives and adventures. It opened on the evening of April 1, 1938, at Carnegie Hall in New York City, an event Belle remembered with great fondness since Osa asked her to stand up and the audience applauded.[6]

During 1938 Clark transformed Osa's public image from that of Martin's partner to that of a glamorous trend-setting celebrity and supporter of popular philanthropic causes. Her exquisitely tailored wardrobe included antelope skin coats, hats made of guinea fowl feathers and bustard wings, zebra skin shoes, and an assortment of beautifully colored fabrics with jungle motifs. In March 1939 the Fashion Academy named her one of America's twelve best-dressed women, along with actress Bette Davis and socialite Mrs. Alfred Gwynne Vanderbilt.[7]

Prior to her selection, Osa had launched a line of designer sportswear for women and children, made from a fabric trademarked as "Osafari." The line included shirts, slacks, shorts, jackets, and skirts, had specially designed wooden buttons in the form of African masks, carried the label "Osa Johnson," and came in a variety of colors including Kedong Gold, Masai Bronze, Kenya Blue, Uganda Flame, Acacia (yellow), and Nandi (brown). In late 1939 Osa marketed a line of pigskin and goatskin gloves called The Congo, which was produced by the Speare Glove Co. of New York City. The gloves came in a variety of colors and were sold in leading department stores including B. Altman & Co.[8]

Hailed as the First Lady of Exploration, Osa also designed a line of stuffed animals known as Osa Johnson's Pets to coincide with the publication of her book *Osa Johnson's Jungle Friends* by J. B. Lippincott in late 1939. J. B. Lippincott, the head of the company, whom Clark described as "cautious and shrewd," insisted that Osa's name as author appear as Mrs. Martin Johnson because of better public recognition. Clark refused to accept Lippincott's claim that no one would recognize Osa's name: "It was clear after many discussions that J. B. Lippincott wasn't going to budge about the wording of the author's name. So I came up with a compromise and suggested that the name Osa Johnson be made part of the title, and much to my surprise, he accepted this. That's how this odd arrangement of title and author, *Osa Johnson's Jungle Friends* by Mrs. Martin Johnson, came about."⁹

Osa Johnson's Pets included eight different animal species, some in two or three sizes. Each toy came with a small booklet explaining the animal's natural history. They held great appeal for children and rapidly became an enormous commercial success. By 1940 they were being sold in department stores around the country. In 1939 the National Toy Show voted them the most original plush toy of the year, and the following year they were endorsed by the National Wildlife Federation for teaching natural history to children.[10]

Designer clothing, recognition as one of America's best-dressed women, public lectures, product endorsements, and a children's book linked to a line of stuffed animals promoting conservation had all served to shape Osa's image. Her activities constantly kept her in the public eye, as did the honors she regularly received. The American Society of Cinematographers named her one of the ten most photogenic personalities outside filmdom in 1940, the same year that the famous horticulturist David Burpee named a new variety of sweet pea after her.[11] In November 1939 she presented the San Diego Zoo with an orangutan and five cheetah, and made national headlines not so much for the donation, but because one of the cheetah clawed her while being loaded for shipment.[12]

In 1938 Clark attempted to interest publishers in Osa's autobiography, but received a cool reception. The publishers resisted taking on a woman's autobiography, claiming inaccurately that Martin had already thoroughly described Osa's life in his books. Finally, in late 1938, with Columbia Studios committed to a biographical film of Martin's life, he was able to interest J. B. Lippincott in a biography of Martin authored by Osa. It was clear to Clark that both the film and book had to be a combination of biography and autobiography since Martin and Osa's lives and careers had been so intimately intertwined.

While Osa's previous children's books had been packaged from heavily edited articles that had appeared in *Good Housekeeping*, there was no such material to draw upon for this new book. It was obvious to Clark from the start that Osa needed a ghostwriter who could not only synthesize previously published materials, but also interview her and those who had known Martin. He chose Winifred Dunn, who was then a free-lance theatrical radio writer living in a Manhattan rooming house. Dunn, who had never written or ghosted a book before, was skilled at writing scripts for short radio shows. She brought to the effort both literary talents and a flair for humor and drama, all of which were bound to make the book highly readable and popular. Dunn spent long hours interviewing Osa and others, traveled to Chanute and Independence, and read all of Martin's books. She took an instant liking to Osa, and wrote admiringly of her prior to the book's publication. The manuscript that resulted was hardly a collaboration, since Dunn wrote all of it and Osa's role was limited to providing information and approving the final copy. Dunn, by her own admission, consciously glided over names and dates, and portrayed Martin and Osa as a stunning example of a uniquely American success story. Martin was cast as both a likeable Peck's Bad Boy and a Horatio Alger hero whose bravery, forceful sincerity, and respect for American values enabled him not only to overcome enormous hardships, but also to inspire others by his example. Conspicuously absent from Dunn's account was Martin's showmanship, his shrewdness in business matters, the complexity of his character, and a description of the role played by so many in making his successes possible. Dunn similarly idealized Osa for audiences of the early 1940s. She emphasized her role as the dutiful wife who sewed, cooked, and planted vegetable gardens, albeit in the wild corners of the world. Osa was courageous, beautiful, gracious, hard working, and above all, obedient to her husband's wishes. That feminists of the time drew inspiration from Dunn's portraiture of Osa reflects the state of their own struggle to prove women the equal of men. What they saw in Osa was not so much a paradigm for the feminist movement, but rather a woman who had successfully faced hardships and dangers usually reserved for men. Although it was important to them that Osa had proven her mettle, it was far more significant that she had been given the opportunity of doing so.[13]

Osa's book *I Married Adventure*, with its distinctive zebra-striped cover, was published on May 17, 1940, and received immediate acclaim. Its selection as a June Book-of-the-Month Club choice helped make it the number one national best-seller in nonfiction for 1940. It occupied first place on the *New York Times* best-seller list for many weeks. Within the first eight months of publication, 288,000 copies were sold, a very significant number considering that the country had not yet recovered from the Great Depression. Eventually 500,000 copies were sold within the first year of publication.[14] The book's success was not just due to the fine quality of its writing, nor to the fact that it appealed to broad audiences of nature lovers, conservationists, amateur photographers, and armchair adventurers. More importantly, the Johnsons' lives validated the ideals and values of American society, and gave hope and inspiration to those who believed in the country's potential opportunities. It was a story that was particularly welcome to a country gripped by the Depression and threats of war. Although their success story had been played out in Africa and the South Seas, they were, as the naturalist Robert Wood Krutch noted, "as American as David Crockett." Reviewers across the country praised the book as "readable and exciting," "unique," "good reading," and "pleasant, forthright . . . exciting." In reviewing it for *Books*, Rose Feld best summed up its appeal when she said, "It is a good human story about two extremely likeable people, told by one of them with simplicity, humor, warmth, and complete lack of side."[15]

Osa went on a speaking tour to promote the book, taking along an eight-by-six-foot mock-up of it in which she collected the signatures of all forty-eight governors and other important personalities.[16] In June she traveled to Florida, where she was the guest of honor at the Florida State World's Fair. At the invitation of Hamilton Holt, the president of Rollins College, she spoke to the college's alumni on Rollins Day. Impressed with her accomplishments and grateful for her presence at Rollins Day at the World's Fair, Holt gave serious consideration to awarding her an honorary degree.

Clark had actually been trying for some time to secure an honorary degree for Osa. In January 1940 he had Osa write to Pomeroy, asking if he could persuade Columbia University to give her one. Two weeks later, Pomeroy benignly replied, "I shall give it thought."[17] Although Osa had little need for an honorary degree, Clark viewed it as providing some academic legitimacy that could compensate for her limited formal education. In addition, as a publicist, he saw it as an opportunity for giving her positive press coverage. When the prospects at Columbia dimmed, Clark pursued the issue with Rollins College at the same time that he agreed to Osa's participation in Rollins Day. The quick quid pro quo he was seeking did not materialize because Holt did not buckle to the sort of pressure Clark could bring to bear. It appears that Holt decided to move ahead on granting Osa an honorary degree only after meeting her at the Florida State World's Fair. He was obviously greatly impressed with her and her accomplishments, and five months later wrote her and said: "I have not forgotten the delightful afternoon at the World's Fair where you spoke so charmingly to our alumni, and where you and I had our pictures taken under a potted bamboo tree with two chimpanzees dressed in children's rompers. . . . Would you let me present to our Trustees your name as one on whom Rollins can confer the honorary degree of Doctor of Science . . . at our annual convocation?"[18]

Osa promptly accepted and traveled to Winter Park, Florida, in February 1941, not only to receive the degree, but also to participate in Rollins's Annual Animated Magazine at which several nationally known writers and men and women of affairs spoke to an audience of several thousand people. Among the participants that year were Archduke Otto Hapsburg and the writer Marjorie Kinnan Rawlings. Osa's address, entitled "A Vanishing World," was less than three hundred words in length, but contained both powerful summations of her life experience and affirmations of the American way of life. It was obviously written in her own words, which were sincere, straightforward, and moving:

> With our old world dissolving before our eyes, most of us are desperately wondering, and trying to hold on to what remains of the good, the true, and the familiar.
>
> For twenty-seven years, Martin and I devoted our lives to trying to capture and arrest a vanishing world, and we have assembled a vast library of film of wild animals and savage human beings and landmarks of natural beauty which we hope will be useful to the future world, if the future world has any interest in things of peace. . . .
>
> Young people seem to me to be most affected by the rapid changes of the moment. Thousands of them write to me for advice of all kinds. Can I help them become explorers? How will they get into some profession or career?
>
> My answer is that all I know is what I have experienced. Martin and I started with very little schooling and no resources nor help. . . . We had only our hopes and our nerve. . . . Opportunity is something that one has to make for himself, with laborious planning and doing and plenty of suffering. . . .
>
> Nothing is impossible, if you want it badly enough, and if you have the imagination to dream and the energy to make your dreams come true.[19]

On the following day, February 24, Osa was presented at the Founder's Day Convocation for the honorary degree of Doctor of Science by Fleetwood Peeples, a well-known naturalist. He recapitulated her career and then succinctly summarized those characteristics and values for which she was best known:

> Osa Johnson, scientist, explorer, aviator, lecturer, author, motion picture producer, for your unique achievements in science and art; for your most daring and adventurous life, probably unequaled by any modern woman; for your splendid example of courage, fortitude and loyalty to high ideals in every walk of life, which has been and will remain a shining mark and an inspiration for all American youth, for these and for all your fine womanly qualities.[20]

It is significant that Peeples added "for all your fine womanly qualities." In so doing, he dispelled all thought that these were lacking in Osa and that they were incompatible with her other accomplishments, which were then mostly associated with men.

The film *I Married Adventure* had its New York premiere on September 23, 1940, at the Plaza Theatre. Prominent among the guests were A. Perry Osborn, the vice-president of the American Museum of Natural History who had negotiated the contract with Columbia Pictures, and Will Hays, a former chairman of the Republican National Committee and former U.S. postmaster general, who was president of the Motion Picture Producers and Distributors of America, a trade organization that established industry standards. Reviewers were quick to point out the film's obvious defects. Bosley Crowther, the *New York Times* critic, said:

> The Johnsons now seem a little stale; the best sequences . . . are familiar clips from their many travel films, while the several re-enactments . . . which are used to knit the story together, are stagy. . . . The resurrected sequences . . . suggest a bit of staging. But the little scenes by which Mrs. Johnson has attempted to give the story a loose chronology—scenes in which she plays herself very badly . . . are pitifully amateurish. By their synthetic nature, they call unfortunate attention to a fault which was often apparent in the earlier Johnson films and which was open to vague suspicion. We presume you know what we mean?[21]

Variety was even more tart in its review:

> It is dated, tiresome and amateurish. The box office prospects are highly doubtful. . . . The narration is over-dramatic. . . . Don Clark and Albert Duffy, who wrote the screen track, have over-emphasized the lan-

guage to the point where it sounds like a campaign speech.[22]

Despite *Variety*'s predictions about the film's doubtful box office appeal, it was a financial success. Nostalgia for the Johnsons was still a powerful force, and coupled with aggressive promotion by Columbia, produced packed movie houses. However, it was now abundantly clear that Osa had little acting talent, despite all the effort she had put into studio shots made in Hollywood and New York City.

Osa and Clark's romantic involvement had long been common knowledge and was a constant concern to Belle, Aunt Minnie, and old Johnson friends like Davison, Faunce, and Pomeroy. However, there was little they could do to intervene, especially since Osa and Clark appeared to love one another, and because he was so clearly responsible for her enormous success. Still, some suspected his motives and worried about what might happen to her once she lost popular appeal. She earned huge sums of money and she and Clark lived a lavish lifestyle at the Waldorf-Astoria Hotel. She developed extremely expensive tastes in clothing and jewelry, which Clark justified on the grounds that she had to maintain a glamorous image for him to attract future commercial projects. While Belle and others advised restraint and wise investments for possible future lean times, Osa and Clark continued to spend very freely.

Ellen Dryden, who was Eastman's niece, and her husband, George, came to accept Clark as a genuine friend. In April 1940 Osa and Clark went to visit the Drydens at Eastman's former retreat, Oak Lodge, in Enfield, North Carolina. On the 29th, they were secretly married at the lodge by a Methodist minister, the Reverend B. D. Gretchen, the Drydens serving as witnesses. In order to insure maximum secrecy, Osa used the name Helen Leighty on the marriage certificate.[23] It is significant that this period coincided with the publication of *I Married Adventure*, which celebrated Osa's life with Martin while at the same time putting it to rest. In a sense, the book represented a widow's final tribute, and left her free to begin a new life. That new life had in fact already begun a few years before, but marriage gave it the kind of completeness Osa needed. Personally satisfying as the wedding may have been for Osa and Clark, it was potentially damaging to the book's commercial prospects and to those of the film, which was to be released in five months' time. The success of both depended in large part on the public's sympathetic perception of Osa as a loving widow paying homage to her fallen heroic husband. Her marriage at this point to the man who was managing the exploitation of Martin's life story would have resulted in public chagrin and adverse commercial consequences. Clark was keenly aware of this, and therefore insisted that the marriage be kept secret. Yet this was not a viable long-term option, since discovery by the press or others would also have proven detrimental to Osa's career. Ever the skilled publicist, Clark eventually turned this potential adversity to great advantage by deciding on a highly public marriage ceremony once the film and book had achieved commercial success.

Osa and Clark were married by Mayor LaGuardia at City Hall on February 3, 1941, at a ceremony that was extensively covered by the press. A. Perry Osborn and his wife served as the witnesses, and following the ceremony there was a wedding breakfast at the Waldorf-Astoria. Although Belle told the *Chanute Tribune* that "Mr. Getts is a very fine man," neither she nor Aunt Minnie attended the ceremony. Yet a number of Osa's old friends came, including the Drydens, Stanfords, Hays, Sikorskys, and Governor and Mrs. Charles Edison of New Jersey. No mention was ever made of the secret marriage several months before, at which Osa had used her middle and maiden names. Clark, who was keenly aware that public reaction to him would have a major impact on Osa's career, told the press that he planned to become an explorer. Osa added that he was "a great outdoor man," which he was not. These public statements were obvious attempts to draw similarities between Clark and Martin, and to give Clark a form of successional legitimacy as Osa's husband.[24]

In 1941 Osa reached the peak of her career and was one of America's best-known celebrities. Although Clark had carefully crafted her public image, it nonetheless rested on the foundation of her life and experiences with Martin. With each passing year, however, the films and the experiences they depicted became increasingly dated, and as a result had diminished public appeal. Clark dealt with this problem in several ways. He had Osa produce books and lecture films that gave a fresh and feminine perspective to experiences previously described by Martin, and kept her in the public eye through lectures, product endorsements, and philanthropic activities. She served as honorary chairman of the National Wildlife Federation's National Wildlife Restoration Week in 1941, and as chairman of the African Wing of the British-American Ambulance Corps. In addition, she regularly received distinctions that gave her considerable public exposure, as, for example, when in 1941 she was named as one of fifty-three leading women by the General Federation of Women's Clubs, along with Eleanor Roosevelt and Anne Morrow Lindbergh.[25]

One would have thought that *I Married Adventure* had exhausted Osa's fund of marketable experiences. However, the book had no sooner come off the best-seller lists, where it had been for almost a year, than Lippincott published a sequel, *Four Years in Paradise*. One of the most appealing of Osa's books, it recounts the almost three years the Johnsons spent at Lake Paradise. Although this period had already been described by Martin in his book *Safari* and in two films, the public had an insatiable appetite for tales that combined high adventure, domestic companionship, and the romance of pioneering. With the help of a ghostwriter, Osa successfully brought these elements forward in an intimate and chatty style that also portrayed her and Martin as very likeable Midwesterners who had achieved happiness in the pursuit of the unusual.

The launching of *Four Years in Paradise* so soon after *I Married Adventure* was dictated by Lippincott's desire to capitalize on the enormous popularity of the latter. This marketing strategy proved successful, as the book quickly got on the *New York Times* best-seller list. Rose Feld, reviewing the book for the *New York Herald Tribune*, succinctly summed up its enormous appeal in saying the following: "One is caught by the essential Americanism of these two intrepid explorers. With engaging honesty and frankness, with something akin to but deeper than naivete, Osa Johnson completely destroys the aura of mystery, bravery, and silent grandeur with which most heroes of the jungle surround themselves."[26]

There was just one dissenting voice in the chorus of praise for *Four Years In Paradise* and it came from an old rival, Mary L. Jobe Akeley. Hardly an unbiased reviewer, she wrote the following in the *New York Times:* "The book is beautifully illustrated. Whereas the format is pleasing, it is obvious that Webster has not been followed in the orthography of certain familiar words . . . nor Taylor for the Swahili terms. But this may be due to the editor-publisher's oversight rather than to the author's leaning toward phonetics."[27] Akeley was high in her praise of Martin's work, but trivialized Osa's accomplishments by stating that they were largely limited to "growing produce," "jungle homemaking," and "hair-breadth escapes from death." She also took pains to remind readers that Osa was "the former Mrs. Martin Johnson, now Mrs. Clark H. Getts." However, Akeley's jealous barbs were no match for the public enthusiasm that rapidly made the book a best-seller.

The publication of *Four Years in Paradise* was linked to the release of a lecture film, *African Paradise*, which premiered on November 4, 1941, at New York's Carnegie Hall.[28] Following the premiere, Osa embarked on a nationwide tour during which she delivered over a hundred lectures. It was while on this tour that she and Clark visited Chanute, where on November 25 she purchased the house where she was born, hoping to convert it into a museum. This small three-room cement block house stood in sharp contrast to Osa and Clark's new six-room apartment on the twelfth floor at 400 Park Avenue in New York City. They had spent $20,000 to decorate the apartment, and had commissioned one of the museum's landscape artists, Arthur August Jansson, to paint African scenes on the walls.[29]

As Osa traveled through the heartland of America and was greeted by large enthusiastic audiences, she did not realize that this phase of her career had in fact reached its high point. Clark, however, knew that there was little left to extract from her overseas travel experiences and felt that she had to convert her enormous popularity into a new career. The prospects for this were extremely good as she had already received offers to host radio shows. What worried him most were her episodic and unpredictable alcoholic binges, which he, like Martin, thought he could control. In Africa, Osa's illness had been easily hidden from public view. However, Clark found this increasingly difficult to do once she left the shelter of his close management on lecture tours and came under the scrutiny of producers and directors.

CHAPTER SEVENTEEN

FINAL YEARS

In March 1942, Osa and Clark returned to New York City from a 17,000-mile nationwide lecture tour. By this time, she was a skilled and entertaining lecturer who, as Clark later commented, "had an extraordinary way with both adults and children." She had a perfect sense of timing, knew her speeches down to the punctuation, and possessed a wonderful ability to amuse, as when she gave perfect imitations of a lion's roar and a zebra's braying. The receipts from this tour were considerable, not least of all because Clark had shifted from a flat payment system to a percentage of the house receipts. While this yielded greater returns, it also presented accountability problems, as some theater managers routinely undercounted the audience. Therefore, before Osa went out on stage, Clark insisted that he and the managers stand together in the wings and simultaneously count the house.[1]

Despite Osa's emergence as a celebrity in her own right, she continuously paid homage to Martin, who since his death had been honored in a number of ways. Chanute renamed its municipal airport Martin Johnson Airport, Senator Arthur Capper of Kansas delivered a tribute to him from the floor of the U.S. Senate, and in 1944 the Liberty Ship *Martin Johnson* was launched in California. Both Martin and Osa received other forms of recognition, as when the state of North Borneo issued a four-cent stamp in 1939 using their photograph of a proboscis monkey. In Nairobi, a prominent hairstyling salon, located on Delamere Avenue behind the New Stanley Hotel, was named Osa's Ltd. in her honor.[2]

In 1943 Osa and Clark moved their office from the Waldorf-Astoria Hotel to the second floor of 430 Park Avenue, a short distance from their apartment. They furnished it with a custom-made mahogany desk and two matching mahogany fireplace mantels between which they spread a large leopard-skin rug. Clark later recalled: "The office had its own private stairway leading to the street. One mantel was sculpted with African motifs and the other with ones from Borneo. The leopard-skin rug was made up of several skins of which only the middle one was Osa's. I bought the others so that we could have a sizable rug that would impress prospective clients. Whenever they left, we rolled it up against the wall."[3]

The move out of the Waldorf-Astoria was primarily dictated by finances. Although Osa continued to give lectures and to earn royalties on books and films, her annual income had begun to decline significantly. Clark, who was unable to make up for this loss with income derived from representing other artists and celebrities, had no choice but to cut expenses. The potential for deriving future books and films from Osa's life and career with Martin was gradually diminishing. Yet Clark showed great ingenuity as when he successfully marketed the children's books *Pantaloons: Adventures of a Baby Elephant* (1941) and *Snowball: Adventures of a Young Gorilla* (1942), even though the stories had been previously published in *Good Housekeeping*. He was able to interest Random House in the books primarily because he had them illustrated in color by Arthur August Jansson, a landscape artist on the staff of the American Museum of Natural History. *Pantaloons* received high praise for its "many fine illustrations in color" and because "the prose is rhythmic and has the charm of storytelling about it." *Snowball* was criticized because of awkward sentence structure and several typographical errors, but overall received favorable reviews.[4]

In 1942 Clark encouraged Osa to produce an adult travel book based on her and Martin's trips to Borneo. Crucial to this was the retrieval of Martin's 1935–1936 diaries, which had been used by Tilton during the 1937 lecture tour and by Lowell Thomas for narrating the film *Borneo*. Unable to find them in Osa's papers, Clark was forced to contact Lillian Seebach, whom he and Osa had fired several years before. Seebach, who was then working at DeLuxe Laboratories, had good reason to be uncooperative. Yet she showed no rancor and was quickly able to locate the blue-lined eight-by-ten-inch looseleaf sheets Martin used as a diary.[5] The manuscript that resulted with the help of a ghostwriter combined both the 1920 and the 1935–1936 trips to Borneo. Despite the draw of Osa's name, Clark was unable to find a publisher for the manuscript. Eventually, it was packed away in a Sphinx bond-paper box and stored with Osa's possessions. However, twenty-four years later, in 1966, it was posthumously published under the title *Last Adventure*.[6]

Interest in the South Pacific greatly intensified during World War II as American armed forces fought the Japanese on atolls and islands most had never heard of before, but which quickly became household words. In order to capitalize on this intense interest, Clark hired a ghostwriter to produce a book about Osa's experiences in the Solomon Islands and the New Hebrides in 1917. Titled *Bride in the Solomons* and heavily illustrated with sixty-four pictures, it was published by Houghton Mifflin in 1944. The title was clearly misleading since Martin and Osa had been married seven years by the time they went on this trip. However, it demonstrated Clark's genius as a publicist, as did his timing of publication, which followed the Battle of Guadalcanal. The latter did not escape perceptive reviewers, one of whom remarked: "Fighting fronts of today recalled in the days of exploratory travel with their primitive aspects obviously dished up for the immediate occasion."[7] Foster Hailey, the *New York Times* critic, best summed up the book's value in saying the following: *"Bride in the Solomons* is not an important book or even a very good travelogue. Mrs. Johnson is vague about the location of many of the places of which she writes. . . . As a story of two adventurous Kansans, starting a career of romanticized travel that later brought them a fortune, it makes first-rate reading."[8]

As with her other adult books, Osa had little to do with the actual writing. In contrast to her previous books, *Bride in the Solomons* contains excessive exaggerations and hyperbole, which were clearly intended to appeal to readers who were following the war in the Solomons. In addition, several events were completely fabricated and much license was taken with others. Despite these defects, the book is considered an important historical resource because it documents people and events not well described elsewhere. Following a well-established promotional strategy, Clark and Osa produced a lecture film, *Tulagi and the Solomons*, with which they toured in 1943 and 1944.

In 1944 Clark also succeeded in marketing what was to be the last of Osa's children's books, *Tarnish: The Story of a Lion Cub*. Published by Wilcox and Follett, it was beautifully illustrated in color by Jansson, and quickly became popular even though the story was derived from a previously published magazine article. It received excellent reviews, the *New York Times* saying that it stood out "among wild animal stories for the younger children."[9]

Aware that television was the mass medium of the future, Clark felt that Osa could redirect her career and become the hostess of different types of shows. She had all of the necessary attributes for this kind of role, including beauty, poise, stage presence, and finely honed public speaking abilities. Yet her unpredictable alcoholic binges made it increasingly impossible for him to secure contracts with either radio or television stations. In describing her problem, he said: "Even when she went out alone shopping, she frequently returned home intoxicated. Once she was so drunk, she took off a valuable necklace and left it on the seat of the cab. Of course, we never recovered it. It was impossible for me to monitor her twenty-four hours a day as I had a business to run."[10]

At social gatherings, Osa invariably became intoxicated and frequently violent. On one such occasion at their apartment, she threw a heavy glass ashtray at Clark. Although the ashtray missed him and others, it crashed into a large wall mirror. Clark reached the end of his patience with Osa's drinking in 1946. He had arranged a speaking tour for Mrs. Vijaya L. Pandit, the leader of India's delegation to the United Nations and the sister of Prime Minister Jawaharlal Nehru. At the reception held for Mrs. Pandit, Osa became drunk and started to yell racial epithets at her. It was Osa's conduct at this reception and her increasing tendency to be physically violent when drunk that prompted Clark to seek psychiatric help for her. In 1946 he had her hospitalized against her will in a psychiatric sanitarium in Connecticut, where she remained for a few months.[11]

Osa eventually obtained a release from the sanitarium, and as Belle later said, "never went back to live with Clark again." She separated from him on November 25, 1946, and a little over a year later, on January 26, 1948, sued for an annulment of their marriage in New York State Supreme Court. The suit drew immediate press attention, especially because of the nature of the accusations she leveled against Clark. Through her lawyer, Bertram A. Mayers, she charged that he had induced her to form a corporation, Osa Johnson Inc., in which he held a 50 percent share, and that over the years he had embezzled from $200,000 to $500,000 by juggling the books. In addition, she charged that, prior to their marriage, she was unaware that he had been a conscientious objector during World War I and that he had been incarcerated in the federal penitentiaries at Fort Leavenworth and at Alcatraz. She also told the press that on February 22, 1920, after his release from prison, he boasted of his record as a conscientious objector in Evanston, Indiana, and urged an audience to "rise and rebel against the government."[12]

Osa's allegation that Clark has been a conscientious objector quickly turned public sympathy to her side. World War II was still a vivid memory for Americans, most of whom viewed draft dodgers with contempt. Military service not only defined government benefits for veterans but also gave them an honored place in American society. Families were extremely proud of children, spouses, and siblings who had served in the war, and defensive about sons who had escaped conscription because of a 4F classification denoting physical or mental disabilities.

Osa also alleged that Clark had hidden his conscientious objector status from her, a charge that did not hold up well under judicial scrutiny since it was reported in some newspapers at the time of their New York City marriage. However, this went down extremely well with the public and gave credence to her other allegation that he had embezzled her assets.

Clark eventually responded to Osa's allegations through his attorney, Frederick P. Bryan. He denied that he had embezzled any funds and stated that the corporation had only $45,000 in cash, the remaining assets consisting of films and photographs. He readily admitted that as a young man he had taken "the quixotic position" that participation in war was wrong and that he had been determined to make a public issue of his principles. He told the press that he had insisted on a court martial, and that he had been confined to Camp Grant in Rockford, Illinois, for thirty months. His story was easily verified by the press since he had been one of the best-known conscientious objectors of the time. Although he tried to portray his actions as those of an idealistic young man and imply that in retrospect he regretted them, the public continued to see him as a draft dodger and to sympathize with Osa.[13]

Osa defamed Clark far and wide, but succeeded best at persuading those who were not close at hand. Eddie Ruben in Nairobi recalled thirty years later that Clark was "a swine to her." Yet this was an unquestioning assessment based on what Osa had written to him and others in Kenya. DeWitt Sage, who was in New York City at the time, expressed a very different opinion: "I always thought she was in good hands as long as she was with Clark Getts. After their divorce, she was always being taken advantage of since she had little business sense. . . . I once visited her at her office when she was meeting with two film industry men I knew to be dishonest."[14]

Vern Carstens also thought well of Clark and believed that the intense anger Belle later felt toward him was the result of "a very bad misunderstanding."[15] However, matters were much more complicated than that, as Carstens realized. As far as Belle was concerned, central casting in a Hollywood studio could not have come up with a more perfect villain than Clark. She had always thought of him as an interloper and an opportunist, and was only too willing to believe Osa's account that she had been fleeced of her fortune. Characterizing Clark in this manner enabled Belle to hide Osa's alcoholism and to depict her as a victim. She based her assessment of Clark on instinct, on what Osa told her, and on her own very strong maternal need to see her daughter as the public did—as an endearing and glamorous celebrity. Without Clark, Belle would have had to find other villains since she could not have come to terms with the harsh reality that Osa's professional decline after her separation from Clark was of her own doing. She explained the demise of Osa's career as a direct result of Clark's alleged larceny. Yet the two issues were quite distinct and only tangentially related.

Over the years, Belle remained implacable in her attitude toward

Clark, consistently characterizing him as a cheat and a thief. Her feelings softened somewhat in 1972 when he sent her a Christmas card, which she reciprocated. Commenting on her response to him she said, "Well, I'm a Christian woman and one must be forgiving. But I will never forget what he did to my Osa." Thus she was willing to forgive but not to admit that she had ever made an error in judgment.

When Clark later offered to donate Johnson memorabilia to the Martin and Osa Johnson Safari Museum in Chanute, Belle rejected the offer and claimed that his possession of any Johnson materials confirmed her belief that he had embezzled Osa's funds. That Clark still held items that he and Osa had collected together in Africa in 1937, as well as some furniture and books, scarcely lent credence to Belle's allegations. What underlay her rebuff was the unspoken acknowledgment that gifts from Clark in the role of benefactor would have challenged her image of him as wholly villainous. So influential were Belle's views of Clark at the time that some museum officials only grudgingly acknowledged his gifts when they arrived, and claimed that he had no right to them in the first place. Taking up her acrimonious cause as their own, they so offended him that he eventually moved some of the materials to another archive.

In the absence of convincing evidence, it is impossible to determine if Clark embezzled funds that were rightfully Osa's. The strongest evidence against him, besides Osa's personal allegations, is circumstantial in nature. Had he wanted to embezzle her money, he was certainly in an ideal position to do so, and to prevent the fact from being discovered. Similarly, the evidence that he did not embezzle, or at least not the amounts she claimed, is also circumstantial. Although Osa earned huge sums from her films, books, and lectures between 1937 and 1943, she and Clark also incurred enormous overhead expenses, including a Park Avenue office and apartment, travel, clothes, jewels, and entertainment. These facts alone indicate that a sizable portion of Osa's earnings went to sustain a very luxurious life-style.

While the annulment suit was before the court, Osa began to sell off possessions at auction in order to raise money. In the process, she sold some of Clark's Chinese porcelain collection along with Martin's rifles.[16] In order to prevent further loss, Clark hurriedly moved his possessions to another warehouse and later admitted that in the process he accidentally took some of Osa's things, none of which had great monetary value. Although he later donated most of these things to the Martin and Osa Johnson Safari Museum and to the University of Wyoming, his admission provided Belle with further justification for her claim that he had embezzled Osa's monies.[17]

Osa's annulment suit was unsuccessful, but the following year she and Clark reached a property settlement in which she received half of the corporation's cash assets, all the films and pictures, and the rights to her books. Clark vividly recalled their final meeting at the 430 Park Avenue office: "The canisters of film were all stacked against the wall. I told Osa that they were all there for her to do with as she wished. I gave Osa the current files and everything else she was entitled to."[18] Osa frequently told Belle that her signature on the settlement agreement had cost her a million dollars, the amount she then believed she could never recover from Clark. With a settlement reached, Osa filed for a divorce in Chicago on April 19, 1949, charging desertion. Nine days later, she was granted an uncontested divorce, and as Belle later remarked was finally free to do as she pleased.[19]

Osa could have achieved further professional success after her divorce if she had not been afflicted by alcoholism. This illness, coupled with her inexperience in business matters and the limited value of her dated films, placed her in increasing financial difficulty. Despite her handicaps, she was successful in marketing some of her films. In 1950 she entered into a ten-year contract with a television film producer who created twenty-six half-hour film segments which aired on many independent television stations as *Osa Johnson's Big Game Hunt*.[20] Her personal appearances on a New York City television station were canceled when she showed up intoxicated. The television shorts were eventually successful, as were re-releases by Morro Films in the 1950s of *Congorilla* and *Borneo* (retitled *Devil Beast of Borneo*). Yet the income from these ventures and from book royalties was scarcely enough to cover her mounting expenses. She moved out of the Park Avenue apartment in 1952 and rented a smaller one in the Woodward Hotel at Broadway and West 55th Street.

Clark kept himself informed about what was happening to Osa and was deeply concerned over the severity of her alcoholism: "She would go into bars and quickly attract a crowd of admirers by telling people who she was. She entertained them with stories, and they bought her drinks."[21]

Osa's lawyer, John Crane, became what Clark and others later termed "a live-in." Clark described him as a gambler and as an inept attorney who was censured for incompetence by the New York State Supreme Court.[22] In late July 1951, Bud Cottar's daughter, Joan, and her Aunt Myrtle visited Osa and Crane at the Park Avenue apartment. Myrtle had a heated argument with Osa about how gerenuk antelopes obtain water, but the high point of the conversation was Osa's claim that she and Crane were planning a trip to Kenya in order to tame the Turkana people. African trips in the planning stage had long become a standard component of Osa's promotional repertoire. But the purpose of this one struck the Cottars as absurd.[23]

One of the few points on which Clark and Belle fully agreed was that Crane was a detrimental influence in Osa's life. Belle angrily recalled that Crane had duped Osa into believing that the jade she had collected in Borneo was soapstone worth only $300. Osa had purchased it for $2,000 and later it had been appraised by an expert for $12,000. "Osa was ironing in the kitchen and told me that Crane had sold the jade for $300. When he came in, I confronted him and said that it couldn't have been worthless soapstone since Martin had an excellent appraiser look at it. On hearing this, Crane left the room. I told Osa that I suspected he had sold it as jade and kept all the money except $300 to either pay off gambling debts or to gamble again. But she refused to believe me."[24]

Dependent on ever-dwindling resources and amorously involved with a man who gambled, Osa soon found herself in desperate financial straits. In addition, she was in poor health, suffering from hypertension and coronary artery disease, for which she was under the care of several physicians. In the absence of lecture and film contracts, she raised capital by selling off possessions, including hunting trophies which were stored at Jonas Brothers Studios in Mount Vernon, New York. However, even by resorting to these drastic measures, she was still accumulating a long list of creditors and was rapidly becoming penurious.

On the morning of Wednesday, January 7, 1953, Osa's maid, Alberta Ward, spoke with her in her suite at 9:00 A.M. Two hours later, Crane arrived and found Osa's fully clad body in the empty bathtub, she apparently having fallen in after suffering a heart attack. He called her Aunt Minnie and Uncle Bill, who lived nearby at 450 West 57th Street, and they immediately came over. Aunt Minnie broke the news to Belle while Crane arranged for one of Osa's treating physicians to pronounce her dead and sign the death certificate. Osa was fifty-eight years old.

Crane gave conflicting stories to the press concerning the circumstances surrounding Osa's death.[25] As reporters from the newspapers and wire services questioned him, he changed his original story and claimed that when he arrived at the apartment, Osa was extremely ill. According to this version, he called her physician, Dr. Samuel A. Levene, a general practitioner, but she died before he arrived. Aunt Minnie corroborated the fact that Crane found Osa dead in the empty bathtub, but to avoid upsetting Belle told her that she had died in her sleep in bed. Crane not only called Dr. Levene but also Dr. David Bloom, another general practitioner, who pronounced Osa dead. Bloom listed chronic myocarditis as the cause of death on the certificate, employing a term for what is more accurately called an acute myocardial infarction (heart attack).[26] Crane also told the press that Osa had been "working night and day" on preparations for a new safari to Africa and that she had "just worked herself out."[27] In creating this fiction, he sustained Osa's public image as an active explorer and linked her death to Africa, with which she had been so long associated.

Aunt Minnie and her husband Bill made the funeral arrangements through Coughlin and Poole, and held a two-day wake at the Columbus Circle Chapel at 43 West 60th Street. On the evening of January 9, a brief religious service was conducted before Aunt Minnie and Crane accompanied the body to Chanute. There, thousands of people, including schoolchildren, filed past the open bier in the Presbyterian Church. The funeral service on Monday, January 12, was conducted by the Reverend Fred Shaw, the retired pastor of the church. In his eulogy, he paid tribute to Osa as a woman who had distinguished herself as an explorer and author. He also praised her for serving as an inspiration for women who had advanced into fields previously reserved for men. During the service, the organist played "Song of Safari," the theme song of the film *Simba*, and two solos were sung, "In the Garden" and "Beyond the Sunset." Following the church service, Osa's remains were carried to nearby Elmwood Cemetery where they were interred next to Martin's.[28]

All across the country, the little girl who had once collected pretty rocks and leaves on the Kansas prairie was remembered as an intrepid and courageous woman. She had inspired the young, affirmed the values of her era, and forever changed America's vision of the exotic and far away.

EPILOGUE

Osa bequeathed her entire estate to Belle, whom she also appointed as her executrix. Despite misgivings, Belle retained Crane to probate the will and settle the estate. She later regretted this decision, recalling that "he made such a mess of things that I had to get another lawyer, Daniel Flynn." The will was not probated until July 30, 1953, by which time the estate owed $5,849.91 to some twenty creditors. The largest group of creditors were physicians, whose bills amounted to close to $2,000, followed by a moving and storage company that presented a claim for $1,800. The remaining creditors largely consisted of merchants but also included Belle, who was owed almost $1,000, and Osa's maid, Alberta Ward, who had a claim for $261 in unpaid wages.[1]

During the last several months of her life, Osa had come close to penury. In order to meet the demands of creditors, Belle was forced to auction off most of Osa's possessions. On September 21 she entered into a public auction agreement with the Plaza Art Galleries in New York City. A total of 237 items were auctioned at two sessions on October 16 and 17, realizing a gross of $5,618.62. The majority of items consisted of household furnishings once used in the Park Avenue apartment. However, there were also artifacts and trophies collected in Africa, including a zebra skin, a leopard skin, carved wooden figures, musical instruments, clubs, and arrows. A Mauser rifle sold for $65, a shotgun for $100, and two cameras brought only $22.50. Five large paintings by Arthur August Jansson were also put up for sale. However, Belle withdrew the one of Songa, the young Meru man the Johnsons had first met in 1921.[2]

Belle had mistakenly anticipated that the auction would bring in large receipts, and was sadly disappointed when she saw valuable items go for a few dollars. The large mock volume of *I Married Adventure*, with which Osa had toured the country, was sold for a mere $10. Its principal value to a buyer was that it contained the signatures of many celebrities and famous people. Jansson's magnificent African canvases went for $20.00 each, and only $17.50 was bid for an elegant robe Osa had worn during her lecture tours. Belle was especially pained by the sale of Osa's lecture robe, which had originally cost $15,000. "The auctioneer just rolled it up in a bundle and held it up as if it were trash. It hurt me so to see it treated that way." In later years, Belle was philosophical about the sale, saying that "they were only material things, most of which could be replaced." Yet she had lingering regrets and frequently consoled herself by saying, "I couldn't have kept all these things. I had no room for them."

Belle held on to thousands of photographs, various artifacts and memorabilia, and the Johnsons' films, which were stored in New York City. She also kept the remaining trophies, which were cared for by the Jonas Brothers Studio in Mount Vernon, New York. However, she allowed the Eastman Kodak Company to continue storing the thousands of still negatives which Martin and Osa had deposited there over the years, later remarking, "What could I have possibly done with them? I had no place to keep them."[3]

In 1956, three years after Osa's death, Belle, Dr. James Butin, a leading Chanute physician, and members of the Chamber of Commerce began planning for a museum to honor the Johnsons. Osa herself had once proposed establishing a museum in the house where she was born. She had offered the house and collections of artifacts to the town, but the offer was turned down. However, by 1956 there was significant support for a museum among members of the Chamber of Commerce and others in the town. Butin, who headed the Chamber's museum planning committee, and Les Matthews, the Chamber's manager, mobilized a broad base of support. In 1957 they secured all of the remaining Johnson trophies from Jonas Brothers and, together with materials provided by Belle, set up a temporary exhibit in a vacant store in Chanute. The success of this exhibit drew even broader support, and a bond issue to finance a museum building was placed before the voters. The bond issue failed to pass, but in 1959 the Santa Fe Railway offered to donate its old freight building for use as a museum. The town and the Chamber of Commerce accepted this proposal, and on June 11, 1961, after five years of planning, the Martin and Osa Johnson Safari Museum was dedicated and opened to the public.[4]

The museum became the major focus of Belle's life, and she frequently met with some of the visitors, whose annual numbers have risen to five thousand. During her lifetime, she remained the driving force behind the museum and was known as Mother Leighty to all who became her close friends. When she died in 1976 in her one-hundredth year, she bequeathed to the museum all of the rights she had to Martin and Osa's films and writings.

Martin's sister, Freda, who had preferred Independence, Kansas, as the site for the museum, also donated items Martin and Osa had given her. In the late 1950s she and her husband, J. Reamey Cripps, worked on a biography of Martin, but never found a publisher.[5]

The recovery of Johnson films and artifacts has always been a major mission of the museum. Osa had kept the film in storage in vaults in New York City. This footage consisted not only of films to which she had legal rights, but also those she had borrowed from the American Museum of Natural History (AMNH) and never returned. Her failure to return considerable amounts of film to the museum was fortunate because it saved them from certain destruction. In the 1960s, the AMNH embarked on a program of deacquisitioning and destroying large quantities of older nitrate-based film. This decision was motivated by limited and inadequate storage facilities and the perceived decreasing scientific importance of some earlier films. That these films had great historical significance failed to prevent their destruction. Large quantities of Johnson film in the museum's collections were destroyed during this program, except for various versions of *Simba*; a nine-minute, 16-mm print called *Children of Africa*, produced in 1937 from film shot in 1924–1927; and small amounts of miscellaneous footage.

During the 1960s, Belle was greatly troubled about the fate of the almost 800,000 feet of negative film stock then stored in New York City. Complicating matters was the fact that she had not paid the storage bill on the film, which by 1966 had amounted to $2,500. Over the years, she had tried to market the film commercially but with little success. In October 1958, for example, she gave power of attorney over the film and also over Osa's writings to a New York City agent, Ethel Paige. However, during the thirty months of the agreement, Paige had little success in marketing either film or writings. Eventually, the Martin and Osa Johnson Safari Museum arranged for the film storage company to transfer all of the footage to the Library of Congress's Motion Picture Conservation Center at Wright-Patterson Air Force Base in Dayton, Ohio. The museum then began the difficult process of cataloging the material. In 1980 William Cayton of Radio and Television Packagers donated a large quantity of film that he had purchased from Osa in the 1940s. He had previously used this film to produce fifty-two quarter-hour programs, which he collectively marketed under the title *Jungle*. It is currently stored at the University of California Film and Television Archive in Los Angeles. Other Johnson films are in the collections of the British Film Institute, the Nederlands Filmmuseum, and the American Heritage Center of the University of Wyoming.

The Johnsons' original still negatives and prints found their way over the years into several institutional collections. Both Martin and Osa routinely stored most of their glass plates and negatives at the Eastman Kodak Company in Rochester, New York. These were later transferred to the International Museum of Photography at George Eastman House, which now has 8,485 negatives and glass plates. In 1987 these were copied onto a laser video disk. Although prints are still made from the original plates and negatives, the video disk greatly facilitates access to the collection. The American Museum of Natural History has several hundred glass plates and negatives, many of which were returned from George Eastman House in the late 1980s. The Museum of Modern Art has a large collection of promotional prints associated with the Johnsons' commercial feature films. Many of the tinted glass slides used by Martin and Osa during their vaudeville tours are now stored with the Jack and Charmian London Collection of the California Department of Parks and Recreation in Santa Rosa, California. The largest collection of still photographs, numbering in the thousands, is held by the Martin and Osa Johnson Safari Museum.

In the late 1960s, the museum's Board of Directors gave serious consideration to expanding the institution's scope to include a permanent exhibit of African art. Belle expressed reservations about this new direction, fearing that it would dilute the museum's original purpose. However, in time, she came to support the concept, and at her request the new exhibit, which occupied the second floor of the museum, was named the Johnson Memorial Hall of African Culture. On January 19, 1974, Belle cut the ribbon at the opening ceremony along with Chanute's mayor, John Schultz, and G. Edward Clark, the former U.S. Ambassador to Mali and Senegal. The museum's African art collection, much of it collected in Africa by one of us (PJI), is among the largest in the Midwest and has over the years been an important resource to both scholars and visitors.[6] In addition to this new hall, the museum also established the Stott Explorers Library and the Selsor Gallery in honor of two prominent museum benefactors. In 1990, the Larry D. Hudson Family Foundation provided a $500,000 donation to renovate Chanute's historic Santa Fe Depot for the purpose of providing space for both the museum and Chanute's public library. By January 1992, an additional $1,500,000 had been raised, and plans were underway for establishing an endowment fund. The new museum, which contains an auditorium and other educational facilities, opened in 1992.[7]

The museum has not only preserved the memory of Martin and

Osa Johnson but, more importantly, promoted a broad range of educational programs fostering cross-cultural understanding and wildlife conservation. Johnson film footage has been regularly used in National Geographic Society specials, by the British Broadcasting Corporation, and by public television stations in the United States. Items in the museum's collections have been loaned for national exhibitions, and its publications on African art and on the Johnsons have been widely circulated.

Clark Getts continued to represent artists and celebrities through the 1960s. In 1955 he married Dorothy Raphun Jones, who had been his and Osa's secretary. They lived for many years in Weehawken, New Jersey, before moving to a retirement community in Clemson, South Carolina, in 1981. Although retired by the 1970s, Clark maintained a telephone answering service and mail drop at 655 Fifth Avenue, and regularly came into Manhattan to attend the monthly luncheon meetings of the Dutch Treat Club at the Regency Hotel on Park Avenue. He was then in his eighties and was one of the oldest and most respected members of this group, which brought together writers, agents, celebrities, and distinguished members of the press and media. He frequently invited one of us (PJI) to these luncheons, which always featured well-known speakers. Clark and Lowell Thomas, who often sat together, were quick in their assessments of a speaker's skills, which they sometimes discussed loudly enough for both the speaker and other guests to hear. Clark was intolerant of those who could not project their voices, and Thomas had no patience with speakers who rambled.[8]

Clark also enjoyed lunching at the Top of the Sixes Restaurant, which then had unobstructed views north toward Central Park. He always arrived early and secured a window table with a superb view. On all these occasions, he spoke of Martin and Osa. He always expressed great admiration for both of them, and his eyes often filled with tears whenever he discussed Osa's alcoholism. It was during one of these frequent luncheons that he agreed to reestablish contact with Belle and donate to the museum office furnishings he and Osa had used. He also donated a large collection of Johnson material to the American Heritage Center of the University of Wyoming, including three of Martin's cameras—a Bell & Howell movie camera, a Speed Graphic, and a Press Graflex. Clark maintained a keen interest in the museum in Kansas and became one of its honorary trustees, along with Vern Carstens, David Martin, Lowell Thomas, Admiral George Wauchope, and others. He peacefully passed away in Clemson, South Carolina, on May 4, 1982, in his ninetieth year, and at his request his ashes were returned to his native Wisconsin.

Vern Carstens retired as chief test pilot and manager of flight engineering at the Beechcraft Corporation in 1966 and moved to Chanute,

Kansas. He became an active supporter of the museum, and over the years, he and his wife Wilma donated collections of his African memorabilia. He died in Chanute on August 13, 1978. James Laneri, who had piloted the Johnsons in Borneo, retired to St. Petersburg, Florida, where he devoted much of his time to inventing. He died on October 9, 1985, and bequeathed to the museum a number of artifacts he had collected in Borneo. Daniel Pomeroy died in his home at Sea Island, Georgia, on March 25, 1965, at the age of ninety-six. During Osa's later years, he acquired a number of her African hunting trophies. Among these was the greater kudu, which she had stalked across Mount Marsabit for several days. Pomeroy's heirs sent this trophy to the Martin and Osa Johnson Safari Museum, but gave the other ones to another institution.

The Big Nambas of Nihapat's village, Tenmarou, on the island of Malekula, eventually left their high mountain home and settled on the coast. In 1980 and 1981, Kirk Huffman, curator of the Vanuatu Cultural Center, carried a portable generator and projector across Malekula and showed the Johnsons' films to the Big Nambas. The films were so popular that he had to project them several times over in each village. Sixty years had elapsed since Martin and Osa had shown these films on the island, and yet the response to them was the same. Nihapat's grandson, Chief Arnhapat, who stood for the Vanuatu parliament in 1980, also saw the films and was deeply moved by them.[9] The governments of both Vanuatu and the Solomon Islands now possess significant collections of the Johnsons' films and consider them an important part of their national cultural heritage.

In the last year of her life, Belle expressed the wish that some earth from Lake Paradise be brought to Martin and Osa's grave in Chanute. The following year, as the mist was still drifting across Marsabit's peaks, we walked down to the lake. A herd of buffalo stood motionless on the other side of the crater as we gathered up some earth with the help of Wako Halake, a Boran guide whose grandfather had worked for Martin and Osa. It was a cold January day when we finally reached Chanute and, as Belle had wished, brought a special part of Africa to their final resting place.

AFTERWORD

I first became aware of Martin and Osa Johnson on a warm August afternoon in 1952. I had gone to the local library with my friends Robby Bach, Jimmy McGarrity, and Jamesy Keane, to explore worlds that lay beyond the horizons of the New York City suburb where I lived. As usual, I headed toward the travel section, at the rear of the library, and happened to pull down from the wooden shelf a copy of Osa's book *Four Years in Paradise*. It had been rebound by the library, a visual cue to an impressionable teenager that it was a popular book. While the encounter was by chance, my reading of the first several pages was not. I had already developed a strong interest in Africa, originally stimulated because my maternal grandfather was born and raised there.

What attracted me most in Osa's first few pages and the picture inserts was not just the lure of adventure, but also her portrayal of Africa. In dramatic contrast to the writings of many other African travelers I had read, Osa's Africa was not a dark and brooding place of constant danger and irrational violence. Rather, it was a natural paradise full of beauty and tranquility, and compatible with her American habits of home gardening and baking apple pies. In describing Africa this way, she sharply challenged the long-established myth that only the bravest of travelers could survive there. Suddenly, she made Africa seem accessible to me.

As I sat with the book at one of the great oak tables, my friends came over to take a look. Seeing the 1920s cars in the photographs, they pronounced the book "old-fashioned" and not worth reading. Peer pressure won, and I reshelved the book. Several weeks later, however, I returned to the library alone and took the book home with the librarian's enthusiastic approval.

It did not take me long to discover Osa's memoir *I Married Adventure*, and several of Martin's books. Yet, as much as I enjoyed them, they did not stir my imagination as had my encounter with *Four Years in Paradise*. It was not only that this was the first of their books that I had read, but more significantly that it described the idyllic high point of their careers when their talents were mustered in the service of wildlife conservation.

Inexperience and limited library resources hampered me from discovering much more about the Johnsons. I already knew that Martin had died in an airplane crash on January 13, 1937, the day I was born. But I wanted to learn more about what had happened to Osa after her last book was published in 1944.

One day in early 1953, as I commuted to high school on one of New York City's last remaining elevated lines, I glanced at a passenger's copy of the *New York Times*, and saw a bold headline announcing Osa's death. I was both startled and saddened; the timelessness of her writings had induced me into thinking of her as almost immortal. The sense of loss I felt had as much to do with missing the opportunity of meeting her as with sadness over her death. At school, I found no one with whom I could share these feelings. In fact, none of my classmates had ever heard of Osa, except for Frank McGuire, who had read her obituary that morning in the *New York Daily Mirror* under the headline "Queen of Jungle Dies." At home, my parents were indifferent, my mother remarking that it was a miracle that she had lived so long given all the stress to which she had subjected herself. I announced my intentions of visiting the funeral parlor where she was being waked. My parents promptly vetoed this idea by saying that a young boy had no business seeing the body of someone he did not know, and that such a visit would be an intrusion into the family's privacy. Although I did not go to the wake, I remembered from the obituary accounts that Osa was survived by her mother, Belle Leighty, of Chanute, Kansas.

My interest in the Johnsons received validation from my English teacher at St. Augustine's Diocesan High School, Brother Brendan Dooley, who praised my essay "They Broke All Records," in which I described their lives in Africa, and by the school's principal, Brother Barnabas Paul, who recommended their books for summer reading. But integrating my interests in a career in science and medicine with my fascination with Africa and the kind of life the Johnsons led seemed an impossible task to me, and one which both my parents and school guidance counselor strongly discouraged. It was only when I met John R. Saunders, an official at the American Museum of Natural History, that I realized it was possible to combine one's vocation in life with diverse avocations.

As I moved on into college, my interest in the Johnsons waned, though I continued to buy copies of their books whenever I found them in used bookstores. At the same time, my knowledge of Africa grew as I read widely on African history, political science, anthropology, and natural history. In my sophomore year in college, I entered a prominent political essay contest on current events in Africa and won the second prize for my paper, "International Security and the Challenge of African Nationalism." Some history and political science majors felt resentful that a biology major had beaten them, while my fellow science students viewed me as being idiosyncratic. After all, I had strayed beyond the accepted intellectual boundaries for someone planning to study medicine. Yet, there were those such as my biology professor, C. William Lacaillade, who viewed my participation in the contest as a challenge to the narrow vocational orientation of many faculty and students, and as an affirmation of his strong belief that the arts and sciences were not mutually exclusive.

In my third year of medical school, I was awarded an overseas fellowship by the Association of American Medical Colleges and the Smith, Kline and French Laboratories to spend several months at Kowak, a Maryknoll medical mission in Tanganyika Territory (now Tanzania). By June 1961, I was on my way to East Africa, my boyhood dreams about to come true. When I arrived in Kenya Colony and Protectorate (now Kenya), Nairobi had not yet become the hub of a huge tourist industry. As in the Johnsons' time, most visitors were wealthy Europeans and Americans who had come on hunting safaris. The country was still a colony where the Union Jack flew over its administrative posts, and Queen Elizabeth's head graced the stamps and coins. I carried into East Africa many preconceptions and attitudes shaped both by American values of the time and by the enormous literature I had read over the years. From the outset, the East Africa that I had vicariously come to know clashed with the reality I found. My visit occurred during the colonial twilight, and I clearly saw the dynamic push toward independence, and met Africans of a kind who had never appeared in the Johnsons' writings. In Tanganyika, I closely worked with African doctors and nurses, government officials, and teachers, who became my friends. Their hospitality and patient teaching enabled me to enter lives which from my readings I never knew existed.

The world of northern Kenya, which the Johnsons knew so well, was much as it had been in their time. Isolated and harsh, it was a closed district still dominated by warring herdsmen and wildlife, and tenuously held together by far-flung administrative posts where the queen's portrait was prominently displayed. Missionaries had not yet come into this area in large numbers, and this, coupled with poor roads and sparse communication links, left people to pursue their lives according to little-changed ancient customs and traditions. My respect and admiration for the Johnsons was affirmed as I crossed this rugged wilderness toward Lake Paradise, where they had lived for a few years. The lake lies in a crater at the top of Marsabit Mountain, which is covered by a dense virgin forest festooned with moss. It was still an isolated and primeval world where humans seldom intruded, the home of elephant and rhino, lion and bush buck.

Early one morning, I climbed up the slope to the crater's rim, much as a pilgrim approaches a shrine, filled with excitement, joy, and apprehension. The view at the top was spectacular, as if created by the brush of a Hudson River School painter. Lake Paradise lay below, as a blue pool surrounded by green meadows and walls of forest. Beyond the forest's slopes, the Kaisoot Desert stretched to the horizons in shades of purple, brown, and gray. Except for the breeze, it was a world full of haunting silence, where even the elephants below created no sound as they moved through the water. The vista that spread out before me was the same one Martin had captured in pictures over three decades before. Yet my exhilaration at this thought was tinged with disappointment as I scanned the crater's southwestern ridge. In Martin's pictures, the ridge was crowded with the thatch roofs of their permanent camp, but now only open spaces appeared between the trees. While I had succeeded in traveling to the place in Africa that I most associated with them, the open spaces on the ridge abruptly told me that I could not travel back into time. The site still contained a few mud-brick walls and the concrete footings of their houses, now worn smooth over the decades by the feet of elephants making their way to the lake. I picked up a small brick from one of the walls and took it back as a souvenir.

On returning to New York City, I wrote to Osa's mother, Belle Leighty, in Chanute, Kansas, telling her I had visited Lake Paradise and had taken photographs of it which she might like to have. I had no idea if she was still alive nor did I have a street address, but a few weeks later, I received a reply. More letters and photographs were exchanged, and finally she invited me to come out to visit the Martin and Osa Johnson Safari Museum which had recently opened. In September 1964, my sister Joyce and I traveled to Chanute, and again I felt like a pilgrim as the train made its way from Kansas City down into the southeastern corner of the state. It was late in the evening when we arrived at Chanute. A group of a half a dozen people stood under the dim station lights and moved toward us as we stepped off the train. In the center was a small woman who stretched out her hand. In touching it, I felt that I had come to the end of a long journey, but in reality, an even greater odyssey had just begun.

Belle was a sweet and charming woman who possessed not only elegance and poise, but also modesty and warmth. We took an immediate liking to one another, and our friendship was to last for a dozen years until her death in 1976. When we first met, she was eighty-eight years old, highly independent and self-sufficient, and had enormous energy and a remarkable memory. She spent hours talking about Martin and Osa, providing me with details about their lives not contained in any of their writings. This was the first of many visits with Belle, and the beginning of constant correspondence by telephone and letters that not only cemented our relationship, but also gave me a new mission in life—to write a biography of the Johnsons. Belle raised the issue on the second day of my visit as we sat in her small living room surrounded by framed pictures of Martin and Osa. Her choice of me, she said, was based on instinct, on my having written a popular book about my experiences in Africa, and because I had been born on the morning Martin died. She attached almost supernatural significance to this coincidence and to my interest in Martin and Osa. She was so confident that I could quickly write the biography that in the ensuing months she began sending me pictures to illustrate it. It was difficult for her, who had lived the Johnson story from beginning to end and afterwards, to fully appreciate how much time and effort would be required just to establish the factual record.

Before I left Chanute, Belle gave me an unpublished manuscript Osa had written about their trips to Borneo in 1920 and 1935–1936. She had kept it safe in a kitchen cabinet, stored in the original Sphinx bond-paper box that Osa had used. My success in having this book published under the title *Last Adventure* (William Morrow and Co., 1966) only strengthened Belle's conviction that I could rapidly write the biography. Yet, as I did some preliminary research, it became apparent to me that a great deal of effort would be required to locate and study all of the archival holdings where primary source materials were housed. My departure for several years in Africa delayed this endeavor, which did not get underway for another decade. In time, I came to know Osa's Aunt Minnie; her second husband, Clark Getts; the Johnsons' pilot, Vern Carstens; their cameraman, Joseph Tilton; and I interviewed others who had worked overseas with them, including James Laneri, David Martin, Douglas Oliver, and DeWitt Sage.

My wife, Eleanor, developed a great interest in the Johnsons and in their role in the evolution of the travel documentary. Soon after our marriage, we traveled to East Africa and not only visited Lake Paradise and other places where the Johnsons worked, but also interviewed many people who knew them. Clark Getts and Vern Carstens became very good friends whom we greatly admired. Our children came to know Vern and his wife Wilma as Grandpa Vern and Grandma Wilma, and John Willey, who as editor in chief of William Morrow and Co. had published *Last Adventure*, became their "Uncle John." These threads from the Johnsons' lives were woven into our own, and we ourselves became part of their posthumous story.

Researching the Johnsons' lives and careers entailed not only establishing the factual record, but also probing the myths they and their publicists had created. Belle herself had lived with the myths so long that she fully accepted some of them. Our discovery of the Martin and Osa behind the myths was a long and painstaking process, but one that was necessary to the writing of a critical biography. What emerged were two people quite different in many ways from the public images they had created for themselves. We were not disappointed by what we found because even in their private lives, Martin and Osa had the power to inspire.

Pascal James Imperato

NOTES

The Johnsons' existing papers and correspondence and other primary source materials concerning them are dispersed in several archival holdings. In citing materials from these archives, we have included catalogue numbers where possible. Martin Johnson authored eight books and Osa ten. We have used the following abbreviations:

WORKS BY MARTIN JOHNSON

TSS	*Through the South Seas with Jack London* (1913)
MJCSS	*Martin Johnson's Cannibals of the South Seas* (Unpublished, 1919)
CL	*Cannibal-Land* (1922)
CA	*Camera Trails in Africa* (1924)
SF	*Safari* (1928)
LN	*Lion* (1929)
CON	*Congorilla* (1931)
OAJ	*Over African Jungles* (1935)

WORKS BY OSA JOHNSON

JB	*Jungle Babies* (1930)
JP	*Jungle Pets* (1932)
IMA	*I Married Adventure* (1940)
FYP	*Four Years in Paradise* (1941)
JF	*Osa Johnson's Jungle Friends* (1941)
PS	*Pantaloons* (1941)
SL	*Snowball* (1942)
BS	*Bride in the Solomons* (1944)
TA	*Tarnish* (1944)
LA	*Last Adventure* (1966)

The following abbreviations are used in the notes to identify the Johnsons and various archival holdings:

MJ	Martin Johnson
OJ	Osa Johnson
AMNH	American Museum of Natural History Archives
HEH	Henry E. Huntington Library, Jack London and Charmian Kittredge London Collections
LC	Library of Congress, Motion Picture Division
NYPL	New York Public Library, General Library and Museum of the Performing Arts (Lincoln Center)
SM	The Martin and Osa Johnson Safari Museum Archives
UW	University of Wyoming, American Heritage Center, Clark H. Getts Collection

PROLOGUE

1. Malekula is the second largest island in the New Hebrides, an archipelago that in 1980 became the independent country of Vanuatu (the name means "the land that has stood up strong for a long time"). It extends 55 miles southeast to north-west and is roughly shaped like an hourglass. It is some 4 miles wide at its narrowest point, but close to 30 miles wide in the south.
2. Three versions of the Johnsons' 1917 trip to the Big Nambas exist. Two of these are published, MJ's *CL*, written a few years after the event, and OJ's *IMA*, written twenty-two years later. MJ's manuscript, *Martin Johnson's Cannibals of the South Seas* (SM), written shortly after the trip, was never fully published, al-though portions appeared as articles in MJ's hometown newspapers, *The Inde-pendence Daily Reporter* and *The Independence Evening Star*. There are significant differences in the details presented in each of these accounts.
3. The Big Nambas were given their name by early European visitors because of the large masses of red-violet pandanus fibers, known as *nambas*, that are used by these people as penis sheaths. A group to the south of them, whose penis sheaths are smaller, were named the Small Nambas. In all their writings, MJ and OJ incorrectly refer to them as the Big Numbers and Small Numbers, respectively. For details on the ethnography of Malekula, see A. Bernard Deacon, *Malekula: A Vanishing People in the New Hebrides*, ed. Camilla H. Wedgwood (London: Rout-ledge and Keegan Paul, 1937; reprinted 1970).
4. For accounts of European depredations in the New Hebrides, see Tom Har-risson, *Savage Civilization* (New York: Alfred A. Knopf, 1937).
5. The Bridges affair and the death of the Corlette boy are recounted in detail by Harrisson, *Savage Civilization*, 405–406, and by Charlene Gourguechon, *Journey to the End of the World: A Three-Year Adventure in the New Hebrides* (New York: Charles Scribner's Sons, 1977), 36–38. This massacre was widely discussed by Europeans in the islands at the time, and MJ and OJ knew of it. MJ refers to it and the subsequent punitive expedition while narrating his film *Across the World with Mr. and Mrs. Martin Johnson* (1930).
6. The name, which is derived from the Portuguese word for sea slug, *bicho de mar*, a principal item of trade beginning in the nineteenth century, was eventually applied by early traders to the pidgin spoken in the New Hebrides. Today, *bêche-de-mer* is known in English as bislama and in French as bichelamar, and is the official language of Vanuatu (the New Hebrides).
7. *CL*, 15.
8. *CL*, 15.
9. *CL*, 15–16.
10. Harrisson, *Savage Civilization*, 405.
11. In all their writings and in their films, MJ and OJ incorrectly refer to Nihapat as Nagapate. The correct spelling of Nihapat's name is discussed by Kirk Huffman of the Vanuatu Cultural Center in a letter to the Martin and Osa Johnson Safari Museum, in *The Johnson Wait-A-Bit News* 2, 4:7–8 (1981).
12. *CL*, 16.
13. *CL*, 16.
14. *CL*, 16.
15. *CL*, 17.
16. *CL*, 17.

17. *CL*, 18–19; *IMA*, 121–122.
18. *CL*, 19.
19. It is entirely possible that Nihapat was merely insisting that MJ and OJ visit his village nearby as his guests.
20. The captain of the *Euphrosine* stopped in Tenmarou Bay in order to leave a letter for MJ from Merton King, the British resident for the New Hebrides. In it, King warned MJ not to penetrate the interior of Malekula. He very pointedly said, "Such an undertaking cannot but be attended with great risk to yourself and to all those who accompany you" (*CL*, 21–22; *IMA*, 124–125).
21. *CL*, 19–20; *IMA*, 122.
22. *CL*, 20.
23. *CL*, 20.
24. MJ makes no mention of being chased by Nihapat's people in either of his two accounts. This detail appears only in OJ's account in *IMA*, 123. MJ's principal concern was not the Big Nambas they had left behind, but those on the beach (*CL*, 20).
25. The question naturally arises concerning the actual danger posed by the Big Nambas to MJ and OJ. Tom Harrisson, who visited the Big Nambas with the Oxford University expedition in 1932, fifteen years after the Johnsons' visit, said: "The Big Nambas are difficult to approach not only because of their own fights, but because they hate the white man. . . . War is the main feature of Big Nambas life" (*Savage Civilization*, 395, 401). Yet he characterized the chief of Tenmarou as "charming" and "friendly" and as one who enabled him "to move freely and unarmed all over this country, even between villages at war with each other" (396). From most published contemporary accounts, it appears that the Big Nambas were warlike, fiercely independent, and resentful of European intrusions into their way of life. Blood feuds among themselves primarily spawned an endless cycle of well-focused revenge killings and cannibalism.

    In MJ's two accounts (*CL* and *MJCSS*) of this Malekula episode, he states that the captain of the *Euphrosine* left a letter from the British resident with their crew on the beach and departed after being told they were a short distance in the interior. The letter warned MJ not to enter the interior of Malekula. In attempting to explain the captain's departure, MJ relates that his crew led the captain to believe that he and OJ were nearby in the bush, in no danger, and about to return to the boat (*CL*, 21). The crew had no way of being certain of these facts, and surely the captain of the *Euphrosine* must have known this. The fact that he left indicates that he either showed poor judgment or else did not think that the Johnsons were in serious danger. The danger to them was actually more potential than immediate, and lay in the unpredictable circumstances that might have arisen while traveling among a warlike people.

1. GROWING UP IN KANSAS

1. For the early history of Lincoln see Dorothe Tarrence Homan, *Lincoln—That County in Kansas* (Lindsborg, Kans.: Barbos' Printing, 1979), 1–127.
2. MJ regretted that he never saw the Kansas frontier as it had been before settlement (interview, Belle Leighty, OJ's mother, Chanute, Kans., May 24, 1966).
3. *IMA*, 18; Kenhelm W. Stott, Jr., *Exploring with Martin and Osa Johnson* (Chanute, Kans.: Martin and Osa Johnson Safari Museum Press, 1978), 10.

4. Interviews, Belle Leighty, Chanute, Kans., May 25, 1966, February 19, 1970; interview, Thelma Harmon, Des Moines, Iowa, January 23, 1989.

5. *IMA* 18; Stott, *Exploring*. In *IMA* (18), OJ relates that John Johnson did not respond to the call for "boots and saddles" when General George Armstrong Custer rode out to the Battle of the Little Big Horn. Johnson had been enticed into a poker game he was winning; as a result, he not only saved his life, but also won two hundred dollars. Belle Leighty expressed doubts about the accuracy of this anecdote (interview, Chanute, Kans., February 20, 1970).

6. Homan, *Lincoln*, 64. The town has been known as both Lincoln and Lincoln Center (Homan, *Lincoln*, 112–113).

7. Advertisements promoting Lincoln ran from the late 1870s through the mid-1880s (Homan, *Lincoln*, 98–99). Lincoln never became a large town. Its population in 1986 was 1,599; see *Encyclopedia Americana* (Danbury, Conn.: Grolier, Inc., 1986), 296.

8. Homan, *Lincoln*, 102.

9. The Johnsons had two other children in addition to Martin, a son who died at the age of four in 1894, and a daughter, Freda (1895–1966). The Johnsons donated a silver cup to the Lincoln Methodist Church in memory of their four-year-old son (Personal communication, Margaret Cripps Sachs, Berkeley, California, October 21, 1991; "Lincoln Has First Claim," *Lincoln Republican*, December 29, 1921). The Johnsons' small frame house on South Second Street, although much renovated, was still standing in 1989 (interviews, Mrs. Richard Erickson [Elizabeth Marshall], Kansas City, Mo., March 24, 1989; Mrs. Evelyn Bolte, Lincoln, Kans., November 14, 1989).

10. For conditions in Lincoln Grade School in the late nineteenth century, see Homan, *Lincoln*, 136. For MJ's early years in school, see Homan, *Lincoln*, 341 and *IMA*, 19. According to Homan, MJ began the first grade in 1888, when he was just four years old (341). The Annual Report of the Lincoln School District No. 6 for June 30, 1893, gives Martin's age as eight years, but not his grade. The June 30, 1894, report similarly lists only his age, which was then nine (courtesy Delwin J. Rathburn, Register of Deeds, Lincoln County, Kans.).

11. OJ states in *IMA* (21) that MJ first ran away from home when he was put back into the sixth grade after receiving failing grades in all subjects except geography. Martin had actually run away a number of times before this (interview, Belle Leighty, Chanute, Kans., May 23, 1966).

12. In *IMA* (22), OJ states that MJ's mother followed him when he ran away for the first time to give him a carpetbag of his things. She also states that when he returned he was received without surprise or comment. These statements are at variance with the observations of other contemporaries who recall that his parents were very upset by his running away (interview, Belle Leighty, Chanute, Kans., February 18, 1970).

13. *IMA*, 13–25, 193–197, 245–251; in real life, OJ called him "Papa Johnson."

14. For a description of John Johnson when MJ was young, see H. C. Ingraham, "Adventure Unlimited! Martin Johnson's Boyhood Pal Recalls Thrill-Filled Life of Renowned Kansan," *Wichita Eagle and Beacon Magazine*, February 17, 1963, 4, 12.

15. MJ's boyhood in Lincoln is described in *IMA*, 18–23; Homan, *Lincoln*, 137–139; *Lincoln Republican*, December 29, 1921. The Marshalls originally lived next door to the Johnsons and Bennie (later Ben) and Martin were very close friends. Ben's

father, Abram Marshall, organized the Saline Valley Bank in 1881. Ben later became president of the bank. He died on April 22, 1948 (interview, Mrs. Richard Erickson [Elizabeth Marshall], Kansas City, Missouri, March 24, 1989; Homan, 133). In May 1935 MJ visited Lincoln, landing with one of his planes, *The Spirit of Africa*, on Ben Marshall's pasture. At that time he visited his former home on South Second Street and met with his old friends (Homan, *Lincoln*, 223; *Lincoln Sentinel-Republican*, May 30, 1935; interview, Mrs. Richard Erickson [Elizabeth Marshall], Kansas City, Mo., March 24, 1989). The Rees family (OJ incorrectly spells the name Reese in *IMA*, 19) first settled in Lincoln in 1872. The mill of which MJ was so fond was destroyed by a fire on January 1, 1942, when spontaneous combustion occurred in a wheat pit (Homan, *Lincoln*, 231).

16. *IMA*, 24.
17. "The Barefoot Boy" in *The Complete Poetical Works of John Greenleaf Whittier* (Boston: Houghton, Mifflin and Co., 1894), 195–196.
18. For an analysis of the characters Tom Sawyer and Huckleberry Finn, see Everett Emerson, *The Authentic Mark Twain: A Literary Biography of Samuel L. Clemens* (Philadelphia: University of Pennsylvania Press, 1984), 78–84; 127–144.
19. Horatio Alger (1832–1899), the popular American writer, shaped the aspirations of youth when Martin was young with his stories about self-supporting boys who through virtue, hard work, and a dash of luck overcome great obstacles and climb up the ladder of success. For an analysis of Horatio Alger's works and their impact on American values, see Edwin P. Hoyt, *Horatio's Boys: The Life and Works of Horatio Alger, Jr.* (Radnor, Pa.: Chilton Book Co., 1974). The changing meaning of the essential message in Alger's works over time is discussed in detail in Gary Scharnhorst with Jack Bales, *The Lost Life of Horatio Alger, Jr.* (Bloomington: Indiana University Press, 1985), 149–156.
20. Clark Hallan Getts, OJ's manager and second husband, thought that Winifred Dunn, who ghosted *IMA*, was successful in making Martin a Horatio Alger hero (interview, New York City, March 16, 1977). OJ's mother, Belle Leighty, expressed the view that MJ's early years were not quite as described in *IMA* (interview, Belle Leighty, Chanute, Kans., May 25, 1966).
21. *IMA*, 23; Homan, *Lincoln*, 139. Leon A. Sherwood, Sr., *The Spirit of Independence* (Independence, Kans.: Tribune Printing, 1970), 30.
22. Sherwood, *The Spirit*, 52; Ken D. Brown, *Independence: The Way We Were* (Independence, Kans.: Independence Arts Council, 1980), 53. Independence, unlike Lincoln, gradually grew in size, reaching a population of 4,851 in 1902 and a population of 10,598 in 1986; see *Atlas of the World* (Chicago: Rand McNally & Co., 1902), 232; *Encyclopedia Americana* (Danbury, Conn.: Grolier Inc., 1986), 296. Independence, the county seat of Montgomery County, is on the Verdigis River. It was founded in 1870 on the site of the former Osage Reservation; see *Kansas: A Guide to the Sunflower State* (New York: Hastings House, 1939), 476.
23. *IMA*, 23–25.
24. *IMA*, 23.
25. MJ not only learned many of his father's technical skills, but also his business and marketing practices, which he used regularly in later years.
26. *IMA*, 24.
27. *IMA*, 26; OJ states that MJ was fifteen, going on sixteen, when these events occurred (*IMA*, 26) and that she was in her seventh year (*IMA*, 15). She also states that eight years elapsed before she learned the name of the itinerant photo-

grapher (*IMA*, 17). Given her March 14, 1894, birthdate, and her hearing of MJ late in 1909, it is likely that the year was 1901 and that Martin was sixteen, going on seventeen.

28. *IMA*, 26–27.
29. *IMA*, 27.
30. *IMA*, 15–17.
31. *IMA*, 15; Chanute's population at the time of Martin's 1901 visit was 4,208; see *Atlas of the World* (Chicago: Rand McNally & Co., 1902). The town was founded in 1872, when the four nearby rival settlements of Chicago, Chicago Junction, Alliance, and Tioga decided to merge. It was named after Octave Chanute, a construction engineer for the Leavenworth, Lawrence, and Galveston Railroad, who later became a pioneer aeronautical engineer; see William Frank Zarrow, *Kansas: A History of the Jayhawk State* (Norman: University of Oklahoma Press, 1957), 290, 292, 297, 319–320.
32. "Osa Helen Leighty Johnson (Mrs. Martin Johnson)," in *The National Cyclopedia of American Biography*, vol. 39 (New York: James T. White and Co., 1954), 39.
33. Margaret Olwine, "The Safari Museum at Chanute, Kansas," *Star: Sunday Magazine of the Kansas City Star*, September 22, 1974, 12.
34. Interview, Belle Leighty, Chanute, Kans., May 25, 1966. Nancy Ann Taylor died in Chanute in 1945 at the age of eighty-nine.
35. Describing her mother's pioneer move to Kansas, Belle said: "The Indians were so bad up here that my family had to go back to Missouri. It was only after the army chased the Indians out that they were able to come back and settle" (interview, Belle Leighty, Chanute, Kans., May 24, 1966).
36. "Wreck Ends 50-Year Service of Engineer," *Wichita Beacon*, September 8, 1934, 2–3; Osa's unusual name was, according to her mother, an abbreviated form of Rosa. "I had a friend named Rosa and liked the name but since there was someone with it already, I dropped the R and called her Osa. Helen was for my husband's mother" (interview, Belle Leighty, Chanute, Kans., October 2, 1964). There is the possibility that inspiration for the name Osa may have also come from local Indian names such as Osage and Osawatomie.
37. Interviews, Minnie Thomas, New York City, 1964–1966.
38. Interview, Belle Leighty, Chanute, Kans., May 25, 1966.
39. Ingraham, "Adventure Unlimited."
40. Letter from Charmian K. London to Ralph D. Harrison, Oakland, Calif., October 3, 1915 (HEH, JL-9960).
41. *IMA*, 30–32.
42. *IMA*, 32; MJ was probably expelled in the fall term of the 1901–1902 school year, when he was seventeen years old. His name appears in the *Autograph Record Book, Montgomery County High School, 1901–1902*, which was a register of students attending school. His age in this document is given as seventeen. The records of the Montgomery County High School were accidentally destroyed during the 1920s. Thus full documentation of the precise time and circumstances of MJ's expulsion is not possible (interview, Pat Helm, Montgomery County Board of Education, January 30, 1989).
43. *IMA*, 32; Stott, *Exploring*, 11.
44. *IMA*, 35–37.
45. *IMA*, 37.

46. Stott, *Exploring*, 12. MJ in *TSS* (59) states that he sailed east across the Atlantic on a cattle steamer in May 1906, several years after he had left school.
47. Ingraham (in "Adventure Unlimited") states that he did not waste any more time with John Johnson but went to see Lucinda and Freda, who "greeted me warmly with tears in their eyes." He quotes Lucinda as saying that her husband "is so stingy with all of us. . . . He thinks we should all slave for him, just like he had to do for his father back in Illinois."
48. Ingraham, "Adventure Unlimited."
49. Letter from Martin E. Johnson to Jack London, Independence, Kans., November 5, 1906 (HEH, JL-8466).
50. The Johnsons' writings and those of others present differing accounts of MJ's European travels. There are significant inconsistencies about the number of trips, dates, his stowing away across the Atlantic, and his working at Luna Park in Paris. The available evidence documents that MJ made three trips to Europe in his early years. The date of the first of these was probably in 1902 (Ingraham, "Adventure Unlimited"). The second occurred between May and June 1906 and lasted several weeks. On the second trip, MJ returned from Liverpool on the *Bovic* (letter from Martin E. Johnson to Jack London, Independence, Kans., November 23, 1906, HEH). The story of his stowing away on one of these trips is questionable because he makes no mention of it in his letters to Jack London, yet he describes the less daring feat of stowing away from Southampton to Antwerp. The third trip occurred in 1909, when he was returning home from the *Snark* voyage. The trans-Atlantic stowaway episode may have taken place at this time, if indeed it ever took place at all. MJ later spoke about it in his *Snark* Theater travelogues, and Ralph D. Harrison described it in his postscript to *TSS* (368–369). The veracity of these accounts is suspect because of MJ's claims at the time of having been to places he never visited.

2. THE URGE TO WANDER

1. Letter from Martin E. Johnson to Jack London, Independence, Kans., November 5, 1906 (HEH, JL-8466).
2. For details of Jack London's early life and career, see Joan London, *Jack London and His Times: An Unconventional Biography* (Seattle and London: University of Washington Press, 1968), 1–250; Richard O'Connor, *Jack London: A Biography* (Boston and Toronto: Little, Brown and Co., 1964), 3–181; John Perry, *Jack London: An American Myth* (Chicago: Nelson-Hall, 1981), 1–125; Clarice Stasz, *American Dreamers: Jack and Charmian London* (New York: St. Martin's Press, 1988), 8–26, 46–68; Irving Stone, *Sailor on Horseback* (Garden City, N.Y.: Doubleday & Co., 1977), 9–170.
3. Perry, *Jack London*, 75–82; Stasz, *Dreamers*, 130–131; Stone, *Sailor*, 141.
4. O'Connor, *Jack London*, 186; Perry, *Jack London*, 176–177; Stasz, *Dreamers*, 144.
5. O'Connor, *Jack London*, 153–154; Stasz, *Dreamers*, 96, 141; *TSSJL*, 38.
6. O'Connor, *Jack London*, 238–239; Perry, *Jack London*, 202–203, Stasz, *Dreamers*, 132–133.
7. Jack London, *The Cruise of the Snark: A Pacific Voyage* (London and New York: KPI, 1986), 13; A. Grove Day, *Jack London in the South Seas* (New York: Four Winds Press, 1971), 1.

8. Jack London, "The Voyage of the Snark," *Cosmopolitan*, December 1906, 115–122.

9. See London, *Cruise of the Snark*, 27–38; O'Connor, *Jack London*, 251–256; Stasz, *Dreamers*, 137–141.

10. O'Connor, *Jack London*, 254.

11. Charmian Kittredge London, *The Book of Jack London* (New York: The Century Co., 1921), 150.

12. Herbert Rowell Stolz (1887–1971) later became a Rhodes scholar and then received his M.D. degree from Stanford University in 1914. From 1925 to 1934 he served as director of the Institute of Child Welfare, University of California at Berkeley. Later, he was chief of the Special Services Division of the California State Department of Education. He and Lois Meek Stolz, Ph.D., authored what is now a classic volume, *Somatic Development of Adolescent Boys: A Study of the Growth of Boys during the Second Decade of Life* (New York: Macmillan, 1951). A veteran of World War I, he died in Palo Alto, California, on January 16, 1971, of a cerebral thrombosis at the age of eighty-four.

13. O'Connor, *Jack London*, 256; Stasz, *Dreamers*, 140; *TSSJL*, 16.

14. Some writers have repeated OJ's inaccurate statement in *FYP* (35) that MJ first became aware of the *Snark* voyage on reading the November 10, 1906, issue of *Cosmopolitan* magazine. Miriam L. Mih, in her *Safari: A Short Travelogue of the Adventures of Martin and Osa Johnson* (Chanute, Kans., 1961), states that MJ "read an ad that Jack London had placed in the *Cosmopolitan* (November 10, 1906)," (6); Kenhelm W. Stott, Jr., presents another variant of this in his *Exploring with Martin and Osa Johnson* (Chanute, Kans.: Martin and Osa Johnson Safari Museum Press, 1978): "The November 11, 1906, issue of *Cosmopolitan*, which Martin described as his favorite magazine, contained an article concerning the proposed round-the-world yachting trip of author Jack London and his wife" (12). The November 1906 issue of *Cosmopolitan* did not carry either advertisements or articles about the *Snark* voyage. However, the December 1906 issue carried Jack London's famous article "The Voyage of the Snark." London received an advance copy of the issue on November 24, 1906, almost three weeks after MJ wrote his November 5 letter (letter from Jack London to Editor, *Cosmopolitan*, Glen Ellen, Calif., November 24, 1906, HEH). Thus MJ's letter to Jack London could not have been based on a reading of the December issue of *Cosmopolitan*. MJ never mentions the magazine in question by name. He merely says, "While passing away an hour with my favorite magazine, my attention was attracted to an article describing a proposed trip" (*TSSJL*, 2–3). In *IMA* (41), OJ states that MJ "leafed the magazine Freda had left in her chair." MJ must have read of the *Snark* trip in the November issue of *Woman's Home Companion*, which carried the only magazine article on the subject up to that date. The fact that it was a women's magazine possibly explains why his sister Freda was reading it and why he and OJ never mention it by name in any of their writings. Their decision not to name the magazine was probably determined by the attitudes of the times. Neither MJ nor OJ could publicly admit to the pivotal role played by an article in a women's magazine in shaping the career of an American male hero.

15. "A Preliminary Letter from Jack London Who Is Going Round the World for the Woman's Home Companion," *Woman's Home Companion* 33, 11:19 (November 1906).

16. *TSSJL*, 3.

17. See n. 1.
18. The photograph showed a smiling MJ standing erect with his hands in his pockets. He wore a long-sleeved shirt with a bow tie and a large fedora.
19. Elsie Whitaker Martinez, *San Francisco Bay Area Writers and Artists*, an interview conducted by Franklin D. Walker and Willa Klug Baum, Berkeley, University of California, Regional Oral History Office, Bancroft Library, 1969, 144–145.
20. Telegram from Jack London to Martin E. Johnson, Glen Ellen, Calif., November 12, 1906 (HEH, JL-12221).
21. *TSSJL*, 3–4.
22. Telegram from Martin E. Johnson to Jack London, Independence, Kans., November 12, 1906 (HEH, JL-8467).
23. Letter from Martin E. Johnson to Jack London, Independence, Kans., November 13, 1906 (HEH, JL-8468).
24. Letter from John A. Johnson to Jack London, Independence, Kans., November 13, 1906 (HEH, JL-8408).
25. *TSSJL*, 4; *IMA*, 44–45.
26. Letter from Jack London to Martin E. Johnson, Glen Ellen, Calif., November 17, 1906 (HEH, JL-12222).
27. Ingraham, "Adventure Unlimited," 4, 12.
28. *TSSJL*, 11.
29. Charmian London, *The Book of Jack London*, 156–157.
30. *TSSJL*, 12–13.

3. APPRENTICE TO ADVENTURE

1. *TSSJL*, 18.
2. *TSSJL*, 18.
3. *TSSJL*, 35–37.
4. *TSSJL*, 38.
5. *TSSJL*, 39–40.
6. *TSSJL*, 47.
7. *TSSJL*, 48.
8. *TSSJL*, 48.
9. Letter from Jack London to Freda Johnson (courtesy State of California, Department of Parks and Recreation, and I. Milo Shepard).
10. *TSSJL*, 51–52, 58.
11. London, *Cruise of the Snark*, 25, 60–66.
12. *TSSJL*, 84.
13. Stasz, *Dreamers*, 171.
14. Diary entries made by Charmian during the last weeks of the sail to Hawaii document how disappointed she and Jack were with both Roscoe and Bert. On May 1, 1907, she wrote, "Mate assembles all hands after breakfast and gives a lecture on ship discipline. Uncle talks back and mate feels pretty sick." This was followed on May 4 by the comment, "Mate more and more disgusted with uncle." She also recorded a number of comments about Bert. On May 9 she said, "Bert's unexpected demoralization, no ambition, grouchy, neglectful," and on May 11 noted that "Bert still impossible"; see Diary, Charmian Kittredge London, 1907 (HEH, JL-200). While the parting with Roscoe was stormy and

unpleasant, the one with Bert was fairly amicable. Bert's knowledge and skills were not well matched to what was needed of him on the *Snark*, and both he and Jack recognized this. In addition, his mother genuinely wanted him to return to his studies at Stanford.

Bert remained on in Hawaii for a while with his uncle and regularly saw the Londons during that time. In fact, Jack based his story "Koolau the Leper" on the true account of a leprosy-afflicted leader and his followers who murdered Bert's father, then a deputy sheriff in Hawaii, in order to avoid being sent to Molokai, the leprosy colony (Stasz, *Dreamers*, 163–164).

Martin's account of what occurred to these two men is interesting because it places both them and Jack in the best possible light, and is at significant variance with what really happened. He attempts to characterize the departures as voluntary, which they were not (*TSSJL*, 88).

15. *TSSJL*, 115.
16. O'Connor, *Jack London*, 262.
17. *TSSJL*, 95.
18. *TSSJL*, 109.
19. *TSSJL*, 87, 89.
20. Jack London, *Martin Eden* (New York: Macmillan, 1909).
21. Charles N. Watson, Jr., "The Composition of Martin Eden," *American Literature* 53:337–408 (1981).
22. Diary, Charmian Kittredge London, August 8, 1907 (HEH, JL-220).
23. Martin states that while in Honolulu, Jack showed him a sheet of paper on which the title *Martin Eden* was written. Jack then told him that he was going to make him a half-hero of the book by using his Christian name and the surname of an old friend called Eden (*TSSJL*, 141–142).

    Despite this firsthand account, Watson (in "Composition") concludes that the full name Martin Eden derives only from Jack's handyman neighbor who lived a somewhat reclusive life in the Sonoma Valley near Wake Robin Lodge. He was a Swedish immigrant who in the words of one writer was "a very plain man, simple, coarse, unkempt"; see Anders Kruskopf, "Martin Eden of Sonoma," *American Scandinavian Review* 31:347–348 (1943). However, the documented evidence seems to point to the untidy possibility that Jack derived the name from the two men and made Martin Johnson a half or a quarter hero.
24. *TSSJL*, 137.
25. Diary, Charmian Kittredge London, October 6, 1907 (HEH, JL-220).
26. Diary, Charmian Kittredge London, July 24, 1907 (HEH, JL-207).
27. Day, *Jack London*, 61.
28. *TSSJL*, 149–150.
29. *TSSJL*, 144–145.
30. *TSSJL*, 169.
31. *TSSJL*, 139.
32. Day, *Jack London*, 112, 113; O'Connor, *Jack London*, 267–269; Stasz, *Dreamers*, 177–178.
33. *TSSJL*, 201.
34. *TSSJL*, 201.
35. Diary, Charmian Kittredge London, March 10, 1908 (HEH, JL-222).
36. *TSSJL*, 215.

37. *TSSJL*, 215–216.
38. Stasz, *Dreamers*, 74, 158.
39. *TSSJL*, 304.
40. *TSSJL*, 303.
41. *TSSJL*, 278.
42. *TSSJL*, 268. Martin later changed his attitude and achieved financial success in vaudeville by showing these pictures to large audiences in the United States and Europe.
43. Diary, Charmian Kittredge London, May 29, 1908 (HEH, JL-222).
44. Jack London, "The Terrible Solomons," *Hampton's Magazine* 24:347–354 (March 10, 1910).
45. London, *Cruise of the Snark*, 297.
46. *TSSJL*, 277.
47. See Elaine Pasco, *Racial Prejudice* (New York: Franklin Watts, 1985), 1–34, 107–110.
48. Charmian Kittredge London, *The Log of the Snark* (New York: The Macmillan Co., 1916), 325–336.
49. For social, economic, and political conditions in the Solomon Islands at the time of the *Snark* visit, see Judith A. Bennett, *Wealth of the Solomons: A History of a Pacific Archipelago, 1800–1978* (Honolulu: University of Hawaii Press, 1987), 78–217; Janet Kent, *The Solomon Islands* (Newton Abbot, U.K.: David and Charles, 1972), 65–717.
50. *TSSJL*, 287.
51. *TSSJL*, 289.
52. *TSSJL*, 291.
53. Charmian London, *Log of the Snark*, 351.
54. Kent, *Solomon Islands*, 101.
55. The posts were shipped home via Australia. Martin later carried his sculpture in a specially made trunk and billed it in his vaudeville act as a "Devil-Devil." Since 1961 it has been on permanent exhibit at the Martin and Osa Johnson Safari Museum in Chanute, Kansas.
56. For a detailed description of *ramo* and their role as hired assassins, see Roger M. Keesing and Peter Corris, *Lightning Meets the West Wind: The Malaita Massacre* (Melbourne: Oxford University Press, 1980), 17–24.
57. The Londons' adventure on the *Minota* was the best publicized event of their trip. They were greatly helped out of their dangerous situation by a missionary, J. St. George Caulfeild, and Captain Keller of the whaleboat *Eugenie*, who was later killed and beheaded by the Solomon Islanders.
58. *TSSJL*, 310.
59. *TSSJL*, 311.
60. Charmian viewed Jack's illnesses as so serious that she made provisions in the event of his death. "I tell Martin if Jack should die and he (M) is competent and I can't sell Snark here, I'll have him take her to S. Fr."; see Diary, Charmian Kittredge London, October 8, 1908 (HEH, JL-222).
61. *TSSJL*, 330–331.
62. From the existing documentation, it is difficult to pinpoint a single cause for Jack's pellagra. While pellagra is often due to a deficiency in dietary intake of niacin, it can also be secondary to disturbances of the intestinal tract and alcohol-

ism that impede the vitamin's absorption, factors which may have been contributory in Jack's case. Certain medications can interfere with the absorption of niacin, another possible factor, since Jack was given to self-medication.

63. Letter from Martin Johnson to Jack London, Sydney, Australia, December 6, 1908 (HEH, JL-8472).

64. Martin may have been suffering from filariasis, a parasitic worm infection caused by *Wuchereria bancrofti*. Transmitted by various mosquito species, it was endemic throughout most islands of the South Pacific at the time of Martin's visit. Its early symptoms include painful swelling of the scrotal contents due to inflammation and blockage of the lymphatics. In 1908 no effective medications were available for treating this disease, even though many drugs were tried. However, the disease and the surgical approaches once used to relieve swelling of the scrotal contents could lead to sterility. In a December 8, 1908, letter to Jack, Martin said that the doctor had told him that the "left side is no good at all and that the right side is perfectly healthy" (HEH, JL-8473).

65. Letter from Jack London to John A. Johnson, Sydney, Australia, April 3, 1909 (HEH). In this letter, Jack suggested that John Johnson wire his son $150 to $300 so that he could see more of Europe and satisfy his yearnings. By January 7, 1909, MJ was in debt to Jack for $411.63, borrowed against future wages (HEH, JL-8473).

66. Before leaving Australia, MJ unsuccessfully tried to join up with former president Theodore Roosevelt's expedition to East Africa. When the *Asturias* reached Port Said, he again tried to reach the Roosevelt expedition, which had left for Mombasa, East Africa, three days before (*TSSJL*, 368). That Martin was anxious to travel through East Africa for several months after his experiences of the previous two years indicates how strong was his desire for adventure.

4. VAUDEVILLE

1. Jack London's articles based on the *Snark* voyage appeared in the *Woman's Home Companion*, *Harper's Weekly*, *Hampton's Magazine*, *Pacific Monthly*, and others; MJ's letters home were published at irregular intervals in 1908 and 1909 in Independence's two newspapers, *The Independence Evening Star* and *The Independence Daily Reporter*.

2. Burton Holmes (1870–1958) coined the term "travelogue" in 1904 in London, England, and originated motion picture travel films. See "Burton Holmes, Lecturer, 88, Dies," *New York Times*, July 23, 1958, 27; and "Burton Holmes," in *The National Encyclopedia of American Biography*, vol. 44 (New York: James T. White, 1962), 510–511.

3. Letter from Martin Johnson to Jack London, Independence, Kans., December 16, 1909 (HEH); Martin's Balance—End of *Snark* Trip, Jack London, February 1915 (HEH).

4. Letter from Martin Johnson to Jack and Charmian London, Independence, Kans., November 25, 1909 (HEH).

5. Letter from Martin Johnson to Jack and Charmian London, Independence, Kans., July 21, 1910 (HEH).

6. Letter from Martin Johnson to Jack London, Independence, Kans., March 17, 1910 (HEH).

7. Letter from Martin Johnson to Jack London, Independence, Kans., December 16, 1909 (HEH).

8. *IMA*, 71–76.

9. Interviews, Belle Leighty and Minnie Thomas, Chanute, Kans., February 18, 1970.

10. Letter from Martin Johnson to Jack and Charmian London, Independence, Kans., May 19, 1910 (HEH).

11. Interview, Belle Leighty, Chanute, Kans., May 25, 1966.

12. See n. 10.

13. See n. 5.

14. See n. 5.

15. See n. 5.

16. See n. 11.

17. Letter from Martin Johnson to Jack and Charmian London, Fort William, Ontario, Canada, October 20, 1911 (HEH).

18. The poor reception in Humboldt was due in part to people having read of Martin's travels in the newspapers. In October 1964, when one of us (PJI) rode through Humboldt with Osa's mother, Belle Leighty, she remarked: "Martin and Osa came up here from Chanute in a buggy and were given a very bad reception by these people." She still felt some resentment over this more than half a century later.

19. Letter from Martin Johnson to Jack and Charmian London, Osborne, Kans., November 10, 1910 (HEH).

20. Letter from Martin Johnson to Jack and Charmian London, Denver, Colo., December 8, 1910 (HEH).

21. Letter from Martin Johnson to Jack and Charmian London, Laramie, Wyo., April 6, 1911 (HEH); OJ occasionally gave solo performances, being billed as "Osaleighty" or as the "Tom Boy of Honolulu."

22. See n. 17.

23. See n. 17.

24. Letter from Charmian London to Martin Johnson, Glen Ellen, Calif., October 28, 1911 (HEH).

25. Letter from Martin Johnson to Jack and Charmian London, Peoria, Ill., November 29, 1911 (HEH); letter from Charmian London to Martin Johnson, Glen Ellen, Calif., December 12, 1911 (HEH); letter from Martin Johnson to Jack London, Independence, Kans., December 7, 1911 (HEH).

26. Charles Edward Bray (1859–1932) was a varieties pioneer who was described as "a suave, handsome chap . . . an excellent 'front'; when he entered a restaurant the waiters did nip-ups to give him a ringside table"; see Douglas Gilbert, *American Vaudeville: Its Life and Times* (New York: Dover Publications, 1940), 210–211. Bray became a close personal friend of MJ and OJ and visited them at their camp on Mount Marsabit in Kenya in 1925; see "Charles E. Bray Dies, Variety Pioneer," *New York Times*, February 15, 1932, 17. MJ signed up with the Orpheum in October, but returned to Independence for the Christmas holidays from early December to January 8, 1912. While there, he helped his father out in the store during the Christmas shopping period.

27. Letter from Martin Johnson to Jack and Charmian London, Fort Wayne, Ind., February 14, 1912 (HEH).

28. MJ and OJ were in Seattle, Washington, on July 26, 1912, when the Londons disembarked from the *Dirigo* on which they had spent five months sailing around Cape Horn from Baltimore. This was OJ's first meeting with the Londons. The two couples went to Glen Ellen, where the Johnsons spent a short time before going on to a San Francisco performance. MJ was extremely keen on purchasing a ranch near the Londons (letter from Martin Johnson to Jack and Charmian London, Salt Lake City, September 26, 1912, HEH; Stasz, *Dreamers*, 245).

29. Letter from Martin Johnson to Jack and Charmian London, Lincoln, Neb., October 22, 1912 (HEH).

30. MJ frequently provided the Londons with his one-week-stand itineraries and even took the trouble to let them know when these were slightly modified.

31. Harrison wrote a total of eleven letters to Jack London between 1911 and 1915 and received three in return. He also corresponded with Charmian London between 1915 and 1917.

32. Letter from Martin Johnson to Jack and Charmian London, Louisville, Ky., December 27, 1912 (HEH).

33. Letter from Martin Johnson to Jack and Charmian London, La Porte, Ind., December 7, 1912 (HEH).

34. Martin Beck (1867–1940) later became president of the Orpheum Circuit and built the famous Palace Theater in New York City. A short, fat, bald man, he enjoyed collecting art and rare books. The Martin Beck Theater in New York City, named in his honor, received landmark status in 1987 ("5 More Theaters Classified as Landmarks," *New York Times*, November 5, 1987, B1–B2).

35. Letter from Martin Johnson to Jack London, London, England, March 25, 1913 (HEH).

36. See n. 35.

37. Letter from Martin Johnson to Jack and Charmian London, New York City, June 21, 1913 (HEH).

38. Cruise of the Snark Lectures. "Jack London's Sail in the South Seas at the Criterion," *New York Sun*, June 16, 1913, 2; "Jack London's," *Variety*, June 27, 1913, 16. The show was advertised in several New York City newspapers (see *New York Sun*, June 16, 1913, 14).

39. It has been erroneously assumed by some that MJ produced a film of the *Snark* cruise entitled *Jack London's Adventures in the South Sea Islands*. In actuality this was the title of his Criterion Theater travelogue, which consisted of lantern slides made by himself and others and motion film footage shot by others; see *Jack London's Adventures in the South Sea Islands*, in *The American Film Institute Catalog of Motion Pictures Produced in the United States: Feature Films, 1911–1921*, ed. Patricia King Hanson and Alan Gevinson (Berkeley: University of California Press, 1988), 468.

40. The fact that no mention is made of the specifics of Osa's operation raises the possibility that it was gynecologic in character. The surgeon who performed it, Dr. William Surber Porter (1867–1948), became a good friend of the Johnsons and later provided MJ with glass eyes with which to trick the peoples of the New Hebrides and Solomon Islands.

41. Letter from Martin Johnson to Jack and Charmian London, Minn., Minnesota, November 22, 1913 (HEH); MJ said that he had written a first rough draft, which Harrison rewrote. After correcting this, he sent it back to Harrison, who wrote up the final draft. Harrison later told Charmian that he had used MJ's

newspaper clippings and letters in preparing the book and had enjoyed the collaboration; MJ claimed in his November 22, 1913, letter that he obtained a list of book publishers and took his manuscript to the first one on the list, leaving before noon of the same day with a contract. Sales of the book were modest, and the two-dollar retail price gave MJ and Harrison little in the way of royalties. The book received respectable reviews, including one in the *New York Times Book Review* on February 22, 1914, VI, 89. The *American Library Booklist* 10:225 (February 14, 1914), made an accurate assessment when it said that the book was "a tale, plain in style, almost too colloquial at times, but on the whole breezy." A facsimile edition of *TSSJL* was published in 1972 by Wolf House Books.

42. See O'Connor, *Jack London*, 258.
43. Letter from Charmian London to Ralph D. Harrison, Oakland, Calif., October 3, 1915 (HEH).
44. Dedication in the Londons' copy of *TSSJL* (courtesy, State of California, Department of Parks and Recreation, and I. Milo Shepard).
45. Pers. comm., Belle Leighty, Chanute, Kans., May 25, 1966.
46. *IMA*, 188–189.
47. MJ bitterly complained to the Londons that he was also saddled with visits from "all of Osa's relatives who get passes over the railroad and sponge on us"; see letter from Martin Johnson to Jack and Charmian London, New York City, November 22, 1914 HEH).
48. Letter from Martin Johnson to Jack and Charmian London, New York City, August 16, 1914 (HEH).
49. Letter from Martin Johnson to Jack and Charmian London, New York City, January 2, 1915 (HEH).
50. MJ had initially thought up the idea of the travel weekly, which at first Bray dismissed. Later Bray asked MJ to organize it and authorized him to purchase the films that were used in it; see letter from Martin Johnson to Jack and Charmian London, New York City, November 28, 1914 (HEH).
51. Letter from Martin Johnson to Jack and Charmian London, Hot Springs, Ark., March 26, 1915 (HEH).
52. Western Union Day Letter from Martin and Osa Johnson to Charmian London, New York City, November 23, 1916 (HEH).
53. Letter from Martin Johnson to Charmian London, New York City, March 24, 1917 (HEH).
54. Letter from Charmian London to Martin Johnson, Glen Ellen, Calif., March 29, 1917 (HEH).

5. SAILING THE SOLOMONS

1. Interview, Belle Leighty, Chanute, Kans., May 25, 1966.
2. *IMA*, 107.
3. Interview, Belle Leighty, Chanute, Kans., February 18, 1970.
4. Letter from Martin Johnson to Charmian London, Aboard the Burns Philp SS *Mindini*, July 2, 1917 (HEH).
5. Bennett, *Wealth of the Solomons*, 135, 151, 153–154, 171.
6. In *BS* (123), OJ incorrectly states that the governor introduced Markham to them. MJ had in fact prearranged with Markham to take them around the Solomons.

7. For a detailed analyis of Bell's life and work in the Solomons, see Keesing and Corris, *Lightning*.

8. *BS*, 3–7.

9. *BS*, 116–117.

10. Bell was brutally killed on October 4, 1927, by a Malaita *ramo*, Basiana, who cleaved open his head with the barrel of a rifle (Keesing and Corris, *Lightning*, 138); OJ later interpreted this murder as an example of native savagery expressed at a moment of relaxed vigilance on the part of the white man (*BS*, 46). In his film *Across the World with Mr. and Mrs. Martin Johnson*, MJ inaccurately claimed that Bell was eaten after he had been killed. In reality, the reasons for Bell's murder were extremely complex and stemmed from resentment against bullying police, the harsh enforcement of tax collection, and the confiscation of rifles (Keesing and Corris, *Lightning*).

11. During the 1980s, the Martin and Osa Johnson Safari Museum in Chanute, Kansas, was visited by Laurence Foanaota of the Solomon Islands National Museum, Honiara, and by Vianney Atpatum, archeologist with the Vanuatu Cultural Center, Vila. Both nations have since acquired Johnson film footage for their national cultural archives; see *The Johnson Safari Wait-A-Bit News* 7,3:7 (1986) and 2,4:5 (1981).

12. *BS*, 14.

13. Bennett, *Wealth of the Solomons*, 179.

14. *BS*, 137–138.

15. *BS*, 141.

16. *IMA*, 112.

17. Bennett, *Wealth of the Solomons*, 143.

18. Letter from Martin Johnson to Charmian London, New York City, August 15, 1914 (HEH).

19. In *BS* (63–91), OJ describes as reality the plantation as it was nine years earlier, when the *Snark* crew visited it. This fabrication includes conversations with people who had left (Bernays and Harding) and with Derbishire, who had died in 1914. Keesing and Corris (*Lightning*, 59) point out that OJ was given to "exaggeration and pure fabrication" in *BS*. OJ's chronology of their travels and her account of events in *BS* differ from those found in other sources.

20. Letter from Martin Johnson to Charmian London, New Hebrides, October 27, 1917 (HEH).

21. Harrisson, *Savage Civilization*, 237–238.

22. A reel of 35-mm motion film holds slightly less than 1,000 feet, and today constitutes around ten minutes of projection time. However, silent films were projected at varying speeds, but most often a reel lasted twelve to fourteen minutes. Thus the Johnsons' 40,000 feet represented about eight to nine hours of running time.

23. Letter from Martin Johnson to Charmian London, Sydney, Australia, January 4, 1918 (HEH).

24. Letter from Martin Johnson to Charmian London, New York City, October 9, 1918 (HEH).

25. Kevin Brownlow, *The War, the West, and the Wilderness* (New York: Alfred A. Knopf, 1979), 403. *Among the Cannibal Isles of the South Pacific* was a film of fact and possessed elements of the narrative documentary later created by Robert Flaherty with his famous film *Nanook of the North* (1922).

26. Samuel Lionel Rothafel (1881–1936), known as "Roxy," was the leading motion picture theater innovator and operator of his time. In New York, he managed the Strand, Rialto, Rivoli, and Capitol theaters. He introduced precision dancing with a group first called the "Roxyettes" and then the "Rockettes," and later managed the Radio City Music Hall; see "Samuel Lionel Rothafel," in *Dictionary of American Biography*, vol. 11, supp. 2, ed. Robert Livingston Schyler and Edward T. James (New York: Charles Scribner's Sons, 1958), 584–585.

27. The lecture film consisted of 5,000 feet. A longer version, totaling 9,200 feet, was redone with titles and called *Cannibals of the South Seas*. It consisted of two parts (part I: 5,200 feet; part II: 4,000 feet) and was released in December 1918. Part II of this longer film was called *Captured by Cannibals*. The film was distributed by Exhibitors Mutual Distributing Corp. and had a trade showing on November 19, 1918, at the Astor Hotel Ballroom, for which George W. Beynon conducted a symphony orchestra in performing his score; see Henson and Gevinson, eds., *American Film Institute Catalog of Motion Pictures Produced in the United States: Feature Films, 1911–1920*, 24.

28. See n. 24.

29. For a summary of popular press and trade publication reviews of the film, see *Motion Picture News*, August 10, 1918, 854.

30. "Movie Man Invades Home of Cannibals," *New York Times*, July 22, 1918, 9.

31. "Seeing Rialto and Rivoli with Rothapfel," *Motion Picture News*, August 3, 1918, 737.

32. Letter from Charmian London to Martin Johnson, Glen Ellen, Calif., March 27, 1918 (HEH).

33. See n. 24.

34. OJ commented on the abuses of labor recruiting in *BS* (208).

35. MJ was unsuccessful in finding a publisher for a book about his experiences, entitled *Martin Johnson's Cannibals of the South Seas* (*MJCSS*). OJ's mother gave this manuscript to one of us (PJI) on May 25, 1966, and requested that we find a publisher for it in New York City. We had previously rewritten and arranged for the posthumous publication by William Morrow and Co. of OJ's manuscript *LA*, which appeared in January 1966. After editing *MJCSS*, we took it to John C. Willey, then editor in chief at William Morrow and Co. He declined interest on the grounds that the public was willing to accept one long-lost manuscript (as *LA* had been advertised), but not a second. The manuscript was returned to OJ's mother and is now in the SM collections.

6. RETURN TO MELANESIA

1. *CL*, 23–27; The Robertson-Cole Company gave a farewell luncheon for the Johnsons at the Hotel Astor on March 24, 1919, hosted by Harry Houdini, the magician.

2. Father Prin had retired to Vila, where MJ and OJ met him. He gave them permission to use his stone house on Vao, where they built a photographic laboratory in one room (*CL*, 39–40; *IMA*, 130).

3. *IMA*, 129.

4. See A. Bernard Deacon, *Malekula: A Vanishing People in the New Hebrides*, ed. Camiela H. Wedgwood (London: Routledge and Keegan Paul, 1934; reprinted 1970).

5. Deacon, *Malekula*, xxxii–xxxiii.
6. *CL*, 56.
7. Paul Mazouyer (also spelled Mazoyer) gained a reputation as a brute and as some-one who mistreated the peoples of northern Malekula, where he regularly re-cruited laborers for his plantation on Aore Island. For a detailed description of his mistreatment of the Melanesians and his death at the hands of the Big Nambas for recruiting abuses, see Charlene Gourguechon, *Journey to the End of the World: A Three-Year Adventure in the New Hebrides* (New York: Charles Scribner's Sons, 1977), 38–39.
8. *CL*, 62, 92–93.
9. *CL*, 63.
10. *CL*, 67–68; *IMA*, 111, 186.
11. *CL*, 77–78. The people of Nihapat's village, Tenmarou, gradually abandoned the highlands for a new settlement of the same name on the nearby coast. By 1989 fewer than a dozen Big Nambas were left in the highlands; see David Stan-ley, *South Pacific Handbook* (Chico, Calif., Moon Publications, 1989), 635.
12. *CL*, 88–89, 118. MJ later confessed that his suspicions of Nihapat wooing Osa were absurd (*CL*, 88).
13. *CL*, 119.
14. *CL*, 134.
15. *CL*, 131, 133–134; *IMA*, 149–150.
16. *CL*, 152–153.
17. For a fuller description of men's clubhouses (*amel*), curing heads, and human effigy figures (*rambaramp*), see Deacon, *Malekula*, which is illustrated with a num-ber of MJ's field photographs.
18. OJ shared the work of developing film and plates in the laboratory at Vao (*CL*, 175).
19. *CL*, 179.
20. *CL*, 181–182.
21. *CL*, 187–189; *IMA*, 159–161; *BS*, 241–243; "Speaking of Pictures . . . Cannibals Roast a Man," *Life* 8:12–13 (March 25, 1940).
22. Letter from Martin Johnson to Charmian London, Sydney, Australia, Novem-ber 9, 1919 (HEH).
23. Letter from Charmian London to Martin Johnson, Glen Ellen, Calif., March 27, 1918 (HEH).
24. Despite the remarkable nature of MJ's New Hebrides film footage, his *Head Hunters of the South Seas* was not released until the fall of 1922, almost three years after it had been completed. His Borneo film *Jungle Adventures* was released in 1921.

7. JUNGLE ADVENTURES

1. In *IMA* (163), OJ inaccurately states that they first returned to the United States before leaving for North Borneo.
2. Interview, Belle Leighty, Chanute, Kans., May 25, 1966.
3. Interview, Clark H. Getts, New York City, May 18, 1977.
4. For a history of early wildlife photographers, see C.A.W. Guggisberg, *Early Wildlife Photographers* (Newton Abbot, U.K.: David and Charles, 1977); and Brownlow, *The War*, 402–566.

5. Sir Joseph West Ridgeway (1844–1930) had previously served as a military officer in Asia and as governor of Ceylon from 1896 to 1903; see "Sir Joseph West Ridgeway," in *The Dictionary of National Biography, 1922–1930*, ed. J. R. Weaver (London: Oxford University Press, 1937). British North Borneo later became Sabah and is presently part of Malaysia.

6. *IMA*, 162–181.

7. *IMA*, 174. The Johnsons' menagerie on leaving North Borneo included Bessie, a young female orangutan they had obtained on a rubber plantation; another gibbon ape; and Papua, a green and red parrot from New Guinea. These were added to Pollyanna, the parrot from Malaita, and Cornelia and Jack, crested cockatoos from Australia that were waiting for them in New York.

8. Letter from Martin Johnson to Charmian London, Sandakan, British North Borneo, July 14, 1920 (HEH).

9. *IMA*, 181; Stott, *Exploring*, 26.

10. *IMA*, 183–185; letter from Osa Johnson to J. Allen, Sandakan, British North Borneo, July 3, 1920 (HEH).

11. Interview, Belle Leighty, Chanute, Kans., January 20, 1974; letter from Osa Johnson to Belle Leighty, Singapore, August 7, 1920 (Belle Leighty). Lucinda Johnson had been ill for some time and regularly obtained animal blood from the butcher, which she used as a tonic (pers. comm., Margaret Cripps Sachs, Berkeley, Calif., October 21, 1991). She may have been suffering from diabetes mellitus (both MJ and his sister Freda later developed it), for which insulin did not become available until 1922. Her remains were later interred in Independence's Mount Hope Cemetery in a plot purchased by MJ.

12. Letter from Martin Johnson to Charmian London, New York City, November 30, 1920 (HEH).

13. Brownlow, *The War*, 410–411; *Shipwrecked among Cannibals*, in Hanson and Gevinson, eds., *The American Film Institute Catalog of Motion Pictures Produced in the United States: Feature Films, 1911–1920*, 829.

14. Johnson's "Jungle Adventures Meet Stiff Competition," *Motion Picture News*, September 24, 1921; the film was copyrighted on December 21, 1921, and a synopsis filed with the Library of Congress (MP 2081).

15. *Exhibitors Trade Review*, October 1, 1921; *Herald*, September 11, 1921.

16. The Capitol program also featured a Harold Lloyd comedy, *I Do*; a personal performance by Arthur Hackett, the concert tenor; several novelty films; a ballet; and performances by a recently recruited eighty-five-man orchestra. Bessie, the Johnsons' orangutan, also made some stage appearances.

17. Suzanne Sexton, "Jungle Adventures," *Morning Telegraph*, September 10, 1921; for the numerous rave reviews of the film, see *Jungle Adventures*, Scrap Book Clippings, MFL-NC #1523 (NYPL).

18. *New York Times*, September 12, 1921, 16.

19. Arthur Hoerl was one of the film industry's most productive producers, directors, and screenwriters. He was involved with some 300 feature films, 150 documentary and industrial films, and wrote, produced, and directed *Play Ball*, the first film on baseball, for the American League.

20. *Jungle Adventures*, in *Variety*, September 16, 1921.

21. *Catalog of National Non-Theatrical Motion Pictures Inc.*, New York, January 1924, 152–155; "Missing Films and Missing Titles," *The Johnson Safari Wait-A-Bit-News* 4,4:10–11 (October 1983).

22. MJ never wrote a book about the 1920 Borneo trip. However, OJ completed a 363-page manuscript in the early 1940s combining both the 1920 trip and a later one made in 1935–1936. OJ's mother gave this manuscript to one of us (PJI) on October 2, 1964, while we were visiting Chanute, Kansas. With the help of a late friend, Everett Morrison, a well-known tenor, and his agent, Alice Murray, we were put into contact with the late Mary Greene, who was then the director of publicity of William Morrow and Co. She liked the manuscript, and sent it to John C. Willey, the editor in chief, who agreed to publish it provided we rewrote it. OJ's mother received an advance of $5,000, and we provided agent and editing services gratis. We rewrote the manuscript in early 1965, and it was published in January 1966 as *Last Adventure: The Martin Johnsons in Borneo*. Following publication, our rewritten manuscript was sent to OJ's mother, and unfortunately, OJ's original 363-page manuscript was discarded by the publisher. *LA* sold around ten thousand hard-cover copies in the United States, and it was later published in Great Britain and Finland.

23. "Realism in the South Seas," *New York Times Sunday Book Review*, December 24, 1922, III, 26.

24. *New Statesman* 20:22 (October 7, 1922); *Boston Evening Transcript*, September 2, 1922, 6.

25. Letter from Martin Johnson to Carl Akeley, Nairobi, British East Africa, June 1, 1925 (AMNH).

26. *Head Hunters of the South Seas* was copyrighted on September 27, 1922 (LU18245). It consists of five reels and is 4,387 feet in length.

27. "Cannibals at the Movies," *New York Times*, May 30, 1920, 56; *Motion Picture News*, October 7, 1922, 1706–1707.

28. For a description of Carl Akeley's life and work, see Mary L. Jobe Akeley, *Carl Akeley's Africa: The Account of the Akeley-Eastman-Pomeroy African Hall Expedition* (New York: Dodd, Mead & Co., 1929); Penelope Bodry-Sanders, *Carl Akeley: Africa's Collector, Africa's Savior* (New York: Paragon House, 1991); Penelope Bodry-Sanders, "Carl Akeley—The Man Who Loved Africa," *Discoverer's Club: Travel News from the American Museum of Natural History* 2,3:1–2,4 (1988); Carl Akeley, "Carl Akeley's Own Story," *The Mentor* 13,12:23–32 (1926); the Akeley Memorial Number, *Natural History* 27:115–179 (1927). For a description of Akeley's plan for the museum's African Hall, see Carl Akeley, "African Hall, a Monument to Primitive Africa," *The Mentor* 13,12:10–22 (1926).

29. Bodry-Sanders, *Carl Akeley*, 208–209.

30. Bayard Dominick, the firm's senior partner, had hunted big game in British East Africa in 1909, and had served as a trustee of the museum ("Bayard Dominick; Broker 43 years," *New York Times*, May 2, 1941, 21); letter from Martin Johnson to George H. Sherwood, Nairobi, British East Africa, December 5, 1923 (AMNH).

31. *IMA*, 194. On leaving New York for Africa, MJ and OJ gave their pets to the Central Park Zoo, except Kalowatt, who traveled with them.

8. SEMPER ALIQUID NOVI

1. C. G. Schillings, *Flashlights in the Jungle* (New York: Doubleday, Page and Co., 1905); Schillings, *In Wildest Africa* (New York and London: Harper and

Brothers, 1907); Bartle Bull, *Safari: A Chronicle of Adventure* (New York: Viking, 1988), 138–143.

2. Former president Theodore Roosevelt arrived in East Africa in April 1909. His safari was one of the largest ever mounted and consisted of five hundred porters plus ancillary personnel. Financed by Andrew Carnegie, it was one of the most important historical events in British East Africa up to that time; see Theodore Roosevelt, *African Game Trails* (New York: Charles Scribner's Sons, 1910).

3. Arthur Radclyffe Dugmore, *Camera Adventures in the African Wilds: Being an Account of a Four Months' Expedition in British East Africa* (New York: Doubleday, 1910); Guggisberg, *Early Wildlife Photographers*, 51–61. James T. Clark eventually became director of preparation and installation at the American Museum of Natural History, and after Carl Akeley's death in 1926 he completed the African Hall, which became known as the Akeley African Hall; see Geoffrey Hellman, *Bankers, Bones and Beetles: The First Century of the American Museum of Natural History* (Garden City, N.Y.: The Natural History Press, 1968), 155, and James T. Clark, *Trails of the Hunted* (Boston: Little, Brown and Co., 1928).

4. James T. Clark joined Kearton as an assistant after the completion of the Dugmore safari.

5. For descriptions of early American safaris to East Africa, see Errol Trzebinski, *The Kenya Pioneers* (New York: W. W. Norton and Co., 1985), 138–139, 171; Bull, *Safari*, 157–261.

6. Guggisberg, *Early Wildlife Photographers*, 21–24, 70–75. In 1913 Kearton accompanied James E. Barnes on his African expedition as photographer and cinematographer; see James E. Barnes, *Through Central Africa from Coast to Coast* (New York: D. Appleton and Co., 1915).

7. Marius Maxwell, a settler in Kenya, and Marcuswell Maxwell began photographing animals shortly after World War I, and also attempted to document animal behavior; Oskar Olsen, a Swedish cameraman, made some superb films at water holes in northern Kenya in 1920 (Guggisberg, *Early Wildlife Photographers*, 93–96).

8. Sir H. Rider Haggard, *The Days of My Life: An Autobiography*, vols. 1 and 2, ed. C. J. Longman (London: Longmans, Green and Co. Ltd., 1926); Bull, *Safari*, 263–271.

9. "African Lion Hunt an Exciting Movie," *New York Times*, June 23, 1914, 11.

10. An account of Rainey's African hunts is given by his dog trainer, ER M. Shelley, in his book, *Hunting Big Game with Dogs in Africa* (Columbus, Miss.: 1924).

11. Rainey, who never married, suddenly died aboard the SS *Saxon* in 1923 while traveling to Africa with his sister, Grace Rainey Rogers. He was buried at sea. After his death, his sister donated a collection of 97 of his East African mammalian specimens to the AMNH to supplement the 133 he had already donated in his lifetime. In 1934 she donated the Paul J. Rainey Memorial Gateway in his honor at the New York Zoological Gardens, and a large tract of land in Louisiana to the Audubon Society which became a wild game preserve in his honor (see "Paul J. Rainey Dies of Stroke at Sea," *New York Times*, September 20, 1923, 4). Some of Rainey's films are preserved in the paper print collection of the Library of Congress; see Kemp R. Niver, *Early Motion Pictures: The Paper Print Collection in the Library of Congress*, ed. Bebe Bergsten (Washington, D.C.: Library of Congress, 1985).

12. *SF*, 204–207.

13. *CA*, 293.
14. *CA*, 293.
15. *IMA*, 231.
16. A full picture of this period in Kenya's history is provided by several authors: Bull, *Safari*, 157–261, Mary Gillett, *Tribute to Pioneers* (Oxford: J. M. Considine, 1986); Jan Hemsing, *Then and Now: Nairobi's Norfolk Hotel* (Nairobi: Sealpoint, 1982); Elspeth Huxley, *Out in the Midday Sun: My Kenya* (New York: Viking, 1985); Huxley, *Settlers of Kenya* (London: Longmans, Green and Co., 1948); Huxley, *White Man's Country: Lord Delamere and the Making of Kenya*, vols. 1 and 2 (London: Chatto and Windus, 1935); Elspeth Huxley and Arnold Curtis, eds., *Pioneers' Scrapbook: Reminiscences of Kenya, 1890 to 1968* (London: Evans Brothers Ltd., 1980); Trzebinski, *Kenya Pioneers*.
17. Nora Kelly, "In Wildest Africa: The Preservation of Game in Kenya, 1895–1933," thesis, Vancouver, Canada, Simon Fraser University, 1978.
18. Although his first name was Arthur, he was formally known as A. Blayney Percival and was born in March 1875 at Newcastle on Tyne. He had two children, Margaret (Kummerfeldt), who lives in Spokane, Washington, and Buster, a son who died in the Second World War at the age of twenty. His brother, Philip Percival, was the leading big game hunter of his time. A. Blayney Percival died of laryngeal cancer on January 20, 1941, at age sixty-five at his farm, Mamandu Estate, near Machakos, (pers. comm., Margaret Kummerfeldt, 1989–1990; "A. Blayney Percival: Pioneer of Game Preservation in Kenya," *East African Standard*, January 21, 1941).
19. Carl Akeley heavily relied on A. Blayney Percival's knowledge of wildlife habitats in designing the African Hall at the American Museum of Natural History.
20. *CA*, 44. Akeley returned to the United States in early 1922. He used the Nairobi laboratory during the Johnsons' absence up north, and left behind one of his Akeley cameras, which MJ used in the environs of Nairobi. The Ackeley camera revolutionized wildlife filmmaking. It was adapted for fast action because it could be quickly moved in any direction; see letter from Martin Johnson to Carl Akeley, Nairobi, British East Africa, May 8, 1922 (AMNH).
21. MJ and OJ were generally sparing in their public acknowledgments of the assistance they received from others in Africa and the South Seas. Notable exceptions to this were Carl Akeley, A. Blayney Percival, and Stanley Taylor, head of the Bureau of Native Affairs in Nairobi, who helped them recruit personnel.
22. Bud Cottar's mother lent Osa kitchen equipment and utensils when they were setting up house in Nairobi (pers. comm., Joan Kennedy, Brooklyn, New York, May 19, 1989). Bud Cottar became a highly respected big-game hunter in East Africa and accompanied many famous clients on safari. He served as a British army scout in German East Africa (now Tanzania) in the First World War, and in the U.S. Navy in the Second World War, when he was severely wounded. He married Tosca Lewis and had one daughter, Joan (Kennedy), who lives in Brooklyn, New York. In later years, he wrote a number of stories for American sporting magazines about his early hunting experiences in Africa. His brother Mike ran the Lake Victoria ferry at Kinesi in the North Mara District of Tanganyika (now Tanzania), and Mike's son Glen and his grandson Calvin currently operate Cottar's Safari Service in East Africa (pers. comm., Pat Cottar, Nairobi, Kenya, 1989; pers. comm., Joan Kennedy, Brooklyn, New York, 1989; Dutchie Reidy, "Sketch of Charles Cottar, Jr.," unpublished ms.)

23. Over the years, a number of members of the Cottar family have understandably expressed their disappointment at MJ and OJ's failure to acknowledge the true extent of Bud Cottar's contributions to the success of their first African trip.
24. OJ's role as the person who held the gun became a prominent feature of MJ's films and gave a unique character to their public marital partnership; MJ, in dedicating his book *Lion*, used the phrase, "To Osa, My Wife, Who Holds the Gun." While this statement is true, it is also equally true that the life-saving shots were sometimes fired by others.
25. *CA*, 69.
26. John Walsh's wife, "Pioneer Mary," was known for her ferocious nature and her *kiboko* whip, which she used on anyone who crossed her path. She and John had first farmed and then operated a transport business using donkey wagons. John also briefly mined salt at Lake Magadi. Known to the Africans as *Bibi Kiboko* (mother of the hippo/rhino hide), she died on June 20, 1922. John died soon thereafter of an accidentally inflicted gunshot wound to the knee (*CA*, 84; Gillett, *Tribute*; Trzebinski, *Kenya Pioneers*, 18–20).
27. The Johnsons set up their camp fifteen miles from the Whitehead sisal plantation.
28. *CA*, 113.
29. Major A. Radclyffe Dugmore, *The Wonderland of Big Game: Being an Account of Two Trips through Tanganyika and Kenya* (London: Arrowsmith, 1925), 86–87, 94. Dugmore also went on to photograph at Marsabit's Crater Lake (138–139).
30. *CA*, 134; letter from Martin Johnson to Carl Akeley, Nairobi, Kenya, May 8, 1922 (AMNH). Martin's description of the pro-Thuku demonstration characteristically reflects the European colonial attitudes of the time.
31. *CA*, 48–49; *IMA*, 203, 206–207.
32. A. Donaldson Smith, *Through Unknown African Countries: The First Expedition from Somaliland to Lake Lamu* (New York: Edward Arnold, 1896), 352.
33. Geoffrey Archer, "British East Africa. I. Recent Exploration and Journey in the North of British East Africa," *Geographical Journal* 42:421–435 (1916).
34. Sir Geoffrey Archer, *Personal and Historical Memoirs of an East African Administrator* (Edinburgh: Oliver and Boyd, 1963), 37.
35. H. B. Sharpe, "Marsabit Political Records, Early History," Kenya National Archives, PR/168 MBT/34, 1928; T. S. Muirhead, "Further Notes on Marsabit District," Kenya National Archives, PRB/167 DC MBT/2/1, 1925.
36. Lieut.-Col. J. H. Patterson, *In the Grip of the Nyika: Further Adventures in British East Africa* (New York: Macmillan, 1909). Patterson was best known for his killing of man-eating lions at Tsavo when the Uganda Railway was being constructed in East Africa; see Lieut.-Col. J. H. Patterson, *The Man-Eaters of Tsavo and Other East African Adventures* (London: Macmillan, 1907).
37. Letter from Dr. Audley D. Stewart to Pascal James Imperato, Rochester, N.Y., January 7, 1961. In 1961 we finally ascertained the precise location of Lake Paradise through the Land and Surveys Office in Nairobi; see Pascal James Imperato, *Bwana Doctor* (London: Jarrolds, 1967), 161–166.
38. Pascal James Imperato and Eleanor M. Imperato, "A Short History of Marsabit: Paradise Lost," *Africana* 6, 8:28–32 (1978); Pascal James Imperato and Eleanor M. Imperato, "Kenya's Lake Paradise," *Explorers Journal* 51, 1:22–27 (1980).
39. For a fuller account of early travelers to Marsabit and northern Kenya, see Pascal James Imperato, *Arthur Donaldson Smith and the Exploration of Lake Rudolf* (Lake Success, N.Y.: Medical Society of the State of New York, 1987).

40. Muirhead, "Further Notes"; John Yardley, *Paregon or Eddies in Equatoria* (London: J. M. Dent, 1931), 223–256, 276–282.

41. Dugmore, *Wonderland*, 88.

42. *CA*, 179.

43. *CA*, 184, 207.

44. John Johnson eventually continued his around-the-world trip, and on returning to the United States settled in Enid, Oklahoma, where he lived with his daughter, Freda, and her husband, J. Reamey Cripps. While in Enid, he briefly reentered the jewelry business. He died in October 1931.

45. Dugmore was high in his praise of MJ and OJ's kindness. He wrote: "I shall never forget the kindness that both he and his charming wife showed me. . . . Considering that we were engaged in the same sort of work . . . we might have been considered in a way as rivals, or at least as competitors, and it would not have been surprising if he had been unwilling to help us. . . . He did all in his power to assist, and I learned from him a great deal about developing, drying, and taking care of cinema film. I owe him a debt of gratitude that I shall never be able to repay" (*Wonderland*, 174–175). MJ referred to Dugmore as a fine personality and an excellent photographer (*CA*, 282).

46. MJ incorrectly spelled his name Boguni in an article in *Asia* magazine, a fact he corrected in *SF*. Boculy (also spelled Bakuli and Bakhari) was later arrested and convicted of poaching rhino in 1929 after MJ and OJ had left Marsabit (H. B. Sharpe, "Marsabit District Annual Report, 1929," Kenya National Archives, AR/1697, 1929).

47. *IMA*, 262.

48. Pliny the Elder (A.D. 23–79), a Roman scholar, popularized this Greek proverb in Latin as "Ex Africa semper aliquid novi."

9. MEN OF HIGH PURPOSE

1. Brownlow, *The War*, 411; "Universal Gets Big Game Picture," *Motion Picture News*, April 14, 1923, 1824.

2. Letter from Carl Akeley to George Eastman, New York City, July 26, 1923 (AMNH).

3. Letter from Carl Akeley to Samuel L. Rothafel, New York City, March 10, 1923 (AMNH).

4. "Advance Publicity, Trailing African Wild Animals," *New York Call*, May 18, 1923; "Trailing African Wilds," *Variety*, April 12, 1923. The Metro Picture Corporation, which distributed the film, was founded in 1915. In 1924 it amalgamated to form Metro-Goldwyn-Mayer (MGM); see Ephraim Katz, *The Film Encyclopedia* (New York: Perigee Books, 1979), 802.

5. "Trailing African Wild Animals," *Exhibitors Herald*, May 12, 1923, 13–17. OJ sold the elephant head to oil producer Frank Phillips in the late 1930s; it is on permanent exhibition at the Woolaroc Museum, which is operated by the Frank Phillips Foundation near Bartlesville, Oklahoma.

6. *Trailing African Wild Animals*, Scrapbook Clippings, MFL 1430 (NYPL).

7. *Women's Wear*, May 19, 1923.

8. "Beauty and the Beast," *New York World*, May 21, 1923.

9. *Evening World*, May 21, 1923.

10. MJ is identified in one scene as going into dense bush to shoot a charging rhino. On seeing the film at a Nairobi benefit showing, Alan Black, a famous white hunter, confronted MJ and said, "That's not you. It's Bud Cottar. I recognize his walk" (pers. comm., Joan Kennedy, Brooklyn, N.Y., May 19, 1989).

11. A number of reviewers expressed regret that these two competing films were playing simultaneously (*Trailing African Wild Animals*, Scrapbook Clippings, MFL 1430, NYPL). The Snows offered MJ $30,000 to delay the release of his film. He was agreeable to a delay but demanded $50,000, which the Snows refused to pay. After consulting with Metro's lawyer, MJ suggested that Akeley sue the Snows for titling their film along the lines of one of his own films. MJ gleefully told Akeley that the suit "could sew them up for weeks . . . and it would absolutely kill their picture, which they deserve"; see letter from MJ to Carl Akeley, Cleveland, Ohio, April 15, 1923 (AMNH).

12. "Close-Ups of Jungle Beasts," *New York Times*, May 21, 1923, 12.

13. See n. 12.

14. A fairly complete listing of MJ's and OJ's book and periodical publications is contained in Gene DeGruson, *Kansas Authors of Best Sellers: A Bibliography of the Works of Martin and Osa Johnson, Margaret Hill McCarter, Charles M. Sheldon, and Harold Bell Wright* (Pittsburg, Kans.: Kansas State College, 1970).

15. *New York World*, March 30, 1924, 6e; *Nation and Athenaeum*, December 6, 1924, 36:supp 386.

16. *New Statesman*, October 11, 1924, 24:supp 7.

17. Letter from Martin Johnson to Henry Fairfield Osborn, New York City, June 6, 1923 (AMNH).

18. Report of the President, *Fifty-Fourth Annual Report of the Trustees of the American Museum of Natural History*, New York, May 21, 1923, 11.

19. Songa was a young Meru warrior whom MJ and OJ had met on their previous African trip. Their plan to make a film of his daily life was inspired by Robert Flaherty's highly successful production *Nanook of the North*, released in 1922. Flaherty's film, which presents the daily life of an Eskimo family, inspired many similar productions (Brownlow, *The War*, 471). At the time of its release, it was "hailed as the first poetic film of fact," and has since become a classic (Brownlow, *The War*, 473). Flaherty is considered by many to be the originator of the documentary, a term first used by John Grierson in a 1926 review in the *New York Sun* of Flaherty's second film, *Moana* (Brownlow, *The War*, 471).

20. See n. 2.

21. Letter from Martin Johnson to Carl Akeley, New York City, August 21, 1923 (AMNH).

22. Letter from Carl Akeley to Martin Johnson, New York City, August 31, 1923 (AMNH); letter from Martin Johnson to Carl Akeley, Chanute, Kans., September 4, 1923 (AMNH).

23. George H. Sherwood, "Martin Johnson African Expedition, Davison-Pomeroy Proposition, History and Present Status of the Plan," October 31, 1923 (AMNH).

24. For a sketch of Pomeroy's life, see "Daniel Pomeroy, Banker, 96, Dies," *New York Times*, March 26, 1965, 35. Pomeroy was an experienced banker who not only supported the museum's conservation mission, but also believed that MJ's films represented a sound investment.

25. Letter from Daniel E. Pomeroy to Henry Fairfield Osborn, New York City, January 2, 1924 (AMNH); letter from Henry Fairfield Osborn to Daniel E. Pomeroy, New York City, November 14, 1923 (AMNH). The corporation offered an 8 percent return on its stock and entered into a contract with MJ; the directors included industrialists, investment bankers, lawyers, and sportsmen, many of whom had an interest in conservation.

26. Letter from Henry Fairfield Osborn to George H. Sherwood, New York City, November 26, 1923 (AMNH).

27. Letter from Martin Johnson to Henry Fairfield Osborn, aboard the *Leviathan*, December 5, 1923 (AMNH).

28. "Museum to Exhibit Martin Johnson Film. President Osborn Announces Arrangement with Traveler Now in Africa," *New York Times*, January 13, 1924, I, pt. 2, 8. Among the stockholders were Percy C. Madeira, a Philadelphia lawyer and business executive who had hunted big game in Africa in 1907 (see *Hunting in British East Africa* [Philadelphia: J. B. Lippincott, 1909]); Governor Gifford Pinchot of Pennsylvania, prominent in the conservation movement; and H. Morton Merriman, the industrialist who had supported the Johnsons' first African trip.

29. *IMA*, 271–272.

10. BWANA PICCER AND MEMSAHIB KIDOGO

1. *IMA*, 273. Gof Sokorte Guda in Boran means "big sweet water crater"; a shallower marsh-filled crater on Marsabit where the Ulanula tourist lodge is now located is known as Gof Sokorte Dika, "small sweet water crater."

2. Letter from Martin Johnson to Carl Akeley, Lake Paradise, Kenya, December 1, 1924 (AMNH).

3. *SF*, 8–9.

4. Letter from Frank B. Kellogg to Lord Curzon, London, England, December 28, 1923 (AMNH).

5. MJ asked Blayney Percival to act as a guide, to cover him and Osa with a rifle when they were filming dangerous game, and to supervise the building of the log and mud houses needed at Lake Paradise. MJ and OJ considered Blayney their closest friend in Africa, and OJ became godmother to his daughter, Margaret (pers. comm., Margaret Kummerfeldt, Spokane, Washington, 1989, 1990).

6. On arriving in Nairobi, MJ rented a post office box (first Box 51 and later Box 3A), secured a cable address (MARJON), and arranged to have the American Consul forward correspondence via Meru. Details of MJ and OJ's preparations for the trip to Lake Paradise are covered in their books, *IMA* (273–276), *FYP* (13–92), and *SF* (3–35). See also letter from Martin Johnson to Daniel E. Pomeroy, Nairobi, Kenya, February 17, 1924 (AMNH).

7. Diary and Reports—The Martin Johnson African Expedition Corporation, Isiolo, February 28, 1924 (AMNH).

8. André Dugand, whom MJ incorrectly referred to as being a Boer, was the head conductor for the Northern Frontier Transport Corps. French by birth, he spoke fluent French, English, and Afrikaans (probably the reason for MJ's mistake). He had supervised the construction of large stretches of the Marsabit Road and was intimately familiar with the Northern Frontier; see Monty Brown, *Where Giants*

Trod: The Saga of Kenya's Desert Lake (London: Quiller Press, 1989), 370–371, 374, 376–377.

9. Muirhead, "Further Notes"; Brown, *Giants*, 321–336. Neither MJ nor OJ acknowledges in their writings that there were previous occupants of this campsite.

10. Letter from Alice L. Seixas to Carl E. Akeley, New York City, April 22, 1924 (AMNH). George Eastman did not invest his $10,000 in the corporation, but made a separate arrangement with MJ. MJ himself bought shares in the corporation with his own funds.

11. Sydney Downey, a prominent white hunter and later a leading conservationist, recalled that the rocks at Wistonia were smoothly indented where the elephants pressed their heads and flapped their ears (interview, Nairobi, Kenya, October 27, 1977). In 1977 we observed buffalo at the Boculy water hole, which was still known by that name to local guides.

12. MJ provides detailed accounts of animal behavior patterns and the techniques of wildlife photography in *SF*, 72–207.

13. Diary, N'Doto Mountains, December 27, 1924 (AMNH).

14. *FYP*, 185.

15. Osa Johnson, "At Home in Africa," *Natural History* 27:561–569 (1927).

16. *SF*, 21.

17. *SF*, 224.

18. Interviews, Belle Leighty, Chanute, Kans., 1966–1974.

19. Percy N. Furber, *I Took Chances: From Windjammers to Jets* (Leicester, U.K.: Edgar Backus, 1954), 248–250.

20. Diary, Lake Paradise, May 3, 1925 (AMNH); *SF*, 139–140.

21. Diary, Lake Paradise, May 12, June 8, 1925 (AMNH).

22. Furber, *Chances*, 250; Diary, Lake Paradise, June 8, 1925 (AMNH).

23. Letter from Martin Johnson to Carl Akeley, Nairobi, Kenya, June 1, 1925 (AMNH). Furber later married Mary Hall, a well-known playwright and actress, and died in Johannesburg, South Africa, in May 1950 (Furber, *Chances*, 250; "Mrs. Beverly H. Furber, 59, Actress and Playwright," *New York Times*, November 7, 1964, 27).

24. Arthur Buchanan Sanderson's son, Ivan Terence Sanderson (1911–1973), was a well-known naturalist. He authored numerous books, and in 1950 narrated *Osa Johnson's Big Game Hunt*, a series of short films that OJ produced for television; see *Contemporary Authors*, vols. 37–40, ed. Ann Evory (Detroit: Gale Research Co., 1979), 477.

25. *FYP*, 167; *SF*, 70–71. Interview, Belle Leighty, Chanute, Kans., February 18, 1970.

26. Diary, Lake Paradise, May 3, 1925.

27. Letter from James L. Clark to Henry Fairfield Osborn, New York City, November 6, 1924 (AMNH).

28. Letter from Daniel E. Pomeroy to Henry Fairfield Osborn, New York City, December 18, 1924 (AMNH).

29. Diary, Nairobi, July 29, 1925 (AMNH).

30. Letter from Martin Johnson to Carl Akeley, Lake Paradise, Kenya, December 1, 1924 (AMNH); letter from Martin Johnson to Daniel E. Pomeroy, Lake Paradise, Kenya, February 26, 1925 (AMNH).

31. *Nanook of the North*, produced by Robert Flaherty using an Akeley camera, was released in 1922 and immediately captured the public's imagination. It has since become a classic of the silent film era; see Brownlow, *The War*, 471–473.

32. Letter from George H. Sherwood to Martin Johnson, New York City, May 3, 1926 (AMNH).

33. Letter from Carl Akeley to Daniel E. Pomeroy, New York City, March 26, 1925 (AMNH).

34. T. S. Muirhead, "Notes on Marsabit Affairs in 1925," Kenya National Archives, PRB/167 DC MBT/2/1, 1925. MJ was made an honorary game warden when he arrived in Nairobi in 1924.

35. Diary, Duke of York, January 29, 1925 (reproduced with the gracious permission of Her Majesty Queen Elizabeth II); MJ recorded the meeting in his diary on February 1, 1925 (AMNH).

36. Diary, Lake Paradise, December 1, 1925 (AMNH); letter from Martin Johnson to Punch Breckenridge, September 10, 1925 (courtesy J.D.T. Breckenridge). Breckenridge recalls Osa taking pictures of wildlife and her "wonderful safari cooking." "For me, it was my first experience of the American sweet tooth with maple syrup on eggs and bacon for breakfast" (letter from J.D.T. Breckenridge to Pascal James Imperato, Kealties, Durrus, Ireland, December 12, 1990).

37. Interview conducted by Reverend Paolo Tablino and Philip Joshua, Marsabit, May 30, 1989 (letter from Paolo Tablino to Pascal James Imperato, Marsabit, Kenya, May 31, 1989). The Johnsons' former vaudeville booking agent, Charles Edward Bray, and his wife visited the lake for two weeks in December 1925.

38. Glenday was later in charge of all the districts in the Northern Frontier and in 1939 became governor of Somaliland. On March 7, 1925, MJ and OJ rescued him and Captain R. Taverner, the district commissioner of Barsaloi, near Laisamis after their donkeys had stampeded with their food, clothing, and camping supplies and left them stranded (Diary, Lake Paradise, March 7, 1925, AMNH). Details of Glenday's life and career are given in Brown, *Giants*, 360–367, and in E.A.T. Dutton, *Lillibullero or the Golden Road* (Zanzibar, 1944). For Miles's career, see Dutton and Mary Gillett, *Tribute to Pioneers* (Oxford: J. M. Considine, 1986).

39. Akeley, *Carl Akeley's Africa*, 2–4; letter from Martin Johnson to Carl Akeley, on the Guaso Nyiro, Kenya, June 25, 1925 (AMNH); Bodry-Sanders, *Carl Akeley*, 204.

40. Robert H. Rockwell, a taxidermist who accompanied the expedition, characterized Pomeroy as "a jovial, happy companion who obviously savored life and cheerful society"; see Robert H. Rockwell with Jeanne Rockwell, *My Way of Becoming a Hunter* (New York: W. W. Norton and Co., 1955), 208.

41. Audley Durand Stewart, M.D. (1883–1972), was a surgeon who received his medical degree from the University of Pennsylvania in 1910; see *JAMA* 221:208 (1972).

42. Aubrey Fitzpatrick Ayre (1886–1975) was born in South Africa and in 1906 arrived in East Africa, where he became a sawmiller, farmer, rancher, and professional hunter. He accompanied the Duke and Duchess of York on their 1925 safari to the Northern Frontier. He was a founder of the East African Professional Hunters' Association, learned to fly when he was seventy, and retired to Durban, South Africa, where he died on January 9, 1975; see Gillett, *Tribute;* Anthony Dyer, *The East African Hunters: The History of the East African Hunters' Association* (Clinton, N.J.: Amwell Press, 1979), 4–5.

43. George Eastman, *Chronicles of an African Trip* (Rochester, N.Y.: Privately printed for the author, 1927), 35. According to Robert H. Rockwell, Eastman "had no

capacity for conviviality, was an extremely hard man to get to know, and always maintained an air of aloofness and reserve" (Rockwell, *My Way*, 208). OJ was able to melt Eastman's reserve, and in the subsequent years she and MJ became his close friends.

44. Eastman, *Chronicles*, 70–72. Mary L. Jobe Akeley, Carl's widow, was later under the impression that portions of MJ and OJ's film *Simba* included footage made by her husband. She requested access to this for use in lectures and articles; see letter from Mary L. Jobe Akeley to George H. Sherwood, New York City, March 14, 1932 (AMNH). MJ replied to Sherwood that only 25 feet of Akeley's film was used in the original prerelease version. This contained shots of the Lumbwa (no lions showing), 15 feet of hyenas on the plains, and a "jerky buffalo charge." All this footage was deleted from the film when it was released; see letter from Martin Johnson to George H. Sherwood, New York City, April 12, 1932 (AMNH).

45. *SF*, 264–266.

46. Letter from Martin Johnson to George H. Sherwood, Nairobi, Kenya, December 11, 1926 (AMNH).

47. Pomeroy was always extremely generous to the Johnsons. He also paid the cost of mounting and installing the impala group shot by OJ that is now on permanent exhibit in the gallery of the Akeley African Hall. This group was mounted by Akeley's successor, Robert H. Rockwell, and bears OJ's name as the donor.

48. Letter from George H. Sherwood to Percy N. Furber, New York City, April 30, 1926 (AMNH); letter from George H. Sherwood to John R. Bradley, New York City, May 11, 1926 (AMNH).

49. Just before closing the camp down, MJ suffered first and second degree burns of his head and face when several flash cartridges exploded (*SF*, 282–285). Earlier in 1926, Kalowatt, their pet gibbon, was electrocuted on wires outside the Norfolk Hotel in Nairobi. The loss of Kalowatt, which had been their surrogate child, plunged OJ into a period of depression (interviews, Belle Leighty, Chanute, Kans., 1966–1974).

50. When Sydney Downey, one of Kenya's leading white hunters and conservationists, visited the Johnsons' Lake Paradise campsite in 1935, the brick fireplace was still standing (interview, Sydney Downey, Langata, Kenya, October 27, 1977). When we visited the site in 1961 and 1977, the footings of the various buildings were still visible and a number of low stone retaining walls were intact.

51. Letter from Martin Johnson to George H. Sherwood, Nairobi, Kenya, December 11, 1926 (AMNH); Akeley, *Carl Akeley's Africa*, 188.

52. MJ had been motivated to climb up Mount Kenya by the Duke of York, who suggested he photograph its harsh beauty (*IMA*, 319).

53. Gerald Victor Wright Anderson received his medical degree from University College Hospital, London, and arrived in East Africa in 1902. He was among those who organized the Flying Ambulance Service, the forerunner of the Flying Doctors Service, and was a member of the Nairobi Health Board (Gillett, *Tribute*; interview of Gerald V. W. Anderson conducted by Errol Trzebinski, June 18, 1978, Nairobi, Kenya, courtesy Errol Trzebinski).

54. Letter from Martin Johnson to Daniel E. Pomeroy, Chogoria Mission near Meru, Kenya, February 15, 1927 (AMNH); *IMA*, 318–321.

55. *SF*, 293.

11. WITH LIONS AND BOY SCOUTS ON THE SERENGETI

1. William C. Everson, *American Silent Film* (New York: Oxford University Press, 1978), 334–338.
2. *Simba* in Kiswahili means lion; "*Simba* (Wild Animal Film)," in *Variety*, January 25, 1928.
3. *Simba* program, Earl Carroll Theatre, New York City, January 23, 1928 (NYPL). The full title of the film is *Simba, King of Beasts: A Saga of the African Veldt*. The AMNH possesses five versions of the film and they vary in length. Some have tinted stock while others are black and white. They are either silent or have a musical sound track and a talking prologue; see Nina J. Root, *Catalog of the American Museum of Natural History Film Archives* (New York and London: Garland Publishing, Inc., 1987), 311–312. Two of Akeley's three bronzes depicting a Nandi lion-spearing episode were displayed on the stage during the Earl Carroll Theatre showings. Together weighing 2,200 pounds, they were transported with great difficulty from the museum to the theater.
4. Pomeroy and the Johnsons later produced a one-reel film, *Naked Man versus Beast*, consisting of lion-spearing sequences from *Simba*. Isak Dinesen saw *Simba* at Government House in Nairobi on October 30, 1928, when it was shown to the visiting Prince of Wales. Writing to her mother, she commented that she had no feelings for films, but found MJ's slow-motion shots of giraffe curious; see Isak Dinesen, *Letters from Africa, 1914–1931*, ed. Frans Lasson (Chicago: University of Chicago Press, 1978), 384. The prince's secretary, Alan Lascelles, also saw the film that evening and reflected the resentments of jealous local colonials in saying that it relied on extremely long telephoto lenses to give false impressions, and that it was by no means "truly face-to-face with nature"; see Duff Hart-Davis, ed., *In Royal Service: The Letters and Journals of Sir Alan Lascelles. Vol. II, 1920–1936* (London: Hamish Hamilton, 1989), 97.
5. Henry Fairfield Osborn, "Lo, The Poor Nordic," *New York Times*, April 8, 1924, 18; Franz Boas, "Lo, The Poor Nordic. Serious Flaws Are Suspected in Professor Osborn's Theories—Views as to Nordic Italians—Pre-War Ethnology as 'Made in Germany,'" *New York Times*, April 13, 1924, 19.
6. Franz Boas, *The Mind of Primitive Man* (New York: The Free Press, 1965), 37.
7. Madison Grant, *The Passing of the Great Race* (New York: Charles Scribner's Sons, 1916). Osborn hosted the Second International Congress of Eugenics at the museum in 1921, and served as its president. In 1932 he hosted the third congress at the museum and served as honorary vice-president. At the latter, he presented a paper, "Birth Selection Versus Birth Control"; see *A Decade of Progress in Eugenics: Scientific Papers of the Third International Congress of Eugenics* (Baltimore: Williams and Wilkins, 1934), 29–41.
8. Ashley Montagu, *Man's Most Dangerous Myth: The Fallacy of Race*, 5th ed. (New York: Oxford University Press, 1974), 236. Racial jokes were a staple of vaudeville and were carried over into films. Virtually every ethnic group was spoofed, not just blacks; see *Unspeakable Images: Ethnicity and the American Cinema*, ed. Lester D. Friedman (Chicago: University of Chicago Press, 1991).
9. *Simba* was placed in a vacuum-sealed container to preserve it for future generations; see "A Noteworthy Gift to the American Museum of Natural History," News Release, March 15, 1928 (AMNH); letter from Alice L. Seixas to Geroge H. Sherwood, New York City, January 3, 1933 (AMNH).

10. See Arthur S. Vernay, "Angola as a Game Country," *Natural History* 27:588–594 (1927).

11. Alfred J. Klein sold his Maasai lion-spearing sequence to the Martin Johnson African Expedition Corporation along with other footage for $30,000; see Memorandum of Conference between Messrs. Pomeroy, Johnson, and Sherwood, Re: Martin Johnson Films, June 3, 1929 (AMNH); Klein, who gained a reputation as one of East Africa's best white hunters, described the Africans in this sequence as Maasai in an article, "Caged," in *Collier's* 80:10 (October 15, 1927), but the copyright material claims they are Nandi. Klein returned to the United States in 1927 to marry his childhood sweetheart, Florence Tintera, and it was at that time that he sold the film to Pomeroy. He died at Shimoni on the Kenya coast on May 9, 1944, at the age of sixty-one. Attempts by Edward Rodwell to find his grave in the Mombasa cemetery in 1989 were unsuccessful; see "Alfred J. Klein, 61, Noted Hunter, Dies," *New York Times*, May 21, 1944, 43; Shirley Victor Cooke, "Mr. A. J. ('Al') Klein, an Appreciation," *Mombasa Times*, May 13, 1944; "Lion Killer," *Time*, June 5, 1944, 74–75; Edward Rodwell, "The Search for a Grave," *The Standard*, May 19, 1989, 15.

12. Mary S. Lovell, *The Sound of Wings: The Life of Amelia Earhart* (New York: St. Martin's Press, 1989), 81, 86–87.

13. Interview with Fitzhugh Green's son, Fitzhugh Green (1918–1990), Washington, D.C., February 2, 1988. Green vividly recalled his father speaking of OJ as "pretty, charming, and gutsy" and describing MJ as "hard-driven and humorless"; Fitzhugh Green, *National Cyclopedia of American Biography* (New York: James T. White and Co., 1950), 93–94. George Palmer Putnam speaks of literary ghosting in his book, *Wide Margins: A Publisher's Autobiography* (New York: Harcourt, Brace & Co., 1942), 156.

14. *New York Herald Tribune*, April 15, 1928, 5; *New York Evening Post*, March 10, 1928, 12; *New York World*, March 18, 1928, 11; *Springfield Republican*, March 20, 1928, 10.

15. Between 1921 and 1953, the *New York Times* carried some one hundred articles about the Johnsons, in addition to reviews of their films and books, and articles authored by both of them. During this period they were featured in numerous newsreels produced by Fox-Movietone, Universal, and others.

16. Interviews, Belle Leighty, Chanute, Kans., 1966–1974.

17. Robert Dick Douglas, Jr., David R. Martin, Jr., Douglas L. Oliver, *Three Boy Scouts in Africa* (New York: G. P. Putnam's Sons, 1928), vi. As the three Boy Scouts were ending their stay with the Johnsons in Africa on August 18, 1928, another Boy Scout, Paul Siple of Erie, Pennsylvania, was being chosen to accompany Richard E. Byrd on his first expedition to Antarctica; see Eugene Rodgers, *Beyond the Barrier: The Story of Byrd's First Expedition to Antarctica* (Annapolis, Md.: Naval Institute Press, 1990), 37. Putnam, who was Byrd's publisher, was the moving force behind this arrangement, and later published Siple's book, *A Boy Scout with Byrd* (New York: G. P. Putnam's Sons, 1931); Siple's experiences with Byrd set him on a career as a geographer and biologist, and eventually he made six trips to Antarctica; see Paul Allman Siple, *Current Biography*, ed. Marjorie Dent Candee (New York: H. W. Wilson Co., 1957), 512–514.

18. *LN*, 234.

19. Albert David Kaiser, M.D. (1887–1954), was an assistant professor of pediatrics at the University of Rochester School of Medicine and Dentistry at the time he

accompanied Eastman. From 1945 until his death he served as health officer of Rochester, New York; see *JAMA* 160:310 (1954).

20. George Eastman, *Chronicles of a Second African Trip*, ed. and with notes and an introduction by Kenneth M. Cameron (Rochester, N.Y.: The Friends of the University of Rochester Library, 1987), 3–24.

21. Eastman, *Chronicles*, 23.

22. Eastman, *Chronicles*, 45–48. MJ posed OJ in Eastman's sedan chair for some humorous photographs.

23. Eastman, *Chronicles*, 62.

24. Eastman's trip back was marred by a fire aboard the train from Khartoum to Cairo. He and Kaiser were forced to flee from the train in their pajamas ("Eastman in Peril in Cairo Train Fire," *New York Times*, March 15, 1928, 1).

25. Martin Johnson, "Taming Elephants," *Saturday Evening Post* 201,37:30 (January 5, 1929). For a history of taming elephants in this area, see Rupert Watson, "The Garamba Elephants," *SWARA* 12,4:15–17 (July–August 1989). The recent status of white rhino in Garamba is described in Jane Perlez, "Rare White Rhino Avoids Extinction in Preserve in Zaire," *New York Times*, June 5, 1990, C4.

26. Douglas et al., *Three Boy Scouts*, 23.

27. Personal communications, David R. Martin, Morro Bay, Calif., May 16, 1986; Douglas L. Oliver, Honolulu, Hawaii, October 5, 1989.

28. "Three Boy Scouts Bag Lion Apiece in Africa"; "Seven Beasts Invade Martin Johnson's Camp," *New York Times*, July 31, 1925, 16. Martin and Oliver attended Harvard, and the former later became an executive in the Boy Scouts of America. Oliver obtained his Ph.D. in anthropology at the University of Vienna and became a leading authority on the peoples of the Pacific. His book *The Pacific Islands*, 3d ed., illustrations by Sheila Mitchell Oliver (Honolulu: University of Hawaii Press, 1989), is considered a classic. His other books include *A Solomon Island Society: Kinship and Leadership among the Siuai of Bougainville* (Cambridge, Mass.: Harvard University Press, 1955); *Ancient Tahitian Society* (Honolulu: University Press of Hawaii, 1974); and *Oceania: The Native Cultures of Australia and the Pacific Islands*, 2 vols., illustrated by Lois Johnson (Honolulu: University of Hawaii Press, 1988). Dr. Oliver is currently Emeritus Professor of Anthropology at Harvard University and the University of Hawaii. Robert Dick Douglas, the third Boy Scout, graduated from Georgetown University School of Law and became a practicing attorney. In 1935, the three Boy Scouts held a reunion in New York City at the Boy Scouts of America headquarters (*New York Times*, September 4, 1935, 14).

29. MJ and OJ were the first professional cinematographers to document this remarkable annual migration; see "Vast Trek of Animals under Way in Africa. Martin Johnson Reports Herds 10 Miles Wide and 30 Miles Long in Tanganyika," *New York Times*, August 21, 1928, 41.

30. A summary of press reviews of the film was published in an article, "Interesting Material in New Johnson Film," *Motion Picture News*, January 25, 1930, 52; *Variety*, January 22, 1930. The film was released under the auspices of the American Museum of Natural History and subtitled *Featuring Three Boy Scouts in Africa*. Although the opening credits state that it was copyrighted in 1929 by MJ, no formal copyright was ever filed with the Library of Congress.

31. *Africa Speaks*, in *The American Film Institute Catalog of Motion Pictures Produced in the United States: Feature Films, 1921–1930*, ed. Kenneth W. Munden (New York

and London: R. R. Bowker Co., 1971), 8. For an account of Hoefler's experiences while making the film, see *Africa Speaks: The Chronicle of Adventure* (New York: Blue Ribbon Books, 1931).

12. GENTLE GIANTS AND FOREST PEOPLE

1. Interview, DeWitt Sage, Links Club, New York City, December 15, 1977.
2. Ephraim Katz, *The Film Encyclopedia* (New York: Perigee Books, 1979), 1072–1073, 1156–1157.
3. Letter from Martin Johnson to Daniel E. Pomeroy, New York City, April 18, 1929 (AMNH).
4. Letter from Martin Johnson to Thomas J. Craig, New York City, October 30, 1929 (AMNH).
5. *New York Times*, April 7, 1929, 4.
6. Mary S. Lovell, *The Sound of Wings: The Life of Amelia Earhart* (New York: St. Martin's Press, 1989), 138.
7. Fitzhugh Green, *Dick Byrd—Air Explorer* (New York: G. P. Putnam's Sons, 1928).
8. *Saturday Review of Literature*, November 15, 1930, 341; *New York Herald Tribune*, November 16, 1930, 10.
9. Katz, *Film Encyclopedia*, 1156.
10. *CON*, 125–126; "The Chapin-Sage Expedition," *Natural History* 27:181–183 (1927); James P. Chapin, "Ruwenzori from the West," *Natural History* 27:615–627 (1927).
11. Interviews, Belle Leighty, Chanute, Kans., 1964–1974.
12. Interview, Belle Leighty, Chanute, Kans., February 18, 1970. Pomeroy affectionately called OJ "Tom," derived from her vaudeville billing as the "Tom Boy of Honolulu"; in letters to her in later years, he often used the salutation, "Dear Tom."
13. Interview, Belle Leighty, Chanute, Kans., January 21, 1974.
14. *CON*, 236.
15. Katz, *Film Encyclopedia*, 1184–1185; Jay Robert Nash and Stanley Ralph Ross, *The Motion Picture Guide*, vol. 8 (Chicago: Cinebooks, 1987), 3518–3519.
16. Paul L. Hoefler, *Africa Speaks: A Story of Adventure* (New York: Blue Ribbon Books, 1931), 127–144. Mike and Bud Cottar served as guides and white hunters for Hoefler's Colorado African Expedition.
17. W. S. Van Dyke, *Horning into Africa* (California Graphic Press, 1931), 182–183.
18. OJ was proud of the fact that she was the first woman to receive a big-game license from the governor of Tanganyika Territory (interview, Belle Leighty, Chanute, Kans., February 18, 1970).
19. Sage, interview.
20. *CON*, 32–38.
21. *CON*, 60, 78–79.
22. Sage, interview.
23. Sage, interview. In *CON* (81), MJ states that his swearing was heard on some of the sound tracks.
24. Sage, interview; *CON*, 60, 117. Visceroptosis had few adherents after 1910; see Thomas S. N. Chen and Peter S. Y. Chen, "Glenard's Disease: The Vagaries of Visceroptosis," *New York State Journal of Medicine* 91:101–105 (1991).

25. *CON*, 111–136, 173.

26. Carl Akeley, "Gorillas—Real and Mythical," *Natural History* 23:429–447 (1923).

27. Akeley, *Carl Akeley's Africa*, 234.

28. Through Carl Akeley's efforts and those of others, a gorilla sanctuary, the Parc National Albert (now the Parc National des Virungas) was firmly established on May 6, 1929 (Akeley, *Carl Akeley's Africa*, 253). By the 1980s, tourist groups were regularly taken into the Virunga Mountains to visit wild gorillas that had become habituated to humans. Such contacts place gorillas at risk for acquiring human diseases such as measles. In 1990 some wild gorillas in the Virunga Mountains were vaccinated against measles with dart guns.

29. Dian Fossey, well known for her studies of the mountain gorilla, said she had never heard of Martin and Osa Johnson (interview, Dian Fossey, Explorers Club, New York City, September 7, 1983); see also Dian Fossey, *Gorillas in the Mist* (Boston: Houghton Mifflin Co., 1983), and George B. Schaller, *The Year of the Gorilla* (Chicago: University of Chicago Press, 1964).

30. Martin Johnson, "Trailing Gorillas in African Jungles," *New York Times Magazine*, August 30, 1921, 6–7, 23; *CON*, 147, 183; *IMA*, 338.

31. Martin Johnson, "Adventures in Akeley's African Park," *New York Times Magazine*, September 6, 1931, 10–12; Mary L. Jobe Akeley, "Carl Akeley's Grave. His Widow Made Arrangements for Its Proper Care," *New York Times*, December 18, 1931, 22. MJ and OJ were very fond of Delia Akeley, Carl's first wife, whom they met in Nairobi on returning from the Congo. Clark Hallan Getts, OJ's manager and second husband, gave the following assessment of Mary L. Jobe Akeley: "She was a horsey-looking woman who felt that she and Carl didn't get the public recognition they deserved for their vast scientific knowledge of Africa. She was intensely jealous of Osa's celebrity, and had such an unpleasant personality that newspaper reporters avoided her. Osa, who didn't have a jealous bone in her body, found it hard to accept Mary Jobe's negative feelings toward her" (interview, Clark Hallan Getts, New York City, March 16, 1977).

32. The White Fathers are an order of missionary priests founded in 1868 by Cardinal Charles Lavigerie, archbishop of Algiers. Their official name is the Order of Our Lady of Africa of Algiers; see Pascal James Imperato, *Historical Dictionary of Mali*, 2d ed. (Metuchen, N.J., and London: The Scarecrow Press, 1986), 254.

33. *CON*, 206. MJ also wired the *New York Times* from Irumu on November 25, claiming that the animals were the largest ever captured. The *Times* ran a short front-page story on the capture the following day ("Three Gorillas Are Captured by Martin Johnson in Africa," *New York Times*, November 26, 1930, 1).

34. Interview, Dr. J. R. Gregory, Norfolk Hotel, Nairobi, Kenya, October 26, 1977.

35. Gregory, interview.

36. Gregory, interview.

37. Ingagi and Congo (later named Mbongo) were presented to Belle J. Benchley, director of the San Diego Zoological Garden, while Okero and Teddy were given as gifts to the National Zoological Park in Washington, D.C., on September 17, 1931. Okero was very much a surrogate child for OJ, who told her mother to consider him a grandchild. Okero did not thrive at the zoo, and when he first became ill in March 1932, Dr. William M. Mann, the zoo's director, called MJ and OJ. OJ spent a day and a night with Okero trying to nurse him back to health, and later in September she and MJ gave the zoo $1,000 to cover

medical expenses for him and Teddy. Okero died on October 7, 1932, of anemia and a bladder tumor, while Teddy died on July 6, 1936 (National Zoological Park Catalog Records 13,713, 13,714, September 17, 1931; "Baby Gorilla Dies at Zoo Here Despite Efforts of Doctors," *Washington Star*, October 8, 1932).

38. Both Sage (interview, 1977) and MJ (*CON*, 276) believed that the Africans' demands for better wages and living conditions were instigated by communists from Harlem.

39. "Big City Startles Two African Boys," *New York Times*, July 5, 1931, 3; "Two African Boys Find Harlem Odd," *New York Times*, July 6, 1931, 19; "Harlem Sharpens Uganda Boys' Wits," *New York Times*, October 3, 1931, 19; "Scorned a Throne, Now Faces Swahilis' Curse: Hot-Dog Man Gets Ominous Note from Africa," *New York Times*, January 22, 1934, 17.

40. "Curse of the Congo Claims Life of Dog Owned by Policeman Who Scolded Africans," *New York Times*, January 26, 1934, 19.

41. During this tour, MJ and OJ attended John Johnson's funeral in Independence, Kansas. They flew by plane for the first time with Vern L. Carstens, the manager of Chanute's airport. They presented their lecture and film at Town Hall in New York City on December 4, 1931 (*New York Times*, December 5, 1931, 21).

42. The Essex House, which was designed by Frank Grad and built in 1930, was only partially full when the Johnsons moved into it because of the severe economic depression; see Thomas E. Norton and Jerry E. Patterson, *Living It Up: A Guide to the Named Apartment Houses of New York* (New York: Atheneum, 1984), 137.

43. Lovell, *The Sound of Wings*, 162.

44. *Boston Transcript*, February 3, 1932, 2; *Outlook* 160:122 (January 27, 1932).

45. Letter from Osa Johnson to Charmian London, New York City, March 18, 1932 (HEH). OJ was generally an infrequent correspondent and, according to MJ, was "the world's champion rotten letter writer. One letter a year is a very good average for her" (letter from Martin Johnson to Charmian London, New York City, March 14, 1932, HEH).

46. MJ served as one of six pallbearers, along with Dr. Audley D. Stewart and Dr. Albert D. Kaiser ("Eastman a Suicide: Note to His Friends Says 'Work Is Done,'" *New York Times*, March 15, 1932, 1; "Thousands Mourn at Eastman Rites," *New York Times*, March 18, 1932, 21). Eastman and the Johnsons developed a very close personal relationship; he carefully saved most of the many personal letters they wrote to him between 1925 and 1932 (Archives, George Eastman House).

47. Letter from Martin Johnson to Charmian London, New York City, March 14, 1932 (HEH).

48. Lowell Thomas (1892–1981) was then a journalist, lecturer, newsreel commentator, and radio broadcaster who had gained fame with his book *With Lawrence in Arabia*.

49. Helen J. Wauchope, "My Experiences with Martin and Osa Johnson," *The Johnson Safari Wait-A-Bit News* 5,3:8–11 (July 1984). Joyce married George Wauchope, the captain of the *City of New York*, whom she met in 1933 while sailing to join the Johnsons in East Africa. He later became president of the Farrell Lines ("George Wauchope, Ex-Navy Officer," *New York Times*, April 14, 1978, II, 2).

50. "Truman H. Talley Rites Tomorrow," *New York Times*, January 18, 1942, 17; "Truman Hughes Talley," *Current Biography, 1942*, ed. Maxine Block (New York: The H. W. Wilson Co., 1943), 816.

51. Letter from Martin Johnson to Charmian London, New York City, February 17, 1932 (HEH).
52. *Congorilla* is a relatively short film, running some sixty-six minutes. Both MJ and OJ are credited as being its producers. Although MJ narrates it and there is dialogue and music, it contains several titles, vestiges of the silent era. The film was rereleased in the 1950s by Morro Films.
53. *Herald Tribune*, July 22, 1932; Irene Thirer, "Johnsons' 'Congorilla' is Grand: Winter Garden Offers Marvels of Africa with Laughs Galore," *New York Daily News*, July 22, 1932; "The Martin Johnsons with Camera and Gun, in the Jungles of Africa," *New York Times*, July 22, 1932, 18.
54. Congorilla, *Variety*, July 6, 1932.

13. AFRICA FROM THE AIR

1. The Johnsons paid $20,000 for the two planes and made an initial down payment of $17,000 on November 23, 1932 ("Cost of Equipment, Supplies, Etc. for New African Safari—Leaving New York December 31, 1932," AMNH).
2. The total projected cost of the expedition was $142,200.12 exclusive of the planes and camera equipment. Of this, $18,973.71 was for salaries, $53,354.64 for travel expenses, $14,265.00 for film from Eastman Kodak, $7,701.88 for developing and printing at H.E.R. Laboratories in New York City, and $2,816.45 for aviation fuel. On November 24, 1932, MJ purchased Wah and another gibbon ape they did not take along from Ellis Joseph for $500.00.
3. Vern Louis Carstens (1901–1978) was born in Rock Island, Illinois, and died in Chanute, Kansas. He later had a distinguished career as chief test pilot and manager of flight engineering for the Beechcraft Corporation in Wichita, Kansas (pers. comm., Vern L. Carstens, Chanute, Kans., 1966–1978). In 1978 we discussed the possibility of a memorial for Carstens in Africa with Errol Trzebinski, who suggested planting a tree at the Bamburi Portland Cement Company Limited's rehabilitation area outside of Mombasa, Kenya. Edward Rodwell, the dean of Kenya's journalists, organized the project, saw to the erection of a monument with a bronze plaque, and officiated at the planting of an African fig tree on February 10, 1979. The actual planting was done by Group Captain Tom James, the company's pilot (Edward Rodwell, "Bamburi Memorial," *Coastweek*, February 9, 1979; Rodwell, "In Memory of a Pioneer Pilot," *The Standard*, February 23, 1979, 24; Jane Blades, "Memorial Tree Honors Vern Carstens," *Chanute Tribune*, May 1, 1979). In 1984 Carstens's widow, Wilma, visited the memorial tree (Rodwell, "Recalling the 'Old Days of Flying in Safari Country . . . '," *Coastweek*, September 14, 1979).
4. Carstens, pers. comm. Aviation was still in its infancy when the Johnsons arrived with their two planes. The Aero Club of Kenya was founded in 1927, and the first plane was registered in 1928 (interview, J. M. Richmond, Nairobi, Kenya, October 28, 1977).
5. *Baboona*, Pressbooks, MFL XXXC.865, MFL N.C.198, MFL 470 (NYPL).
6. Hugh Stanton arrived in Kenya as a young boy in 1907. He served as a white hunter for Baron Louis Rothschild's expedition and was one of the hunters who protected actors during the 1929 filming of *Trader Horn*. For many years, he trapped animals for the San Diego Zoo and, along with his wife Jane, operated

"Bushwackers," a rustic camp near the Athi River; see 1987 addendum to Gillett, *Tribute*. MJ paid the Stantons $1,507.69 to trap animals, which he filmed in his studio.

7. Sydney Downey recalled that "There was a board on their gate which read 'No Visitors' to keep people out. . . . They took their hyena out to the plains to become wild, but the morning after it was back in Muthaiga again" (letter from Sydney Downey to Pascal James Imperato, Langata, Kenya, November 15, 1979).

8. MJ told the *East African Standard* (May 16, 1934) that he had to have animals brought to his home so that he could record their sounds. The paper noted that "among the animals at his house were 51 baboons."

9. Ray Nestor, "Kenya Memoirs, 1912–1950," unpublished (courtesy Errol Trzebinski).

10. Interview, E. A. Ruben, Nairobi, Kenya, October 26, 1977.

11. Letter from F. Trubee Davison to Martin Johnson, New York City, January 14, 1935 (AMNH).

12. Ruben, interview.

13. Interview, Dr. J. R. Gregory, Norfolk Hotel, Nairobi, Kenya, October 26, 1977.

14. *OAJ*, 151, 218, 220.

15. John Cloudsley-Thompson, *Animal Migration* (New York: G. P. Putnam's Sons, 1977), 81.

16. Letter from Sir Vivian Fuchs to Pascal James Imperato, Cambridge, England, January 26, 1989. See V. I. Fuchs, "The Lake Rudolf Rift Valley Expedition, 1934," *Geographical Journal* 86:114–142 (1935).

17. Carstens, pers. comm. An apocryphal story still in circulation among bush pilots in Kenya is that the Johnsons landed their amphibians on Lake Paradise.

18. *OAJ*, 78.

19. Davison's friends gave him a farewell dinner in the Perroquet Suite of the Waldorf-Astoria Hotel in New York City on May 29, 1933. The *New York Times* (May 30, 1933) noted that the only "woman" present was Mishi, a three-year-old chimpanzee.

20. Letter from George H. Sherwood to H.E. the Governor of Kenya, New York City, May 22, 1933 (AMNH).

21. Quesada became head of the Federal Aviation Agency during the Eisenhower Administration, and later president of the Washington Senators. For Dorothy Davison's account of the trip, see Franz Lidz, "On the Scene, One Elephant Hunt Was Enough for African Trekker Dorothy Davison," *Sports Illustrated* 62:92–93 (March 11, 1985).

22. *OAJ*, 94, 96.

23. *OAJ*, 101, 103, 105, 239–240.

24. Copyright Descriptive Material, *Baboona, an Aerial Epic over Africa*, 1935, LP 5343 (LC).

25. Carstens, pers. comm.

26. Letter from Dorothy Davison to Pascal James Imperato, Locust Valley, New York, May 15, 1986.

27. *OAJ*, 218–219. The Johnsons and their party spent three days traveling by road to and from Gangala Na Bodio, the elephant training farm where they shot extensive film footage.

28. MJ purchased one Wall sound camera for $11,200 and a new Bell & Howell Eyemo Aerial camera for $1,860. He also had two other Bell & Howell motion picture cameras, but did not use any Akeley cameras on this trip.
29. Vern L. Carstens, "A Pilot on Safari, Sixth Installment," *The Sportsman Pilot* 15,1:28–29, 40–42 (January 1936).
30. Interview, Iris Roberts Mistry, Nairobi, Kenya, October 27, 1977.
31. Carstens, "A Pilot on Safari," 40.
32. Quotes from a letter from Marthe Adcock to Pascal James Imperato, Mombasa, Kenya, April 24, 1979, and an interview conducted for the authors by Edward Rodwell at the Mombasa Club, Mombasa, Kenya, April 18, 1988.
33. Carstens, pers. comm.
34. *East African Standard*, June 26, 1934.
35. Gregory, interview.
36. Letter from Martin Johnson to E. A. Ruben, Nairobi, Kenya, July 13, 1934 (courtesy of the late E. A. Ruben).
37. Carstens, pers. comm. The Johnsons' former home has been remodeled over the years, including additions to the front and rear. Since 1970, it has been owned by Yusuf Abdulgani, a prominent Nairobi businessman, who purchased it from a Mexican national, Mario Pascoe. The ambassador of Greece leased the house for five years in the 1970s, after which the Abdulgani family lived in it. In 1991 it was leased to Paolo Garbosa, the ambassador of Portugal. When we visited it in 1977, MJ's laboratory building was being used as a laundry and storeroom (pers. obs. and information provided by Yusuf Abdulgani to Dilawar Khan, Bruce Safaris Ltd., Nairobi, Kenya, December 31, 1990, and March 1, 1991).
38. "Barrage of Flour Stops Jungle Lion, Johnsons Back from Another African Trip, Tell of Their Latest Adventures," *New York Times*, August 10, 1934, 10.
39. Eastman Kodak provided the Johnsons with a small amount of experimental 16-mm Kodachrome film and a custom-made camera to use it; see Kenhelm W. Stott, Jr., "Color Photography on Johnson Expeditions," *The Johnson Wait-A-Bit News* 1,4:7–8 (October 1980).

14. RETURN TO THE RAIN FOREST

1. Robert H. Richards, "Wreck Ends 50-Year Service of Engineer," *Wichita Beacon*, September 8, 1934, 1, 14; "Two Killed, 3 Badly Injured, in Train Wreck," *Chanute Tribune*, September 7, 1934, 1, 2.
2. "Rites for Three Victims of Wreck," *Chanute Tribune*, September 10, 1934, 1; "Mrs. Leighty Is Awarded $8,000," *Chanute Tribune*, October 11, 1934, 2. In later years, Osa's mother lived in a small frame house at 402 South Steuben Avenue in Chanute.
3. Letter from Martin Johnson to Charmian London, New York City, September 17, 1934 (HEH); RKO Circuit Agreement, January 30, 1935 (AMNH). Around this time, MJ and OJ contracted with illustrator, William A. Steward, to produce a comic strip entitled "Danger Trails." It appeared as a syndicated feature in numerous newspapers and chronicled the Johnsons' careers. In 1935 a number of illustrations from this comic strip were published in a small book entitled *Danger Trails in Africa*. A few years later, OJ contracted with illustrator Glen Cravath to produce a comic strip entitled "Diana Daring in Jungle Depths."
4. Letter from Osa Johnson to Charmian London, October 20, 1934 (HEH).

5. See n. 4.

6. "Baby Elephant to Go to St. Louis by Plane," *New York Times*, October 10, 1934, 46.

7. *Baboona*, Pressbooks, MFLXXXC.865, MFL N.E. 198, MFL 470 (NYPL).

8. Martin Johnson's Invitation List for "Baboona" Premiere (AMNH).

9. For a summary of press and trade reviews of *Baboona*, see *Motion Picture Herald*, February 2, 1935, 38; Andre Sennwald, "Aerial Safari in Africa with Mr. and Mrs. Martin Johnson in 'Baboona' at the Rialto," *New York Times*, January 23, 1935, 21; Richard Watts, Jr., "Baboona," *New York Herald*, January 23, 1935, 26.

10. "Theatre Receipts," *Motion Picture Herald*, February 2, 1935; 74; February 9, 1935, 88; "What the Picture Did for Me," *Motion Picture Herald*, March 16, 1935, 57.

11. Copyright descriptive material, *Baboona, an Aerial Epic over Africa*, 1935, LP5343 (LC).

12. Letter from Martin Johnson to Jack and Charmian London, Denver, Colo., December 8, 1910 (HEH).

13. Pers. comm., Belle Leighty, Chanute, Kans., 1966–1974; *Manchester Guardian*, December 18, 1935, 17; Henry E. Armstrong, "The Martin Johnsons over Africa," *New York Times Book Review*, October 20, 1935, 9.

14. "Bid Johnsons Bon Voyage," *New York Times*, August 9, 1935, 20. Osa, who was the only woman member of the Circus Saints and Sinners Club, was made an honorary member of the Adventurers Club at this luncheon.

15. "Johnsons on Way to Wilds of Borneo," *New York Times*, August 14, 1935, II, 2.

16. Agnes Newton Keith arrived in North Borneo in November 1934, about a year before the Johnsons' return there; see Agnes Newton Keith, *Land below the Wind* (Boston: Little, Brown and Co., 1940), 69–75; *LA*, 33.

17. Pers. comm., Joseph Tilton, Pittsburgh, Pa., 1980–1987; Tilton also recalled that Martin frequently spoke of Jack London during the long hours they filmed together from blinds.

18. Letter from Osa Johnson to Belle Leighty, British North Borneo, April 18, 1936 (courtesy Belle Leighty).

19. Letter from Martin Johnson to Charmian London, Sandakan, British North Borneo, June 15, 1936 (HEH).

20. Pers. comm., Joseph Tilton, Pittsburgh, Pa., 1980–1987; James Laneri, St. Petersburg, Fla., 1981.

21. Keith, *Land below the Wind*, 73. Martin also lashed out at Tilton once, claiming that the sound track was of poor quality. Later he apologized when Fox cabled back, "It's the best sound you've ever gotten" (pers. comm., Joseph Tilton, Pittsburgh, Pa., February 13, 1980).

22. Agnes Newton Keith, who was aware of the Johnsons' marital difficulties, greatly admired them "for their courageous way of meeting the many problems of their own lives" (letter from Agnes Newton Keith to Pascal James Imperato, Oak Bay, Victoria, B.C., Canada, April 1, 1966).

23. Virtually all of the movie film was black and white except for a small amount of 35-mm Kodachrome color footage that Eastman Kodak provided. Although Technicolor was available, it then required a three-reel camera system and development in specialized laboratories in the United States and Europe. It was unacceptable to the Johnsons because they had to develop film in the field in order to verify results quickly. In addition, full-length color features had not yet won

widespread public acceptance. Eastman Kodak also provided a dozen experimental 3-by-4-inch color starch plates, which MJ gave to Tilton, who used them primarily for making still pictures of OJ (pers. comm., Joseph Tilton, Pittsburgh, Pa., May 5, 1986).

24. Keith, *Land below the Wind*, 73.
25. "Johnsons Return with Largest Ape, 300-Pound Orang-utan Is One of Explorers' Trophies of Year's Borneo Hunt," *New York Times*, October 26, 1936, 19.
26. Frank Buck, in Katz, *The Film Encyclopedia*, 179.

15. 1937

1. "Wild Ape Is Met at Museum Show" *New York Times*, November 1, 1936, II, 7; "Martin Johnsons Return with Wild Boy of Borneo," *New York Post*, October 26, 1936, 9.
2. Saudin bin Labutau, "The Story of Saudin by Himself," trans. Agnes Newton Keith, *Atlantic Monthly* 161:227–231 (1938).
3. "Clark H. Getts," in *Who's Who in America* (Chicago: Marquis Who's Who, 1981), 1193. Some sources state that Getts was on the staff of a life insurance company while he was in China ("Osa Johnson, Former Whitehall Man Married," *The Winona Republican*, February 3, 1941, 12).
4. "Johnson et al. versus Western Air Express Corporation et al.," *Pacific Reporter*, 2d ser., 45 Cal. App. 2d 614, 114, 688–698 (1941).
5. "One Killed, 10 Hurt as Plane Crashes in California Hills: The Martin Johnsons Escape Death, but Are Critically Injured When Big Airliner Plows into Rugged Area," *New York Times*, January 13, 1937, 1, 25.
6. Burnap charged $1,150 for the approximately twelve hours of medical care he gave MJ. This was an exorbitant amount for the times, as was the $3,000 he charged for the five weeks he cared for OJ.
7. Interviews, Belle Leighty, Chanute, Kans., 1964–1976; Martin Johnson, Standard Certificate of Death, State of California, Department of Public Health, Local Registered Number 1656, January 26, 1937 (Registrar–Recorder, Los Angeles County, California); "Mrs. Johnson Is Told Her Husband Died: Bears Shock Bravely, Tells of Crash," *New York Times*, January 15, 1937, 7. Margaret Cripps Sachs, MJ's niece, commented: "Osa was devastated by Martin's death. He was everything to her, and she was really lost without him" (pers. comm., October 22, 1991).
8. Note by Charmian London, Glen Ellen, Calif., undated (HEH); letter from Agnes Newton Keith to Pascal James Imperato, Oak Bay, Victoria, B.C., Canada, April 1, 1966.
9. Interviews, Clark H. Getts, New York City, 1972–1980.
10. "Osa Johnson Goes Home," *New York Times*, February 24, 1937, 25; "2,000 Attend Rites for Martin Johnson," *New York Times*, February 28, 1937, II, 9.
11. Last Will and Testament, Martin Johnson, Surrogate's Court, County of New York, probated March 12, 1937, 150.
12. Letter from Osa Johnson to Freda Cripps, On Safari, East Africa, August 31, 1937 (AMNH).
13. Judicial Settlement of the Account of Proceedings of Osa Johnson as Executrix of the Estate of Martin Johnson Deceased, Release and Discharge of Osa Johnson as

Executrix of the Last Will and Testament of Martin Johnson, Deceased, Surrogate's Court, County of New York, P-150/1937, 1940.

14. OJ later sold the elephant head to oil producer Frank Phillips, who kept it at his country home, Willaroc, outside of Bartlesville, Oklahoma. Among MJ's unpaid bills was one for $465 from Frank Edward Smith, M.D., for OJ's medical care prior to January 12, 1937. Smith's son, Frank E. Smith, Jr., M.D., recalled that his father had treated OJ for several years, often spoke of both her and MJ to his family and greatly admired them (pers. comm., Frank E. Smith, Jr., M.D., Salisbury, Conn., February 13, 1991). See also Last Will; Judicial Settlement.

15. Pers. comm., James Laneri, St. Petersburg, Fla., March 19, 1981; June 9, 1981.

16. Letter from Osa Johnson to Marshall McLean, On Safari, July 24, 1937 (AMNH).

17. Letter from Marshall McLean to Osa Johnson, New York City, July 30, 1937 (AMNH).

18. Seebach also cut the color film MJ and Tilton had shot in Borneo for use in OJ's upcoming fall lecture tour.

19. Letter from Osa Johnson to Lillian Seebach, On Tour, May 1, 1937 (AMNH).

20. Getts, interview. *Stanley and Livingstone*, which starred Spencer Tracy, Walter Brennan, Charles Coburn, and Sir Cedric Hardwicke, was released in 1939.

21. Letter from Osa Johnson to Daniel Pomeroy, On Safari, August 16, 1937 (AMNH). While in Kenya, OJ and Clark stayed at Closeburn Estates, a farm on the outskirts of Nairobi then owned by Rob Grahame Bell. OJ complained that the suspended plow share that was used to signal the beginning and end of work made a terrible noise. On returning to the United States, she shipped out a Santa Fe locomotive bell (letter from Rob Grahame Bell to Pascal James Imperato, Ballitsville, Natal, South Africa, July 7, 1978). The bell was still in use at Closeburn when we visited there in 1977.

22. Getts, interview.

23. "Theatre Receipts," *Motion Picture Herald*, September 25, 1937, 60; October 2, 1937, 66.

24. Copyright Descriptive Material, *Borneo*, 1937, LP7914 (LC).

25. John Mosher, "Borneo," *New Yorker*, September 11, 1937, 94.

26. *Film Daily*, September 7, 1937, 7; *Variety* (Hollywood), September 11, 1937, 3; *New York Herald Tribune*, September 4, 1937, 8; *Variety*, September 8, 1937, 19; *New York Times*, September 4, 1937, 8.

27. See Judicial Settlement.

28. OJ produced several news stories for the *New York Times*: "Couple Survives Jungle Crash," August 1, 1937, II, 1; "Grass Fires Kill African Wild Life," October 10, 1937, II, 1; "Africans Rebel at Playing Slaves," October 17, 1937, 29; "Natives Endanger the Johnson Party," October 24, 1937, 29; "Lions Prey on Band Fleeing Ethiopia," November 14, 1937, 25. The first story describes a rescue mission headed by OJ and Al Klein in search of Phillip Whitemarsh and his wife, who had crash-landed in their small plane while en route to Kisumu to pick up OJ and Clark. The Whitemarshes had purchased the Johnsons' Muthaiga home in 1934.

29. Letter from Lillian Seebach to Clark H. Getts, New York City, September 20, 1937 (AMNH); letter from Lillian Seebach to Osa Johnson, October 5, 1937 (AMNH).

30. Dr. J. R. Gregory, OJ's personal physician in Kenya, observed: "It didn't seem

right to many of us that she had become involved with someone else so soon after Martin's death." E. A. Ruben recalled that Clark understandably came under suspicion since OJ was a wealthy widow whom he had known for less than a year (interviews, Dr. J. R. Gregory, Norfolk Hotel, Nairobi, Kenya, October 26, 1977; E. A. Ruben, Nairobi, Kenya, October 26, 1977).

31. Interview, Belle Leighty, Chanute, Kans., May 23, 1966.

16. GLAMOROUS OSA

1. "Mrs. Johnson Sues Again," *New York Times*, December 23, 1937, 17; interview, Vern Carstens, Chanute, Kans., January 30, 1978.
2. Carstens, interview.
3. "Johnson et al. versus Western Air Express Corporation et al.," *Pacific Reporter*, 2d ser., 45 Cal. App. 2d 614, 114, 688–698 (1946).
4. Pomeroy stored all of the corporation's papers in the basement of his Englewood, New Jersey, home until 1952, when he turned them over to the AMNH along with the rights to the film *Simba*.
5. Letter from Wayne M. Faunce to Roy Chapman Andrews, New York City, March 20, 1935 (AMNH).
6. *Jungles Calling*, Clipping File (NYPL); interview, Belle Leighty, Chanute, Kans., May 25, 1966.
7. "12 Women Get Style Awards," *New York Times*, March 19, 1939, 4.
8. Mary Wells Ridley, "Osa Johnson Slicks Up Jungle Sport Wardrobe," *New York World-Telegram*, March 11, 1939, 32; Eve Richardson, "Osa Johnson Designs Clever Outdoor Togs," *Beverly Hills Shopping News*, May 1, 1939, 1; "Osa Johnson's Famous Congo Gloves," *New York Sun*, December 5, 1939, 20.
9. Interview, Clark H. Getts, New York City, June 3, 1974.
10. The toys were manufactured by the F. W. Woolnough Co. of New York City; "Mrs. Johnson Honorary Head of Wildlife Week," *Boston Post*, March 2, 1940, 4.
11. "Cameramen Pick 10 Personalities," *New York Sun*, March 17, 1940, 2; "New Sweet Peas," *New York Herald Tribune*, March 13, 1940, 6.
12. "Osa Johnson to be Honored at San Diego Zoo Ceremony," *Los Angeles Times*, November 2, 1939, 2.
13. When *I Married Adventure* became a national best-seller, Dunn sued OJ for additional compensation. "She had been paid a fixed amount for the job and thought the book would sell a few thousand copies. When it became a runaway best-seller, she felt cheated and tried to get additional money out of Osa, which she failed to do" (interview, Clark H. Getts, New York City, June 10, 1976).
14. Alice Payne Hackett and James Henry Burke, *80 Years of Best Sellers, 1895–1975* (New York and London: R. R. Bowker Co., 1977), 129–130. The original edition of *I Married Adventure* remained in print for over twenty years. In the early 1960s, a thousand copies a year were being sold (Royalty statements for the J. B. Lippincott Co., 1960–1963, courtesy Belle Leighty). A slightly revised edition was published in 1989.
15. Joseph Wood Krutch, *Nation* 150:736 (June 15, 1940); Rose Feld, *Books*, May 19, 1940, 1.
16. In March, OJ had a reunion with her mother at Vaughn's summer place in Fort Worth, Texas ("Tragedy Passed, Osa Johnson Has Learned to Live Alone," *Fort*

Worth Press, March 7, 1940, 2). Clark Getts was frustrated on the tour by the fact that Lippincott would print only ten thousand copies of the book at a time. As a result, the book was sometimes unavailable in cities where Osa spoke.

17. Letter from Osa Johnson to Daniel Pomeroy, Los Angeles, Calif., January 31, 1940 (AMNH); letter from Daniel Pomeroy to Osa Johnson, New York City, February 14, 1940 (AMNH). As he often did, Pomeroy addressed OJ in this letter as "Dear Tom."

18. Letter from Hamilton Holt to Osa Johnson, Winter Park, Fla., November 20, 1940 (courtesy Department of Archives and Special Collections, Rollins College).

19. Osa Johnson, "A Vanishing World," The Annual Animated Magazine, February 23, 1941 (courtesy Department of Archives and Special Collections, Rollins College); "Celebrities Speak from the 'Animated Magazine,'" *Winter Park Topics*, February 21, 1941, 1.

20. Founders' Day Program, Rollins College, Winter Park, Florida, February 24, 1941; Citation for Honorary Degree of Doctor of Science for Osa Johnson, Fleetwood Peeples, Public Orator (courtesy Department of Archives and Special Collections, Rollins College).

21. Bosley Crowther, "'I Married Adventure,' the Story of the Martin Johnsons, at the Plaza—Two New Foreign Films," *New York Times*, September 24, 1940, 26.

22. *I Married Adventure*, in *Variety*, September 25, 1940.

23. Marriage Certificate, Clark H. Getts and Helen Leighty, State of North Carolina, County of Halifax, Office of Register of Deeds, April 29, 1940 (courtesy Register of Deeds, Halifax County, N.C.).

24. "Osa Johnson Wed Here: Mayor Performs Ceremony at City Hall for Widow of African Explorer," *New York Times*, February 4, 1941, 23; "Osa Johnson Wed to Her Manager: LaGuardia Ties Knot and Bride Gets an Orchid," *New York Sun*, February 3, 1941, 5; "Osa Is Married to Clark Getts by N.Y. Mayor," *Chanute Tribune*, February 3, 1941, 1; "Osa Johnson Eager for Peace So She Can Go Hunting Again: Newlywed and Her Husband Will Return to the Jungles, She Says, When War Is Over," United Press International, February 7, 1941.

25. "Off to the Front in East Africa," *British American Ambulance Corps*, September 1940, 1. An ambulance sent to Kenya was named "Osa Johnson". "53 Women Named As Leaders of Sex," *New York Times*, May 9, 1941, 17.

26. Rose Feld, "Home Folks from Kansas, in the African Jungle: How Osa and Martin Kept House, Raised Corn and Watermelons, and Photographed Lions," *New York Herald Tribune*, December 14, 1941, IX, 5. Clark Getts claimed that he played a major role in the writing of this book, and many years later said: "The ghostwriter we hired got bogged down, and I ended up writing a good deal of it myself" (interview, Clark H. Getts, New York City, June 3, 1974).

27. Mary L. Jobe Akeley, "Life in an Unspoiled Wilderness of Equatorial Africa," *New York Times*, January 4, 1942, VI, 6. Mary L. Jobe Akeley differed from OJ in many ways. She was extremely well educated and an accomplished explorer and scientist in her own right before she married Carl Akeley. She saw herself as far superior to OJ in her scientific knowledge of Africa, its peoples, and its wildlife. Yet, in one important respect, she was very similar to OJ. Although she survived her husband by forty years, she lived primarily through his name and accomplishments (Bodry-Sanders, *Carl Akeley*, 254).

28. Invitation to World Premiere, *African Paradise*, Clipping File (NYPL); "Osa

Johnson's "African Paradise" to Have Premiere at Carnegie Hall," *The Baldwin Citizen*, October 23, 1941, 1.

29. "Osa Purchases Place of Birth for a Museum: Mrs. John Fohler of Dallas Sells Corner at Seventh and Malcolm," *Chanute Tribune*, November 25, 1941, 1; interview, Belle Leighty, Chanute, Kans., May 23, 1966.

17. FINAL YEARS

1. Interviews, Clark H. Getts, New York City, 1972–1980.
2. "In Memoriam—Martin Johnson," Speech of Hon. Arthur Capper of Kansas, in the Senate of the United States, May 18, 1938; C. Jackson Selsor, "Proboscis Monkey of Borneo," *Explorers Journal* 56, 2 (1978): 54–55.
3. Getts, interview.
4. *Christian Science Monitor*, November 3, 1941, 9; *Library Journal* 66:1096 (December 15, 1941); *Library Journal* 67:1069 (December 1, 1942).
5. Letter from Clark H. Getts to Lillian Seebach, New York City, June 6, 1942 (AMNH).
6. OJ's original manuscript was untitled and was dedicated to "our servicemen fighting overseas"; *LA* received numerous positive reviews, including "Yesterday's Frontiers Live Again," *Detroit News*, January 23, 1966; "Posthumous Story of Love and Fearless Adventure," *Savannah Morning News*, January 30, 1966; "Book about Exploring Johnsons Stirs Memories," *Portland Evening Express*, January 29, 1966; "Trip to Borneo Lively Reading," *Dayton Daily News*, April 24, 1966; "Johnsons in Borneo: The Last Expedition," *Washington Star*, March 6, 1966; "Last Expedition of the Johnsons," *Rochester Democrat and Chronicle*, February 13, 1966; "Osa Johnson's Last Safari," *Milwaukee Journal*, January 30, 1966; "More Martin Johnsons," *New York Times*, December 6, 1965.
7. *Bulletin from Virginia Kirkus' Bookshop Service* 12:294 (July 1, 1944).
8. Foster Hailey, *New York Times*, October 8, 1944, 4.
9. *New York Times*, March 18, 1945, 28.
10. Getts, interview.
11. Getts, interview. Interviews, Belle Leighty, Chanute, Kans., 1964–1974.
12. Harry Coren, "Ex-Explorer Sues Her 2nd Hubby as 'Fake,'" *New York Daily Mirror*, January 27, 1948, 2; James L. Kilgallen, "Osa Johnson Says 2nd Mate Stole $300,000," *New York Journal American*, January 26, 1948, 1; Leeds Moberley, "Osa Sues to Unwed Adventure No. 2," *New York Daily News*, January 27, 1948, 2; "Osa Johnson Sues Mate, Tells Past," *Chicago Daily Tribune*, January 27, 1948, 7.
13. "Denies His Alcatraz Career Put Marriage on the Rock," *New York Daily Mirror*, May 8, 1948, 4; "Getts Explains 'Prison Term,'" *New York Journal American*, January 27, 1948, 3; "Osa's Mate Calls Her Suit a Jungle Jumble," *New York Daily News*, May 8, 1948, 6; "Osa's Suit Lies Says Husband," *New York Journal American*, May 7, 1948, 3.
14. Interview, E. A. Ruben, Nairobi, Kenya, October 26, 1977; interview, DeWitt Sage, Links Club, New York City, December 15, 1977.
15. Interview, Vern Carstens, Chanute, Kans., January 30, 1978.
16. Getts, interview. Carstens corroborated the sale of the rifles, having seen them in a pre-auction display at the auctioneers, Parke-Bernet.

17. Getts, interview; Leighty, interview. MJ's sister, Freda Cripps, also believed that Clark had embezzled OJ's monies (pers. comm., Margaret Cripps Sachs, Berkeley, Calif., October 22, 1991).
18. Getts, interview.
19. Roy Topper, "Osa Johnson Plans Divorce," *Chicago Herald-American*, April 17, 1949, 24; "Widow of Explorer Wins Divorce," *Los Angeles Herald*, April 29, 1949, 2.
20. Memorandum from Lloyd Mann to Walter F. Meister, June 2, 1953, New York City (AMNH). A number of the films in *Osa Johnson's Big Game Hunt* were narrated by Ivan Terrence Sanderson, a well-known naturalist and nature writer whose father, Arthur Buchanan Sanderson, worked for the Johnsons at Lake Paradise.
21. Getts, interview.
22. Getts, interview; Leighty, interview. In the Matter of John Crane, an Attorney, Supreme Court of the State of New York, Appellate Division, First Judicial Department, September 1953 (courtesy First Judicial Department).
23. Pers. comm., Joan Kennedy, Brooklyn, N.Y., 1989.
24. Leighty, interview.
25. "Osa Johnson Dies: A Noted Explorer," *New York Times*, January 8, 1953, 30; "Osa Johnson, Explorer, Found Dead," *New York Daily News*, January 8, 1953, 8.
26. Certificate of Death, Osa Johnson, No. 156-53-100564, City of New York, Department of Health, Bureau of Records and Statistics, January 7, 1953. There is no evidence to support the widespread rumor that OJ accidentally committed suicide through a combination of alcohol and drugs. This rumor is primarily based on the perception that OJ's penurious state provided sufficient motive.
27. "Osa Johnson, Explorer, Found Dead."
28. "First Woman Explorer, Tribute to Osa Johnson in Last Rites," *Chanute Tribune*, January 13, 1953, 1.

EPILOGUE

1. Last Will and Testament, Osa Johnson, Surrogate's Court, County of New York, probated July 23, 1953, 2026, 427.
2. Auction per Order of Estate of Osa Johnson, Plaza Art Galleries Inc., Sale No. 3417, October 16–17, 1953.
3. Interviews, Belle Leighty, Chanute, Kansas, 1964–1974.
4. For a history of the museum, see Martin and Osa Johnson Safari Museum and Johnson Memorial Hall of African Culture, 1961–1981, suppl., *Chanute Tribune*, June 11, 1981; and "Martin and Osa Johnson Safari Museum. 30 Years: 1961–1991," *Chanute Tribune*, June 8, 1991.
5. Letter from Freda Johnson Cripps to President, American Museum of Natural History, Albany, Calif., October 20, 1962 (AMNH); letter from Freda Johnson Cripps to Walter F. Meister, Albany, Calif., November 10, 1962 (AMNH).
6. John Povey, "The Johnson Memorial Hall of African Culture," *African Arts* 7,3:74–75 (1974); "Dignitaries Open Museum's Cultural Hall," *Chanute Tribune*, January 21, 1974, 1. In 1991 the museum's Board of Trustees renamed the Johnson Memorial Hall of African Culture, the Imperato African Hall (Conrad G. Froehlich, "Safari Museum News," *Chanute Tribune*, April 17, 1991, 3).

7. "Renovation Project Needs Community," *Chanute Tribune*, September 11, 1990, 1; "Depot Drive Tops $1 Million Mark," *Chanute Tribune*, December 13, 1990, 8; "Depot Drive Reaches Goal," *Chanute Tribune*, January 2, 1992, 1.

8. Lowell Thomas frequently said: "Martin and Osa were my pals."

9. Letter from Kirk Huffman, Vila, Vanuatu, to the Martin and Osa Johnson Safari Museum, *The Johnson Safari Wait-A-Bit News* 2,4:7–8, (1981).

FILMOGRAPHY

FULL-LENGTH FEATURE AND LECTURE FILMS

Year of Release	Title	Type of Film
1918	*Among the Cannibal Isles of the South Pacific*	Silent lecture film
1918	*Cannibals of the South Seas* (divided into two parts, with Part II being called *Captured by Cannibals*)	Silent feature
1921	*Jungle Adventures*	Silent feature
1922	*Head Hunters of the South Seas*	Silent feature
1923	*Trailing African Wild Animals*	Silent feature
1928	*Simba*	Silent and sound feature
1928	*Adventuring Johnsons*	Silent lecture film (2 reels)
1930	*Across the World with Mr. and Mrs. Martin Johnson*	Sound feature
1931	*Wonders of the Congo*	Silent lecture film
1932	*Congorilla*	Sound feature
1934	*Wings over Africa*	Silent lecture film
1935	*Baboona*	Sound feature
1937	*Jungle Depths of Borneo* (also called *Adventuring through Borneo*)	Silent lecture film
1937	*Borneo*	Sound feature
1938	*Jungles Calling*	Silent lecture film
1940	*I Married Adventure*[a]	Sound feature
1941	*African Paradise*	Silent lecture film
1943	*Tulagi and the Solomons*	Silent lecture film

Note: Some sources list a 1913 silent feature film, *Jack London's Adventures in the South Sea Islands* (also called *Jack London's South Sea Island Adventures*). This was not a film but rather the title of the Johnsons' 1913 Criterion Theatre illustrated lecture in which borrowed and purchased film footage was shown.

[a]This film was produced by Columbia Pictures using extensive Johnson footage.

SHORT FILMS

Year of Release	Title	Type of Film
	On the Borderland of Civilization[a]	Series of 10 one-reel silent films
1918–1919	*The City of Broken Old Men* (Noumea)	One-reel silent
"	*Cruising in the Solomons*	"
"	*Domesticating Wild Men*	"
"	*The Home of the Hula Hula*	"
"	*Lonely South Pacific Missions*	"
"	*Marooned in the South Seas*	"
"	*Recruiting in the Solomons*	"
"	*Saving Savages in the South Seas*	"
"	*Through the Isles of the New Hebrides*	"
"	*Tulagi—A White Spot in a Black Land*	"
1919	*Animals of Australia*	"
"	*Cruising in the New Hebrides*	"
"	*The Leuneuwa Lagoon*	"
"	*South Sea Fishing*	"
"	*Tahiti*	"
1921–1922	*Martin Johnson's Voyages* (also called *Martin Johnson South Sea Films*)[b]	Series of 22 one-reel silent films
"	*At Colombo and Port Said*	One-reel silent
"	*Bessie the Adventuress*	"
"	*Ceylon*	"
"	*China Comes to Borneo*	"
"	*Coolie Women of Borneo*	"
"	*Dance of Joy in the South Seas*	"
"	*An Expedition into the Solomon Islands*	"
"	*In Search of the Lost Tribe*	"
"	*Into the Setting Sun*	"
"	*Nipa Workers*	"
"	*On a Chinese Junk*	"
"	*People You Meet in the South Seas*	"
"	*Rapid Transit in Borneo*	"
"	*Raratonga*	"
"	*Sandakan, the Seductive*	"
"	*Search for the Unknown River*	"
"	*Singapore*	"
"	*South Sea Kids*	"
"	*South Sea Preparedness*	"
"	*Through the Valley of Rubber*	"

[a]Distributed by Robertson-Cole.
[b]There were originally nineteen single-reel films in this series which were distributed by National Non-Theatrical Motion Pictures, Inc.

Year of Release	Title	Type of Film
"	*Up the Sekong River*	"
"	*Wild and Wooly Hunt*	"
1921	*Traveling East of Suez* (also called *East of Suez*)	Three-reel silent
1928	*Johnsons at Home*	Three-reel silent
"	*Naked Man versus Beast*	One-reel silent
"	*Safari*	Three-reel silent
1937	*Children of Africa*[c]	One-reel silent

[c]This film was edited by Agnes G. Kelly Saunders of the American Museum of Natural History using Johnson film produced in 1924–1927.

BIBLIOGRAPHY

Martin Johnson authored eight books, of which seven were published, and also some sixty periodical articles. Osa Johnson wrote ten books and some forty periodical articles. Of the latter, twenty-four appeared in *Good Housekeeping* magazine and were later synthesized into several children's books. The Johnsons, their lectures, films, and books were the subjects of numerous periodical articles and thousands of newspaper accounts. Many of the newspapers have long since ceased publication, and the absence of indexes to them makes retrieval of articles extremely difficult. The *New York Times* alone carried over a hundred articles about them during the thirty-two-year period 1921–1953; some of these were front-page stories. Significant collections of newspaper articles that deal with the Johnsons exist at the New York Public Library, General Library and Museum of the Performing Arts (Lincoln Center), the Martin and Osa Johnson Safari Museum (SM), and in the Clark H. Getts Collection at the American Heritage Center, University of Wyoming. Contemporary motion picture industry coverage and assessments of their films are extensive and found primarily in trade publications such as *Exhibitors Herald, Motion Picture News, Moving Picture World, Variety, Wid's Film Daily*, and others. Except for *Variety*, none are indexed, and accession is possible only through painstaking examination of individual issues on microfilm.

There are three published bibliographies on the Johnsons; together they provide extensive information about their books, periodical articles, and secondary sources. Gene DeGruson's *Kansas Authors of Best Sellers* (1970) contains information about published books and articles primarily listed in standard indexes such as the *Reader's Guide to Periodical Literature*. Sondra Updike Alden's "A Bibliography of the Books Written by Martin Johnson" (1984) presents detailed listings of various American and foreign-language editions, of which there are many. Evelyn V. Alden's "A Bibliography of the Books Written by Osa Johnson" (1985) approaches Osa's books in much the same manner. The existence of these bibliographies provides access to a broad range of published materials, except for newspaper articles and stories that appeared in motion picture industry publications.

This bibliography presents a chronological listing of all first American edition books and selected periodical articles written by the Johnsons. Important secondary sources and publications describing the larger historical context of their times are also included and listed alphabetically.

BIBLIOGRAPHIES

Alden, Evelyn V. A Bibliography of Books Written by Osa Johnson. *The Johnson Wait-A-Bit News* 6,2:1–7 (1985).

Alden, Sondra Updike. A Bibliography of Books Written by Martin Johnson. *The Johnson Safari Wait-A-Bit News* 5,1:B1–B7 (1984).

DeGruson, Gene. *Kansas Authors of Best Sellers: A Bibliography of the Works of Martin and Osa Johnson, Margaret Hill McCarter, Charles M. Sheldon, and Harold Bell Wright.* Pittsburg, Kans.: Kansas State College of Pittsburg, 1970.

Imperato, Pascal James. *New York Times* articles dealing with Martin and Osa Johnson, 1921–1953 (typescript), 1976. SM Archives.

BOOKS BY MARTIN JOHNSON

Johnson, Martin. *Through the South Seas with Jack London.* New York: Dodd, Mead and Co., 1913 (republished by Wolf House Books, 1972).
————. Martin Johnson's Cannibals of the South Seas. Unpublished, 1919. SM Archives.
————. *Cannibal-Land: Adventures with a Camera in the New Hebrides.* Boston and New York: Houghton Mifflin Co., 1922.
————. *Camera Trails in Africa.* New York and London: The Century Co., 1924.
————. *Safari: A Saga of the African Blue.* New York and London: G. P. Putnam's Sons, 1928 (republished by Tower Books, 1971).
————. *Lion: African Adventure with the King of Beasts.* New York and London: G. P. Putnam's Sons, 1929.
————. *Congorilla: Adventures with Pygmies and Gorillas in Africa.* New York: Brewer, Warren and Putnam, 1932.
————. *Over African Jungles: The Record of a Glorious Adventure over the Big Game Country of Africa 60,000 Miles by Airplane.* New York: Harcourt, Brace and Co., 1935.

SELECTED PERIODICAL ARTICLES BY MARTIN JOHNSON

Johnson, Martin. Camera Man in Borneo. *Asia* 21:125–140 (1921).
————. Cannibals at the Movies. *Asia* 21:425–431 (1921).
————. Wild Men of the New Hebrides *Asia* 21:568–611 (1921).
————. In the African Blue. *Asia* 23:442–446 (1923).
————. Martin Johnson's Photographs of Wild Animals in Africa, with a Commentary by Carl E. Akeley. *World's Work* 46:184–192, 293–300 (1923).
————. What I Am Trying to Do. *World's Work* 46:373–383 (1923).
————. Scenes from the Plains and Jungles of Africa. *Natural History* 24:289–296 (1924).
————. Extracts From The Diary of Martin Johnson. *Natural History* 25:571–578 (1925).
————. Scenes about Lake Paradise: Reproductions from Photographs Taken by the Martin Johnson African Expedition. *Natural History* 25 (1925). 16-page insert.
————. Hunting Lions with a Flashlight. *World's Work* 52:135–150 (1926).
————. The Camera as an Aid to the Naturalist. *Scientific American* 137:152–153 (1927).
————. Laughs and Thrills in Camera Hunting. *New York Times Magazine*, July 31, 1927, 4–6, 21.
————. Wild Neighbors of the African Jungle. *New York Times Magazine*, August 14, 1927, 8–9.
————. Picturing Africa. *Natural History* 27:539–560 (1927).
————. Scenes from Akeley's Africa: Reproduced From Photographs Taken by Martin Johnson during the Present Martin Johnson African Expedition. *Natural History* 27:172–173 (1927). 8-page insert.
————. The Land of Glorious Adventure: A Series of Sixteen Photographs by Martin Johnson Shot during the Four Years He Spent in Africa Making His Motion Picture Record of African Wildlife and African Natives. *Natural History* 27:544–545 (1927). 16-page insert.

_____. Giraffes and Their Enemies. *Saturday Evening Post* 200:35 (1928).

_____. Taming Elephants. *Saturday Evening Post* 201:37, 130 (1929).

_____. Giving a Jungle Show to a Lion Audience. *Literary Digest* 101:60–64 (1929).

_____. Little Men and Little Women. *World's Work* 60:42–48, 113–115 (1931).

_____. Trailing Gorillas in African Jungles. *New York Times Magazine*, August 30, 1931, 6–7, 23.

_____. Adventures in Akeley's African Park. *New York Times Magazine*, September 6, 1931, 10–11.

_____. Matching Wits with the African Beasts. *New York Times Magazine*, September 13, 1931, 8–9, 20.

_____. Sky Trails in Africa. *Natural History* 33:131–138 (1933).

_____. Wings over Africa. *Natural History* 34:596–611 (1934).

_____. Camera Safaris. *Natural History* 37:46–62 (1936).

_____. In Borneo with the Martin Johnsons. *Natural History* 39:3–18 (1937).

_____. Tree-Climbing Fish. *Natural History* 40:676 (1937).

BOOKS BY OSA JOHNSON

Johnson, Osa. *Jungle Babies*. With 21 illustrations from drawings by Margaret Flinsch. New York and London: G. P. Putnam's Sons, 1930.

_____. *Jungle Pets*. New York and London: G. P. Putnam's Sons, 1932.

_____. *Osa Johnson's Jungle Friends*. Philadelphia and New York: J. B. Lippincott Co., 1939.

_____. *I Married Adventure: The Lives and Adventures of Martin and Osa Johnson*. Philadelphia and New York: J. B. Lippincott Co., 1940 (rev. ed., William Morrow and Co., 1989).

_____. *Four Years in Paradise*. Philadelphia and New York: J. B. Lippincott Co., 1941.

_____. *Pantaloons: Adventures of a Baby Elephant*. Illustrations by Arthur August Jansson. New York: Random House, 1941.

_____. *Snowball: Adventures of a Young Gorilla*. Illustrations by Arthur August Jansson. New York: Random House, 1942.

_____. *Tarnish: The Story of a Lion Cub*. Illustrations by Arthur August Jansson. Chicago: Wilcox and Follett Co., 1944.

_____. *Bride in the Solomons*. Boston: Houghton Mifflin Co., 1944.

_____. *Last Adventure: The Martin Johnsons in Borneo*. Edited by Pascal James Imperato. New York: William Morrow and Co., 1966.

SELECTED PERIODICAL ARTICLES BY OSA JOHNSON

Johnson, Osa. My Home in the African Blue. *Good Housekeeping* 78:48–49, 167–170, 173 (1924).

_____. I Told You So. *Good Housekeeping* 85:24–25, 148, 151–152, 154, 156, 158, 161 (1927).

_____. At Home in the Jungle. *Natural History* 27:561–569 (1927).

_____. Mirrors of the Jungle. *Collier's* 80:10–11 (1927).

_____. Jungle Babies. *Good Housekeeping* 88:36–37, 246, 249, 250–254 (1929).

_____. Bad Boy. *Good Housekeeping* 90:58–59, 96 (1930).

————. Toto Tembo, the Baby Elephant of the African Jungle. *Good Housekeeping* 90:58–59, 296 (1930).

————. Toto Twiga. *Good Housekeeping* 90:58–59, 240, 243–244 (1930).

————. Ringside Seat. *Good Housekeeping* 91:60–61 (1930).

————. Teddy Tantrum. *Good Housekeeping* 94:44–45, 116–121 (1932).

————. Snowball. *Good Housekeeping* 95:80–81, 166–168 (1932).

————. Flying Flame: The Story of a Flamingo City on Lake Nakuru. *Good Housekeeping* 95:26–27, 161–162 (1932).

————. Baboons to You, but Blah-Boons to Mrs. Martin Johnson. *Good Housekeeping* 101:64–65, 154, 156 (1935).

————. Pantaloons. *Good Housekeeping* 101:34–35, 98, 100, 102 (1935).

————. Polka Dot Pets: An African Adventure with A Happy Ending for Four Orphans of the Wilderness. *Good Housekeeping* 103:38–39 (1936).

————. Jungle Dinner. *Hearst's International Cosmopolitan* 162:74–76, 79 (1937).

————. Wah Wah's Wings. *Good Housekeeping* 104:38–39 (1937).

————. Jungle. *American Magazine* 124:146 (1937).

————. I Am a Woman of Adventure. *Everybody's Weekly. Philadelphia Inquirer*, May 12, 1940, 1, 4.

————. Lady, or the Elephant? Excerpt from *I Married Adventure. Scholastic* 37:19–20 (1940).

————. Life in the Solomons. *Collier's* 110:32–34 (1942).

SELECTED PUBLICATIONS RELATED TO THE JOHNSONS

Akeley, Carl E. Martin Johnson and His Expedition to Lake Paradise. *Natural History* 24:284–288 (1924).

————. Martin Johnson's African Photographs, *World's Work* 46:184–192 (1923).

Alden, Sondra Updike. Martin Johnson, Photographer. *Explorers Journal* 62, 2:86–89 (1984).

Alden, Sondra, and Stott, Kenhelm W., Jr. Safari Museum: Chanute Memorializes Famous Exploring Couple. *Explorers Journal* 59, 2:58–63 (1981).

Bodry-Sanders, Penelope. *Carl Akeley: Africa's Collector, Africa's Savior.* New York: Paragon House, 1991.

Carstens, Vern L. A Pilot on Safari. *The Sportsman Pilot*, August 1935–May 1936.

Douglas, Robert Dick, Jr.; Martin, David R., Jr.; and Oliver, Douglas L. *Three Boy Scouts in Africa: On Safari with Martin Johnson.* New York and London: G. P. Putnam's Sons, 1928.

Foster, George. Osa Again Finds Civilization Unkind. *The American Weekly*, June 27, 1948, 4.

Green, Fitzhugh. *Martin Johnson: Lion Hunter.* New York and London: G. P. Putnam's Sons, 1928.

Ingraham, H. C. "Adventure Unlimited! Martin Johnson's Boyhood Pal Recalls Thrill-Filled Life of Renowned Kansan." *Wichita Eagle and Beacon Magazine*, February 17, 1963, 4, 12.

Houston, Dick. The Boy and Girl Next Door Made Movies Far Away. *Smithsonian* 17, 8:144–155 (1986).

Imperato, Pascal James. *Bwana Doctor.* London: Jarrolds, 1967.

————. *The Cultural Heritage of Africa.* Chanute, Kans.: Safari Museum Press, 1974.

————. The Johnsons in Africa. *Africana* 2,9:18–20, 29–30 (1966).

Martin Johnson and His Wife, Explorers, Go to Conquer Cannibals with a Camera. *The Picture Show* 1,4:18–19 (May 10, 1919).

Martin and Osa Johnson Safari Museum and Johnson Memorial Hall of African Culture, 1966–1981. *Chanute Tribune*, special suppl., June 11, 1981.

Martin and Osa Johnson Safari Museum. 30 Years: 1961–1991. *Chanute Tribune*, special suppl., June 8, 1991.

Mih, Miriam L. *Safari: A Short Travelogue of Martin and Osa Johnson*. Chanute, Kans., 1961.

New Edition of Johnson Memoirs Published. *Chanute Tribune*, April 14, 1989, 1, 8.

A Partial Listing of Johnson Films Held by the Library of Congress (typescript), Chanute, Kans., Martin and Osa Johnson Safari Museum, 1985.

Preston, Douglas J. Shooting in Paradise. *Natural History* 93, 12:14, 16, 18, 20 (1984).

Ray, J. Karen. Osa Johnson. In *The Kansas Chautauqua: Understanding America, Land, People, and Culture*, 28–32. Emporia, Kans.: The Center for Great Plains Studies, Emporia State University, 1988.

Rodwell, Edward. Pioneers of Wildlife Photography. *The Standard*, October 27, 1978, 29.

Ross, D. G. Martin Johnson and His Camera. *Mentor* 13:33–40 (1926).

Saudin bin Labutau. Story of Saudin by Himself. Trans. Agnes Keith. *Atlantic Monthly* 161:227–231 (1938).

Selsor, C. Jackson. Proboscis Monkey of Borneo. *Explorers Journal* 56,2:54–55 (1978).

Speaking of Pictures . . . Cannibals Roast a Man. *Life* 8:12–13 (March 25, 1940).

Starr, Cecile. Women on the Verge . . . Pioneer Documentary Filmmakers That History Ignored. *International Documentary*, Fall 1990, 15–19.

Stebbens, Fred, and Stebbens, Ruth. Safari Museum: Memorial to Adventure. *Kansas*, Summer Leisure Issue, 1965, 10–12.

Stott, Kenhelm W., Jr. *Exploring with Martin and Osa Johnson*. Chanute, Kans.: Martin and Osa Johnson Safari Museum Press, 1978.

———. The Johnson Museum. *Swara* 3,3:22–23 (1980).

———. Martin and Osa Johnson: Exploration Was Their Way of Life. *Explorers Journal* 58, 3:106–109 (1980).

Thomas, Lowell. The Story of Martin Johnson. *Natural History* 39:154–167 (1937).

Weilert, Mary. ESU Teacher Delves into Osa Johnson. *Chanute Tribune*, April 15, 1988, 10.

Woolf, S. J. A Quarter Century of Jungle Adventure. *New York Times Magazine*, April 21, 1940, 10, 17.

OTHER PUBLICATIONS

Akeley, Carl E. *In Brightest Africa*. New York: Doubleday and Co., 1923.

Akeley, Mary L. Jobe. *Carl Akeley's Africa: The Account of the Akeley-Eastman-Pomeroy African Hall Expedition*. New York: Dodd, Mead and Co., 1929.

———. In the Land of His Dreams. *Natural History* 27:525–532 (1927).

———. *The Wilderness Lives Again: Carl Akeley and the Great Adventure*. New York: Dodd, Mead and Co., 1940.

Archer, Geoffrey. *Personal and Historical Memoirs of an East African Administrator*. Edinburgh: Oliver and Boyd, 1963.

Baxter, P.T.W. Social Organization of the Boran of Northern Kenya (shortened version of a D. Phil. thesis). Oxford, Lincoln College, 1954.

Bennett, Judith A. *Wealth of the Solomons: A History of a Pacific Archipelago, 1800–1978.* Honolulu: University of Hawaii Press, 1987.

Binks, H. K. *African Rainbow.* London: Sidgwick and Jackson Ltd., 1959.

Brown, Ken D., *Independence: The Way We Were.* Independence, Kans.: Independence Arts Council, 1980.

Brown, Monty. *Where Giants Trod: The Saga of Kenya's Desert Lake.* London: Quiller Press, 1989.

Brownlow, Kevin. *Behind the Mask of Innocence.* New York: Alfred A. Knopf, 1990.

————. *The War, the West, and the Wilderness.* New York: Alfred A. Knopf, 1979.

Bull, Bartle. *Safari: A Chronicle of Adventure.* New York: Viking, 1988.

Buxton, Edward North. *Two African Trips: With Notes and Suggestions on Big Game Preservation in Africa.* London: Edward Stanford, 1902.

Cullen, Anthony, and Downey, Sydney. *Saving the Game: The Story of the Destruction and Attempts at Preservation of the Wildlife of East Africa, under the Stewardship of Mankind.* London: Jarrolds, 1960.

Day, A. Grove. *Jack London in the South Seas.* New York: Four Winds Press, 1971.

Deacon, A. Bernard. *Malekula: A Vanishing People in the New Hebrides.* Edited by Camilla H. Wedgwood. London: Routledge and Keegan Paul, 1937 (reprinted 1970).

Dinesen, Isak. *Out of Africa.* New York: Random House, 1938.

Du Chaillu, Paul. *Explorations and Adventures in Equatorial Africa.* New York: Harper and Brothers, 1861.

————. *Stories of the Gorilla Country: Narrated for Young People.* New York and London: Harper and Brothers, 1909.

Dugmore, Arthur Radclyffe. *African Jungle Life.* London: Macmillan and Co., 1928.

————. *Autobiography of a Wanderer.* London: Hurst and Blackett, 1930.

————. *Camera Adventures in the African Wilds: Being an Account of a Four Months' Expedition in British East Africa.* New York: Doubleday and Co., 1910.

————. *The Wonderland of Big Game: Being an Account of Two Trips through Tanganyika and Kenya.* London: Arrowsmith, 1925.

Dutton, E.A.T. *Lillibullero or the Golden Road.* Zanzibar: Privately printed, 1947.

Dyer, Anthony. *The East African Hunters: The History of the East African Professional Hunters' Association.* Clinton, N.J.: The Amwell Press, 1979.

Eastman, George. *Chronicles of an African Trip.* Rochester, N.Y.: Privately printed for the author, 1927.

————. *Chronicles of a Second African Trip.* Edited and with notes and an introduction by Kenneth M. Cameron. Rochester, N.Y.: The Friends of the University of Rochester Libraries, 1987.

————. In Collaboration with Dr. Audley D. Stewart, a Safari in Africa. *Natural History* 27:533–538 (1927).

Everson, William K. *American Silent Film.* New York: Oxford University Press, 1978.

Gilbert, Douglas. *American Vaudeville: Its Life and Times.* New York: Dover Publications, 1940.

Gillett, Mary. *Tribute to Pioneers.* Oxford: J. M. Considine, 1986.

Gourguechon, Charlene. *Journey to the End of the World: A Three-Year Adventure in the New Hebrides.* New York: Charles Scribner's Sons, 1977.

Gregory, J. R. *Under the African Sun: A Memoir of Dr. R. W. Burkitt of Kenya.* Nairobi: Colourprint Ltd., 1977.

Guggisberg, C.A.W. *Early Wildlife Photographers.* Newton Abbot, U.K.: David and Charles, 1977.

Haggard, H. Rider. *The Days of My Life: An Autobiography.* 2 vols. Edited by C. J. Longman. London: Longmans, Green and Co., 1926.
_____. *King Solomon's Mines.* New York: Longmans, Green and Co., 1938.
Hanson, Patricia King, and Gevinson, Alan, eds. *The American Film Institute Catalog of Motion Pictures Produced in the United States: Feature Films, 1911–1920 Film Entries.* Berkeley, Los Angeles, London: University of California Press, 1988.
Harcombe, David. *Solomon Islands: A Travel Survival Kit.* South Yarra, Australia: Lonely Planet Publications, 1988.
Harpole, Charles (general editor), and Musser, Charles. *The Emergence of Cinema: The American Screen to 1907,* vol. 1 of *History of the American Cinema.* New York: Charles Scribner's Sons, 1991.
Harpole, Charles (general editor), and Bowser, Eileen. *The Transformation of Cinema, 1907–1915,* vol. 2 of *History of the American Cinema.* New York: Charles Scribner's Sons, 1991.
Harpole, Charles (general editor), and Richard Koszarski. *An Evening's Entertainment: The Age of the Silent Feature Picture, 1915–1928,* vol. 3 of *History of the American Cinema.* New York: Charles Scribner's Sons, 1991.
Harrisson, Tom. *Savage Civilization.* New York: Alfred A. Knopf, 1937.
Hellman, Geoffrey. *Bankers, Bones, and Beetles: The First Century of the American Museum of Natural History.* Garden City, N.Y.: The Natural History Press, 1968.
Heminway, John. *African Journeys: A Personal Guidebook.* New York: Warner Books, 1990.
Hemsing, Jan. *Ker & Downey Safaris Ltd.* Nairobi: Sealpoint Publicity, 1989.
_____. *Then and Now: Nairobi's Norfolk Hotel.* Nairobi: Sealpoint Publicity and Public Relations, 1982.
Hoefler, Paul Louis. *Africa Speaks: A Story of Adventure.* Philadelphia and Chicago: The John C. Winston Co., 1931.
Homan, Dorothe Tarrence. *Lincoln—That County in Kansas.* Lindsborg, Kans.: Barbos' Printing, 1979.
Huxley, Elspeth. *Nine Faces of Kenya.* New York: Viking, 1991.
_____. *Out in the Midday Sun: My Kenya.* New York: Viking, 1985.
_____. *White Man's Country: Lord Delamere and the Making of Kenya.* 2 vols. London: Chatto and Windus, 1935.
Imperato, Pascal James. Africa's Lands of Forbidden Rites. *Sportsman* 13,2:15–17, 69–83 (1965).
_____. *Arthur Donaldson Smith and the Exploration of Lake Rudolf.* Lake Success, N.Y.: Medical Society of the State of New York, 1987.
_____. Count Samuel Teleki's 1888 Expedition to Lake Turkana. *Swara* 11, 2(1988):31–33.
_____. Dr. Arthur Donaldson Smith: Pioneer Desert Traveller. *Swara* 4,5:12–15 (1981).
_____. Early Modern Medical Services at Marsabit, Kenya. *East African Medical Journal* 58,1:769–776 (1981).
_____. Gateway to Kenya's North. *Off Hours* 1,6:4–8 (1983).
_____. *Medical Detective.* New York: Richard Marek, 1979.
Imperato, Pascal James, and Imperato, Eleanor M. Kenya's Lake Paradise. *Explorers Journal* 51,1:22–27 (1980).
_____. A Short History of Marsabit: Paradise Lost. *Africana* 6,8:28–32 (1978).
_____. Up North in Kenya. *Explorers Journal* 57, 1:22–29 (1979).

Jansson, Arthur August. Natives of East Africa: From Pen and Ink Studies Made in Kenya Colony during the Eastman-Pomeroy-Akeley East African Expedition of 1926–1927. *Natural History* 27:594–595 (1927). 4-page insert.

Katz, Ephraim. *The Film Encyclopedia*. New York: Perigee Books, 1979.

Kearton, Cherry. *The Animals Came to Drink*. New York: Robert McBride, 1933.

———. *Wildlife across the World*. New York: Doran and Co., 1913.

Keesing, Roger M., and Corris, Peter. *Lightning Meets the West Wind: The Malaita Massacre*. Melbourne: Oxford University Press, 1980.

Keith, Agnes Newton. *Land below the Wind*. Boston: Little, Brown and Co., 1940.

Labor, Earle; Leitz, Robert C. III; and Shepard, I. Milo. *The Letters of Jack London*: Vol. 1 (1896–1905), Vol. 2 (1906–1912), Vol. 3 (1913–1916). Stanford, Calif.: Stanford University Press, 1988.

Leigh, W. R. *Frontiers of Enchantment: An Artist's Adventures in Africa*. New York: Simon and Schuster, 1940.

———. Painting the Backgrounds for the African Hall Group. *Natural History* 27:575–582 (1927).

London, Charmian Kittredge. *The Book of Jack London*. 2 vols. New York: The Century Co., 1921.

———. *The Log of the Snark*. New York: The Macmillan Co., 1916.

London, Jack. *The Cruise of the Snark*. New York: The Macmillan Co., 1911.

———. First Boat Letter (Snark Voyage): A Preliminary Letter from Jack London Who Is Going Around the World for the Woman's Home Companion. *Woman's Home Companion* 33,11:19 (November 1906).

Lovell, Mary S. *The Sound of Wings: The Life of Amelia Earhart*. New York: St. Martin's Press, 1989.

Lumbacher, James L., comp. and ed. *Feature Films: A Directory of Feature Films on 16 mm and Videotape Available for Rental, Sale, and Lease*. New York and London: R. R. Bowker Co., 1985.

Lundquist, James. *Jack London: Adventure, Ideas, and Fiction*. New York: Ungar, 1987.

Lydekker, R. *The Game Animals of Africa*. London: Rowland Ward Ltd., 1908.

Marciel, Mervyn. *Bwana Karani*. Braunton, U.K.: Merlin Books Ltd., 1985.

Markham, Beryl. *West with the Night*. Boston: Houghton Mifflin Co., 1942.

Maxwell, Marcuswell. *Big Game Photographs from The Times*. London: The Times Publishing Co., 1929.

———. *Elephants and Other Big Game Studies from The Times*. London: The Times Publishing Co., 1930.

Maxwell, Marius. *Stalking Big Game with a Camera in Equatorial Africa: With a Monograph on the African Elephant*. London: William Heinemann Ltd., 1925.

Millais, John G. *A Breath from the Veldt*. London: Henry Sotheran, 1895.

———. *Wanderings and Memories*. London: Longman, Green and Co., 1919.

Munden, Kenneth W., ed. *The American Film Institute Catalog of Motion Pictures Produced in the United States: Feature Films, 1921–1930*. New York and London: R. R. Bowker Co., 1978.

O'Connor, Richard. *Jack London: A Biography*. Boston and Toronto: Little, Brown and Co., 1964.

Oliver, Douglas L. *Oceania: The Native Cultures of Australia and the Pacific Islands*. 2 vols. Honolulu: University of Hawaii Press, 1988.

———. *The Pacific Islands*. 3d ed. Honolulu: University of Hawaii Press, 1989.

Olwine, Margaret. The Safari Museum at Chanute, Kansas, *Star*. *Sunday Magazine of The Kansas City Star* 5,38:6–8, 10, 12, 14 (September 22, 1974).

Osborn, Henry Fairfield. The Vanishing Wildlife of Africa. *Natural History* 27:515–524 (1927).

Pease, Alfred E. *Travel and Sport in Africa*. London: Arthur L. Humphreys, 1902.

Percival, A. Blayney. *A Game Ranger's Note Book*. Edited by E. D. Cuming. London: Nisbet and Co., 1924 (reprinted by the Amwell Press, with forewords by Margaret Kummerfeldt and Jim Rickhoff, 1985).

———. *A Game Ranger on Safari*. Edited by E. D. Cuming. London: Nisbet and Co., Ltd., 1928 (reprinted by the Amwell Press, with forewords by Margaret Kummerfeldt and Jim Rickhoff, 1985).

Percival, Philip. Picturing Africa. *Natural History* 27:570–574 (1927).

Pern, Stephen. *Another Land, Another Sea: Walking Round Lake Rudolph*. London: Victor Gollancz, 1979.

Preston, Douglas J. *Dinosaurs in the Attic: An Excursion into the American Museum of Natural History*. New York: St. Martin's Press, 1986.

Ramsaye, Terry. *A Million and One Nights: A History of the Motion Picture Through 1925*. New York: Simon and Schuster, 1926.

Reece, Alys. *To My Wife 50 Camels*. London: Harvill Press, 1963.

Richmond, J. M., and Hemsing, Jan, comps. and eds. *Aero Club of East Africa, 1927–1977*. Nairobi: Aero Club of East Africa, 1977.

Rockwell, Robert H., with Rockwell, Jeanne. *My Way of Becoming a Hunter*. New York: W. W. Norton and Co., 1955.

Rodwell, Edward. *And So It Goes: Some of the Best of Edward Rodwell*. Nairobi: Ian Parker and Westlands Sundries Ltd., 1984.

———. In Memory of a Pilot. *The Standard*, February 23, 1979, 24.

———. *The Mombasa Club*. Mombasa, Kenya: The Mombasa Club, 1988.

———. The Search for a Grave. *The Standard*, May 19, 1989, 15.

Roosevelt, Theodore. *African Game Trails: An Account of the Wanderings of an American Hunter-Naturalist*. New York: Charles Scribner's Sons, 1910.

Root, Nina J., ed. *Catalog of the American Museum of Natural History Film Archives*. New York and London: Garland Publishing Co., 1987.

Sadoul, Georges. *Dictionary of Films*. Translated, edited, and updated by Peter Morris. Berkeley and Los Angeles: University of California Press, 1972.

———. *Dictionary of Filmmakers*. Translated, edited, and updated by Peter Morris. Berkeley and Los Angeles: University of California Press, 1972.

Schillings, C. G., *Flashlights in the Jungle: A Record of Hunting Adventures and of Studies of Wildlife in East Equatorial Africa*. New York: Doubleday, Page and Co., 1905.

———. *In Wildest Africa*. New York and London: Harper and Brothers Publishers, 1907.

Shelley, ER M. *Hunting Big Game with Dogs in Africa*. Columbus, Miss., 1924.

Sherwood, Leon A., Sr. *The Spirit of Independence*. Independence, Kans.: Tribune Printing, 1970.

Slide, Anthony. *The Vaudevillians: A Dictionary of Vaudeville Performers*. Westport, Conn.: Arlington House, 1981.

Smith, A. Donaldson. *Through Unknown African Countries: The First Expedition from Somaliland to Lake Lamu*. London and New York: Edward Arnold, 1896.

Spencer, Paul. *Nomads in Alliance: Symbiosis and Growth among the Rendille and Samburu of Kenya*. London: Oxford University Press, 1973.

———. *The Samburu: A Study of Gerontocracy in a Nomadic Tribe*. London: Routledge and Keegan Paul, 1965.

Stanley, David. *South Pacific Handbook*. Chico, Calif., Moon Publications, 1989.

Stasz, Clarice. *American Dreamers: Charmian and Jack London*. New York: St. Martin's Press, 1988.

Stein, Charles W., ed. *American Vaudeville: As Seen by Its Contemporaries*. New York: Alfred A. Knopf, 1984.

Stewart, John. *Filmerama*, vol. 1, *The Formidable Years, 1893–1919*. Metuchen, N.J.: Scarecrow Press, 1975.

Tablino, Paolo. *African Traditional Religion: Time and Religion among the Gabra Pastoralists of Northern Kenya*. Marsabit, Kenya: Marsabit Catholic Parish, 1989.

————. *The Diocese of Marsabit: Some Historical Notes*. Marsabit, Kenya: Catholic Diocese of Marsabit, 1989.

————. *I Gabbra del Kenya*. Bologna, Italy: E.M.I., 1980.

Ternes, Alan, ed. *Ants, Indians and Little Dinosaurs*. New York: Charles Scribner's Sons, 1975.

Thurman, Judith. *Isak Dinesen: The Life of a Storyteller*. New York: St. Martin's Press, 1982.

Trench, C. C. *The Desert's Dusty Face*. Edinburgh and London: William Blackwood and Sons, 1964.

Trzebinski, Errol. *The Kenya Pioneers*. New York and London: W. W. Norton and Co., 1986.

————. In Search of Karen Blixen's Kenya. *New York Times*, January 12, 1986, 10, 15.

————. *Silence Will Speak: A Study of the Life of Denys Finch Hatton and His Relationship with Karen Blixen*. London: Heinemann, 1977.

Watson, Charles N., Jr. *The Novels of Jack London: A Reappraisal*. Madison: University of Wisconsin Press, 1983.

Weaver, John T. *Twenty Years of Silents: 1908–1928*. Metuchen, N.J.: Scarecrow Press, 1971.

Were, Gideon S., and Wanjala, Chris, eds. *Marsabit District Socio-Cultural Profile*. Nairobi: Ministry of Planning and National Development at the Institute of African Studies, University of Nairobi, 1986.

Van Dyke, Woodbridge Strong. *Horning into Africa*. California Graphic Press, 1931.

Vaucaire, Michel. *Paul Du Chaillu: Gorilla Hunter*. Translated by Emily Pepper Watts. New York and London: Harper and Brothers, 1930.

OTHER SOURCE MATERIALS

Johnson, Martin. *Diary and Reports—The Martin Johnson African Expedition Corporation*. Nos. 1–7, December 1923–December 1925. Mimeographed. New York, American Museum of Natural History (59.9:08).

Martin Johnson Negatives at the American Museum of Natural History. Nos. 108065–108580, 250569–250958. New York, American Museum of Natural History, 1940.

Photographs of Osa and Martin Johnson. Video Disc I, Frames 43334–51818, Interactive Catalog 1. Rochester, N.Y., George Eastman House, 1987.

Vern Carstens: A Memorial to an Exceptional Pilot. Produced by Amber Davis and Karma Haines, based on an interview with Wilma Carstens and published sources. A Royster Junior High School Local History Production, Chanute, Kans. Videotape, 30 min. in length, January 1990 (courtesy Wilma Carstens).

INDEX